Some Architectural Writers
of the Nineteenth Century

Some
Architectural Writers
of the
Nineteenth Century

BY

NIKOLAUS PEVSNER

CLARENDON PRESS · OXFORD

1972

Oxford University Press, Ely House, London W. 1

GLASGOW NEW YORK TORONTO MELBOURNE WELLINGTON
CAPE TOWN IBADAN NAIROBI DAR ES SALAAM LUSAKA ADDIS ABABA
DELHI BOMBAY CALCUTTA MADRAS KARACHI LAHORE DACCA
KUALA LUMPUR SINGAPORE HONG KONG TOKYO

PRINTED IN GREAT BRITAIN BY WILLIAM CLOWES & SONS LIMITED,
LONDON, COLCHESTER AND BECCLES

PREFACE

THIS book is a considerably enlarged version of the Slade Lectures I gave at Oxford in the session 1968–9. Thirty-five years earlier H. S. Goodhart-Rendel had given them. His dealt with *English Architecture since the Regency* altogether, and it is most unfortunate that they were not published until 1953. For they must have been a delightful series, brilliantly worded and full of discoveries which younger scholars were to make again. Lord Clark in the re-issue of 1950 of his *The Gothic Revival* calls Goodhart-Rendel 'the father of us all' and records his 'kindness to his unworthy children'. That is decidedly generous; for *The Gothic Revival* was first published in 1928. Goodhart-Rendel in the foreword promised a bigger book for the future, and it is doubly unfortunate that he never got down to writing it. For his knowledge of the material was unmatched in the early fifties. But he lacked stamina, a lack counterbalanced by all the fascinating qualities which those of us remember who have known him. Not that I agree with the way he presents Victorian and post-Victorian architecture in the book of 1953. He is pretty consistently for what I am against and against what I am for, and no one can as yet write of the nineteenth century without fors and againsts. Goodhart-Rendel throughout backs the Parisian *Beaux-Arts* principles and style and throughout sneers at the moderns of the twenties and after and at their forerunners—'the gelatinous ismus', he writes, into which abroad 'Mackintosh's childish imitation of Beardsley's drawings' was converted. This is too bad, and matters were made worse, indeed tragic, by Goodhart-Rendel as Principal of the Architectural Association being put into a position in which he could try to enforce *Beaux-Arts* against the wish of students who were longing to be helped into the modern style.

But Goodhart-Rendel's book remains brilliant. The like of it could not now be written. We now know too much. That this is so is largely due to Professor Henry-Russell Hitchcock whose stamina no one in his senses would call in doubt. Busy ploughing the field he kept to it, i.e. kept to nineteenth- and twentieth-century architecture for well over twenty years. The outcome is two monumental books, *Early Victorian Architecture in Britain* of 1954 and the volume on *Architecture of the Nineteenth and Twentieth Centuries* of 1958. And whereas Goodhart-Rendel kept to his England and his France, Hitchcock in the *Pelican History of Art* is international. International also are my *Pioneers of Modern Design* which first came out in 1936, but which is brief and—I can see that now—as partisan as Goodhart-Rendel's lectures were—only, as I have already indicated, on the opposite side. The late Sigfried Giedion's *Space, Time and Architecture* which joined the growing troop of architectural histories of the nineteenth century in 1941 is partisan too, but has dangers in this which I hope to avoid by making it clear in my title that I will only deal with certain selected people and trends. Giedion conveys the impression that his nineteenth century was *the* nineteenth century. That this is not so has since been obvious to a host of younger scholars. Not a year passes without the presentation of new material in the *Architectural Review*, *Architectural History*, and other journals, and not a month passes without the Victorian Society, founded in 1958, fighting for some Victorian building.

So it was a matter of course to me that my Slade Lectures, thirty-five years after Goodhart-Rendel's, should present a specialized aspect of Victorian architecture. I chose architectural writing, because it has always been a passion of mine to read what architects have to say about architecture, and also because the first chapters of my book of 1936 had been largely just that, only for the decades before Morris very sketchily done. For the time around 1850 I had probed a little deeper in two small books dealing with one architect, Sir Matthew Digby Wyatt, and one event, the Great Exhibition of 1851 (*Sir Matthew Digby Wyatt* (Cambridge, 1949), *High Victorian Design* (London, 1951)). All this did not amount to much, and so I thought it high time to gather the contents of extracted books and papers and give the whole of the material some shape.

Some shape—the title of this book contains a 'some' too. Its chapters deal with some architectural writers, not all. It would be impossible to get all of them together. Professor Peter Collins's *Changing Ideals in Modern Architecture* (London, 1965, now also paperback) for instance contains much, especially of French material, which will be looked for in vain in my book, and I have no doubt that younger colleagues will be able without much effort to point out gaps. Mr. Peter Howell has in fact already done that. I have also much profited by contributions from pupils and their theses, in the first place Phoebe Stanton, Robin Middleton, Priscilla Metcalf, and George McHardy. I am grateful to them, as I am to St. John's College, Cambridge for hospitality to Judy Nairn for reading proofs and making the index, and to Dorothy Dorn and Winifred Bailey for the crystal-clear typing of a maddeningly complicated manuscript.

The quality of the manuscript reflected the way the book came about. The Slade Lectures amounted to fourteen. That gave no more than a framework. The filling in with detail after detail and quoted passage after quoted passage may well have obscured the course which the lectures were intended to take, and the final outcome may strike the reader as no more than *matériaux pour servir* . . . Perhaps I should have heeded Byron's

> Small have continual plodders ever won,
> Save base authority from others' books.

Perhaps I should have kept away from the temptation of an oversized *florilegium*. Anyway, I know only too well that this book is not a painting with the Titian or Rembrandt sweep but a mosaic where the subject and the pictorial effects are put together *tessera* after *tessera*.

Furthermore, even the selection of who should be in and who out may at times seem arbitrary. May I therefore in conclusion explain it? The writers of neo-Classicism are on the whole left out. No Soane will be found, little Schinkel and little Quatremère de Quincy where needed, and hardly any Cockerell, because the material has not even yet been collected. The real start is with the English archaeologists of the late eighteenth and early nineteenth century, and the first biographical chapter is on Rickman. As will be expected the great Gothicists follow: Pugin, the Cambridge Camden Society, Ruskin, and Scott—Lord Clark's straight run, but strengthened by a chapter on Caumont and a chapter on Viollet-le-Duc including his predecessors. But the Italianate line is followed as diligently: Hübsch and Hope, Donaldson and Hittorff, Kerr and Fergusson, and so to Semper. American writers are left out, because the Americans have published so much already themselves. I refer only to Phoebe Stanton: *The Gothic Revival and American Church Architecture* (Baltimore, 1968), and to the reprinting of Horatio Greenough's essays *Form and Function* (ed. H. A. Small, Berkeley, 1947, also as a paperback), of Montgomery Schuyler's *American Architecture and other Writings* (ed. W. H. Jordy and R. T. Coe, Cambridge, Mass., 1961), of Henry van Brunt's essays, (ed. W. A. Coles, Cambridge, Mass.,

1968), and of the writings of John Wellborn Root (ed. D. Hoffmann, New York, 1967)—let alone Sullivan's essays, republished more than once.

I end with William Morris who died in 1896, largely for the personal reason that my book of 1936 carries on from him with writers such as van de Velde and those of the *Deutsche Werkbund*. But Morris is not only the pioneer of the twentieth century, he is also the consummation of the Gothic Revival and especially of Ruskin, and so I decided that it would be right and proper to end this book with Morris as I had started my earlier book with Morris thirty-five years ago.

POSTSCRIPT

Two books came out too late to be made use of. *Die verborgene Vernunft*, catalogue of an exhibition held in the Neue Sammlung in Munich in 1971 contains a whole string of quotations from Winckelmann to 1901. Some duplicate what is in this book, others ought to be in it. The case of Robert Macleod's *Architectural Ideology in Britain, 1835–1914* is different. It poses itself many problems which were mine as well, and as it is much briefer than my book, it is more lucid. But the two books rarely duplicate, though Mr Macleod takes in Greek Thomson, Fergusson and Kerr. Moreover, nearly half his book deals with events and writings of after 1880. Its climax is the chapter on Lethaby.

CONTENTS

LIST OF PLATES

(At end)

LIST OF FIGURES

CHAPTER I

Walpole and Essex

HORACE WALPOLE bought Strawberry Hill in 1747,[1] 'a little plaything house'.[2] In 1749 he spoke for the first time of his 'future battlements'.[3] His liking for what he called 'the charming venerable Gothic'[4] dated back further. 'Venerable' he and his friends did not take too seriously, and 'charming' is an epithet well suited to characterize what indeed he did build at Strawberry Hill. In a letter of 1750[5] he could refer to Gothic and Chinese side by side and attribute to both of them 'a whimsical air of novelty'. His staircase for instance he calls 'so pretty and so small that I am inclined to wrap it up and send it you in my letter',[6] and he speaks of the windows of the staircase as 'lean windows fattened with rich saints'.[7] So the house grew between 1753 and 1776 with room after room added, the Library in 1754, the Holbein Room in 1759 [Pl. 1], the Gallery with its plaster fan vault in 1763, the Round Tower in 1761–71, the Beauclerk Tower in 1776. At first Horace Walpole and some of his friends did the designing, but the Beauclerk Tower was designed by a professional architect, James Essex, and the new offices near the house were built—much later, in 1790—by James Wyatt, another professional architect. Horace Walpole respected both highly.[8]

There is in fact a development of Gothicism noticeable in Strawberry Hill, and, as it heralds the nineteenth century, it must be pointed out here. The character of Horace Walpole's rooms is indeed charming and whimsical, but among the elements which make them up, there are accurate copies of genuine Gothic items,

[1] On Horace Walpole the best general book is R. W. Ketton Cremer (London, 1940, third ed. 1964). The letters are in course of total publication by the world's leading Horatian, W. S. Lewis: *The Yale Edition of Horace Walpole's Letters*, so far 34 vols. (New Haven, 1937–69).
[2] Letter to Conway, 8 June 1747, *Letters of Horace Walpole*, ed. Mrs. Paget Toynbee, I (Oxford, 1903).
[3] Letter to George Montagu, *Yale Ed.*, IX, 102.
[4] Letter to Montagu, 25 July 1748, ibid., 64.   [5] Ibid., XX, 166.
[6] Ibid., 361.   [7] Ibid., 381.
[8] For all matters concerning the history of the house see W. S. Lewis, 'The Genesis of Strawberry Hill', *Metropolitan Museum Studies*, V, 1934–6.

and this interest in archaeological accuracy is in contrast to Rococo mentality. The bookcases in the library were taken from Dugdale's illustration of the side doorways of the chancel screen of Old St. Paul's, the chimney-piece in the same room from the monument to John of Eltham, the chimney-piece of the library from the monument to Archbishop Peckham in Canterbury Cathedral, the chimney-piece in the Holbein Chamber from Archbishop Warham's monument also in Canterbury Cathedral, and the gallery vault from the aisles of Henry VII's Chapel. No incongruity was felt yet in using a monument for a fireplace, but the wish for accurate reproduction remains memorable.

Horace Walpole's interest in Gothic architecture as it was really built, was genuine, however much he played with Gothic horror. On 15 March 1769 he wrote[9] that he intended to prepare a 'history of our architecture, . . . especially the beautiful Gothic'. It is this interest which had attached him to James Essex, whereas his admiration later in life for James Wyatt had quite different reasons. Only a few months after the letter just quoted, he told William Cole[10] that Essex had asked for his advice in connection with the history of Gothic architecture on which he was working, and that he, Horace Walpole, had suggested three parts for the book: part one to be written by himself and to provide the history 'from the round Roman arch to Gothic perfection', and then to the 'bastardized Gothic' and the barbarous style of James I. This first part was to end with Inigo Jones. Part two should be 'observations on the art, proportions, and method of building', and this should be by Essex; part three, whose purpose would be to 'ascertain the chronological period of each building', Cole ought to write. However, both Walpole and Cole dropped out, and Essex carried on alone.[11] In fact, on 15 Dec. 1770 Walpole tells Cole that 'Mr Essex has all his materials ready', but also that 'it will never appear, while I am in being'.[12] It did not, nor has it since.

James Essex more than anyone else represents the incipient passion for Gothic accuracy. In work he was commissioned to do as an architect for cathedrals he wanted to match the original work exactly. An example is the high altar surround of Lincoln Cathedral [Pls. 2 & 3]. This he did in 1761, and it still deceives quite experienced visitors now.

9 Letter to H. Zouch, *Yale Ed.*, XVI, 27.   10 Ibid., I, 190–1.
11 Letter to George Montagu, 24 Oct. 1772, Ibid., X, 285.   12 Ibid., I, 204.

Essex was born in 1722, five years after Horace Walpole. He was the son of a joiner and trained as an architect. He worked as a restorer on Ely Cathedral, Lincoln Cathedral, Winchester College, and in the year of the Beauclerk Tower designed a new altar-piece for King's College Chapel at Cambridge [Pl. 4]. He had met Horace Walpole already in the thirties at Cambridge, and his archaeological interest goes back to that time. We know of it from unpublished drafts, notes, drawings etc. in the British Museum.[13] They would have remained unknown and might have been destroyed, if it had not been for T. Kerrich, University Librarian of Cambridge, who kept them and ultimately donated them to the British Museum and who also made use of them to a very limited extent in a paper he read to the Society of Antiquaries in 1809.[14] However, that paper belongs in a different context and will be referred to again later.

Essex's manuscripts show that already in 1737 he made a careful drawing of the Norman chapel of Barnwell near Cambridge,[15] in 1740 planned a book to be called *Antiquille* or *The Antiquities of Cambridge*,[16] and in 1756 worked on a book of measured drawings of King's College Chapel. Some of those which remain are better than any done before.[17] Shortly after that the idea must have come to him of an illustrated history of architecture. Careful drawings of plans of the Basilica of Maxentius (the so-called Temple of Peace), Old St. Peter's, and other buildings including Salisbury Cathedral survive and are dated 1758. In the course of the years this became a history of Gothic architecture, though still intended to start at Stonehenge and cover architecture in the Bible, Roman architecture, early Christian architecture, the contribution or otherwise of the Goths, and so on. There are among the manuscripts a number of drafts, some of them identical, and there are also references in letters of 1769 and 1779.[18]

Among the intended introductory passages one calls the programme of the book 'to consider what are the parts of which

---

[13] Add MSS. 6760–73, 6776, also letters in other volumes of Add. MSS., especially to William Cole. The only publication which has made use of this material is Donald R. Stewart, 'James Essex', *The Architectural Review*, CVIII, 1950. Paul Frankl's *The Gothic; Literary Sources and Interpretations through Eight Centuries* (Princeton, 1960), which is the most thorough book by far on writings about the Gothic style (875 pages of it!) is relatively weak on England, and especially weak on Essex. Also, his point of view differs substantially from mine.

[14] 'Some Observations on the Gothic Buildings abroad . . .', *Archaeologia*, XVI, 1810, 309 ff. See below, p. 20.

[15] Add. MS. 6770.

[16] The drawn title-page is in 6770.

[17] A printed prospectus is in 6772, the best drawings are in 6776.   [18] See Stewart op. cit.

Gothick architecture in General is composed [and] what Parts belong to each stile in particular';[19] another starts from Vitruvius' and Wotton's principles of convenience, strength, and beauty, and insists that Gothic beauty also is based on fixed rules: 'neither proportion nor regularity are wanting';[20] yet another defines architecture against building as 'governed by Proportions, Order, and Regularity'. Building comes from necessities, architecture from religion.[21] The best introduction to Gothic architecture is this:

There is no Stile or Architecture so little observed and less understood than that which we call Gothic, though it is not by any means so barbarous and inelegant as is generally supposed . . . For whoever considers their works with attention will find many of them judiciously designed and admirably executed . . . [They can] afford Pleasure to a curious Spectator and instruction to the Studious Architect . . . Nothing can be more wonderfully contrived than many of their vaulted roofs . . . nothing more bold and surprising than the manner of supporting such masses of stone upon such seemingly slender pillars.[22]

But in order fully to understand, Essex continues, 'time must be spent in measuring their parts'. So here is a defence of Gothic on aesthetic as well as structural grounds. Now to go into more details, Essex agrees with writers before him that 'the principal characteristic of that stile of building which we improperly call Gothick is the pointed Arch',[23] but he discounts the three then current theories on how the pointed arch began in the north. One is romantic, the second historical, the third purely formal. The first two seem to have been first formulated about 1700.[24]

The romantic explanation derives the Gothic style from lines of trees in forests. J. F. Félibien in his *Dissertation touchant l'architecture antique et l'architecture gothique*, published in 1699, writes that the many slender piers and the vaults standing on them are 'comme autant de rameaux et de tiges d'arbres' (p. 173). The historical explanation is that the Saracens in Spain used Gothic forms before

[19] 6762, 11v.   [20] 6762, 62v.   [21] 6765, 1.
[22] 6771, 23.   [23] 6771, 23.
[24] See R. Middleton, 'The Abbé de Cordemoy and the Graeco-Gothic Ideal', *Journal of the Warburg and Courtauld Institutes, XXV*, 1962, 303 and 301. This paper and its continuation ibid., XXVI, 1963 are the most important account of early Gothicism in France. A much more detailed account is in Dr. Middleton's Ph.D. Thesis, 'Viollet-le-Duc and the rational Gothic Tradition' (Cambridge, 1958). Cf. also two excellent papers: E. S. de Beer, 'Gothic: Origin and Diffusion of the term', *Journal W. and C.I.*, XI, 1948 and A. O. Lovejoy, 'The first Gothic Revival', in *Essays in the History of Ideas* (Baltimore, 1948).

the north. This theory is first found in the second edition of John Evelyn's 'Account of Architects and Architecture' in his translation of Fréart's *Parallèle*.[25] The edition is dated 1707, but the dedication to Wren 1697, and Wren in fact believed in this theory and put it forward himself in his Memorandum on Westminster Abbey in 1713.[26] He may even have done this before Evelyn. In any case it also appears in France already in 1699.[27] Bishop Warburton incidentally in his edition of Pope managed to combine both theories: The Goths after they had occupied Spain 'having been accustomed ... to worship the Deity in Groves ..., when their new religion required covered edifices, they ingeniously projected to make them resemble Groves ... They executed the project by the assistance of Saracen Architects, whose exotic style of building very luckily suited their purpose ... A regular Avenue of well grown trees [is reminiscent of] the long Visto through a Gothic Cathedral.'[28]

The third theory of the origin of the Gothic style or rather of the pointed arch is English. It is based on the fact that, if blank arcading of round arches is done with intersecting arches, as it is quite frequent in the Norman style in England, the intersecting forms pointed arches. This view seems first to have been held by Thomas Gray, the poet, who was a friend of Horace Walpole and Essex and who died in 1771. William Mason, editing his poems, tells of his 'great knowledge of Gothic architecture' which enabled him to 'pronounce, at first sight, on the precise time, when any particular part of any of our cathedrals was erected'.[29] However, Gray never published his ideas on Gothic architecture.[30] The theory of the intersecting arches was first put forward publicly by James Bentham in his *The History and Antiquities of the Conventual and Cathedral Church of Ely* in 1771[31] without any reference to Gray.

[25] *A Parallel of the ancient Architecture with the modern* (1707). On this book and Evelyn's views on architecture see K. Downes, 'John Evelyn and Architecture', in *Concerning Architecture,* ed. Sir John Summerson (London, 1968), 28 ff.

[26] S. Wren, *Parentalia* (1750), 297.

[27] Florent le Comte, *Cabinet des Singularitéz,* I, II. Sulzer incidentally, author of the *Theorie der Schönen Künste,* the standard German treatise on aesthetics (1771) also believed in the Saracen origin (see J. von Schlosser: *Präludien* (Berlin, 1927), 288). It is also worth noting that as late as 1849 E. A. Freeman (see p. 101) in his *History of Architecture,* p. xi, wrote that without 'Arabian Architecture ... Gothic cannot be understood'.

[28] *The Works of Alexander Pope,* edited and annotated by Bishop Warburton, (London, 1751), III, 267.

[29] W. Mason, *The Poems of Mr Gray* (York, 1778), IV, 45.

[30] They were printed only in 1814 ('Architectura Gothica'), *The Works of Gray,* ed. Milford (London, 1843), V, 325–32. See P. Frankl, *The Gothic,* 403.

[31] (Cambridge, 1771), 37 and Frankl, *The Gothic,* 411.

Essex makes no comment on the tree theory. He calls the Saracen theory 'not at all probable'[32] and accepts Gray's and Bentham's theory only in so far as 'they accidentally as it were stumbled into the pointed arch';[33] it would not have become a fashion, if it had not been found to possess more serious advantages. Here Essex is entirely original—he calls his view new himself[34]—and what he wrote influenced the next generation. He points out with drawings that for the vaulting of bays of other than square plan, if masons wanted an even height of the crown of the vault, round arches and ribs would have to be mixed with segmental or stilted ones, whereas, once pointing is accepted, it all becomes a matter of varying degrees of pointing.[35]

Series of drawings also were done by Essex to show in great detail how arches are to be set out,[36] and what kind of Gothic vaults exist.[37] There are moreover series of windows as an illustration of the development of tracery, and also series of buttresses and niches,[38] and even the types of Greek temples[39] and Early Christian churches, including e.g. S. Costanza (called S. Agnese), S. Stefano Rotondo, the Church of the Holy Sepulchre in Jerusalem, and the Church of the Nativity at Bethlehem.[40]

Essex divides Gothic architecture in England into five periods: 370 years before the coming of the pointed arch—Anglo-Saxon architecture was still obscure, 130 years of Ancient Gothic, i.e. what we call Norman, 150 years from the death of Henry III, 100 years of the Modern Gothic from Henry IV to Henry VII, and fifty years of the decline from Henry VIII onwards.[41] Gothic architecture should, he adds, repeating Walpole's view, include 'the time of Elizabeth and James' and only terminate with Inigo Jones.[42] Decline he defines in general as that which in all styles follows after the rise from the start to perfection and is characterized by 'confusion of parts' and 'multiplicity of ridiculous ornaments'.[43] Perfection to him is the thirteenth century, which is interesting, in so far as the favourite style of serious Gothic imitation up to 1840 was the

---

[32] 6762, 21.   [33] 6771, 27.   [34] 6771, 27.
[35] 'where arches of different diameters are required to be of equal heights' (6762, 25 ff., also 6771, 230–277). This argument is still used in the literature of the twentieth century—see e.g. Francis Bond, *Gothic Architecture in England* (London, 1906), 309.
[36] 6762, 47 ff.   [37] 6771.
[38] 6762, 29 ff.   [39] 6765, 41v.
[40] 6765, 56v, 47v, 58v, 67v.   [41] 6771, 203 ff.
[42] 6771, 201.   [43] 6762, 5.

Perpendicular,[44] and Essex's perfection only became recognized for imitation from 1840 onwards.

Essex is not kind to the Gothic imitators of his own day: the 'Conceited Surveyor' who spoils an old building by his 'folly and ignorance' in restoring it, and the architect who collects 'together a jumble of discordant parts' and 'puts a string of pointed arches [on] a row of broom sticks'.[45] He had every reason to feel like that, considering the outstanding work which he himself did in cathedrals and the painstaking surveys he made and wrote up of Lincoln and Ely Cathedrals,[46] Croyland Abbey,[47] and the old bridge at Rochester.[48] In fact the note books abound in descriptive notes and little drawings of buildings, so much so that one of the notebooks was later provided with a topographical index.[49] We can follow Essex on a study tour in 1766 which takes him e.g. to Derby ('the silk mills are worth seeing'), to Birmingham and Hagley, Winchester, Portsmouth, Salisbury, Longford Castle, and Stourhead.[50] In other books are accounts of expenses,[51] and Essex also collected passages from other authors on buildings and occasionally book titles, e.g. Frézier's *La Théorie et la pratique de la coupe des pierres* of 1737.[52] So he extracts Gervase on Canterbury, Warton on the *Faerie Queene*, Whitaker on the history of Manchester, Grelot's *Voyage to Constantinople*, Montesquieu's *Essay on Taste*, and other books[53] and also documents, e.g. for the history of Great St. Mary's at Cambridge.[54]

Finally, Essex's notebooks contain a glossary of French terms[55] and a brief one of English terms[56] (memorable because it shows that terms such as billet, nailhead, zigzag, corbel-table were already familiar in his time), and several chronologies.[57] A table of the sizes of Roman bricks[58] and another of the price of corn through six

[44] Thus e.g. for Bentham in his book on Ely (see pp. 5 and 41) Henry VII's Chapel in Westminster Abbey is the climax of English architecture.

[45] 6762, 62v, 16v.　　　　　　　　　　[46] 6761, 72 ff.; 6763, 1 ff.; 6764; 6769, 174–152.

[47] 6760, 45 ff.

[48] 6763, 29 ff.

[49] 6768, 301 ff.

[50] 6767.

[51] 6768, 6769.

[52] 6769, 15.

[53] 6769, 17 ff.; 6771, 290; 6762, 65; 678, 179; 6768, 3; 6771, 222 ff.

[54] 6761, 37 ff.; also 6770.

[55] 6772, 113 ff.

[56] 6770, 167.

[57] e.g. 6771, 190 ff.

[58] 6760, 54.

hundred years[59] are a sign indeed of the scholar's passion for tabulated information. One of the notebooks is called 'Theory and Practical Perspective, Part I'[60] and two contain bound-in letters.[61]

Taking it all in all, the wealth of what Essex left is as amazing as his endeavour towards accuracy.

[59] 6761, 84.   [60] 6773.   [61] 6771, 6772.

CHAPTER II

Goethe and Schlegel

THERE is ample evidence to show that Horace Walpole admired Essex's scholarship; what impressed him in the Gothicizing buildings of James Wyatt was something different: 'sober dignity' and exquisite execution. Wyatt's Lee Priory is to him 'the quintessence of Gothic taste'.[1] More we cannot expect him to say; for Fonthill [Pl. 5] was only begun in 1796, and so the change in attitude between Strawberry Hill Gothic and Wyatt's mature Gothic belongs to the years after Walpole's death. Now Wyatt's mature Gothic, if facile and somewhat operatic, demonstrates the Romantic interpretation of the Gothic style, totally different from the Rococo interpretation of Strawberry Hill. For England Wyatt marked that change; for the Continent it had taken place nearly twenty-five years before, in Goethe's *Von deutscher Baukunst*. *Von deutscher Baukunst, D. M. Ervini a Steinbach* was written and published in 1772. Erwin of Steinbach was master mason of Strasbourg Cathedral, and Goethe believed that the glorious façade of the cathedral was all his. So his paper is a dithyrambic evocation of the greatness of Strasbourg Cathedral.[2] One cannot do better than quote passages from it, and little is needed by way of comment.[3]

I wandered round thy grave, noble Erwin, and searched for thy tombstone, to have revealed to me 'Anno domini 1318 XVI Kal. Febr. Obiit Magister Ervinius, Gubernator Fabricae Ecclesiae Argentinensis'. And I could not find it, and none of thy countrymen could show it me, that my veneration might be poured out at the holy place; . . .

[1] Letter to Hannah More, 25 June 1790, *Yale Ed.*, XXXI, 343.
[2] For the early German writings on the Gothic style see now the outstanding book by Professor W. D. Robson-Scott, *The Literary Background of the Gothic Revival in Germany* (Oxford, 1965). The extensive German literature on Goethe and the Arts and Goethe and architecture is referred to in my paper 'Goethe and Architecture', reprinted in *Studies in Art, Architecture and Design* (London, 1968), I, 164 ff. Since then Herbert von Einem, *Goethe-Studien* (1970) has come out, an enlarged edition of his *Goethe und die Kunst*, including two new papers.
[3] I quote from the translation by Geoffrey Grigson and myself in the *Architectural Review*, XCVIII (1945), 156 ff.

Yet why needst memorial! Thou hast set up to thyself one most glorious. And if the ants crawl round and care not for thy name, thou sharest the destiny of that architect who piled mountains into the clouds . . .

It has been granted to few to create a Babel-thought within their souls, whole and great, and by necessity beautiful to the smallest part, like the trees of God. . . .

Why needst memorial! And from me! It is superstition or blasphemy, when the rabble pronounces sacred names. Before thy colossus, the weak mannikins of taste reel giddily, and spirits that are whole will know thee without interpreter. Only, O excellent man, thus, before I venture my patched-up skiff back upon the Ocean, more likely toward death than prize—behold; here in this sacred copse, where all around the names of my beloved are in leaf, I cut thine into a beech-tree rising slenderly like thy spire, . . .

In a small taste, says the Italian, and goes by. Childish things, babbles the Frenchman after him; and clicks open his snuff-box à la Grecque, in triumph. What have ye done, that ye dare despise! Has not the Genius of the Ancients, rising from its tomb, chained thine, O Latin foreigner! Creeper in the mighty fragments to cadge proportions, cobbler of summer houses out of the holy wreckage, looking upon thyself as guardian of the mysteries of Art because thou canst account, to inch and to fraction, for gigantic buildings! Hadst thou but felt, more than measured—had the spirit of the masses thou gapest at come upon thee, then hadst thou not imitated only because they did it and it is beautiful. Then by necessity and truth hadst thou created thy designs, and living beauty might plastically have welled from them . . .

This is the way things wag: the artist's whim serves the rich man's wilfulness: the topographer gapes, and our dilettanti, called philosophers, lathe out of protoplastic fables rules and history of the fine arts down to now, and true men are murdered by the evil Genius in the forecourt of the mysteries.

Rules, more than examples, harm the man of genius. Before his day, a few people may have worked out a few parts. He is the first, from whose soul emerge the parts grown together into one eternal whole. But school and rule fetter all power of perceiving and acting. What does it profit us, O neo-French philosophising connoisseurs, that the first man who sensed his needs, rammed in four tree-trunks, joined up four poles on top, and topped all with branches and moss?[4] . . .

When for the first time I went towards the Minster, general notions of Taste filled my head. By hearsay, I honoured the harmony of the masses, the

---

[4] This refers to Laugier's *Essai sur l'architecture,* published in 1753. Goethe is unfair to Laugier who was in fact himself, though in a more moderate way, a defender of the Gothic style. On Laugier see now W. Herrmann's excellent *Laugier and eighteenth century French Theory* (London, 1962).

purity of the forms, was a sworn enemy of the tangled arbitrarinesses of Gothick ornament. Under the Gothick heading, I piled up, like the article in a dictionary, all the synonymous misunderstandings of the confused, the unregulated, the unnatural, the patched-up, the botched, the overladen, which had ever passed through my head. Foolishly as a people, which calls all the foreign world barbaric, I named Gothick all that did not fit into my system, from the neatly-turned, gay-coloured cherub-dolls and painting our bourgeois nobility adorn their houses with, to the solemn remnants of older German Architecture, whose few fantastical frettings made me join in the universal song: 'Quite squashed with ornament.' And so, as I walked towards the Minster, I shuddered in prospect of some malformed curly-bristled ogre.

With what unlooked for emotions did the sight surprise me, when I stepped before it! A sensation of wholeness, greatness, filled my soul; which, composed of a thousand harmonising details, I could savour and enjoy, yet by no means understand or explain. So it is, men say, with the bliss of Heaven. How often have I come back to enjoy this sacredly profane bliss, to enjoy the gigantic spirit of our elder brethren in their works ... 'All these masses are there of necessity, and dost thou not see them in all the older churches of my town? Only have I raised their arbitrary proportions into harmony. How above the main porch, which lords over two smaller ones to either side, the wide rose-window opens, answering to the nave; and commonly but a hole for daylight, how, high above, the bell-loft asked for the smaller windows! All that was necessary; and I shaped it into beauty.'

Goethe's debt in all this to Herder, to Hamann, to Young need not be documented. It is patent in his jeering at taste, his admiration of the primeval and of wholeness, and his plea for feeling instead of measuring by rules.

Soon, however, as is equally well known, he moved away from this fervour for Gothic architecture. The journey to Italy in 1786–8 was only the end of an inner development towards classicism, Palladio, and the Winckelmann ideal of calm Greek greatness ('stille Grösse'). And though, fired by the enthusiasm of the Boisserée brothers, he once more for a few years, from 1810 onwards, appeared convinced or at least tolerant of the Gothic style, on the whole the Romantics knew that they could not count on him. Yet his *Von deutscher Baukunst* remained the point of departure of the Romantics in their admiration of Gothic buildings. The vehement feelings and the vehement style of Goethe at the age of twenty-three towers over their writings. The key documents are Georg Forster's *Ansichten vom Niederrhein* of 1791–4, Wilhelm Heinrich Wackenroder's *Herzens-ergiessungen eines kunstliebenden Klosterbruders* of 1797, Ludwig Tieck's *Franz Sternbalds Wanderungen* of 1798, Ernst Moritz Arndt's *Reisen durch einem Theil Deutschlands, Ungarns, Italiens, und Frankreichs in den Jahren 1798 und 1799*, of 1804, and so to the Schlegels.[5]

Forster calls Cologne Cathedral glorious, thrilling, sublime, Arndt speaks of the 'tiefen Ehrfurcht und heiligen Schauer' on entering St. Sebaldus at Nuremberg and specifies the 'tönende Dunkel', the 'hohen und schlanken Säulen' and the 'schwindelnde Decke',[6] Wackenroder calls Dürer manly, vigorous, true, earnest, upright, and writes the famous passage: 'Not only under Italian skies . . . beneath pointed vaults as well true art can grow'—for 'are not Rome and Germany on one earth?', and Tieck exclaims on Strassburg 'I kneel in my thoughts before the spirit who designed and carried out this mighty structure . . . an image of infinity.'

Friedrich Schlegel, the more creative of the two brothers, has written more in praise of early painting than of architecture: painting 'industriously finished . . . of severe, even meagre forms and precise outlines . . . no chiaroscuro and dirt . . . and half-shades . . . childlike ingenuousness and limitations'.[7] These early works, Schlegel writes, 'indicate the original idea and purpose of art more purely and truly than the later works'[8] and ought therefore to be 'imitated faithfully until they have become second nature'.[9] Rubens is a remarkable man, though owing to the taste of the time all wrong,[10] Poussin's art is 'stiff school pedantry',[11] Raphael after his superb early years 'abandoned the way of pious love', seduced by Michelangelo.[12]

In one way Schlegel heralds the problems which became central to German art history in the twentieth century. He has a tendency to set up illuminating polarities, and he is a nationalist. 'The German who has a sense of manliness and greatness, is in danger of being coarse, the Frenchman for love of lightness and graciousness, is

---

[5] See H. Lippuner, *Wackenroder und Tieck und die bildende Kunst* (Zurich, 1964)—apart from Robson-Scott and Frankl.

[6] [IV, 347. For comments on Cologne Cathedral see H. Lützeler, *Der Kölner Dom in der deutschen Geistesgeschichte*, Bonn 1948 (Akademische Vorträge und Abhandlungen XII).]

[7] *Europa*, ed. E. Behler (Stuttgart, 1963), pt. I, 114. Also of course in *Kritische Friedrich Schlegels Ausgabe*, IV (Munich-Paderborn-Vienna, 1959). For more Schlegel literature see now the monumental bibliography in E. L. Stahl and W. E. Yuill: *German Literature of the Eighteenth and Nineteenth Centuries* (London, 1970). For older literature one should still go to E. Sulzer-Gebing: *Die Brüder Schlegel in ihrem Verhältnis zur Kunst* (Munich, 1897).

[8] *Europa*, pt. II, 2, p. 2.   [9] Ibid., pt. II, 2, p. 144.   [10] *Krit. Ausg.* 173.
[11] *Europa*, pt. II, 2, p. 29.   [12] Ibid., pt. II, 2, p. 26.

exposed to the danger of becoming *mesquin* and affected.'[13] Equally penetrating and influential are Schlegel's comparisons of the medieval and the modern painter: the masters of the school of Cologne were 'modest fellows of the gild', a great painter today must 'think deeply and endeavour to find serious and worthy tasks'. Only out of religion and philosophical mysticism can paintings be created to become 'hieroglyphs . . . true symbols of the divine'.[14]

Of his nationalism on the other hand, the less said the better. The Germans are 'the noblest people in the world'.[15] St Denis belongs to that ancient age when in France still 'many traces of German faithfulness and warmth survived'. So Louis IX and Joan of Arc are claimed for the Germanic heritage,[16] Flanders was 'put back many steps', when the country moved away from its Germanic past,[17] and so on.

As for Gothic architecture Schlegel's attention was initially drawn to it by the Boisserée brothers on whom more will be said later. He met them in Paris in 1803, they moved into his house, and he travelled with them to Flanders and the Rhineland. Following Goethe, Schlegel defines the Gothic style beautifully as the synthesis of infinity on the large scale, fulness of nature on the small:[18] 'I have a great liking for Gothic architecture.' It possesses 'an unfathomable artistry of elaboration' and yet 'in the totality of the work . . . greatness and a sense of the immeasurable and portentous'.[19] It should be called German, as Fiorillo in his *History of Painting* had done, and not Gothic. Even abroad the great works of Gothic architecture were built by German masons. All this is romantic in feeling, in thought and expression, and so it is not surprising to find Schlegel use the term romantic as a synonym for Gothic.[20] Cologne Cathedral marks for him 'the flowering style of romantic architecture'.[21]

The influence of August Wilhelm Schlegel, Friedrich's elder brother, was wider though not deeper. In his lectures on literature and art held in Berlin in 1801, but not published till 1884[22] he outlined a system of architectural theory which included passages on the character of Gothic architecture. In all architecture, so Schlegel began, beauty must 'first and foremost consist of the appearance of utility'. 'Fantasy must be subordinated to reason.' The same is true of the making 'of three-dimensional objects for

[13] Ibid., pt. I, p. 105.   [14] Ibid., pt. II, 2, pp. 137–44.   [15] *Krit. Ausg.* 189.
[16] Ibid., 158.   [17] Ibid., 164.   [18] Ibid., 199 ff.
[19] Ibid., 160.   [20] Ibid., 162–3.   [21] Ibid., 185.
[22] A. W. Schlegel, *Kritische Schriften und Briefe*, II (Die Kunstlehre) (Stuttgart, 1963).

durable use'. Architecture does not imitate nature, but 'the method
of nature' and that means 'the demonstration of mechanical forces
and zoomorphic decoration'. Also included is a reference to the
geometrical forms of crystals, 'mathematically constructible'. The
vertical stands for gravity, the horizontal for balance; hence symmetry is demanded—but only externally, as our inner organs are
not disposed symmetrically.[23]

Gothic architecture—here the lectures are only recorded sketchily
—has as its principle 'the innumerable as against the simplicity of
Greek architecture'. After that Schlegel seems to have spoken of part
after part of a major church (a Catholic cathedral) according to
function: altar, nave, choir, organ, side altars, chapels, towers,
bells, portals.[24] In his contribution to his brother's *Europa* in 1803
he is a little more explicit: Gothic architecture 'appears to touch the
limits of the impossible. Its parts are not as compact as those of
ancient architecture, but rather like the muscles in the body of an
animal'.[25] The arrangement by parts will reappear in Rickman and
Caumont, the comparison with muscles (or sinews) in Ruskin.

If the Schlegels received international attention that was largely
due to Madame de Staël. August Wilhelm stayed at her house at
Coppet on Lake Geneva in 1804–5. Friedrich visited him there, and
August Wilhelm travelled with her in Europe. Her *Corinne ou
l'Italie* was translated by Friedrich, and in 1810 she completed her
De l'Allemagne. It was published in 1813. Her treatment of national
characters and her comparisons between French and German features
are evidently inspired by the Schlegels—frivolity but *bon goût* in
France, depth but a tendency to exaggeration in Germany. But
France has nothing, Madame de Staël writes, to emulate the German
wealth of ideas, philosophical bent and enthusiasm. Most of the
book deals with literature, but there is the occasional paragraph on
the German primitive painters whose work 'ne dédaignerait pas
l'école Italienne',[26] and on Gothic architecture which the 'nouvelle
école' considers in a novel way. Madame de Staël herself quotes from
Görres the comparison of the Gothic church with 'a forest whose
branches and leaves death has petrified'.[27] This does not amount to
much, but what Madame de Staël achieved was to draw attention in

[23] A. W. Schlegel, 140–7.
[24] Ibid.   [25] *Europa,* pt. II, 1, p. 30.   [26] chap. XXXII.
[27] Ibid. This Félibien-Warburton conceit also appears in Arndt's impressions of St. Sebaldus
at Nuremberg mentioned a few pages back: 'One stands in a forest of sacred firs' (*Reisen,* 1804,
IV, 347).

other countries to the German contribution to romantic thought and feeling. For England this proved particularly inspiring. We know that Coleridge and Carlyle and later Kenelm Digby were drawn by her to the Schlegels.[28]

So the German contribution to early nineteenth-century architectural thought—minor as it is in comparison with that to philosophical thought—is one of emotional involvement. But in England not all was emotions and romanticism. Research and theorizing on Gothic architecture, following Essex's example, went on too, and this must now be presented.

[28] Carlyle in an article in 1830 calls M. de Staël 'the parent of whatever acquaintance with German literature exists among us' (*Critical and Miscellaneous Essays,* Centenary ed., XXVI, 476), and in a notebook of 1826 mentions Schlegel side by side with Chateaubriand (J. A. Froude, *Thomas Carlyle* (London, 1882), I, 372). On August Wilhelm Schlegel and England see W. F. Schirmer in *Shakespeare Jahrbuch* LXXV, 1939, on Coleridge and England, E. C. Mason, *Deutsche und englische Romantik* (Göttingen, 1959).

CHAPTER III

English Antiquarians

THESE English publications of the late eighteenth and the early nineteenth century are without exception minor in scale and value, but in the aggregate they are significant, and they made an impact on France, stronger than their quality and extent would make one expect. The late Paul Frankl in his *The Gothic* has dealt with most of them, and they can thus here be treated briefly. The relevant books and papers are Michael Young's 'The Origin and Theory of Gothic Architecture', published in 1790, John Carter's *Some Account of the Collegiate Church of St Stephen, Westminster* of 1795 and his *Ancient Architecture of England* of 1795 etc, Sir James Hall's 'Essay on the Origin and Principles of Gothic Architecture' of 1797, James Bentham's *History of Gothic and Saxon Architecture in England* of 1798, James Milner's *Historical Account of Winchester Cathedral* of 1798, the *Essays on Gothic Architecture* by Thomas Warton, Bentham, F. Grose, and Milner of 1800, and many more thereafter. Milner's Essay, 'On the Rise and Progress of the Pointed Arch', derives it, following Gray and Bentham, from the intersecting arches of the Norman style, but Milner shows that he belongs to the romantic generation by also admitting the 'impression of awe' which Gothic buildings convey more than any others, because they produce what he calls, using a term of Burke's, 'an artificial infinite' in the mind of the spectator.[1]

The series of dedicated antiquaries with valuable contributions to make begins with the Revd. Michael Young's 'The Origin and Theory of Gothic Architecture.'[2] It is a curious paper, remarkable because the author discards at once as 'fruitless' the theories of groves and Goths and intersecting arches and Saracens, and asks instead: What are 'the actual properties of the arch which might have recommended its introduction into architecture'? (p. 72.) They are of course all structural. It diminishes 'the lateral pressure';

[1] Frankl, *The Gothic*, pp. 445–6.
[2] *Trans. R. Hibernian Academy*, III, 1790, 55 ff. Not mentioned by Frankl.

it requires less abutment, and so on. Young uses engineering treatises and algebraic calculations. The result of this promising procedure is decidedly odd: The pointed arch is

peculiarly adapted to the style of those religious buildings, which were in fashion in the middle ages, where the roof was to be raised to an extraordinary height, and no great weight immediately incumbent on the point of the arch, or where one tier of arcades was to be raised over another. But where a very high building is to be erected upon a Gothic arch, the quantity of matter over the crown . . . must be very much lightened by windows or other perforations. (p. 83)

Otherwise, Young insists that the elliptical arch is preferable for strength and has less deviation from a true balance.

After 1790, 1797—the original date of publication in the *Transactions of the Royal Society* of Sir James Hall's 'Essay on the Origin and Principles of Gothic Architecture'. In 1813 a much more sumptuous publication as a book followed and incidentally was read by Friedrich Schlegel.[3] Where Young tries to be scientific, Hall is nothing if not fanciful. To him the Gothic style originated in building of oziers, and the frontispiece to the edition of 1813 shows this in a delightfully irresponsible way [Pl. 6]. Behind all this lies no doubt the Félibien-Warburton idea of the Gothic forest.

Hall's 'Essay' in order of time was followed by James Anderson's 'Thoughts on the Origin, Excellencies and Defects of the Grecian and Gothic Styles of Architecture', published in *Recreations in Agriculture*, volumes II–IV in 1800–1. Anderson's papers are treated in detail by Frankl (pp. 493–6), and they deserve it. Anderson was a Scotsman, principally interested in rational farming. He moved to London in 1797 and died in 1808, aged sixty-nine.[4] The papers are a ferocious attack on classical architecture in England, and a plea on several grounds for the Gothic. He does not accuse the Greeks but today's 'bigotted advocates for the Grecian system'.[5] Greek is an architecture of the colonnade. It does not adapt itself. It does not allow for windows or internal subdivisions.[6] Inigo Jones's Whitehall is 'a puerility', St Paul's Cathedral an 'absurdity of the most glaring sort'.[7] Now take Gothic instead. Anderson sets down its structural

---

[3] *Krit. Ausg.* IV, 198.

[4] He is not the James Anderson who published a design for a suspension bridge of iron across the Firth of Forth. This anyway dates only from 1818 (*Report relative at a Design of a Chain Bridge . . . over the Firth of Forth*).

[5] *Recreations in Agriculture*, IV, 394.   [6] Ibid., IV, 274 ff.   [7] Ibid., IV, 282 and 286–7.

advantages as Essex and Young had done. Gothic to him is 'a peculiar application of scientific principles to a particular department of art', i.e. sacred structures.[8] The pointed arch allows the 'pressure outward (to be) diminished', the buttressing, the heavy pinnacles 'to give stability' to the buttresses, the windows which become 'merely adventitious screens'.[9] But Anderson is not limiting himself to structural comments. He also writes romantically of 'stupendous structures which will excite the admiration of future ages',[10] and calls Westminster Abbey 'one great whole of immense magnitude'.[11]

The Revd. James Dallaway's *Observations on English Architecture* of 1806 are the very reverse of Anderson.[12] Half the book is on classical, the other half on medieval architecture, and there is no intention of playing one up against the other. Chapters on Oxford and Cambridge and on Bath for instance freely praise the eighteenth-century Palladians. The comments on the phases of medieval architecture are indifferent, and dating is often wrong. Dallaway's preference is the Gothic of the fifteenth century. The choir of Gloucester Cathedral which is dated after 1400 'includes every perfection to which the Gothic had attained'.[13] He also pays his tribute to the Gothic masons as constructors and refers as witnesses to Wren and also to Soufflot.[14] For occasionally Dallaway looks across the channel, and it is worth noting *en passant* that he dates Saint Denis almost correctly (completed in 1140) and says: 'It will be contended by the French antiquaries that this new mode [i.e. the Gothic] . . . appeared, if not earlier, at least in the same century . . . in France'.

However, considering how erratic Dallaway's dates are that means nothing. Nor does the same assertion made much more peremptorily in F. Sayers's *Disquisitions* (Norwich, 1808). Sayers is convinced that 'many specimens' of pointed architecture on the Continent are earlier than the English examples, but among them he lists the grand entrance of Strasbourg Cathedral with a date 1027 and incidentally Monreale in Sicily as seventh-century (pp. 230–8). So that cannot be taken seriously.

When about the same time or a few years earlier G. D. Whittington

---

[8] *Recreations in Agriculture*, IV, 383.   [9] Ibid., II, 424, 427; III, 130.
[10] II, 418.   [11] IV, 386.
[12] Dallaway's best-known book is the *Anecdotes of the Arts in England* (London, 1800) specially informative on sculpture.
[13] *Observations*, pp. 30, 67.
[14] Ibid., p. 42. On Soufflot and Gothic principles see R. Middleton, 'Viollet-le-Duc and the Rational Gothic Tradition' (Ph.D. Thesis, Cambridge, 1958).

said the same that was a different matter; for Whittington who died in 1807 aged twenty-six was at the time of his death working on a book on French Gothic architecture. We know this from the preface to *An Historical Survey of the Ecclesiastical Architecture of France* published posthumously in 1809.[15] The preface is by the fourth Earl of Aberdeen, himself a great philhellene and the founder of the Athenian Society—Byron's 'travelled thane, Athenian Aberdeen'. The preface to Whittington's book was his first published piece of writing. In it he tells of travels in France and Italy which the two undertook together in 1802 and 1803. The book was left unfinished. A third part to deal with the origin of Gothic architecture remained undone. But what we have is a brief history of French medieval architecture, the earliest according to Frankl except for le Comte's of 1699. It is faulty in many ways—for instance the great Flamboyant buildings of the Late Gothic had remained unknown to Whittington —but its thesis is highly important. It is the 'prior excellence of the French style' over the English. On the initial origins Lord Aberdeen pleads for the East, and one is left to wonder whether this represents Whittington's view as well.[16]

Be that as it may; Whittington certainly had recognized the supreme importance of Saint Denis for the Gothic style. He has the right date and calls it 'perhaps the oldest perfect specimen of ornamental [Gothic] building remaining in France' and adds: 'Our belief that the English artists were prior to those of other nations in the use of the pointed arch must be considerably shaken'.[17] Whittington's own taste by the way is not like Dallaway's for the Perpendicular, but for the French High Gothic of the thirteenth century—'the utmost point of excellence of the middle ages', 'never surpassed in any other age or country' (p. 64)—an interesting preference which, as has once before been observed apropos James Essex, became universal only with Pugin and Scott about 1840.[18]

In the year of Whittington's death a book called *Essays of the London Architectural Society* came out. Frankl does not mention it. It contains a paper by E. Aiken ('On modern Architecture', part I)

[15] My quotations are from the second edition, 1811.
[16] pp. vi, ix, xix.   [17] pp. 137, 139.
[18] But even Whittington could still make elementary mistakes. For instance the choir of La Charité he calls pre-1084, and Bourges 'in its present form' *c.* 1324. Whittington's book was attacked by Milner, and the Revd. John Haggitt published *Two Letters to the Fellows of the Society of Antiquaries* in its defence (Cambridge, 1813), rightly stressing that Milner thinks in terms merely of the pointed arch, Whittington in terms of a style (pp. 8, 49). Haggitt like Lord Aberdeen believes in the Near Eastern sources of Gothic architecture.

praising the 'magic of construction' of Gothic buildings, the ingenious infilling of the cells of a vault in lighter materials, and the saving in centering in the erection of Gothic vaults. S. Beazley Jun.'s 'An Essay on the Rise and Progress of Gothic Architecture' is more conventional. Warburton, Dallaway, Young and also Murphy on Batalha and Payne Knight are quoted. Such motifs as billet, nailhead, and chevron are called Saxon.

Again one year later, i.e. in the year of publication of Whittington's book T. Kerrich, University Librarian of Cambridge, read the paper to the Society of Antiquaries to which reference has already been made because of the paragraphs on Essex. The paper, which was published in *Archaeologia*, vol. xvi (1810), is called 'Some Observations on the Gothic Buildings abroad, particularly those of Italy, and on Gothic Architecture in general'. Kerrich calls the older architecture of England Norman Gothic and the following periods Gothic, Ornamented Gothic, and Florid Gothic, and the early Italian style Lombard,[19] and, like Young before, he refuses to accept the origin of the pointed arch as a problem of importance. 'We ought carefully to distinguish between invention, and what might lead to the use of things . . . invented'. 'The pointed arch alone does not constitute Gothic architecture. . . . Its light pillars, long, thin shafts, elegant foliages and vaultings; its traceries, and numerous other graceful . . . forms . . . are equally essential to its general character (pp. 295–6). Kerrich incidentally goes out of his way to deprecate the restoring of Gothic buildings in his own day. It is 'lamentable to see [Gothic buildings] modernized or (as they call it) improved'. 'It is absolutely impossible to improve them', and if the alterations convince, then they are 'fraud'.[20]

---

[19] Frankl traced the English terminology of styles back to Thomas Warton's *Observations on the Faerie Queene of Spenser* of 1763 where the sequence is Saxon, Gothic Saxon (1200–1300), Absolute Gothic (1300–1441), and Ornamental Gothic (1441 onwards); he also lists John Britton's sequence in *Architectural Antiquities* (vol. I, 1807); Anglo-Saxon, Anglo-Norman, English (1189–1272), Decorated English (1272–1461), Highly Decorated English (1461–1509), Debased English or Anglo-Italian (1509 onwards). Schlegel refers to the English use of the term Norman in his *Letters from his Journey through the Netherlands, the Rhineland, Switzerland and part of France* (*Krit. Ausg.*, IV, 162). Young uses Saxon, Norman, Gothic and compares their character nicely with Tuscan, Doric and Ionic, and Corinthian and Composite (56). Anderson calls Norman Old Gothic and Gothic Modern Gothic (II, 420). Dallaway uses Saxon, Anglo-Norman, Semi or Mixed Norman, Lancet Arch Gothic, Pure Gothic (1300–1400), Ornamented Gothic (1400–60), and Complete or Florid Gothic (after 1460; pp. 49 ff., also 32). Sayers wants to call everything Norman. So we have Ornamented Norman for 1300–1460 and Florid Norman for after 1480 (70–5).

[20] 298–9. John Carter in his anonymous articles of 1798–1817 in the *Gentleman's Magazine* had preceded Kerrich in complaining of what he called the 'innovators'.

Two years later, in 1811, George Saunders, a minor architect who was Surveyor to the County of Middlesex and author of an interesting *Treatise on Theatres* (1790), read a paper to the Society of Antiquaries which was later published in *Archaeologia*, (vol. xvii, 1814). It is called 'Observations on the Origin of Gothic Architecture' and deals chiefly with vaulting. Ribs, Saunders says, serve to fortify groin vaults where otherwise they would be weakest and allow the cells (which he calls pannels) to be very thin. The ribs, he emphasizes, were constructed before the cells, and, by varying the degree of pointing, vaults could be made over bays of oblong plan without the disagreeable appearance of stilting. This latter argument, it will be noticed, Saunders took over from Essex and Kerrich and the thinness of the vaulting cells from Beazley, but otherwise he is original, and his stress on the vault instead of the arch as the generating station of the Gothic style is important. Like Dallaway, incidentally, he refers to Soufflot.

In the same volume of *Archaeologia* Samuel Ware, another architect—he built the Burlington Arcade—had a paper which he had read to the Antiquaries in 1812. The title is 'Observations on Gothic Vaulting', and it is a remarkably systematic affair. Ware distinguishes vaults resting on walls (tunnel vault, dome, domical vault) and vaults resting on piers. These include the groin vault, the 'groined rib' vault, and the vault with ribs 'of the same curvature' —by which he means fan vaults. He gives higher marks to Gothic than to classical building because of the 'higher science' involved, and he discusses the structural advantages of pointed arches and rib-vaults because of the reduction of thrust and the need for less centering. For the former he refers to E.-M. Gauthey's *Traité de la Construction des Ponts* (Paris, 1809–16), which Young and Beazley used as well, for the latter to Wren.

The contributions of this little group of antiquaries may appear minor to us; but they did not appear so to the founders of French archaeology. They were Augustin Le Prévost, M. de Gerville, and Arcisse de Caumont.[21] Le Prévost, best known for his edition (with Léopold Delisle) of Orderic Vitalis, was born in 1787, Gerville in

---

[21] On Le Prévost see the preface by A. Pessy to A. Le Prévost, *Memoires et notes pour servir à l'histoire du Département de l'Eure,* I (Evreux, 1862), p. viii. On M. de Gerville, L. Delisle, *Notice sur la vie et les ouvrages de M. de Gerville* (Valognes, 1853). I owe the reference to both these books to Mlle Geneviève Le Cacheux of the Municipal Library at Caen. For Arcisse de Caumont see M. E. de Robillard de Beaurepaire, *M. de Caumont, sa vie et ses oeuvres* (Caen, 1874), and for early French archaeology altogether P. Léon, *La vie des monuments français* (Paris, 1951), also the older J.-A. Brutails, *L'archéologie du moyen-âge et ses méthodes* (Paris, 1900).

1769, Caumont, by far the most important of the three, in 1801. Le Prévost had been introduced to archaeological scholarship by James Anderson in 1813 and translated Whittington, Gerville went to England as a refugee from the revolution in 1793 and stayed, with one interruption, till 1801. In 1824 he wrote: 'Ni l'architecture romane, ni celle qu'on appelle communement gothique, n'ont attiré l'attention des antiquaires français. Je n'en connais aucun qui s'en soit directement occupé . . . C'est en Angleterre que nous devons chercher des auteurs pour nous diriger dans l'étude de notre architecture ecclésiastique'. By 'notre' he means Normandy in particular,[22] and there was indeed a whole English literature on Normandy and her buildings. It will be surveyed presently. But Gerville also refers to Bentham, Whittington, and Milner.[23] Caumont borrowed English books from Gerville and wrote: 'Je cite les antiquaires anglais, parce que je n'en connais pas d'autres qui se soient occupés de l'architecture du moyen-âge.'[24]

Gerville and Caumont are confirmed by Stendhal who wrote in 1838: 'Notre archéologie nous est venue de l'Angleterre, comme la diligence, les chemins de fer et les bâteaux à vapeur.'[25]

It is natural that Gerville and Caumont should have thought primarily of the literature on Normandy, and there the books which they acknowledged with gratitude were Ducarel's *Anglo-Norman Antiquities* (London, 1767, translated by Caumont, Caen, 1823); J. S. Cotman's *Architectural Antiquities of Normandy* (2 vols.) of 1820–2 with text by Dawson Turner; Charles Nodier, le Baron Taylor, and de Cailloux's *Voyages romantiques et pittoresques dans l'ancienne France* (20 vols.) of 1826–64,[26] and John Britton, A. C. Pugin, and J. and H. Le Keux's *Specimens of the Architectural Antiquities of Normandy* of 1825–8.

[22] P. Yvon, 'La renaissance gothique en Angleterre dans ses rapports avec la Normandie', *Bulletin de la Société des Antiquaires de Normandie*, XXXVIII, 1927–9, 554 ff. Also, not seen by me, P. Yvon, *Le Gothique et la renaissance gothique en Angleterre* (1750–1880) (Caen and Paris, 1931).
[23] *Mémoires de la Société des Antiquaires de Normandie*, I, pt. 1, 1824, 781.
[24] *Mém. Soc. Ant. Norm.*, I, pt. 2, 537 and 606. Also *Cours d'Antiquités Monumentales*, IV (Paris, 1831), pp. 8 ff.
[25] Quoted from Paul Léon op. cit., 91.
[26] See E. Maingot, *Le Baron Taylor* (Paris, 1963).

CHAPTER IV

Moller, Britton, and Willson

THESE three publications of the 1820s and especially the first two of them are totally different from those of the English antiquaries of the early nineteenth century. They are large and costly picture books, and such books, not dealing with Italy, ancient Rome, and ancient Greece—for these had long existed—but with the northern countries and their architectural heritage, became the fashion now.

The earliest of the three was German, and this for its text as much as its illustrations deserves a few pages to itself. It is Georg Moller's *Denkmähler der deutschen Baukunst*, a folio which began to appear in 1815 and was complete in 1821. The illustrations go from Lorsch of the time of Charlemagne to Oppenheim of the fourteenth century and include the Romanesque Mainz, the Transitional Gelnhausen and Limburg, and the thirteenth-century Marburg. The text is of remarkable maturity for its date. It starts from the necessity 'to fix the age of ancient buildings' and to do this not simply by believing all recorded dates (1015–28 e.g. for Strasbourg as it is now), but to try and match documentary dates against the appearance in comparison with earlier, contemporary, and later buildings.[1] This method allows Moller to give a fully convincing account of the German transition from Romanesque to Gothic. He draws attention to the 'deviations' and 'anomalies' of such a situation which may well be 'momentarily discordant and disagreeable', and he is sharp-sighted in spotting that the full Gothic of the thirteenth century is one and the same style 'almost at the same time in all the countries of Europe'. The mid-thirteenth to the late fourteenth century is the architectural climax.

Moller enumerates the various theories of the origin of the Gothic style but does not believe in any of them. As for the country of

---

[1] See the English translation by Priestley and Weale published in 1824 under the title *An Essay on the Origin and Progress of Gothic Architecture*, pp. 1–8. W. H. Leeds published another translation in 1836 under the title *Moller's Memorials of German Gothic Architecture*.

origin he limits the field by accepting as candidates only those which have a northern climate. He makes shamefully short shrift of France and England, using only Notre Dame for France—evidently his knowledge of French cathedrals was extremely scanty—and only York Minster for England. So—a foregone conclusion—Germany wins. No wonder perhaps in the mind of the man who in 1814 had discovered the original design for Cologne Cathedral which was later used for the completion of the gigantic fragment.

This being so, when Moller comes to the question of whether the Gothic style should be used for new buildings today, it is doubly interesting to see that his answer is No. 'We must admire . . . these works, but we cannot produce the like, because the circumstances under which that style of building arose are now no longer the same.' What we would produce would be 'an incongruous and absurd composition'. All this does not, according to Moller, apply to the Grecian style, because this is 'the result of an enlightened understanding and of a correct sense of the beautiful. Hence 'it will never cease to be capable of application',[2] and indeed Moller was an architect in the classical and Italian tradition, as his classical theatre at Darmstadt and his Italian theatre at Mainz show.[3]

Moller's engravings were eagerly studied outside Germany as well, side by side with Sulpiz Boisserée's *Geschichte und Beschreibung des Domes zu Köln*, a sumptuous publication which began to appear in 1823 and was complete in 1831.[4] Moller's text in its English translation was also avidly read. Proof of the regard in which it was held is the fact that Moller was in the first batch of elected honorary members of the newly founded Institute of British Architects, together with Schinkel, Otte of Brunswick, Klenze and Gärtner of Munich, Percier, Fontaine, Le Bas and Gau of Paris, and six others (4 May 1835).[5] Alongside Rickman Moller represented the most respectable scholarship up to 1825.

As for publications of engravings of English medieval architecture

---

[2] pp. 51–3.

[3] On Moller see M. Frölich and H. G. Sperlich, *Georg Moller, Baumeister der Romantik* (Darmstadt, 1959).

[4] On all German literature and problems Frankl's *The Gothic* cannot be bettered. It is required reading.

[5] It may be interesting to parallel this with Corresponding Members of the Société des Antiquaires de Normandie. In 1825 Britton and Pugin Sen. were elected, in 1827–8 Douce and Sir Walter Scott, but also the classicists Raoul-Rochette (see p. 198 ff.) and later Quatremère de Quincy (1829–30) and Hittorff (1831–3), both also classicists. Of Englishmen specially notable is Goodwin the architect (1843–4), of Germans Wetter (1843–4).

John Britton became the great entrepreneur.[6] He was born in 1771. After various picturesque adventures he turned to publishing with *The Beauties of Wiltshire* in 1801. They developed into the celebrated *Beauties of England and Wales* which were issued in twenty volumes between 1801 and 1814. During the years of *The Beauties* Britton moved into more scholarly and more architectural fields. *The Architectural Antiquities of Great Britain* came first (1807 ff), the *Cathedral Antiquities of England* followed (1814 ff) and were never completed. They are publications of great importance; for they first offered the architect and the scholar accurate details of medieval architecture to copy or to study.

Britton crowned these efforts at accuracy with the *Specimens of Gothic Architecture* which came out in 1823–5. Britton's name does not appear on the title-page, though he was the publisher. The authors were A. C. Pugin, the more famous Pugin's father, for the drawings, and E. J. Willson, a Lincoln architect, for the text. The illustrations are of the highest order [Pl. 7], and the text is a considerable contribution to architectural scholarship.[7] Volume five of the *Architectural Antiquities* also contains a long historical text, but this was not issued until 1826, i.e. three years after Willson's. Both must be briefly surveyed, and it must be remembered from the outset that both came out after Rickman's epoch-making little book to which we shall move presently.

Yet what Willson has to say is interesting in its own right.[8] Gothic, he writes in the introduction to volume one, was 'brought into disrepute' by the Late Perpendicular 'overwrought refinement in elaborate details'. The 'barbarous mixtures' of Elizabethan and Jacobean followed, and then the 'pedantic affectation of Italian taste'. When Gothic was taken up again in the eighteenth century Kent was 'miserably deficient in fidelity' and Strawberry Hill no more than 'a heap of inconsistencies'.[9] This changed with Essex who 'was the first professional architect whose works displayed a correct taste in imitation of ancient English architecture. His works

[6] A full account is now at last available: J. Mordaunt Crook, 'John Britton and the Gothic Revival', in *Concerning Architecture*, ed. Sir John Summerson (London, 1968), 98 ff. Valuable also is P. Ferriday's article in *The Architectural Review*, CXXII, 1957. Mr. Howell kindly told me that Mr. Weinreb has two volumes of the Moller edition of 1815 into which is tucked a letter from Moller to Britton introducing a pupil.

[7] On Willson see S. Lang, *Journal of the Society of Architectural Historians*, xxv, 1966, 240–67. John Britton also wrote an obituary for Willson: *Builder*, xiii, 4 (6 Jan. 1854).

[8] Though he has only two lines of footnote in Frankl's book.

[9] *Specimens of Gothic Architecture*, I, ix–xiv.

'cannot be exceeded in their fidelity to ancient examples', but they tend to be meagre and lack boldness. Willson ends this introduction with Wyatt, but he wrote another for the second volume two years later, and here he refers briefly to earlier authors and then ventures upon a Chronological Sketch of English architecture.[10] For Anglo-Saxon he says that nothing is 'yet satisfactorily ascertained', for Norman he suggests the name Romanesque which had in fact been introduced into English by William Gunn in 1819, following the example of M. de Gerville's plea for 'Roman' in 1818.[11] The period 1189–1272 Willson leaves open between Early Gothic, Simple Gothic, Lancet Gothic, English and Early English, 1272–1377 between Pure Gothic, Absolute Gothic, and Decorated English. Willson calls the window tracery of the period 1277–1377 'extremely beautiful', and his examples (York West, Carlisle East, and Lincoln South Transept) show that he does not mean the geometrical tracery of 1250–1300 which became the undisputed favourite of the High Victorians, but the flowing tracery of the Decorated. After 1377 follow Ornamented Gothic, and after 1460 Florid Gothic, or Florid English or Highly Decorated English. Perpendicular English is also mentioned, and this of course—not invented by Willson—carried the day.

As regards the neo-Gothic of his own time Willson is critical: 'We see . . . city merchants inhabiting castles', although 'the ignorance of artificers' tends to produce 'an insipid caricature' and although 'the refinements of modern interior demands' cannot be satisfied in imitation Gothic.[12] A Glossary called 'Technical Terms descriptive of Gothic Architecture' is bound in, and this can serve us as a convenient indication of what present-day terms were already in use in 1822, the date of the glossary. Among them are ambulatory, billet, bowtel (for torus), chevron, corbel table, crocket, cusp, fillet, finial, hood-mould, mullion, ogee, oriel, parclose, pendant, respond, spandril, squinch, stauncheon, transom, wall-plate, zigzag—remarkably many.

But medieval scholarship moved quickly in these years, and Willson's pages in volume two were surpassed already three years

[10] *Specimens of Gothic Architecture*, II, xi–xvii.

[11] For Gunn see *An Enquiry into the Origin and Influence of Gothic Architecture* (1819), for Gerville a letter of 18 Dec. 1818 in which he calls Roman 'un mot de ma façon qui me paraît heureusement inventé' (M. F. Gidon, 'L'invention de l'expression architecture romane', *Bull. Soc. Ant. Norm.*, XLII, 1934, 285–8.

[12] *Specimens,* II, xix–xxiii.

later, in 1826, by Britton's own 180 pages in volume five of the
Architectural Antiquities. The title of this long section is 'Chronological History of Christian Architecture in England'. Compared
with Willson's text Britton's is rather a compilation, but it is a
useful one. There is for instance a long survey of all that had been
written on English medieval architecture from Wotton, Aubrey,
and Wren to 1825. The English translation of Moller (1824) is of
course also referred to.[13] Britton lists sixty-six items altogether. At
the end are appendices including an alphabetical list of architects
and founders of buildings, chronological lists of buildings, monuments, pulpits, fonts, and crosses, and a ten-page glossary. Among
today's terms not in Willson are archivolt, clustered columns,
groin, herringbone, label, nail-head, reredos, rose-window, set-off,
severy, tabernacle, triforium, weepers. As for the names of the styles
Britton is non-committal. He has Saxon (and says like Willson that
'it may . . . be questioned, whether there is even a single specimen of
a complete Saxon Church now remaining in England'),[14] Norman,
and then Pointed First, Second, and Third Division. His highest
praise is, like Willson's, for the time of Edward III ('perhaps for
grace, and elegance of proportion, for richness of decoration without
exuberance, and for scientific skilfulness of execution' the climax[15]),
but the Westminster Chapter House, i.e. what the Victorians called
the Second Pointed, comes in for nearly as much praise (it is on the
way 'to highest eminence').[16]

There is little otherwise of a personal nature in Britton's essay.
He is anti-Catholic ('the unnatural and superstitious profession of
celibacy', 'blind . . . agents of papal avarice', 'the encroachment of
papal tyranny'[17])—three years before Catholic Emancipation—and
he appears a functionalist as regards architecture, though only in a
few sentences at the beginning: 'Architectural excellence consists
in the judicious and skilful adaptation of an edifice to its specific
destination, and in the appropriate and tasteful display or its internal
and external ornaments. Every building of magnitude should be
distinguished by decisive and positive marks of its purpose'.[18] But
Britton does not follow up this statement at all, and altogether
remains throughout the popularizer rather than the scholar. The
contrast between Britton's essay and that of a few years before with
which Rickman appeared on the scene, is in fact striking.

---

[13] And incidentally misdated as being of 1821.   [14] *Architectural Antiquities*, V, 129, 30.
[15] Ibid., 154.   [16] Ibid., 151.   [17] Ibid., 19, 28.   [18] Ibid., 5.

CHAPTER V

Rickman and the Commissioners

RICKMAN did not at once meet with the recognition which he deserved. This is due to the fact that his first paper came out in an obscure Liverpool journal.

Thomas Rickman was born in 1776 and died in 1841. He was the son of a grocer and chemist, first worked in his father's shop, then studied medicine and practised as a doctor at Lewes for two years, and then worked in a firm of corn-factors in London from 1803 to 1808 and in a firm of Liverpool insurance brokers from 1808 to 1813. While in Liverpool he went round drawing churches, and travelled in the north and also as far as Lincolnshire. About 1812 he wrote an architectural history of Chester Cathedral which was not printed until 1861.[1] In the same year he started his career as an architect, a career in which he at last held out and was successful. St George at Everton, Liverpool, dates from 1812–14, St Michael-in-the-Hamlet at Toxteth, Liverpool from 1814–15. Many other churches followed. Mr Colvin lists fifty-five, including eight alterations. He also did a number of secular buildings, best known among them New Court of St John's College, Cambridge. This was done in 1827–31 by Rickman and Henry Hutchinson, his pupil. Hutchinson became a partner in 1821 and died in 1831. Between 1835 and 1841 R. C. Hussey was Rickman's partner and did most of the work owing to Rickman's failing health.

But it is as an author that Rickman has achieved lasting fame. In 1815 he brought out in James Smith's *Panorama of Science and Art* (Liverpool, 1815) a paper called 'An Attempt to Discriminate the Styles of English Architecture from the Conquest to the Reformation'. Only when in 1817 it was published as a book did England begin to notice it, and after a while France as well. It went through

---

[1] In the *Journal of the Architectural, Archaeological and Historic Society for . . . Chester*, II, 277 ff. The printed version is preceded by a Memoir written by Canon Blomfield. More of Rickman in H. M. Colvin's *A Biographical Dictionary of English Architects, 1660–1840* (London, 1954), a book which never seems to fail you.

seven editions, the last one as late as 1881. What the layman knows about it, is that it established Early English, Decorated, and Perpendicular as the terms for the three phases of the Gothic style in England.[2] In fact Rickman does not only say Early English, but also Decorated English, and he justifies the introduction of English by saying that this is done not so much because Gothic is English, though—he adds—'in many instances [the English indeed introduced elements] prior to their continental neighbours', but because each country has its own Gothic[3]—a truth which was to stimulate Whewell and Willis in the thirties. This remark shows at once that there is more to Rickman than just nomenclature.

It is interesting from the start that Rickman at the very beginning of his book calls its purpose twofold: 'to afford the guardians of our ecclesiastical edifices such clear discriminative remarks on the buildings now existing, as may enable them to judge with considerable accuracy of the restorations necessary to be made' and 'to render them more capable of deciding on the various designs for churches in imitation of the English styles'. Both these purposes have more than a touch of self-advertisement. But Rickman also states though not so prominently that the book ought to enable 'most persons to judge at once, at the sight of a plate or a drawing of its correctness'[4] and 'to distinguish the difference of age and style', of a church.[5]

All these were practical purposes, and Rickman was indeed a practical man, or else he would not have become so successful an architect. Thus, for instance, though nearly all his own churches are Gothic of one kind or another, he has no objection to the classical styles. In fact he praises for use in his own age 'the massive Doric' (this was the heyday of the Greek Revival and the so-called Waterloo churches), and the 'beautiful plain Grecian Ionic' and looks forward

---

[2] The priorities on the three terms are not established. For Early English Mr. Howell drew my attention to G. Millers, *A Guide to the Cathedral Church at Ely* (Cambridge, 1805), 7. Decorated English occurs in volume one of Britton's *Architectural Antiquities*, i.e. in 1807. For Perpendicular Rickman seems to have been first. Another terminology which was favoured was Geometrical–Curvilinear–Rectilinear. The latter two were introduced in *The British Critic*, II, 1826, 378. They were adopted and Geometrical was added by Edmund Sharpe in 1849 in *A Treatise on the Rise and Progress of Decorated Tracery in England*, pt. II, chap. I, p. 57 ('It is proposed to apply the term geometrical . . .'), although Rickman had already in the *Attempt* called geometrical tracery as such geometrical. Sharpe's *Treatise* incidentally is dedicated to Willis on whom see Chap. VIII.

[3] *An Attempt . . .* (1817), 37.

[4] Ibid., 109.

[5] Ibid., 37.

to a time 'when we shall have Grecian, Roman and English edifices erected on the principles of each'.[6]

Only the principles of Gothic architecture are less familiar than those of Greek and Roman architecture, and so he had to write his book. The development to him is this. The Roman style 'became debased into the Saxon and early Norman'. Improvement began when columns became piers, i.e. with the 'introduction of shafts'. This emphasis on shafts for the creation of the Gothic style is remarkable. However, he accepts the origin in the intersection of round arches as well (the Gray-Bentham theory) though adding that the pointed arch was accepted because of its 'superior lightness and applicability'. 'The perfection of the English mode' is the Decorated English style, and after it the decline begins with the Perpendicular 'series of pannels' which end by fatiguing the eye with 'the constant repetition of small parts' until the Elizabethan style replaces it, 'rather a debased English than anything else'.[7]

These general introductory remarks are followed by a glossary in which one finds crockets, finials, mullions, spandrels, transoms, as in Willson's and Britton's glossaries later, and also e.g. 'arches of four centres' called Tudor arches, bases 'which will hold water', and 'spherical equilateral triangles.[8] After the glossary comes a more detailed treatment of the styles one after the other, each being dealt with under doors, windows, arches, piers, buttresses, tablets (i.e. cornices etc.), vaults, niches etc., and ornament. Such an arrangement, it will be remembered, had already been adopted by August Wilhelm Schlegel. For Saxon, again like Willson and Britton afterwards, Rickman only says that no datable building has so far been ascertained, though he mentions Barton-on-Humber and Clapham in Bedfordshire,[9] but for Norman and after he is detailed, and pertinent observations follow each other.

His descriptions are more precise than any before. Here he is for instance on the spire of Newark church in Nottinghamshire.[10]

It rises engaged in the west end of the church, and the lower parts are Early English, but it is the upper story of the tower and the spire which are its

---

[6] *An Attempt* . . . (1817), 7. Only on the age of Wren Rickman has reservations. He pronounces regret that Wren did not study the English as well as the Roman style. He gave us, Rickman writes, 'the most magnificent modern building we possess' (i.e. St Paul's) 'but disfigured the English edifice he had to complete' (i.e. Westminster Abbey—mistaking Hawksmoor for Wren).

[7] Ibid., 1–8.

[8] Ibid., 39–42, 57, 59.

[9] Ibid., 45.

[10] Ibid., 82–3.

principal beauties. This story rises from a band (which completely surrounds the tower) of sunk panels. The story consists of a flat buttress of
not much projection on each side, thus making eight round the tower;
these are in three stages, the two lower plain with small plain set-offs, the
upper panelled with an ogee head, and an ogee canopy, above which is a
triangular head to the buttress richly crocketed, which finishes the buttress
under the cornice. Between these buttresses are two beautiful two-light
windows, with rich canopies on the dripstone, and a general canopy over
both, crocketed, and finishing in a rich finial; in the point of this canopy,
between the heads of the windows, is a statue in a small plain niche, and on
each side of the windows are other statues in niches with ogee crocketed
canopies. The tracery of these windows is very good, and the architraves,
both of windows and niches, are composed of shafts. The cornice is filled
with flowers and other ornaments at small intervals, and from the corners
rise short octagonal pedestals, on which are beautiful pinnacles finishing
in statues for finials. The parapet is enriched with sunk quatrefoil panels,
and the spire has plain ribs and additional slopes on the alternate sides;
there are four heights of windows in alternate faces, all except the top row,
richly crocketed. On the whole, perhaps there are no specimens superior
in composition and execution, and few equal.

And here he is on a Perpendicular detail [Pl. 8]:

The small buttresses . . . attached to screen-work . . . are different from
any before used, and they form a good mark of the style. The square
pedestal of the pinnacle being set with an angle to the front, is continued
down, and on each side is set a small buttress of a smaller face than this
pedestal, thus leaving a small staff between them; these buttresses have
set-offs, and this small staff at each set-off has the moulding to it, which
being generally two long hollows and a fillet between, has on the staff the
appearance of a spear head. It is not easy to describe this buttress in words,
but when once seen, it will be easily recognized.[11]

If, with such passages in mind, one goes to Rickman's New Court,
St John's College, Cambridge, one is surprised to see that none of
this antiquarian correctness is to be found. The crowning spire or
pinnacle is not sanctioned by any authority, an arcade like that
dividing the court from the Backs is derived entirely from post-
medieval examples (All Souls, Oxford, by Hawksmoor, for instance,
and the then recent screen of King's College, Cambridge by Wilkins),
and the gatehouse towards the court has a classical pediment
decorated with tracery—a Georgian solecism which the coming

[11] Ibid., 95.

generations were to despise. Just as incorrect is Rickman's Gothic design for the Fitzwilliam Museum competition of 1829, one of three, the others being Grecian and Roman so-called [Pls. 9, 10, 11]. The Gothic one is less Georgian than romantic with its Fonthill tower and its apparent disregard of museum functions.

In the case of churches Rickman could be far more accurate, and his least accurate is in fact his earliest, St George, Everton, Liverpool of 1812–14 with its delightfully licentious cast iron arches and tracery [Pl. 12]. The material was not chosen by Rickman, but by John Cragg, an iron-master, and Rickman complained: 'His ironwork is too stiff in his head to bend to any beauty'.[12] But, seeing the result, one feels that he must have enjoyed himself. In fact, he can as a practising architect never have considered it, as it were, a moral duty to design according to his principles of accuracy. How far superior to most of his fellow-Gothicists he could be is patent in such a church as Hampton Lucy near Charlecote in Warwickshire, built with Hutchinson in 1822–6 [Pls. 13, 14]. The interior in particular is quite convincing, whereas the exterior—the polygonal apse is an addition of 1856 by Sir George Gilbert Scott—has the tightness, the closely set thin buttresses and the high pinnacles on the west tower which are characteristic features of the so-called Commissioners' churches. Rickman indeed designed more of the Commissioners' churches himself or with Hutchinson than any other architect—twenty-one altogether, and some as plain as any of them.

For cheapness—'a proper accommodation for the largest number . . . at the least expense'[13] was one of the demands of the Commissioners, though at first evidently not the decisive one, and since the Commissioners' churches stand at the beginning of the prodigious church building activity of nineteenth-century England, a paragraph or two must be devoted to them.

After some years of intense lobbying an Act was passed in Parliament in 1818 to set aside £1,000,000 for the building of new churches. The main reason was that, owing to the industrial revolution, many thousand people had moved from village to town, and that in these towns there were not enough churches, or, as it was called, not enough sittings. Manchester with a population of 80,000 had only 11,000, Sheffield with a population of 55,000 only 6,300, Stockport

[12] T. Miller Rickman, *Notes on the Life and . . . Work of Thomas Rickman* (London, 1901), 13.
[13] M. H. Port, *Six hundred New Churches* (London, 1961) has assembled all the relevant information. For this quotation see p. 24.

with a population of 34,000 only 2,500. To us this may appear ample, but to a parliament which took it for granted that any self-respecting person attended church regularly, it seemed not only distressing but disgraceful and indeed dangerous.

In the Memorandum handed to the Prime Minister in 1815 by those who worked for a bill, one reads of 'the danger to which the constitution of this country both in church and state is exposed for the want of places of public worship, particularly for persons of the middle and lower classes'. The *Quarterly Review* in 1820 spoke out more sweepingly: 'The edifices which we have erected are manufactories and prisons, the former producing tenants for the latter'; and it concludes: The 'only way of making the people good subjects is by making them good Christians and good men'.[14] Carlyle once said the same more trenchantly: 'Believe in God so that . . . the Manchester operatives be got to spin peaceably'.[15]

The £1,000,000 in the end built 96 churches, obviously not extremely cheaply. Thirty-three of them were in London, 19 in Lancashire, 16 in Yorkshire. The cost was on an average between £5,000 and £15,000, 62 costing over £10,000 and some even more than £20,000, and the Commissioners paid up fully. The style was mostly a Gothic which, if elaborate, was archaeologically far from an accurate reproduction, and, if plain, Gothic hardly more than in pointed windows. An example of the one is St Mary at Sheffield by J. Potter, built in 1826–9 for nearly £14,000 [Pls. 15, 16]. Here are the typical tightly set buttresses and the high pinnacles. The entrance bays left and right of the west tower are typical too, as are internally the wide nave, the aisles as high as the nave, the long, thin windows (here of three lights), the three galleries, the fancy plaster vault on very thin piers, and the short chancel. In short the total impression inside the church has little to do with real interiors of medieval churches. And when it comes to a very cheap church— St Matthew at Duddeston near Birmingham, built in 1839–40, designed by William Thomas and not paid for by the Commissioners but by the Birmingham Church Building Society [Pl. 17]—then Gothic really means no more than a long, narrow body and long, lean pointed windows—Early English, if it must have a historical label. The style was chosen because it 'survives more starvation than

14 Port, 27; *Qu. Rev.*, XXIII.
15 *Past and Present*, Book III, Chap. 15. See also H. L. Sussman, *Victorians and the Machine* (Cambridge, Mass., 1968).

4

any other', as Burges put it.[16] It is this type of minimum Early English, people usually think of when they speak contemptuously of Commissioners' Churches. Such churches are nearly always of the second, not the first, grant. For in 1824 another £500,000 was voted, and that went into 450 churches, i.e. they received only contributions, varying from 5 per cent to 50 per cent and averaging 10 per cent. Ninety-four were in London, 90 in Yorkshire, 63 in Lancashire.

Of Rickman's twenty-one Commissioners' churches some were among the lavish ones, a few also among the archaeologically most respectable (Hampton Lucy has already been mentioned), but others fit the popular image. St George, Chorley (1821–5), St Paul, Preston (1823–5) and Holy Trinity. Darwen (1827–9) all have the Commissioners' characteristics of three galleries, north, south, and west, and thin buttresses. At Chorley and Preston the galleries are on iron columns. Darwen has long, thin two-light windows, Preston pairs of long, thin lancets, Chorley and Preston flat ceilings, and so on.

This is the first time in these pages that a discrepancy is noticed between what a nineteenth-century architect writes and what he builds. More cases and more alarming cases will be presented later. For the unevenness in the character and quality of Rickman's buildings has no parallel in his writings. When, in 1832, he wrote 'Four Letters on the Ecclesiastical Architecture of France' which were published in *Archaeologia*, xxv (1833), the power of his observations and formulation is unimpaired. The letters are the outcome of 'a few weeks' travelling. One hundred and thirty-one buildings in Normandy and Picardy were visited, yet the whole of Letter III is about England. Rickman now felt able to enlarge on Anglo-Saxon architecture, mentioning Brixworth, Barton-on-Humber, Earls Barton, Barnack, St Benet at Cambridge, St Michael at Oxford, Kirkdale, Laughton-en-le-Morthen, and Repton.[17] He then goes on as before, to Early English and to Decorated which 'had the shortest reign'. But the 'best point' remains to him the late fourteenth century; after 1500 'debasement' set in.[18] In this partiality for Perpendicular the majority of architects of the 1830s, and of their patrons too, agreed with Rickman. After all, the Houses of Parlia-

---

[16] *Art applied to Industry* (London, 1865), 110–11.

[17] In 1833 he wrote yet another letter to *Archaeologia*, and this was published in 1834 (vol. XXVI). In this he deals exclusively with Anglo-Saxon buildings, describing for instance long-and-short work (5), triangles instead of arches and rude balusters in windows.

[18] *Archaeologia* (1833), 17–19.

ment are Perpendicular in style. Letter IV deals with the earliest French buildings and then the development from the eleventh century to the Flamboyant. For the thirteenth century Rickman already contrasts Amiens with Salisbury.[19] His own taste is on the English side. He finds French portals with their abundance of figure sculpture confusing and of 'very unsatisfactory appearance'. French Flamboyant also is compared unfavourably with English Perpendicular. The French basket-arch is noted as against the English four-centred arch, but mouldings are noted as similar in both countries. Round piers with arches 'jumping out of the pier side',[20] i.e. with no capitals or abaci at all, get a special remark.

[19] I still could not find a better comparison in my *Outline of European Architecture* well over a hundred years later.

[20] *Archaeologia* (1833), 30.

CHAPTER VI

Caumont

AMONG those whom Rickman met on his journey in 1832 were Augustin Le Prévost at Rouen and Arcisse de Caumont at Caen. Both have already briefly been referred to[1] because of their indebtedness to English archaeologists. Caumont was by far the greater of the two. But though Montalembert, author much later of *Les Moines d'Occident*, wrote of him in his *Le vandalisme dans l'art* in 1839: 'Il a tout vu, tout étudié, tout deviné, tout écrit', yet in Caumont's first and most important writing, *Sur l'architecture du moyen-âge particulièrement en Normandie*[2] which came out in 1824, Rickman's name is absent. *An attempt to discriminate* had not made its impact yet. So Caumont had not the benefit of this the most scholarly treatise to date. His *Sur l'architecture du moyen-âge* is essentially his own, and as a work of scholarship it surpasses Rickman's. Caumont, initially as interested in natural history, geology, and agriculture as in buildings, soon established himself as the most knowledgeable of French antiquarians.[3]

His aim, he states at the start of *Sur l'architecture*, is to make others 'reconnaître du moins d'une manière approximative l'âge d'un monument à la première vue' and at the same time 'rendre populaire ... la science des monuments'.[4] He then divides medieval architecture into the 'Roman'—he adopts Gerville's term—primordial, which is what we would call pre-Norman, 'Roman secondaire', 'Gothique primordial ou à lancettes', 'Gothique secondaire ou rayonnant', and 'Gothique tertiaire ou flamboyant. The terms 'Gothique à lancettes', 'Rayonnant', and 'Flamboyant' incidentally Caumont took over from Le Prévost.[5]

[1] Above, pp. 21–2.   [2] *Mémoires de la Société des Antiquaires de Normandie*, I, 1824, pt. 2.

[3] As Frankl is weak on Caumont, one has to go to de Robillard de Beaurepaire and to Paul Léon (*La vie des monuments français*) for a more general treatment. For both books see note on p. 21.

[4] *Sur l'architecture*, 536–7.

[5] Le Prévost, like Caumont, was also interested in natural history. From 1834 to 1848 he was Deputy for Bernay. He accompanied Taylor and Nodier on their tour through Normandy in preparation of the *Voyage Pittoresque*.

For early buildings Caumont quotes from the sources: Gregory of Tours for the building of Perpetuus at Tours and of Namantius at Clermont Ferrand, and also Bede for Monkwearmouth and Eddius for Hexham[6] But he does not rely solely on written sources, and when it comes to Coutances which, on the strength of written sources alone, M. de Gerville had dated before 1056 although it has lancet windows, Caumont is obviously too polite to his friend to contradict him in so many words.[7] What he did in the end instead was to translate considerably later another English travel-book in which that contradiction is explicitly made.

The book in question is Henry Gally Knight's *An Architectural Tour in Normandy*. The tour was made in 1831, one year before Rickman's, and published in 1836.[8] Gally Knight was an amateur and a Member of Parliament, and followed up his book on Normandy by a sequel on the Normans in Sicily and in 1842–4 by a spectacular two-volume book on *The Ecclesiastical Architecture of Italy* (see below, p. 67). He was with Peel, William Ewart, Thomas Hope, Monckton Milnes, and others a member of the Select Committee on the Fine Arts in 1841 which was to initiate historical fresco paintings in the new Houses of Parliament.[9] The committee had been called together by the Royal Commission for the Promotion of the Fine Arts whose chairman was Prince Albert. Faithful to his German upbringing and his romantic sympathies he admired the Nazarenes and especially Cornelius and collected paintings of the time before the maturity of Raphael. So Gally Knight's works fitted in extremely well. On the Norman tour, undertaken in his English carriage,[10] Knight was accompanied by Richard Hussey who, it will be remembered, was Rickman's partner. So the apostolic succession was secured. The book is less strictly archaeological than the books so far reported: 'Dieppe is an old-fashioned, respectable town, principally of brick'[11] or 'In rambling through Rouen, the artist is arrested at every step by the variety and picturesque combination of gable ends of all heights

---

[6] *Sur l'Architecture*, 547–56.

[7] Ibid., 590. Looking back on pre-Caumont archaeology in France, one should not be too hard on Gerville. Such learned men as Mabillon and Montfaucon had still regarded twelfth-century sculpture as Merovingian and Carolingian, the west tower of St Germain des Prés as sixth-century and the west front of St Denis as eighth-century. Alexandre Lenoir as late as 1806 called the Corbeil *figures colonnes* sixth-century.

[8] The quotations are from the second edition, 1841. Caumont's translation was published in the *Bulletin Monumental*, IV, 1838, 41 ff.

[9] See T. S. R. Boase, 'The Decoration of the new Palace of Westminster', in *Journal of the Warburg & Courtauld Institutes* XVIII, 1954.

[10] *An Architectural Tour in Normandy*, 87.   [11] Ibid., 2.

and dimensions'[12] or 'The old convent [of Saint Wandrille] might easily be converted into a delightful residence and park in the English taste'[13] or 'A ... beautiful valley, or rather glen, of which the steep banks are varied with copse and crag, and watered by the little river ... which hurries and winds along the bottom'.[14]

He comments on the generally bad roads[15] and on farmers pulling down ancient buildings.[16] He says that every village has a *Salon de Biliard*[17] and every town a public library',[18] and he is also capable of quoting Latin from medieval sources,[19] and, as for dating, he is remarkably knowledgeable and to the point. 'In matters of anti-quarian research', he writes in his foreword, 'truth depends upon accurate dates'.[20] 'The French', he says later have 'an indescribable anxiety ... to establish the existence of something Carolingian[21], and this leads to dating too early. Coutances, which brought up this *excursus* on Gally Knight, is the paramount example. It cannot be of 1030–6 as the *Société des Antiquaires de Normandie*, i.e. M. de Gerville, says.[22] 'Does it resemble St Stephen's of Caen [which "disdaining to be decorated, seeks to be sublime"[23]] ... Does it resemble any building ... at that time ... in any part of the world?' And he follows this up with evidence pointing to the thirteenth century. And Coutances is followed by Mortain, also misdated by Gerville.[24] The same treatment is applied to Mortemer.[25] In the case of Bernay he recognizes that it is 'the most ancient building of any consequence ... in Normandy",[26] and has again proved right. Lisieux cannot be of the eleventh century, a consecration of 1178 will apply, Séez cannot have anything to do with a date 1053. The nave must have been built after a fire of 1150, the east end after a fire of 1353.

His observations are throughout excellent. 'The best evidence is in ... buildings themselves ... This evidence is a fact, and a fact is of more weight than bushels of inferences, conjectures, and opinions.' Wide joints for example are early, squared blocks of stone in regular courses begin in the later eleventh century.[27] His taste on the other hand is ambiguous. As a liberal he is hostile to the Middle Ages as such, calling them 'priest-ridden',[28] and to medieval sculpture in

[12] *An Architectural Tour in Normandy*, 22.   [13] Ibid., 10.   [14] Ibid., 110.
[15] Ibid., 92.   [16] Ibid., 91, 95, 110. [17] Ibid., 41.
[18] Ibid., 53.   [19] Ibid., 10–11.   [20] Ibid., iii.
[21] Ibid., 120.   [22] Ibid., 99 ff.   [23] Ibid., 56.
[24] Ibid., 129, also the summing up, 209.   [25] Ibid., 40.   [26] Ibid., 173.
[27] Ibid., 196.   [28] Ibid., 64.

particular: 'appalling images', 'misshapen brood'.[29] Even in architecture he at least once confesses to his preference for 'the buildings
of classic times as the objects of our imitation'.[30] But in Gothic
architecture he calls the Golden Age the time from the late thirteenth
to the middle of the fourteenth century,[31] i.e. the Sainte Chapelle
and Saint Ouen at Rouen,[32] and sees decline in 'the Florid'.[33] Late
Gothic architecture is 'surcharged and obtuse', and there are 'seeds
of debasement' even in King's College Chapel.[34]

King's College Chapel is English, and Gally Knight follows his
thirty-five-page treatment of the development of architecture in
Normandy with forty pages on the parallel development in England.
Here also there are interesting remarks. He accepts no Anglo-
Saxon vestiges, except the towers of Barnack and Whittingham. He
rightly begins the Norman with Edward the Confessor, i.e. before
the Conquest. He names as Transitional to the Gothic both Roche
and Kirkstall, picking what Bilson and Professor Bony were to pick
generations later, and he follows Whittington in insisting that
France preceded England in the use of the pointed arch and in
stressing the importance of Saint Denis.[35]

But then Gally Knight of course had available Caumont's *Sur
l'architecture du moyen-âge*, and to this epoch-making work of scholarship we can now return. Not that *Sur l'architecture* is scholarship
only. Caumont also acknowledges the emotional aspects of the
Gothic style—'tout prit une direction vers le ciel'[36] —and mentions
Mme de Staël and romantic literature.[37] But it is rarely that words
like *mystérieux* and *mélancolique* occur, and on the whole Caumont
just describes and on the strength of description dates. It is characteristic that the hoary question of the origin of the pointed arch
recedes.[38] Intersected round arches—maybe. Imported from the
Orient—may be. In any case the Gothic style was created in France[39]
and England was for quite a time *en retard*,[40] and a note on pointed
arches in Romanesque contexts follows. On the 'Gothique Primordial', to give but one example of Caumont's observation, he
lists as motifs and discusses lancets in pairs and triplets, roses or
quatrefoils or trefoils in the spandrels between, capitals nearer the
Corinthian than the Ionic, columns with rings, parapets with pointed
or pointed-trefoiled arches, vaults on almost unbelievably 'légers

[29] Ibid., 193, 204.   [30] Ibid., 195.   [31] Ibid., 254.
[32] Ibid., 215, 24.   [33] Ibid., 216.   [34] Ibid., 216, 257.
[35] Ibid., 210.   [36] *Sur l'architecture*, 600.   [37] Ibid., 601.
[38] Ibid., 585–93.   [39] Ibid., 596.   [40] Ibid., 640–1.

faisceaux de longues colonnes' and with 'plusieurs nervures . . . en ogives', spires of octagonal shape on towers very rarely octagonal, but turrets square or octagonal, and flying buttresses which come in only in the late twelfth century. All such features are instructively illustrated too [Pl. 18]. Caumont's own taste is like Gally Knight's. The climax of Gothic architecture is the time of Louis IX with the Sainte Chapelle, Reims (cathedral and Saint Nicaise), Royaumont, and others.[41] After the thirteenth century decadence set in: 'surcroît d'ornements, défaut de rectitude dans les lignes', though Saint Ouen at Rouen, begun in 1318, has still no signs of decadence.[42] But in spite of decline Caumont goes on analysing dispassionately, though more briefly—capitals with *choux frisés*, leaves in two tiers, etc.[43]

That Caumont at the start pays his tribute to the English archae-ologists has already been said. Of acknowledgements to German literature there is in *Sur l'architecture* only one: Boisserée's folio on Cologne which—it will be remembered—had just (1823) begun to appear but was not completed till 1831.

1831 is also the year in which volume four of Caumont's *Cours d'antiquités monumentales* appeared, the volume on medieval church architecture. The *Cours* is the printed version of lectures given in 1830. Caumont had now moved from the narrow Norman to the national French field and from a survey of medieval styles to a survey starting with Celtic and Gallo-Roman antiquities. Here English literature has Britton and Pugin added: Gally Knight has been 'impatiently awaited for several years', and Rickman is now mentioned at least once.[44] That much French literature is quoted too goes without saying. There is also some Italian and some German literature, though in the end Caumont reiterates: 'Les ouvrages publiés à Londres sont les plus instructifs de tous'.[45] For Germany Caumont has now apart from Boisserée Moller, of course, and also Stieglitz[46] and Wiebeking.[47] Caumont calls Stieglitz not very

---

[41] *Sur l'architecture*, 632–3, also 641: 'l'époque la plus brillante de l'histoire de l'architecture gothique'.

[42] Ibid., 642.   [43] Ibid., 645, 52.

[44] *Cours d'antiquités monumentales*, 293, 13–17.   [45] Ibid., 36.

[46] Christian Ludwig Stieglitz, *Von altdeutscher Baukunst* (Leipzig, 1820). When W. H. Leeds brought out a third edition of Moller, he added to it notes from Stieglitz.

[47] *Mémoire sur l'état de l'architecture civile dans le moyen-âge* (Munich, 1824). I have not been able to find a copy of this book in England or Germany. Frankl (p. 519) was no more successful. The British Museum copy was burnt. However, the British Museum has a copy of Willis's *Remarks on the Architecture of the Middle Ages* (see Chap. VIII below) with manuscript notes by Cresy (see p. 67), and among these are a few pages from a book by Wiebeking, quite probably the one in

reliable, but the book contains much of interest in our context. Stieglitz states that only the Greeks and the Germans have produced totally original styles of architecture. The Greek is *plastisch*, the German *romantisch*. Great indeed was the influence of the Schlegels! Gothic architecture is the result of a mood not of motifs like the pointed arch. The romantic mood created the 'vaults reaching up to heaven' and the details appearing to originate in a 'free play of fantasy'.[48] But Stieglitz also discusses quite a number of German Gothic buildings. On Moller enough has already been said.[49]

The fourth volume of Caumont's *Cours* runs to well over 300 pages. It is an enlargement of *Sur l'architecture*, and, like *Sur l'architecture* it is intended to be a presentation of facts 'avec la plus stricte impartialité'.[50] Roman primordial is now 'Roman primitif', and there is a 'Roman tertiaire ou la transition'. In each chapter the architectural elements or members are discussed first, examples second. The number of detail observations is impressive [Pl. 19]. The origin of Gothic has forty pages to itself, and Caumont attributes it rather to the 'besoin irrésistible d'innover'[51] than to individual motifs. The earliest dates of Gothic motifs Caumont treats intelligently, but he clearly avoids an explicit answer which would have hurt Gerville. Hence, as had already been said, his later translation of Gally Knight. After that he runs through what is now called 'Ogival primitif' of the late twelfth and the thirteenth century, 'Ogival secondaire', i.e. the fourteenth century, 'Ogival tertiaire', i.e. 1400–*c*. 1480, and 'Ogival quartaire' which includes the early Renaissance.

The climax for Caumont, 'la belle époque', is, just as for Gally Knight, the thirteenth century with its 'effet magique', its 'élancement vers le ciel' and its 'hardiesse'.[52] This is also the epoch when the former anonymity of masons, due to the fact that 'il n'y eut point d'individus, pour ainsi dire', began 'à s'individualiser'. Caumont

---

question. Wiebeking also wrote an *Architecture civile* in seven volumes, but otherwise mostly on matters of engineering (hydraulics, bridge building, road building). In the passage copied by Cresy he describes how medieval vaulted churches were built. The pinnacles on flying buttresses e.g. are not 'vaines décorations' but a structural necessity. The most interesting paragraph is on rib-vaulting and especially the controversial matter of how the webs or cells were constructed, after the arches and the ribs had been built on special centering. In the webs one places 'des lattes flexible sur les centres des nervures; on commence les voûtes d'encadrement dans les angles et près des nervures, et on avance vers les arrêts. Dans les petits vides on voûte sans échafaudage. L'on exécute les cintres servant à l'exécution des nervures à moises pendantes, et on attache les échafaudages aux entraits du comble qui portait les chèvres. C'est par ces moyens qu'on termine les voûtes entre quatre arcs doublaux'.

[48] Frankl, *The Gothic*, 466.   [49] See p. 23.   [50] Caumont, *Cours*, IV, 5.
[51] Ibid., 214.   [52] Ibid., 269.

ends proudly: 'Personne ne m'a devancé dans la carrière que je
viens de parcourir', and he was right. He is the first professional
antiquarian, and being French that means that he was not satisfied
with talking and writing, he wanted to organize as well. And so it
was Caumont in the first place who created the Société des Antiquaires de Normandie in 1823 (the name formed on that of the
Society of Antiquaries) and the Société française d'archéologie in
1834. In that year also he began to hold Congrès Archéologiques
and to bring out a journal, the *Bulletin Monumental*, both still the
principal media of architectural research in France. In the *Bulletin
Monumental* Caumont did some of his most interesting writing.[53]

And he also wrote and published the first inventory of monuments, the *Statistique Monumentale du Calvados* issued in five volumes
in 1846–67 but already announced by Caumont at the start of volume
four of his Cours.[54] Inventorisation in France admittedly had a long
prehistory, beginning with the Académie des Inscriptions et Belles
Lettres in 1810 asking the prefects of the departments for lists of
buildings. Caumont also acknowledges that M. de Gerville from
1814 onwards had studied 400–500 churches in La Manche with a
view to an inventory. However, in all these activities Caumont was
ahead of all others. In England the British Archaeological Association was started only in 1843, and inventorization began only with
the establishment of the Royal Commission on Historical Monuments in 1908. Since then twenty-three volumes have come out,
less than one-twentieth of what will be needed to cover the country.[55]
The countries of the highest achievement in inventorization are
Germany, Switzerland, and Austria. According to a recent count of
all published volumes in what is now the Federal Republic of
Germany,[56] about 450 volumes have so far come out. It is hard to

---

[53] The Société francaise also had foreign members, and they show especially clearly that at
that time France was archaeologically less nationally confined than she has become since. In
1840 the following whom we have already met or are soon to meet were foreign members:
Rickman, Parker (see p. 123), Britton, Gally Knight, Whewell (see the next chapter), Wetter
(see below), and Lassaulx (see below and p. 46), and in 1842 Boisserée and Hübsch (see p. 64,
n. 2,) were elected.

[54] 'J'ai commencé . . .', p. 1.

[55] This figure takes into consideration that until very recently no building later than 1714
was included—which of course leaves out the bulk of the architecturally valuable buildings of
England. At the rate at which the Commission is allowed by the Treasury to work completion
of the Royal Commission's task will take another 600 years at the most generous estimate.
Scotland has so far brought out twenty-two volumes covering eighteen counties, Wales eleven
for nine counties.

[56] *Deutsche Kunst und Denkmalpflege*, XXVI, 1968 and XXVII, 1969; *Kunstchronik*, XXII,
1969, 132 ff. Also for earlier lists, *Deutsche Kunst und Denkmalpflege* 1940–1, 71 ff. and XI, 1953,

say when Germany started, as the date would depend on what should be called the first real inventory. Anyway, speed began to be gathered after the Franco-Prussian war, whereas France herself after Caumont's valiant start gave up totally.

One more means by which Caumont communicated information deserves mention, the reports he put into the *Bulletin Monumental* from 1841 onwards of journeys of exploration he made, mostly in France, but also in Germany. A German journey, for instance,[57] brought him several hours with Johann Claudius von Lassaulx, official architect (Bezirksbauinspektor and Stadtbaumeister) at Koblenz who had already written a letter to Caumont in 1838 which was published in the *Bulletin Monumental*.[58] It listed German antiquarian publications, starting with Boisserée and Moller, and recommended the use of round rather than pointed arches where cheapness mattered. On the same journey Caumont had hoped to meet Boisserée, but this proved impossible, because Boisserée had gone on a trip with the King of Prussia. Lassaulx (whom we shall come across again) had published in *Crelles Journal für die Baukunst* in 1829 a suggestion how vaults could be constructed 'aus freier Hand' ('Beschreibung des Verfahrens bei Anfertigung leichter Gewölbe'). The paper had at once been translated into English (*Journal of the Royal Institution of Great Britain*, I. 1830–1) and French (*Journal du génie civil*, 1833; also *Bulletin Monumental*, IV, 1838, 458).[59] Caumont also several times met Johannes Wetter who lived at Mainz and in 1835 had produced a memorable guide to Mainz Cathedral in which he had defined the Gothic style by an analysis of

70 ff. The same journal XXVII, 1969, 54 ff. and 197 ff. has most gratifyingly added the lists for East Germany, the former German east territories, Denmark, Holland, Belgium, Luxembourg, Switzerland, Austria, Czechoslovakia, Alsace-Lorraine, and Alto Adige. I have to thank Dr. Wolfgang Götz for information on German inventorization and for drawing my attention to the papers of 1968 and 1969. The Reich in 1936–9 managed to bring out forty-two volumes, the Bund in 1948–67 eighty-four volumes. Switzerland's score for 1936–67 is forty-seven volumes. It all puts us to deep shame. J. Braun, 'Die Inventarisierung der Denkmäler im Deutschen Reich', in *Stimmen der Zeit*, XCII, 1917, 680 ff. is still worth reading.

[57] Made in 1842, published vol. ix, 1843.

[58] Vol. IV, 458 ff.

[59] The English translation is by Whewell on whom see the next chapter (p. 45 ff.). Lassaulx ends this paper by saying that, if in future he will have to build churches, he is going to build them in the *Rundbogenstil*. This indeed he did. His earlier churches had been Gothic. From 1824 they were Romanesque. See Albrecht Mann, *Die Neuromanik* (Cologne, 1966) and Frank Schwieger, *Johann Claudius von Lassaulx* (Neuss, 1968), a disappointing book from the point of view of Lassaulx's style. It contains a descriptive catalogue and stresses Lassaulx as a restorer. He visited Paris in 1822. He knew Schinkel and Moller as well as Caumont and Whewell. That he was a foreign member of the Société française has already been said. He was also an Honorary Corresponding Member of the Royal Institute of British Architects by 1838 (see the *Transactions*).

its elements: the vault, its support by piers, buttresses and flying buttresses, and the pointed arch, reducing lateral thrust. The result, he writes, was a 'lofty aspiring skeleton of stone and interstices either open or filled by thin cells of light materials'.[60] It is gratifying to see the workings of this little commonweal of medieval archaeologists, which knew no national boundaries yet. Indeed England in the 1830s had a considerable part to play in its internationality, thanks largely to two men, William Whewell and Robert Willis, neither of them a professional in Caumont's sense.

[60] Frankl, *The Gothic*, in great detail.

CHAPTER VII

Whewell

WILLIAM WHEWELL, the future Master of Trinity College, Cambridge, was born in 1794.[1] His father was a carpenter. The son went to a grammar school and in 1812 to Cambridge. He did well there, became President of the Union in 1817 and in the same year was elected a Fellow of Trinity. His subject was mathematics, but in 1819 he wrote a textbook on mechanics which was highly successful. In 1820 he was made an FRS, in 1825 he was ordained priest, in 1828 he became Professor of Mineralogy, in 1838 Professor of Moral Philosophy, and in 1841 Master of Trinity. He married first Cordelia Marshall, of the Leeds flax-spinning family which built the celebrated Marshall Mills with its egyptianizing façade and ingenious drainage,[2] and after her death, Lady Affleck. From them and also from his stipend and his royalties he accumulated enough money to purchase the site of Whewell's Court and pay for the buildings. The total cost is estimated at £100,000.[3] He died in 1866, and in 1867 out of part of his wealth a chair of International Law was established at Cambridge.

Already in 1823 he had travelled through Picardy and Normandy to look at buildings. He was accompanied by, or rather he accompanied, Kenelm Digby whose tutor he was and whom we have come across already a propos Schlegel and shall soon come across again. In 1829–31 Whewell travelled again in Normandy and also in Germany, and it is the book resulting from his 'hasty tour of a very few months' in Germany that secures him a place in the present context. The *Architectural Notes on German Churches* came out

[1] On Whewell in the present context see N. Pevsner in *German Life and Letters*, XXII, 1968, 37 ff. Also Mrs. Stair Douglas, *Life and Selections from the Correspondence of William Whewell* (London, 1881), and I. Todhunter, *William Whewell*, 2 vols. (1876) which contains a list of all Whewell's publications. The entry in the *DNB* is by Sir Leslie Stephen. Recently R. Robson and W. F. Cannon have done two papers for the *Notes and Records of the Royal Society*, XIX, 1964, 168 ff.

[2] See for a quick reference my *Studies in Art, Architecture and Design* (London, 1968) I, 213 and the bibliographical note 10 on 246.

[3] I owe this information to Mr. Robson.

anonymously in 1830, and named in a second edition in 1835 and a third, much enlarged, in 1842.[4] The principal additions of the second and third editions are a translation of the notes on Rhineland churches contributed by Lassaulx to Klein's *Rheinreise* of 1835,[5] and notes written during an architectural tour in Picardy and Normandy, a tour undertaken in 1831 with Rickman, the tour in fact which made Rickman write his letters to *Archaeologia*. So as Whewell is linked with Rickman by companionship, Lassaulx, whom he calls 'my valued friend',[6] links him with Caumont who, as has been reported, met Lassaulx in 1842, the year of Whewell's enlarged edition.[7]

Whewell apparently knew Moller's text and plates well, and he also owed much to Rickman, 'that excellent and sagacious man' and 'his fixation of the language of science'.[8] Whewell himself was keen on an accepted glossary and said that Rickman's ought to be extended,[9] and devoted a special section to it, adding the page-number in his text to the individual terms.[10] Among the terms introduced by him and now universally used are cushion-capital and sexpartite vault.[11] The terminological list is contained in the chapter called 'Suggestions on the Manner of Making Architectural Notes', a chapter that states at the start: 'Any sound speculation must be founded on the accurate knowledge of an extensive collection of particular instances',[12] a collection which incidentally ought to include 'profiles of mouldings' to be carefully copied.[13] And indeed the strength of Whewell's book which was unmatched in 1830 in England is the combination of closely observed specimens with sound speculation.

In fact, sound speculation—'something of theory and system', as he writes[14]—is the most impressive quality of the book. A table of contents shows: a preface to the first edition *c.* 30 pages, preface to

---

4 The following page references are to the edition of 1842.
5 Koblenz, 1835, 439 ff.
6 Preface to the third edition.
7 Lassaulx (on whom see the note to the preceding chapter, p. 43) was also quoted by Edmund Sharpe in *The Ecclesiologist,* I, 1841, 120 ff. Sharpe is best known for his publications on the development of tracery with the terms geometrical, curvilinear and rectilinear (see p. 29, n. 2), but two of the churches he designed in the mid-forties are of considerable interest, because they are built almost entirely of terracotta, and even the fitments are in that material. They are St Stephen, Lever Bridge, Bolton (1844) and Holy Trinity, Fallowfield, Manchester (1845). See R. Jolley, 'Edmund Sharpe and the Pot Churches', *The Architectural Review,* CXLVI, 1969, 427 ff. It need hardly be said that *The Ecclesiologist* castigated them (IX, 1849, 137 ff.). On *The Ecclesiologist* see below, p. 124.
8 *Architectural Notes on German Churches,* XIV.
9 Ibid., 41.   10 Ibid., 136 ff.   11 Ibid., 71, 72.
12 Ibid., 133.   13 Ibid., 43.   14 Ibid., 18.

the second edition *c*. 15 pages, preface to the third edition *c*. 15 pages, all mostly discussing general points; Chapter One, 'On the Causes of Pointed Architecture' *c*. 40 pages; Chapter Two, 'On the Characters of Transition in Early German Architecture' *c*. 40 pages; and then the 'Suggestions on the Manner of Making architectural Notes' already referred to. The chapter ends with a list of the principal churches examined, about 100 of them, and is followed only by the long addenda of the third edition also already noted.

Yet the core of the book remains Chapter Two. It is highly remarkable both for its sagacity and for the fact that it makes the book the first to deal essentially with one historical problem in one country. The problem is this, explained in terms of today. The Romanesque style is essentially the same in all countries; so is the High Gothic from Chartres to about 1300. The latter, initiated in France just before 1200, in Germany in 1235 with St Elizabeth at Marburg (as Whewell knows and as Moller knew before him), in England in 1245 with Westminster Abbey, is, as Whewell writes in 1835, 'very nearly identical in a great part of Europe'.[14a] But in between lies the Early English in England, and what corresponds chronologically to it in Germany is totally different. Whewell calls it Early German, which has turned out to be an unfortunate term, characterized by mixing a florid indigenous Late Romanesque with not yet fully understood French Gothic motifs, particularly from Laon. Moller had seen that more clearly than Whewell (see p. 23). The best examples are St Gereon at Cologne of 1219-27, Gelnhausen with a date 1243 on its latest part, and Limburg an der Lahn, with the consecration of an altar in 1235. To these is to be added the west choir of Worms Cathedral which is undated but must belong to the first quarter of the century. The principal characteristics are the many-towered, still German-Romanesque skyline— 'like a fine city', says Whewell[15]—some Romanesque decoration still, especially at Worms, capitals partly Romanesque, partly of the French Early Gothic crocket type, and—inspired by the same French style—galleries (or triforia) with twin or triple openings of pointed arches, and sexpartite rib-vaults. At Worms, in the midst of Late Romanesque exuberance, is a Gothic rose-window.

Now Whewell has seen and describes all this, but he describes it as a sequence of events, the sequence formed not on the strength of dates of beginning or consecration of buildings. He apologizes in

[14a] Ibid., 232. [15] Ibid., 96.

the first preface for the shortage of dates assembled by himself; but he insists that the scholar ought to be able to show 'consistency of development' on the strength of 'the internal evidence of derivation and succession'.[16] Whewell in this appears the first ever to establish the autonomy of criteria of style for the dating of architecture—*Stilkritik*, as German art historians were to call it much later.[17]

Armed with these tools handled of course more expertly by a scientist than by an amateur archaeologist or even an architect Whewell examined German churches—fourteen at Cologne, the cathedrals of Mainz and Worms, Limburg, Bonn, Koblenz, and so on, including such smaller places as Andernach and Sinzig, and extending to Bamberg, and for later Gothic buildings to Landshut, Nuremberg, Regensburg, and other places. Descriptions are of the kind of this one for Bamberg: 'It has pointed pier arches, and pointed vaulting; the piers have slender shafts attached, the mouldings are small rolls; there are clustered and banded shafts with capitals of upright foliage'.[18] But true to his programme he rather describes by motifs than by buildings, and so in his Chapter Two he runs through the plan (apses at both ends, apses turning polygonal, west as well as east transepts, and towers also to west and east), vaulting (often sexpartite), arches (often unmoulded), galleries which had been absent in the Romanesque style, windows in 'groups of three stepped lancets or sometimes of fan-shape', corbel-tables of 'circular notches' on pilaster-strips,[19] dwarf galleries etc.

The general character and development of the German Late Romanesque, as abstracted from all these details, comes out with far greater clarity than in any contemporary German literature. Lassaulx in fact called Whewell's book 'excellent' and 'not sufficiently known' in Germany.[20] Nor has Whewell's treatment of the German Late Romanesque been superseded between Lassaulx and today. The transition, Whewell writes, came 'by gradations of more or less, by changes of one part or another, the style advancing over the interval without apparently finding any intermediate position of equilibrium ... from the just wavering Romanesque of Mentz or Worms, to the multiplied but not quite Gothic elements of Limburg and

[16] *Architectural Notes on German Churches*, 25.

[17] M. de Gerville's mis-dating of Coutances Cathedral appears here quoted earlier in fact than in Gally Knight. But Whewell is still ready to accept the eighth century for St Mary-in-Capitol at Cologne which is one of the best and most typical buildings of the mid-eleventh (83). Friedrich Schlegel incidentally had made the same mistake. See *Briefe von einer Reise . . .*, in *Krit. Ausg.* IV (1959), 175.

[18] *Architectural Notes*, 28.   [19] He means Lombard friezes.   [20] *Architectural Notes*, 204.

'Gelnhausen'.[21] The result is, in total contrast to the harmony of the Early English, 'for a considerable period . . . an image of conflict and indecision'.[22]

To see the transition so clearly Whewell had to have an equally clear picture of what is Romanesque and what is Gothic, and here again he was far ahead of his time. Frankl, in *Gothic Architecture* (Pelican History of Art, Harmondsworth, 1962), defined as one of the basic contrasts of the two styles Romanesque frontality and Gothic diagonality. That is precisely what Whewell recognized: Romanesque has 'a prevelance of rectangular faces and square-edged projections'. In the Gothic style 'the square edges disappear'.[23] The square abacus is Romanesque, and 'where it occurs . . . the Gothic is not complete'.[24]

Naturally the much fought-over ground of the origin of the Gothic style had to be entered by Whewell too. It need hardly be said that in discussing this problem he proves himself once more a pioneer. To treat it as the problem of how the pointed arch was discovered is 'a trifling enquiry' and has by now 'become both frivolous and insoluble'.[25] The intersection of round arches may indeed have '*offered* the pointed arch; but what induced men to *take* it?'[26] Gothic is the result of a general development from the 'horizontalism of column and architrave' to verticalism.[27] The piers are given shafts, the shafts send up the vaulting shafts,[28] or, to put it the other way, the pointed arch was adopted because of 'the requirement of vaulting, and . . . the necessity of having arches of equal heights with different widths'.[29] That is of course Essex's theory, (see p. 6), and Whewell indeed quotes Saunders, Ware, and also Kerrich's references to Essex.[30] Nor is this to Whewell merely an argument of 'utility and convenience'; for utility and convenience 'can never elevate. . . forms and artifices . . . into an object of taste'. Gothic is 'a principle of vitality and unity'. 'A cotton mill or an engine house are constructed with a perfect adaptation to their purposes . . . but never have given rise to a style of architecture.'[31]

---

[21] Ibid., 24. [22] Ibid., 126. [23] Ibid., 47–9.

[24] Ibid., 111. Thomas Hope incidentally in his book of 1835 (see p. 69) took this up and describes (p. 435) how 'piers face each other with their angles'.

[25] Ibid., 306–7. [26] Ibid., 324. [27] Ibid., 313.

[28] Ibid., 308. The emphasis on shafts comes from Rickman, see p. 30. [29] Ibid., 19.

[30] Ibid., 55–6. Whewell also stresses as a 'distinct principle' of Gothic structure 'the admission of oblique pressures'. He quotes 'a friend' in this context—no doubt referring to Willis—but something like oblique pressures had played a part already in Young and Anderson (see pp. 16 and 18).

[31] Ibid., 321–2.

5

So much on the German Late Romanesque and on the Gothic in general. Whewell also knew the later German Gothic well. He notes the hall-church principle, 'aisles of the same height as the nave', as one of its outstanding features[32] and actually wrote a special paper on it some years later[33] in which he promises a 'theory of the dissolution of Gothic architecture' and indeed lists and discusses six principles. Among them are the difference between 'the real construction' and 'a superinduced decorative structure',[34] the difference between 'framework' and 'wallwork',[35] the 'interpenetration of coexisting forms'[36] and an ornamentation which is 'only fanciful, not organic'.[37] He also describes how 'the vaults rest on cylindrical or polygonal piers, out of which the vaulting ribs spring abruptly with a discontinuous impost.[38]

Whewell takes it for granted that the Late Gothic is not liked in any of the types into which the international style of the thirteenth and early fourteenth century broke up. 'Most architectural eyes', he writes, 'feel repugnance at first sight of the French Flamboyant', and indeed the tracery of the English Perpendicular has 'more truly the aspect of good architecture than the later tracery of Germany or of France'.[39]

In his dislike of the Late Gothic Whewell is at one with Caumont, but, as against Caumont (and before him Essex and Whittington), he does not regard the French Cathedral Gothic or the late thirteenth century as the acme; for to him the flying buttresses are merely 'an exterior scaffolding' and destroy externally 'all possibility of well proportioned dimensions and parts'.[40] What to him is the classic moment he never says. If it is not the late thirteenth century and not the Late Gothic, is it the Decorated, as praised above the others by Willson and Britton? The Gothic Revival of his own day he recognizes, and he seems to approve of it, though a remark like the following remains ambiguous. The Gothic, he writes, was 'first despised, then tolerated as convenient, then wondered at as whimsical and lawless' but is now 'admired as beautiful and excellent'.[41] That he

[32] *Architectural Notes*, 63.
[33] 'Remarks on the Complete Gothic and After-Gothic in Germany', *Archaeological Journal*, VII, 1850. The term After-Gothic he took over from Willis.
[34] Ibid., 224–5.   [35] Ibid.
[36] Ibid., 229. This is again taken over from Willis—see below, p. 56.
[37] Ibid., 232.   [38] Ibid., 233.
[39] Ibid., 234. For Rickman, it will be remembered, the climax was the early fourteenth century (see p. 30).
[40] Ibid., 258.   [41] Ibid., 2.

dislikes the Italian Renaissance ('unprofitable magnificence')[42] goes
without saying. Italian Gothic comes in only occasionally and
marginally, and it must be admitted that he knew little of France
other than his Picardy–Normandy corner, and of Spain less. For
how could he otherwise have said that tunnel-vaults rarely occur in
churches, tunnel-vaults being, if any, the standard Romanesque
vaults of France?[43] Saint Riquier he had never heard of when he
saw it,[44] and of Spain all he has to say is that 'it is said that there are
in Spain good cathedrals of Gothic architecture'.[45] For the Italian
Gothic his source is his younger Cambridge friend Robert Willis—
but only for the second and third editions. Concerning the first
edition he specifically emphasizes that it was written 'in entire
ignorance' of Willis,[46] which must of course be true, since Willis's
book came out only in 1835. In his later years Whewell wrote less
and less on architecture[47] though his interest in Germany kept alive.
He translated Schiller's and Bürger's poems into verse, and *The
Professor's Wife* by Berthold Auerbach, and he wrote on Goethe's
Hermann und Dorothea and *Wilhelm Meister*. He also reviewed Ruskin's
Seven Lamps of Architecture, read a paper in the session of 1862–3 at
the Royal Institute of British Architects on whether architecture
ought to be called an imitative art, and commented interestingly on
the exhibition of 1851.[48]

[42] Ibid., 18.   [43] Ibid., 60.
[44] Ibid., 235.   [45] Ibid., 33.
[46] Ibid., 14. Whewell refers to Willis's book on pp. 4 and 34.
[47] But his fame as an architectural scholar lasted. Eastlake in his *A History of the Gothic Revival in England* in 1872 still speaks of his 'vast and comprehensive store of information' (p. 130). Bartholomew incidentally in 1839 (see p. 90) acknowledged the 'gigantic strides' made by Whewell (paragraph 252).
[48] The comments on Ruskin and on the 1851 exhibition are referred to below, pp. 152 and 161–2. On all this see Todhunter op. cit., I.

CHAPTER VIII

Willis

ROBERT WILLIS was born in 1800, the son of a physician to the
King.[1] In 1819 he patented a gadget connected with the pedal of the
harp. He went to Caius College as a pensioner in 1821, took his B.A.
in 1826, was ordained deacon in 1827 and in the same year priest,
became a fellow of Caius in 1826, dean in 1827, steward in 1829, a
Fellow of the Royal Society in 1830, and Jacksonian Professor of
Natural and Experimental Philosophy at Cambridge in 1837. He
was obviously a brilliant man, and, incidentally, skilful at music. In
1832 he had married the daughter of Charles Humfrey, a minor
Cambridge architect. Perhaps he was already interested in what
architects were doing. In any case, in 1835 he published as his first
book a volume entirely devoted to problems of architectural history.
It was called *Remarks on the Architecture of the Middle Ages, especially
of Italy*, and it was at once taken very seriously; for in the first
volume of the *Transactions* of the newly founded Institute of British
Architects, the volume for 1835–6, Willis and with him Whewell
appear as Honorary Members. Willis's *Remarks* are indeed as much
pioneer work as Whewell's book on Germany and as much ahead of
others in precision of description, clarity of thought, and expansion
into general theory.

Like Whewell Willis begins by apologizing. The book is the
result of no more than 'a rapid tour through France, Italy and
Germany',[2] a tour undertaken in 1832–3. The aim of the book is 'a
comparison of [the] European styles' within Gothic, and Willis
promises that it is to be more 'extensive . . . [than] has ever been
made'.[3] Existing literature useful to his pursuit is listed in an appendix and acknowledged, especially 'the author of the *Architectural*

---

[1] The following pages are an expanded version of a lecture I gave in honour of Henry-
Russell Hitchcock at Smith College, Northampton, Mass., in 1968. It was printed and published
very handsomely by the college in 1970. On Willis see the *DNB*. The account there is by John
Willis Clark on whom see note 29 below. In addition I used John Venn, *Biographical History of
Gonville and Caius College*, II (Cambridge, 1898).

[2] *Remarks on the Architecture of the Middle Ages*, iii.   [3] Ibid., vi.

Notes on German Churches',[4] and Rickman 'without whose admirably systematic method' Willis could not have written his book.[5] Like Rickman and Whewell Willis is keen on terminology. Among terms mentioned and now familiar one notices continuous mouldings, Saxon mid-wall shafts, tracery bars, and compound piers.[6] In accuracy of description Willis even surpasses Whewell. The technique is that of the engineer rather than the architect. For example: 'at Geneva, Plate III, fig. 23 m p n is the section of the pier arch, which differs from a b, fig. 22, only in having edge-beads m n applied to the first order, and chamfers to the second, p.'[7]

However, like Whewell, he arranges his descriptions not simply by buildings, but by their various elements. So there are chapters on imposts, shafts, tracery, and—the longest chapter—vaulting, and exactly like Whewell Willis proceeds beyond this kind of analysis to what he considers the characteristics of the Gothic style in Italy. But his attitude differs in one way from Whewell's. Whewell was obviously thrilled by what he saw in Germany. Willis—it cannot be denied—felt only contempt for what he calls 'the inferiority of the Italian to all other Gothic styles'.[8] Especially he finds the horizontal striping of e.g. Siena Cathedral so beloved of Butterfield and Ruskin —'streaky bacon' as later cynics called it—'disagreeable' and 'destructive of architectural grandeur'[9] and states much more sweepingly (and pertinently) at the very start that 'there is, in fact, no genuine Gothic in Italy',[10] and he has good arguments. Gothic architecture, he says, incites simultaneously the ideas of height, length and breadth (the latter must refer to vistas across the arcades into the aisles). But in Italy the height is more than twice the breadth of the nave, and the spans of the arcade arches are as wide as those of the transverse arches. It is these wide arcade arches that prove 'actively destructive of the effect of the whole as a Gothic composition'.[11] Only Milan and Siena possess more Gothic proportions. In another place, equally judiciously, Willis explains the particular nature of Italian Gothic architecture from the fact that it 'presents a serious mixture' of Gothic and classical elements, 'taking

---

[4] Ibid., v.   [5] Ibid., 13.   [6] Ibid., 28, 50, 53, 86.
[7] Ibid., 102.   [8] Ibid., 138.   [9] Ibid., 12.
[10] In this judgement, incidentally, he had been preceded by August Wilhelm Schlegel who stated: 'Gothische Baukunst . . . Ihr Charakter in Italien verfälscht'. See *Die Kunstlehre,* ed. E. Lohner (1963), 157.
[11] Willis, *Remarks,* 130.

sometimes one side . . . and sometimes another', stressing now the verticals and now the horizontals and—we are at once reminded of Whewell—using flat, pilaster-like surfaces, mostly with square edges'.[12]

So, even more than Whewell, Willis used the specific subject-matter of his book predominantly as a vehicle to convey more general observations on the nature of Gothic. The most interesting and prophetic observation is that on the difference between 'mechanical and decorative construction'. The eye, he writes, demands to see 'the weights . . . duly supported'. Hence part of Gothic decoration represents construction, though 'this apparent frame is often totally different from the real one'. So we must always watch 'how weights are really supported and how they seem to be supported'.[13] This is exactly the argument Pol Abraham put forward in 1934 to defeat Viollet-le-Duc's thesis.[14]

Vaulting was clearly what fascinated Willis most, and so his next publication dealt with vaulting exclusively; for, unlike Whewell, once Willis had turned to architecture, he went on researching and writing, without however neglecting the duties of his chair.

1841 is the *annus mirabilis* of the story of the Gothic Revival in England. In that year—the year of Rickman's death—Pugin published his *True Principles*, the first volume of *The Ecclesiologist* came out, and Willis wrote his paper 'On the Construction of Vaults in the Middle Ages'. This, which was published in 1842 by the newly founded Institute of British Architects,[15] is epoch-making indeed; for much as we may admire the precociousness of Whewell on Germany and Willis on Italy, Willis's long paper on vaults and its illustrations established a standard of insight and meticulous accuracy which has never since—in England or anywhere else—been surpassed [Pls. 20, 21]. In fact, from 1841 onwards to his death in 1875 one can say of Willis's writings what Delacroix said of Titian: 'Ce que il fait, est fait'.[16] Willis's first question in this treatise is: How did medieval masons set out vaults as complicated as those of the Late Gothic period in England? To answer it he goes to the French literature on the 'taille de pierre' from Delorme in 1568 to

[12] Willis, *Remarks,* 156.
[13] Ibid., 15–16.
[14] *Viollet-le-Duc et le rationalisme médiéval* (Paris, 1934).
[15] *Transactions,* I, pt. 2. On the R.I.B.A. see p. 24 and below, p. 80.
[16] *Journal d'Eugène Delacroix* (ed. A. Joubin, edition of 1950), II, 282. Entry of 4 Oct. 1854.

Frézier in 1738;[17] for in England 'this art has been rather neglected.'[18] His research leads him to the study of the upper surface of vaults where it happened to be exposed to view,[19] and to individual stones on which the incised lines happen to survive which masons drew to mark where and with what profiles the ribs should spring from the tas-de-charge. Such he found at Southwark Cathedral on the demolition of the nave in 1838-9 and at Canterbury Cathedral on the demolition of Lanfranc's tower in 1834.[20]

Willis then discusses in great detail rib-vaults from the simplest to the most complicated. His drawings are still used as the best now, and his descriptions read like those of engineers' technical illustrations: 'Now supposing a rib consists of a single arc of a circle, we may either place the centre of this arc on the impost level, or we may allow it to be placed above or below it.' Then it goes on: 'Let fig. 9 be a vault of which the plan is given, and of which the height of the apices of each rib E, g, f, C, e, D are also determined, as well as the middle plan p, v, s, n, r, m . . . Let ABCD be the plan of the vault.'[21] In all this Willis remains aware of the distinction between 'decorative and mechanical construction', as established in his previous book.[22] He is incidentally also aware of a problem rarely touched on today, namely that complicated vaults which look orderly in plan and are then easy to understand may look wholly confusing when viewed from below because of the differences of curvature in the vault. This the masons must have known, and to take the visual effects into consideration 'argues a great power of fore-seeing'.[23] But they were not always successful, and it is neglect of foresight of this kind which makes, for example the pattern of lierne ribs[24] in the vault of the choir at Wells Cathedral look 'disagreeably distorted', although it is uncommonly regular in plan. The last chapter is on fan-vaults, and Willis already ventures forward with the suggestion that those of the Gloucester cloister might be the earliest in existence, though—typical of his severe scholarship—he checks

[17] On this French literature see now R. Middleton 'Viollet-le-Duc and the Rational Gothic Tradition' (Ph.D. Thesis, Cambridge, 1958).

[18] 'On the Construction of Vaults . . .', I. Willis incidentally also quotes Lassaulx and, with a compliment, Ware (see below, pp. 21, 43, and 46), and, as a source of good illustrations, Pugin's *Specimens* (see p. 25).

[19] Ibid., 6.

[20] Ibid., 10-12. On the demolition at Canterbury see below, p. 172.

[21] Ibid., 16 and 19.

[22] Ibid., 25.

[23] Ibid., 40.

[24] A new term of Willis's at least in English; for he says: 'I have denominated . . . (28).'

himself at once: 'I know the danger of indulging in such specula-tions.'[25]

Finally, as he is writing for architects he looks occasionally to the situation of his own day. He recommends his method at the start, because it may make architects who 'design works in the style of any required age'[26] design them more accurately conforming to Gothic patterns than 'modern practice' usually does.[27] That modern practice allows us to be 'imitators of all styles', whereas 'in the old time one style alone was practised'[28], he accepts without comment.

In fact Willis occasionally practised himself. We are told that he designed the west window of St Botolph at Cambridge and the ceiling of the Great Gate at Trinity,[29] and just once he designed a whole building, the King's Walk Cemetery Chapel at Wisbech, now alas demolished [Pl. 22]. This was in 1841, the same *annus mirabilis*, and there is indeed something *mirabilis* about this little building. As one looks at it, one will at once notice the difference between the Commissioners' practice and the unassuming solidity achieved by Willis. His chapel is in the style of the late thirteenth century rather than the Perpendicular, and it looks as convincing as the rare best of Rickman, and indeed as convincing as the works of 1841 and after by the great mid-century reformers such as Pugin and Gilbert Scott.

But we have not yet done with Willis. For although his chapel showed the preference for the late thirteenth century which only in 1841 began to establish itself and oust the Late Gothic, he wrote a special paper in 1842 for the Institute of British Architects on French Late Gothic architecture. It is called 'On the characteristic Interpenetrations of the Flamboyant style,'[30] and again his analysis of the interpenetration of mouldings is superb. His chief example is a doorway in the north transept of Nevers Cathedral, where in the drawing he isolates the parts which interpenetrate [Pl. 23].

Again 1841 is the year in which Willis turned to the English cathedrals, and there he was to achieve his greatest glory. He did a report on Hereford which came out in 1842.[31] In the next year the British Archaeological Association was founded, and in the year

[25] Ibid., 57.   [26] Ibid., 2.   [27] Ibid., 17.
[28] Ibid., 23-4.
[29] A. E. Shipley, *A Memoir of John Willis Clark* (London, 1913). John Willis Clark was Willis's nephew and completed Willis's great book on the architecture of Cambridge University.
[30] *Trans*. I.B.A., I, pt. 2.
[31] *Report on a Survey of the dilapidated Portions of Hereford Cathedral.*

after that the Archaeological Institute of Great Britain and Ireland. The latter was the result of a secession. In the first volume of the *Journal of the British Archaeological Association*, published in 1846, the story of the schism is told in the preface. The *Archaeological Journal* had begun publication in 1845 and was then still the responsibility of the B.A.A. The second volume changed that, and the Archaeological Institute was now responsible. Willis moved to the Archaeological Institute. The B.A.A. for their descriptions of cathedrals made use of Edward Cresy, a versatile architectural scholar without specific Gothic commitments. He published for instance an *Encyclopaedia of Civil Engineering* in 1847, and a book on bridge building in 1839. He was inspector to the General Board of Health and took a professional interest in sewers.[32] In yet another capacity we shall meet him again.[33] Cresy did Winchester and Gloucester for the B.A.A. in volumes I (1846), and II (1847); and in 1840 published an illustrated account of Stone church in Kent. Willis read a paper on Canterbury Cathedral to the B.A.A.'s meeting on 11 Sept., 1844. and this, his second cathedral paper, came out in the next year. His Winchester paper was read in 1845 and published in 1846.[34] The York paper was read in 1846 and published in 1848.[35] After that nothing was published for a number of years, but Willis read papers all the same, even if he found no time to get them ready for publication. He lectured on Norwich in 1847, on Salisbury in 1849,[36] on Oxford in 1850,[37] on Wells in 1851. His Chichester paper was read in 1853 and published there in 1861, the Lichfield paper came out in the *Archaeological Journal*, XVIII (1861), the Worcester paper in the *Archaeological Journal*, XX (1863). In addition, in 1860 he read a Gloucester paper, in 1861 a Peterborough paper, and in 1863 a Rochester paper.[38] His account of Glastonbury Abbey was given in 1865 and published at Cambridge in 1866 and finally a paper on *The Conventual Buildings of the Monastery of Christ Church in Canterbury* in 1869.[39]

[32] These were, it must be remembered, the years of Chadwick's *Inquiry into the Sanitary Conditions of the Labouring Population of Great Britain* (1842).

[33] See below, p. 67.

[34] *Proceedings of the Annual Meeting of the Archaeological Institute.*

[35] Memoir illustrative of the History and Antiquities of the County and City of York.

[36] See *Arch. J.*, VI (1849), 300 ff., the fairly detailed preparation Cambridge University Library Add. MS. 5036, and a long report in *The Guardian*, 1 Aug. 1849.

[37] *Arch. J.*, VII (1850), 315.

[38] *Arch. J.*, XVII, 335 (Gloucester); XVIII, 397 (Peterborough); XX, 389 (Rochester).

[39] London, 1869. The Cambridge University Library has no more than some preparatory notes on these.

In these cathedral and abbey or priory reports Willis maintained
his powers of observation and description on the same supreme
level as before. An example is the demonstration of how at Winchester the Norman nave was converted by William of Wykeham.[40]
Willis first describes the elevation of the Norman nave, then that of
Wykeham, and he then continues:

We have now to consider the process by which the Norman structure
was converted into that which we have just described. The pier-arch and
mass of masonry, B, C, D, E, was entirely removed, leaving, however, the
pier A, B, (shorn of its bases and capitals). Also the pillar F above, and the
double arch G, which rested on it, was taken down. The arch over this
would of course remain, and indeed the back part of it does, to this day.
The clerestory arches and the window behind were also taken down, but
the piers between were left standing, to the very top of the wall. It must be
remembered that a Norman structure consists of a mere shell of wrought
stonework or ashlaring, applied against a central mass or core of hard
rubble work firmly compacted together, so firmly indeed that in most cases
the ashlaring or skin, arch-voussoirs and all, may be entirely taken away
and the rubble structure will stand firmly for ages. Examples of this may
be often seen in Norman ruins when the ashlaring has been stripped for
building material, while the rubble has not been worth the labour of
destruction. Thus at Bury St Edmund's, Thetford, Binham, Castle Acre,
and in many other monastic ruins, Norman rubble walls still stand upright
without a particle of ashlaring remaining. This process is assisted by the
very slight bond which these rude workmen thought it necessary to establish
between the skin and the body of the work, as well as by the superabundant
and unnecessary strength which the enormous dimensions of their walls
gave to the buildings, and which made them quite able to stand alone when
they had lost their ashlar decoration. It is necessary fully to understand
this before we can conceive the possibility of such changes as those which
we have now to investigate.

I have shewn that the lower arches were cut away from between the
piers and the upper work also taken down, leaving only the separating
piers themselves, which stood untouched from the pavement to the top
of the wall, and connected by one range of the original arches only, namely
those of the triforium. Besides this, the ashlaring was stripped off the
whole inner face of the rubble, with the exception of a small portion of pier
below. The left hand portion of fig. 34 shews half of a compartment of the
Norman work in this intermediate state, as seen from the nave. On the
other side of the pier the ashlaring was left undisturbed throughout the
greatest part of it. Thus at the top the flat Norman buttress may still be

[40] *Proceedings* (1846), 70–5.

seen on the leads under the clerestory, dividing the Perpendicular windows; and in the roof of the triforium, as already stated, the arches, S T, still remain, and are separated by the usual flat Norman buttress.

The portion of ashlaring on the outside of the piers at P, Q, R, which was allowed to remain, was wrought into Perpendicular moldings, a process which was comparatively easy, because, as I have shewn, the plan of the new pier was very little different from that of the old one.

Such a description as this is the result of the closest observation. But Willis was not only the greatest observer; he was also an indefatigable collector of data, both visual and literary. Proof of this are his architectural papers which are now in the Cambridge University Library.[41] The papers contain many pages of little drawings in series of blank arcades, canopies, sedilia [Pl. 25], roofs, pier mouldings, plans etc., lists of churches visited arranged by counties, long chronologies of dated buildings, folders with material on cathedrals etc. Other folders deal with the literary sources left to us, and there again Willis was already aware of most of what we now use as the most illuminating passages on buildings such as Centula, Fontanella, Saint Bénigne at Dijon, Saint Aignan at Orléans, Hildesheim, Petershausen.

The same passion for exact quotation and interpretation made him publish a short book in 1844 which he called *The Architectural Nomenclature of the Middle Ages*. In this he collected the terms used in documents of the English Middle Ages and in French and Italian books. At the end is a list of twenty-two chronicles, indentures etc. which he used, and an alphabetical index of all the terms. He acknowledges as his predecessor Willson's appendix to Pugin's *Specimens*. Willis also watched whether new material was brought out on the Continent which was of outstanding importance to medieval archeology, and so, when Ferdinand Keller in 1844 had for the first time published the ninth-century plan for St. Gall[42] Willis presented it to English readers in 1848.[43] In 1858 J. B. A. Lassus and A. Darcel had first published Villard de Honnecourt's Lodge Book,[44] in 1859 Willis's translation came out,[45] and when in

---

[41] Add. MSS. 5023-91, 5127-42, 7574. Bequeathed by John Willis Clark. I have gone through the Willis papers, but I cannot pretend to have read every page. There are thousands of them, and a student in search of a thesis would find them rewarding. The earliest is a diary of 1819-21. This of course is pre-architectural.

[42] *Bauriss des Klosters St Gallen vom Jahr 820* (Zurich, 1844).

[43] *Arch. J.*, V.

[44] *Album de Villard de Honnecourt*, annoté . . . etc.

[45] *Fac-Simile of the Sketch Book of Wilars de Honecourt* etc.

1863 Sir George Gilbert Scott's *Gleanings from Westminster Abbey* were published, the documentary part of the work was provided by Willis.

No wonder then that Willis, though he was not a rich man like Whewell, assembled a prodigious library. When he had to sell it in 1872, it consisted of 1458 items.[46] There were of course plenty of books on engineering and—reminiscent of his early days—on theology and on music. As for architecture, Vitruvius appears in 26 editions, Alberti in 6, the *Hypnerotomachia* in 2, Serlio in 7, Vignola in 15, Palladio in 10, Scamozzi in 7, Lomazzo in 3, and so on via Barbaro and Cataneo to Falda, Ferrerio, and Rossi, to Borromini and Guarini and even Vittone. France is represented among others by Delorme, Ducerceau, Fréart, A. Lepautre, the elder Blondel; Cordemoy, Marot, Briseux, Boffrand, Le Roy, the younger Blondel, Frézier, and Durand; Germany by Dietterlin, Speckle, Furttenbach, Goldmann and Sturm, Fischer von Erlach, and so to Boisserée and Moller; the Netherlands by Vredeman de Vries, de Keyser, Post and Vingboons; England by Wotton, and then Kent's *Inigo Jones*, Gibbs, Castell's *Villas of the Ancients*, Wood's *Palmyra* and *Balbec*, Stuart and Revett, Major's *Paestum*, Chambers's *Chinese Buildings*, *Kew*, Robert Adam, Cameron, Chandler, and Wilkins's *Magna Graecia*. That the English literature of about 1800 on the Gothic style is well represented, goes without saying (Milner, Whittington, Gunn, Dallaway, Hawkins). With Caumont and Didron and Montalembert Willis's own time is reached (Caumont's *Statistique monumentale du Calvados*, his *L'architecture du moyen-âge*, his *Terms d'architecture* and his *Abécédaire*, Didron's *Annales archéologiques* volumes I–XXVI and his *Manuel*, Montalembert's *Vandalisme*), and he kept up with the books coming out, while he was at work, whether on medieval or post-medieval themes. The latter were represented by Leeds on Barry's Travellers' Club, Loudon's *Encyclopaedia of Villa Architecture*, the four volumes of Letarouilly, and the five of the Official Catalogue of the 1851 Exhibition, the former by so wide a selection as e.g. Owen Jones's *Alhambra*, Gally Knight's *Ecclesiastical Architecture of Italy*, Quast's *Altchristliche Bauwerke von Ravenna*, Kallenbach's *Christliche Kirchenbaukunst*, Heideloff's *Ornementation du moyen-âge*, and E. B. Lamb on ancient domestic architecture. The majority of these will have to occupy

[46] *A Catalogue of the valuable and extensive Library of the Rev. Robert Willis,* sold by Messrs. Hodgson Apr. 3–12, 1872. The R.I.B.A. has a copy.

us in future chapters. In addition Willis also possessed the *Instru-menta Ecclesiastica* of the Cambridge Camden Society, Fergusson's *Principles of Beauty*, some of Pugin's unpolemical publications, Ruskin's *Stones of Venice* and Beresford Hope's *English Cathedral*, and Pugin and the Cambridge Camden Society, and Ruskin and Fergusson require whole chapters. But they cannot be the next. For Pugin, the Camdenians and Ruskin were all committed to the Gothic style, and we must now first have a look at those who during the years we have examined so far sacrificed at other altars.

CHAPTER IX

Hübsch and the Rundbogenstil; Hope and the Neo-Renaissance

So far nearly all that has been presented has been scholars' work, though among them were architect-scholars such as Rickman. Rickman in the middle of his antiquarian writings gives advice occasionally to those wanting to build now, and some of the amateurs did the same. But nobody asked the fundamental question whether new buildings should be imitation-Gothic anyway or indeed imitation-anything. Nobody asked the question, in what style we should build in the nineteenth century. This question was first asked by a German architect, Heinrich Hübsch.

We have carried the German story—very sketchily—up to the Schlegels. Now, to place Hübsch, we must cast a glance at the greatest German architect of their (and Goethe's) age, at Carl Friedrich von Schinkel.

Schinkel, before designing the most beautiful neo-Grecian buildings in Europe and long before becoming Prussian *Ober-baudirektor* in 1831, had been a passionate Gothicist, though in drawings and paintings rather than buildings. In 1810 he wrote[1] 'Antique architecture has its effects, scale and solidity in its material masses, Gothic architecture affects us by its spirit. It is daring, to achieve much with small means. Antique architecture is vain and pompous . . . Gothic buildings refuse meaningless pomp; all is deduced from an idea; hence its character of the necessary, grave, dignified and sublime.' Later of course Schinkel wrote in the opposite vein, just as his buildings were Grecian now, and the dreams

[1] This and many of the Schinkel quotations are taken second-hand from pp. 17–38 of L. Ettlinger, *Semper und die Antike* (Halle, 1937). Schinkel's theory would deserve far more space than can here be given to it. I have also used, and quoted from, H. Kauffmann: Zweckbau und Monument in *Eine Freundesgabe . . . für Ernst Hellmut Vits* (Frankfurt, 1963), 135 ff.; G. Peschken, 'Schinkels nachgelassene Fragmente eines architektonischen Lehrbuchs', *Bonner Jahrbücher*, CLXVI (1966), 293 ff., and 'Technologische Aesthetik in Schinkels Architektur', *Zeitschrift des Deutschen Vereins für Kunstwissenschaft*, XXII (1968). A Basel Ph.D. thesis of 1940 by K. G. Kaehler, called 'Schinkels Kunstauffassung', I have not seen.

of Gothic cathedrals on rocks or in groves were a thing of the past. 'To build Greek is to build right . . . The principle of Greek architecture is to render construction beautiful, and this must remain the principle in its continuation.'

Schinkel was working on a book on architectural theory, and had he completed it, it would have been an important if not a philosophically easy book. 'The scope of architecture is to render beautiful what is usable, useful and purposeful.' 'The ideal of architecture is achieved only if a building completely shows its purpose spiritually and physically, as a whole and in all its parts.' There are to Schinkel three aspects of architecture: Construction, Custom, i.e. acknowledgement of history, and Nature, i.e. a beauty based on nature. On the side of function there are again three aspects: plan, construction, and adornment. The plan must have the maximum of space-saving, of order in the disposition of rooms, and of commodity. The construction must make use of the best material, the best working technique, and the best visible indication of both. Adornment must have made the best choice for the placing of decoration, and must then use the best ornament and the best technique of producing it. The fulfilment of function alone is not enough: 'Mere need cannot give us beauty'; it would result in 'dryness and rigidity' as long as the other two necessary elements, 'the historic and the poetic' are lacking.

Such are the rules. They are general enough to be a safeguard against mere Greek imitation. Indeed, Schinkel wrote: 'If one could, within the scope of Greek architecture, maintain its spirited principle, to cope with the conditions of our new period in the world's history . . . one would probably have found the most suitable answer to the problem' of what a style for today should be like. The stress is placed on the new conditions; for Schinkel explicitly deprecates imitation: 'History has never copied previous history', and—the most telling passage—'Every epoch has left behind its own style in architecture. Why should we not try whether a style for our own might not also be found?' Schinkel's own late buildings are the answer. The Academy of Architecture in Berlin and the church of 1826 for the Oranienburger Vorstadt which was never built are functional and beautiful and not Grecian. But what are they then? There is North Italian Quattrocento in the Academy of Architecture, and in the design for the church which is on a circular plan there is without any doubt something of the Romanesque of Italian baptisteries. The windows have round-arched heads anyway, and that in particular, in 1826, is memorable and helps to explain Hübsch's pamphlet which was published in 1828 and is challengingly called: *In welchem Style sollen wir bauen?* (In what style should we build?). The title, alas—this will be shown—is bolder than the argumentation. It is also bolder than Hübsch's own buildings. For they are in the *Rundbogenstil*, the style of the Schinkel design of 1826, but handled much more conventionally.[2] Hübsch's dilemma is not like Schinkel's between the Grecian style and a new style for the nineteenth century, but between the Grecian and the *Rundbogen* style. He praises the Greek of the Periclean age for its truthfulness,[3] but finds that already with the introduction of the pilaster the 'conventional lie' entered architecture and then grew, until, if we build Grecian now, the result can only be 'strident inconsistency'.[4] If architects are satisfied with 'the dead imitation of Antiquity', they can only do it out of 'dishonest vanity', because they have become known for Grecian buildings, or with 'feigned reasons', or else 'in despair', because they do not believe that it is possible 'to produce a suitable style with the aid of reflexion'. But such a style is obtainable, if one starts 'from the angle of needs', from commodity and firmness,[5] and if one considers 'climate and building materials' which he calls the techno-static conditions.[6] The history of architecture to Hübsch is a development from the most massive to the lightest, the beginning being Egyptian and the end Gothic.[7] The greatest single innovation in this development was the arch, and no style suitable for today can be anything but arcuated. Hence alone Grecian is unsuitable. But among the arcuated styles Hübsch does not take the Gothic, i.e. the lightest, as his point of departure—and this is where, as so often, taste interferes with the logic of the argument. For while the principle of the pointed arch is, Hübsch writes, the same as that of the semicircular arch and while

[2] Hübsch lived from 1795 to 1863. He was a pupil of Weinbrenner, visited Italy, Greece, and Constantinople in 1817–19, wrote in 1822 *On Greek Architecture,* but in 1825 an *Entwurf zu einen Theater mit eiserner Dachrüstung* (Frankfurt, 1825), i.e. on iron roof construction for theatres, and built e.g. the Kunsthalle and the Theatre at Karlsruhe (1836 ff. and 1847 ff.), the Trinkhalle at Baden-Baden (1839 ff.), and a number of churches. He was made a foreign honorary member of the Institute of British Architects in 1837 or 1838 and a Foreign Member of Caumont's Société Française in 1842 (see above p. 42, n. 53). *In welchem Style sollen wir bauen?* is a rare book. Dr. Reinhold Behrens had the kindness to borrow a copy for me which I could read on a visit to Hanover. Two theses on Hübsch's ecclesiastical and his secular building have been done recently under the late Professor Tschira by J. Göricke and G. Vilmar respectively and should soon be published.

[3] *In welchem Style sollen wir bauen?* 18.

[4] Ibid., 20–2.   [5] Ibid., 1–27.   [6] Ibid., 6–8.   [7] Ibid., 10.

Gothic structure is 'organically carried through according to the construction of the vault'—a very interesting remark—Romanesque architecture as against Gothic is like 'a pre-Raphaelite painting in comparison with a post-Raphaelite'. The former may be faulty in drawing, but in the latter 'one looks in vain for the touching simplicity of the former'.[8] So, if today 'one chose instead of the semi-circular the pointed arch, an organic style would be the result as well; but everybody would soon see in the execution that the verticalism of the pointed style 'does not correspond to our demands'. With this the final result is determined. Hübsch can end with this paragraph:

I have reached the goal I have set myself and have established a strictly objective skeleton for the new style, sufficiently detailed, I think, for an architect to enliven it by his own individuality. Everyone will see at once that the new style is most similar to the *Rundbogen* style—nay, that it is essentially the *Rundbogen* style, as it would have become, if it had developed freely and unrestrictedly, without detrimental reminiscences of Antiquity. The similarity results from the nature of the situation, and not from any . . . personal preference . . . The new style will be capable of solving with suppleness the most varied tasks in the most direct way . . . It will move freely in the present and respond to every reasonable require-ment . . . The buildings will no longer have a historical and conventional character, . . . [and] no longer will feelings be required to receive instruction in archaeology before they can manifest themselves.[9]

It is an interesting result. Here for the first time we find what we shall find time and again later on, that the theory of a new style for the new century and the proposals for a style to be used by the new century clash.

Hübsch's decision to plead for the *Rundbogenstil* was less *recherché* in Germany than it would have been in England. The Rhineland seems to have come first. Lassaulx turned from neo-Gothic to neo-German-Romanesque as early as 1824, and thereafter remained faithful to it, at least for exteriors. His first Romanesque church was St Martin at Valwig,[10] and Urbach church by F. Nebel followed in 1825.[11] Also of 1825 is the Protestant church of Wuppertal-Unterbarmen by Hübsch himself, and many of his followed. Yet two or three years earlier the King of Prussia, Friedrich Wilhelm IV, sketched for a cathedral for Berlin an Early Christian basilica

8 Ibid., 42. Shadows of Schlegel (see p. 12).
9 Ibid., 51–2.
10 P. F. Schwieger *Johann Claudius von Lassaulx* (Neuss, 1968), 50 and plates 33–5.
11 A. Mann op. cit., *Die Neuromanik* (Cologne, 1966), pp. 16 and 17.

with two campanili.[12] This never materialized, nor did Schinkel's church of 1826 already referred to, but Ludwig I King of Bavaria was luckier. At his request, and in the style commanded by him, Klenze began the All Saints Hofkirche in Munich in 1827 [Pl. 26], and in 1826 already the king had sent Ziebland, a younger architect, to Italy to study Early Christian and Romanesque basilicas with a view to designing St Boniface which was begun in 1835.[13] Six years before, the King had laid the foundation stone of the better-known Ludwigskirche designed by Gärtner. Meanwhile Persius's Heilandskirche at Sacrow near Potsdam was begun in 1841, and in 1845 Persius's Friedenskirche at Potsdam.[14] The *Rundbogenstil*, it will have been noticed, could fluctuate between Early Christian, Italian Romanesque, and German Romanesque.[15]

Side by side with such buildings must be seen a whole stream of mostly lavishly illustrated books on Early Christian and Romanesque architecture. Preceding them—this must not be forgotten—were the illustrations of Italian Romanesque churches in Kerrich's essay of 1810. They show the cathedrals of Piacenza, Parma, and Modena; and Moller's *Denkmähler* of 1815–21 of which, as we have seen, an English edition appeared in 1824[16] had illustrations of German Romanesque buildings. So had Boisserée's *Denkmale der Baukunst vom 7. bis zum 13 Jahrhundert am Niederrhein* (1833), and later Hübsch's *Bau-Werke* (1838 ff.), and Carl Alexander Heideloff's *Die Ornamentik des Mittelalters* (Nuremberg, 1838–52 ff.).[17] Christian K. J. Baron Bunsen's *Die Basiliken des Christlichen Rom* had begun to appear in 1823 but was only completed in 1843.[18] It illustrates in beautiful engravings views and plans of buildings from Old St

---

[12] L. Dehio, *Friedrich Wilhelm IV von Preussen; ein Baukünstler der Romantik* (Berlin, 1961), 34 ff.

[13] B. Stubenvoll, *Die Basilika und das Benediktinerstift St Bonifaz in München* (Munich, 1957).

[14] In France sympathy with the basilican, apsidal plan and with columns instead of piers goes back much further, in fact to the years of the very start of opposition to the Rococo. Laugier comes into this story, as Dr. Herrmann (see above, p. 10, n. 4) has shown, and R. Middleton in his thesis ('Viollet-le-Duc and the Rational Gothic Tradition') notes examples as early as Potain's design of 1764 for St Louis at St Germain-en-Laye, Chalgrin's design of the same year for the famous and very influential St Philippe-du-Roule, and Trouard's design, again of the same year, for St Symphorien. Trouard's was actually begun first (1767), Chalgrin's second (1771), and Potain's last (1787).

[15] R. N. Wornum in his post-mortem on the Exhibition of 1851, 'The Exhibition as a Lesson in Taste' (*The Arts Journal Illustrated Catalogue*, 1851, pp. i–xxii), treats Norman and Lombardic as varieties of Byzantine and calls all three Romanesque.

[16] See above, p. 23, n. 1.

[17] Heideloff was later a contributor to the Art Union's *Art Journal*. For the forties, Dr. Stefan Muthesius gave me the following two titles: L. Runge: *Beiträge zur Kenntnis der Backstein-Architektur Italiens* (Berlin, 1846) and F. Osten: *Die Bauwerke der Lombarden* (Darmstadt, 1847).

[18] Plate 4 of the Atlas is dated 1822.

Peter's and S. Paolo fuori le Mura to S. Maria sopra Minerva and S. Agostino.[19]

Meanwhile, in 1829, one year before Whewell's book on the Late Romanesque in Germany, Edward Cresy, whom we have met as a Gothicist (p. 57), and G. Ledwell Taylor issued lavish illustrations of the Romanesque buildings of Pisa in a book called *Architecture of the Middle Ages in Italy*.[20] Only six years later followed *L'Architecture moderne de la Sicile* by the distinguished anti-Gothic Parisian architect J. I. Hittorff and Ludwig Zanth (1835), and another seven or eight years later A. F. von Quast's *Die alt-christlichen Bauwerke von Ravenna* (1842),[21] and Gally Knight's *The Ecclesiastic Architecture of Italy from the Time of Constantine to the fifteenth Century* (1842–4). This was a sumptuously illustrated sequel to an unillustrated book by Gally Knight called *The Normans in Sicily, being a Sequel to An Architectural Tour in Normandy*, with which we are familiar. *The Normans in Sicily* came out in 1838 and was to prove that Norman buildings in Sicily have the earliest pointed arches in Europe and that they must be derived from Saracen work. *The Ecclesiastic Architecture of Italy* is a folio in two volumes, picturesquely illustrated by lithographs.[22] Small or not so small figures populate the scenes, yet the architectural details are reliable—more so than Gally Knight's chronology, with e.g. S. Michele at Pavia as seventh-century and S. Ambrogio in Milan as ninth-century.[23]

[19] Bunsen (1791–1865) was an interesting man. He served as a Prussian diplomat in Rome from 1818 to 1838 and was ambassador in London from 1842 to 1854. He is best known to theologians for his biblical criticism of the fifties, but he also wrote a five-volume work on Egyptian history. He was one of the founders of the Prussian (German) Archaeological Institute in Rome. Ruskin mentions him occasionally, e.g. in the paragraph where he explains why he deprecates German philosophy without having read it, because, as he says, of a 'preconceived opinion' (see *Modern Painters*, III, Libr. Ed., V, 424). In the last chapter of his *Basiliken*, incidentally, Bunsen comes out as a partisan of the German Gothic style for his own day as against the Roman and the Byzantino-Romanesque styles, though he wishes to see domes used. Gothic with a dome had, it will be remembered, been Schinkel's early dream of a cathedral. The Gothic style 'alone', says Bunsen, 'speaks the language and absorbs the feelings of Germanic peoples' (*Die Basiliken*, 82). On Bunsen see W. Höcker: *Der Gesandte Bunsen als Vermittler zwischen Deutschland und England*, Göttingen 1951, an attractive book.

[20] There is more to Cresy than this. We have already (p. 57) come across his books on civil engineering and bridge building, and his descriptions of some cathedrals. Manuscript notes to Willis's *Architecture of the Middle Ages* and Caumont's *Terms* are in the British Museum, and he also wrote a book on cottages for agricultural labourers (1847).

[21] Quast (1807–77) was the first Konservator der preussischen Kunstdenkmäler. The appointment was made in 1843. In 1853 he brought out a book on the Romanesque cathedrals on the Middle Rhine. Mr George McHardy in a yet unpublished thesis on Henry Clutton has collected still more titles.

[22] The two coloured title-pages are by Owen Jones.

[23] A long review by Sir Francis Palgrave of Gally Knight and Bunsen is in the *Quarterly Review*, LXXV, 1845, 334 ff.

Gally Knight nowhere actually pleaded for a *Rundbogen* style for today. This needs saying, because in the forties England had a fashion for the round-arched styles and especially the Anglo-Norman. The fashion had been initiated by such churches as P. F. Robinson's Christ Church at Leamington of 1825, D. Robertson's St Clement at Oxford of 1828 and Pugin's St James at Reading of 1837–40—Norman and not Gothic, because close to the genuinely Norman ruins of Reading Abbey.[24]

Revived Early Christian and Italian Romanesque was rarer in England, but by no means missing. The most famous examples are Christ Church, Watney Street by John Shaw, Christ Church Streatham by Wild, and Wilton Parish Church by T. H. Wyatt and David Brandon [Pl. 27], all three begun in 1840.[25]

The parallel to these buildings among writers are James Barr and John Shaw. James Barr in a book called *Anglican Church Architecture*, published in 1842, writes that 'The Anglo-Norman style possesses many peculiarities and elements of beauty that ought to recommend it to occasional adoption', and John Shaw in 1839 writes that Lombardic architecture 'contains in an eminent degree the qualities now so important', i.e. suitability for galleries, for slender iron shafts to support them, for brick as the building material and for simplicity altogether.[26]

---

[24] A list of other early examples of the Norman Revival may be useful, though no doubt it will be a very incomplete one. Castles received the Norman treatment early. The porch for the south wing of Arundel Castle was designed in 1795, it is said, by the eleventh Duke of Norfolk, Broadway Tower in Worcestershire dates from 1797–1800 and is by James Wyatt, as Dr. Alistair Rowan found in the Croome d'Abitot estate papers, and Patterson of Edinburgh built Brancepeth Castle *c.* 1817 ff. Among churches Henry Hakewill's Holy Trinity, Old Wolverton, is as early as 1815, Calverton in Bucks. as early as 1818; also in 1818 Soane made his famous drawing for the Church Commissioners to show how the same area and volume of church can be rendered in a variety of styles. Of 1823 is Patey's church at Teignmouth in Devon, of 1825 G. Smith's church at London Colney in Hertfordshire, of 1828 Robertson's at Kennington in Berkshire. Blore did St John's, Potters Bar in 1835 and St Mark's College, Chelsea in 1838 ff., Fowler St John's at Honiton in Devon in 1835–8, R. Palmer Brown Christ Church, Tunbridge Wells in 1836, Edmund Sharpe whom we have met as a scholar of Gothic tracery, several neo-Norman churches in Lancashire in the mid-thirties (St Mark's, Blackburn in 1836, Cuerden 1837, Chatburn 1838, Farington 1839). Mr. Robin Fedden has collected neo-Norman evidence, chiefly in books of cottages and villas in *The Architectural Review*, CXVI, 1954, 380–4, and the introductions to the volumes of my *The Buildings of England* always have summaries of Neo-Norman churches.

[25] Completely exceptional is the church at Wreay in Cumberland built in 1836–42 to designs of Miss Sarah Losh. See N. Pevsner in *The Architectural Review*, CXLII, 1967, 65 ff. Miss Metcalf, ibid., CXLIII, 1968, 255, has suggested convincingly that Hope's book may have acted as the stimulus. On this see below.

[26] The pamphlet is called *A Letter on Ecclesiastical Architecture, applicable to Modern Churches*. It and the book by Barr are quoted on p. 42 of Basil Clarke's indispensable *Church Builders of the Nineteenth Century* (London, 1938).

John Shaw speaks of Lombardic, not Norman, and that in 1839 most probably presupposes a book which dealt with the Italian Romanesque and many other things and was highly influential. This was Thomas Hope's *An Historical Essay on Architecture* of 1835.[27] Hope had died in 1831. He was a very rich man and had, when he was young, been an indefatigable supporter of the French Empire style—see his *Household Furniture* (1807) and the furnishing of his own house in Duchess Street. Later, chiefly in 1823, in adding to his Surrey country house, The Deepdene, with the help of the architect William Atkinson, he had abandoned the Franco-Grecian in favour of a much freer Italian Renaissance villa style which was then still extremely uncommon. Nash had used it about 1802 at Cronkhill in Shropshire.[28] and its chief characteristic, the loggia of arches on slender columns occurs also in Ledoux's *Architecture* (1804) and Durand's *Précis des leçons* (1802–5).[29] The attractions of the style were the possibility it provided of composing asymmetrically and the greater variety of usable motifs. It culminated between *c.* 1835 and the mid-forties in Barry's Trentham Park and in 1845–51 in Prince Albert and Thomas Cubitt's Osborne.

Prince Albert's role in the Italian Renaissance revival is important in more than one way. He was chairman of the Royal Commission appointed to decide on the internal decoration of the Houses of Parliament (see above, p. 37). His sympathies, it will be remembered, were all for the German Romantics led by Cornelius who were busy reviving brotherly teamwork and the fresco technique. The movement had begun with the frescoes by the Nazarenes first for the Villa Bartholdy in Rome of 1816–17 (now in the Berlin Nationalgalerie) and then in the Casino Massimi of 1820–9. Cornelius visited London for the Royal Commission in 1841, and in 1844 Prince Albert had his own little Casino (the term was actually used) built in the garden of Buckingham Palace. It was decorated by frescoes chiefly from Milton's *Comus* and the works of Walter Scott, the painters selected being Etty, Landseer, Maclise, Eastlake, Leslie, Ross, Stanfield, and Uwins.[30] But not one of these

---

27 On Hope there is now David Watkin's admirable *Thomas Hope and the Neo-classical Idea* (London, 1968).

28 Nash incidentally—so David Watkin tells me—had used *Rundbogen* for Sir Uvedale Price's villa at Aberystwyth *c.* 1790. It is mentioned as castellated and whimsical in Lipscomb's *Journey into South Wales* in 1799. See *Country Life*, CXII, 1952, 33.

29 An amazingly early case is the Gloriette at Schönbrunn outside Vienna by Ferdinand von Hohenburg. This was built in 1775. Valadier's Loggia on the Pincio is of 1806–14.

30 It was demolished in 1928.

was fully in sympathy with the pre-Raphaelite ideals of the Nazarenes which included of course the style of Raphael himself. The only one of whom that was true is Dyce, and his frescoes in the Queen's Robing Room in the Houses of Parliament which were begun in 1848 are the most Nazarene of paintings in England. As for the Casino, Ludwig Gruner, the artistic *confidant* of Prince Albert published it lavishly in 1846 [Pl. 28].[31] Apart from this book he did one in 1854 called *Description of the Plates of Fresco Decorations and Stuccoes of Churches and Palaces in Italy during the fifteenth and sixteenth centuries*[32] and one in 1867 called *The Terracotta Architecture of North Italy* (text by V. Ottolini and F. Lose) and with aid from Prince Albert collected in albums photographic reproductions of the works of Raphael.[33] He also appeared in the Great Exhibition of 1851 as a designer for metalwork, tiles, and textiles in the Italian Renaissance taste.[34]

Yet another aspect of the Italian Renaissance revival and in fact the earliest is Charles Barry's Travellers' Club built in 1829–32 in the late Quattrocento *palazzo* style. When, in 1839, W. H. Leeds published excellent illustrations of the building with an introduction, rather pompously called 'An Essay on Modern English Architecture',[35] he called the Palladian of Sir Robert Taylor and Wyatt 'feeble', 'insipid', and 'spiritless',[36] and the amateurs usually responsible for accepting one design rather than another, especially in competitions, 'superficial dabblers'.[37] What he wants to put in the place of the Palladian and Grecian is emphatically not the neo-Elizabethan—'tasteless mimicking of the most tasteless qualities of the extravagant Elizabethan style.[38] but Barry's Italian, because it allows for 'many diversities', for instance astylar, i.e. columnless

[31] Ludwig Gruner (1801–82) spent the years 1826–36 in Milan and 1831–41 in Rome. In 1841 he settled in England, and he finally went to Dresden in 1856 as head of the Print Room, Mr. Winslow Ames, author of *Prince Albert and Victorian Taste* (London, 1968) is working on him at present.

[32] This contains an essay by Hittorff, on whom see pp. 193 and 214.

[33] These are in the library of Windsor Castle.

[34] See vol. II of the *Descriptive and Illustrated Catalogue*, sec. III, class 23, no. 140 for a jewel case. Two illustrations of textiles are in my *Studies*, II.

[35] The whole volume is called *Studies and Examples of the Modern School of English Architecture* and was published by Weale. On Weale see p. 129.

[36] 'An Essay on Modern English Architecture', 3.

[37] Ibid., 8. Barry had won the Club in a competition. Competitions became a characteristic of major Victorian architecture—after the Travellers' Club, the Fitzwilliam Museum and of course the Houses of Parliament. Pamphlet followed pamphlet right into the sixties on the unfairness of competitions.

[38] Ibid., 14.

and pilasterless, façades,[39] rustication of several kinds, and the horizontal emphasis of a *cornicione*.[40]

To return to Thomas Hope, in his *Historical Essay* he calls all Renaissance and post-Renaissance imitation *Cinque-cento*, an unfortunate term. But on the whole Hope was a writer who took his writing seriously—he wrote a long novel too: *Athanasius* which on publication was attributed by many to Byron. His style in the *Historical Essay* tends to be formal and somewhat portentous, with long sentences—on pages 400–3 one may sample one of 85 lines— and no acknowledgement to preceding authors. In fact, the preface largely gives the impression that all in this book will be first-hand. Hope proudly refers to his travels in Egypt, Greece, Turkey and Syria, along the African coast, in Spain, and four times in Italy.

The book then starts on its historical procession which is to lead from Egyptian via Moorish, Persian, and Russian buildings and very many others to end in what Hope calls the *Cinque-cento*. Hope had indeed observed very much himself, and it is interesting to see an out-of-the-way church like that of Parenzo in Dalmatia (Porič) described accurately with the bench for the clergy running round the apse. Hope always describes in great detail and with reference to many examples.[41] The following is a fair example:

... At times, columns have no direct support whatever on the ground, but at a distance from it rise on brackets; as in the front of the edifice called the Palace of Theodoric at Ravenna, around the steeple of the small church serving as chapel to the palace at Milan, in the cupola of the Certosa near

[39] Nicholas Taylor in *Monuments of Commerce* (R.I.B.A. Drawings Series, London, 1968) suggests Barry's former 16–17 Pall Mall of 1833 as the earliest post-and-beam office façade.

[40] Leeds had already praised the Travellers' Club in his *Illustrations of Public Buildings of London* in 1838, also published by Weale. In the book of 1839 he gives a very useful bibliography of mostly French books dealing with the Italian Renaissance. They are Percier and Fontaine's *Palais ... modernes ... à Rome* (1798), the *Choix des plus belles maisons de plaisance de Rome* (1801), Grandjean de Montigny and Farmin's *Architecture Toscane* (1806), T. F. Suys and L. P. Haudebourt's *Palais Massimi à Rome* (1818), P. Gauthier's *Les plus beaux édifices de ... Gènes* (1830–2), J. I. Hittorff and L. von Zanth's *Architecture moderne de la Sicile* (1835), J. Bouchet and Raoul-Rochette's *La Villa Pia* (1837), L. Cicognara's *Le fabbriche e i monumenti conspicui di Venezia* (1838–40) and of course P. Letarouilly's *Edifices de Rome moderne* (1840). A very early case of a *palazzo* actually built is Klenze's Leuchtenberg Palais in Munich of 1816. The Königsbau of the Munich Royal Palace is later (1826–35) and was, when built, the most monumental of all the new *palazzi*. The French development is fully treated by Hautecoeur. In this context the design for the Royal Exchange submitted in 1839 for the competition by the Hamburg architect Alexis de Chateauneuf ought to be mentioned. Its portico is a loggia *à la Loggia dei Lanzi*. See G. Lange, *Alexis de Chateauneuf, ein Hamburger Baumeister*, Hamburg 1965. Also K. Esdaile in *Architect and Building News* Jan. 9 1831 and S. Tschudi Madsen, 'Chateauneuf and England,' *The Architectural Review*, CXL, 1966, 366 ff.

[41] So many that Cresy in 1836 brought out an index to the book.

Pavia, against the steeple of Santa Croce in Gerusalemme at Rome, in the front of the dome of Lodi, in the nave of St Saturnin at Toulouse, in the east end of the cathedral at Poitiers, over the side porch of the cathedral of Worms, and in Frederic Barbarossa's palace at Gelnhausen. The larger and more essential columns are generally round and plain; the smaller and more ornamental, frequently polygonic, or fluted, or reeded, or formed of ribands or basket work, or smaller columns twisted together perpendicularly, spirally, or in zigzags, or other whimsical ways; as we see in the cloisters of San Giovanni Laterano and San Paolo at Rome, those of St Sauveur at Aix, and a number of others; or adorned with foliage, as in the great west entrance of the cathedral of Autun: sometimes we see small columns, as if broken; witness the gallery on the north side of the cathedral at Vienne in Dauphiné, and the south side porch of that of Worms. Sometimes even a pair or a quartetto of slender shafts form together a true lover's knot; the former in the town hall of Como, the latter in the porch of San Quirico.[42]

Another, briefer example is the description of the system of Lombard friezes:

Where walls are not adorned with columns, they commonly, and sometimes, but more rarely, where they are, have their surface divided into recessed panels, and their corners strengthened by a species of margin or buttress, slightly projecting, which at the top connects and grows into one of the range of Corbel tables, forming wall plates, made in almost all buildings in the Lombard style.[43]

Similarly accurate passages deal with normal corbel-tables, with wheel-windows (including that of Saint Étienne at Beauvais) and many other motifs. The importance of tunnel-vaults in the South of France is recognized (Hope calls them 'trunk-headed' vaults), and the specific character of Gothic architecture well formulated. Hope compares the structural system with the skeletons of vertebrate animals[44] and with timber-framing.[45]

On the other hand Hope is extremely weak on dates. Not only does he offer us few, but he did not possess the scholarship to recognize what accepted dates could be trusted, though, as we have seen, several scholars in England and France by 1835 were capable of reliable dating. Zigzag and cable mouldings he calls Saxon,[46] Worms Cathedral appears without comment as 996–1016, Chartres

[42] *An Historical Essay on Architecture*, 254–5.   [43] Ibid., 257.
[44] Wetter did the same in the same year; see p. 44.
[45] *An Historical Essay*, 349–51.   [46] Ibid., 212.

Cathedral once as 1020–8 and another time as 1170.[47] Similarly Hope has nothing to contribute to the problems of which school of Romanesque or Gothic influenced which, i.e. how types and elements travelled. Instead he has a wild theory that the great uniformity of medieval and particularly Romanesque architecture is due to the Freemasons conquering Europe from Lombardy and working as the 'protégés' of the Papacy.[48]

The architects of all the sacred edifices of the Latin church, wherever such arose—north, south, east, or west [Hope sums up] thus derived their science from the same central school; obeyed, in their designs, the dictates of the same hierarchy; were directed in their constructions by the same principles of propriety and taste; kept up with each other, in the most distant parts to which they might be sent, the most constant correspondence; and rendered every minute improvement the property of the whole body, and a new conquest of the art.[49]

This theory does not seem to have impressed readers. The influence of Hope's book lies in another field, a field already indicated. At a time when, as we shall see, nearly all the scholars and theorizing architects concentrated on the Gothic style, Hope preferred the *Rundbogenstil* and made this known in several ways. On the Gothic he is not always complimentary: 'pinnacles and spires, . . . cusps and corbels, and tabernacles and tracery [like] a mass of network, or rather a cluster of mere conductors'.[50] Within Gothic, incidentally, he deprecates the later stages, with architects abusing their resources 'to astound the vulgar',[51] and the 'fullest bloom and perfection' is the early thirteenth century; however even that he calls 'a maze of intricate and useless lines and tracery'.[52] How different sounds what he says about the Byzantine style. Their domes, 'the noblest offspring of the arch', are 'the most glorious addition to church architecture since the suppression of the Greek.' 'All which in the temples of Athens had been straight, in the churches of Constantinople became curved and rounded—concave within, convex without.'[53]

But stronger yet than such a message of Hope's text must have been that of the plates, and they are predominantly Italian and German Romanesque [Pl. 29], though they include some Gothic

[47] Ibid., 331, 379, 428.
[50] Ibid., 360–1.
[53] Ibid., 355, 124.

[48] Ibid., 224 ff.; 525.
[51] Ibid., 443.

[49] Ibid., 238.
[52] Ibid., 419.

of the same two countries as well. Here was, even if implied rather than said, an invitation to imitate.

Explicitly Hope's is yet another message and one often repeated after him. His last fifty pages deal with his *Cinque-cento* style, from Brunelleschi (whom incidentally he calls a pupil of Donatello), whose Pazzi Chapel becomes the Capella di Piazza[54] to the Baroque. Hope tries to explain how the Renaissance could come about out of a 'new direction of men's minds to objects of beauty and pleasure', out of the growing wealth of laymen and skill of lay artificers and out of the vacuum which the disappearance of the medieval free-masons had left. But however perfect in detail, Renaissance building as building is scientifically inferior to Gothic building,[55] and even the detail is 'a mere masquerade'[56] taking forms independent of the institutions for which they had been required. This judgement did not prevent Hope from recognizing the 'sublime genius' of Palladio and the 'mighty genius' of Michelangelo.[57] But Michelangelo 'wholly wanted taste', his upper pilasters of the Farnese Palace are 'stilted, and sliced, and clustered',[58] and after him came Bernini, Borromini, and Fontana, who 'far outstripped in bad taste the worst examples of the worst era of pagan Rome',[59] and so to the French Rococo which should be called 'the inane or frippery style,'[60] and to today, when some even try to revive the Rococo.[61]

What then ought we to do? *In welchem Style sollen wir bauen?* Hübsch's answer, we have seen, is the Early-Christian-cum-Italian-Romanesque. What made him choose it and defend it with far from complete argument is that it is less severe than the trabeated Grecian, and that round arches are more accommodating and allow more varied, including asymmetrical, composition. The same advantages applied to the use of Italian Renaissance elements and details. As Hittorff had written in the prospectus to his *Architecture moderne de la Sicile* in 1835; 'le plus grand nombre de ces productions peut devenir pour les architectes une source féconde de motifs, heureux, facilement applicables à nos moeurs, nos usages, et à notre climat'.[62] But Hope's final answer, though he recommended both the *Rund-bogenstil* and his *Cinque-cento*, was neither. It was instead Eclecticism,

---

[54] *An Historical Essay*, 533.

[55] Ibid., 512–27.   [56] Ibid., 529.   [57] Ibid., 555, 538.

[58] Ibid., 539.   [59] Ibid., 557.   [60] Ibid., 559.

[61] Hope no doubt thinks of Benjamin Dean Wyatt's interiors of the twenties in such houses as Crockford's Club, Londonderry House, and others.

[62] K. Hammer, *J. I. Hittorff* (Stuttgart, 1968), 106.

and eclecticism was going to be one of the catchwords of a certain type of architectural writer of the second third of the century. It is these we shall now examine.

Hope's last paragraph runs as follows: Why is it that

no one seems yet to have conceived the smallest wish or idea of only borrowing of every former style of architecture whatever it might present of useful or ornamental, of scientific or tasteful; of adding thereto whatever other new dispositions or forms might afford conveniences or elegancies not yet possessed; of making the new discoveries, the new conquests, of natural productions unknown to former ages, the models of new imitation more beautiful and more varied; and thus of composing an architecture which, born in our country, grown in our soil, and in harmony with our climate, institutions, and habits, at once elegant, appropriate, and original, should truly deserve the appellation of 'Our Own'.[63]

[63] *An Historical Essay*, 561.

CHAPTER X

The earliest magazines and Professor Donaldson

LEO VON KLENZE (1784–1864), Honorary Corresponding Member of the Institute of British Architects already by 1836, chief architect to King Ludwig I of Bavaria, was a versatile man. He was neither a pleasant man nor a man of deep convictions. We have met him twice so far, as the architect of the earliest *Rundbogen* church in Germany and the earliest Renaissance *palazzo* in Germany. Now in 1834 he brought out at governmental request a folio called *Anweisung zur Architektur des Christlichen Kultus*.[1] It was intended to be sent to municipal councils to offer them patterns for new churches. The book has 38 engraved plates and a text of about 25 pages, and as if Klenze had never built the church of All Saints [Pl. 26] and the Leuchtenberg Palais, Chapter Three called 'Of the general Principle of Architecture' states: 'Greek architecture is not only the most perfect, best and most beautiful . . . but also the only true architecture'.[2] Hence it must be right for Christian buildings too. The statement sounds apodictic. It certainly proves that Klenze's heart was in the Grecian Glyptothek, his first major building, and in the Walhalla near Regensburg. But the statement does not in fact mean what it says. Without any explanatory comment Klenze includes Roman, i.e. vaulted, buildings with Greek,[3] and indeed nearly all his proposed churches have *Rundbogen* windows, i.e. are Graeco-Roman, just as the exterior of the Glyptothek had a Greek portico but the interior a sequence of vaults in the succession of the Roman baths.

---

[1] On Klenze see O. Hederer, *Leo von Klenze* (Munich, 1964) and R. Wiegmann, *Der Ritter von Klenze und Unsere Kunst* (Düsseldorf, 1839), and on his views on church architecture in particular an article by B. Zittel in *Das Münster*, V, 1952, 343–4.

[2] *Anweisung*, 8.

[3] As for other styles, Klenze calls Gothic churches 'grand' and '*hinreissend*' but arbitrary. So they should only very occasionally be used as a pattern for today. St Peter's in Rome is designed on a bad ground plan and has had fatal effects for centuries. Two recent basilican schemes are praised: Chalgrin's St Philippe-du-Roule and Hansen's Church of Our Lady at Copenhagen, special praise is given to 'the excellent Schinkel', and a swipe is directed in a footnote against English and French but also German innovators who canvass for a new style and originality.

An English architectural critic felt furiously outraged by this. He was Joseph Gwilt (1784–1863), and he published his *Elements of Architectural Criticism* in 1837 for the explicit purpose of opposing the views of an anonymous reviewer who had in the *Foreign Quarterly Review* held up Schinkel, Klenze, and Moller as examples for English architects. As for Moller, whom we know as a Gothicist, the building chosen is the Catholic church at Darmstadt, a building of Pantheon type. For Schinkel the building is the superb Altes Museum, for Klenze the Glyptothek. Gwilt was an experienced writer. He had re-edited Chambers's *Civil Architecture*, made a new translation of Vitruvius, and brought out a book called *Rudiments of the Anglo-Saxon Tongue*. In 1845 he was to do a new *Encyclopaedia of Architecture* which reached a sixth edition in 1889. To show up the impurities of the German buildings from a severely Greek point of view was an easy job. Gwilt's argument is that the Grecian style must in any re-use be accurate to the last moulding and hence is 'unsuitable to modern habits'.[4] Gwilt's position is that he refuses to appear the partisan of any one style. He praises Gothic, he praises the Italian Renaissance, he praises Perrault, the Dôme des Invalides, Gabriel, and Soufflot (Sainte Geneviève), and is nasty (apart from the German Grecians) only to the Adams ('the miserable taste of the Adamses'), and Wilkins (that 'wretched pile of building, the National Gallery').[5] If one wants to locate his own taste, these are the clues. Barry deserved his victory in the competition for the Houses of Parliament, but if only Barry had been allowed to build them in the 'Italian style'![6] For 'the Italian school has been and still is the foundation upon which all the buildings of Europe are designed'.[7] Yet as for today, the French hold 'the highest rank in Europe'.[8]

Gwilt dedicated his book to Cockerell, C. R. Cockerell, S. P. Cockerell's son (1788–1863).[9] In 1839 Cockerell became Professor of Architecture at the Royal Academy. The post had been Soane's till 1837 and then had gone to Wilkins—to Gwilt's horror, expressed with three exclamation marks. But Cockerell was another matter, as his lectures show. They were never published as a book, but summaries appeared in *The Athenaeum* and, taken from these, in *The Builder*.[10] Not that Cockerell necessarily agreed with Gwilt.

---

[4] *Elements of Architectural Criticism*, 19, 23.
[5] Ibid., 31.   [6] Ibid., 28.
[7] Ibid., 38.   [8] Ibid., VII.
[9] See E. M. Dodd in *Victorian Architecture*, ed. P. Ferriday (London, 1963).
[10] I (1843), III (1845), IV (1846).

He said for instance that he had 'great faith' in Schinkel[11] who by the way also was an Honorary Member of the R.I.B.A. Also, he spent much of the available time on matters of ancient architecture and indeed archaeology. For he was as competent a classical scholar as he was an inspired architect. Now what do the lectures give us of theory and of topical criticism? 'In the present day all styles [are] in request',[12] but of all of them, 'the Roman [is] most practicable for us'.[13] Students are warned against 'the exclusive desire for imitation', but also 'the excessive love of novelty and originality'.[14] Castellated country-houses are absurd: 'On entering the baronial hall . . . you are addressed by a powdered footman'.[15] But Pugin gets a compliment for his gateway of Magdalen College at Oxford[16] and the Cambridge Camden Society a bad mark for being 'in pursuit of other subjects than those of the art'.[17] The programme today must be 'the acceptance and employment of every useful element . . . and to engraft new features, and bend it to the march of human improvement'.[18] One might think that that remark implies some recognition of the works of the engineers. But no; their 'modern influence' is deprecated, because they are 'entirely utilitarian', and that architecture must not be.[19] Cockerell's most consistent recommendation is that of Inigo Jones and, even more forcefully, Wren. In his diary he wrote in 1823: 'I hold those as coxcombs and impertinent who decry Palladio, Jones and Wren . . . as some of our professors presumed to do'.[19a] On Wren specifically these are Cockerell's words: 'Character was the basis of [his] art, and poetry has appeared in all [his] conceptions'.[20] St Paul's is held up as a Protestant cathedral, and Cockerell is Protestant in his Christianity. The climax of the lectures seems to have been the description of a Protestant Cathedral. In the reports it sounds a very weird building,[21] with a polygonal nave and circular projections, a large vestibule and a spacious chancel, a lofty dome and a smaller dome, and two towers. Cockerell must of course have known Wightwick's two Protestant Cathedrals of 1840 and 1845, but for them we are not quite ready yet.

Cockerell was the most powerful architect England possessed

[11] III, 85.   [12] III, 31.
[13] III, 85.   [14] IV, 98.
[15] I, 80.   [16] III, 38.
[17] IV, 38. On Pugin see Chapter XIII, on the Cambridge Camden Society Chapter XIV.
[18] I, 60.   [19] III, 31, 38.
[19a] 21 Jan. 1823. Quoted by J. M. Crook in *The Country Seat*, ed. H. Colvin and J. Harris (London, 1970), 227.
[20] IV, 75–6.   [21] IV, 98 ff.

about 1840. He belonged firmly to the classical tradition and was in sympathy with the recent Beaux-Arts developments in Paris. The Ashmolean Museum in Oxford shows his originality, his design for the Royal Exchange his indebtedness to Wren, and both his endeavours towards a more Baroque classicism. The Royal Exchange [Pl. 30] was the object of another competition—this one held in 1839—and in the end William Tite won, with a design also Wrenian but in a vague and muddled way. Tite as an architect was inferior to Cockerell. Robert Kerr to whom a whole chapter is to be devoted later, called him, not unjustly, 'a prosperous commercial practicioner' and an adherent of the convenient abstract eclecticism of the thorough 'man of business'.[22] As regards the Wren Revival Cockerell was indeed not the only one to point to Wren as an example, though his *Tribute to Sir Christopher Wren*, a huge composite drawing of all the Wren churches exhibited in the Royal Academy in 1839 helped the cause considerably [Pl. 31]. He had already been inspired by Wren plans in his Hanover Chapel in Regent Street of 1823–5 and his Holy Trinity, Hotwells, Bristol, of 1829–30, but the first pointer in the Wren direction, or perhaps rather the direction of the John Webb of King Charles Building at Greenwich Hospital, had been Philip Hardwick's splendid Goldsmiths' Hall of 1829–31. Then, in the year of Cockerell's *Tribute*, followed, apart from the designs for the Royal Exchange, the full representation of Wren in George Godwin's *Churches of London*. *The Builder*, whose editor Godwin became in 1844, protested in 1845[23] against the demolition of St Benet Fink, and finally in 1848 Clayton's folio on the Wren churches appeared.

The Builder which started in 1843 was going to be the most important professional paper of the Early and High Victorian decades. The term professional is used in this context advisedly; for these are the years when architecture became a profession.[24]

---

[22] *Trans. R.I.B.A.*, 1883–4, 219. The whole article from which this passage comes is reprinted as Appendix I to this book, pp. 291–314.

[23] III, 497.

[24] On all these developments see Barrington Kaye, *The Development of the Architectural Profession in Britain* (London, 1960). Also Frank Jenkins, *Architect and Patron* (London, 1961). A very recent and very useful summing-up incorporating some little-known material is J. Mordaunt Crook, 'The pre-Victorian Architect; Professionalism and Patronage', in *Architectural History* XII, 1969. On the architectural journals see Frank Jenkins: 'Nineteenth Century Architectural Periodicals', in *Concerning Architecture*, ed. Sir John Summerson (London, 1968). On the Architectural Association see Sir John Summerson's brilliant *The Architectural Association* (London, 1947).

1835 saw the foundation of the Institute of British Architects, and in 1834 John Claudius Loudon, gardener and prolific journalist, had started the *Architectural Magazine*. *The Civil Engineer and Architect's Journal* followed in 1837, and *The Builder*, as has just been said, in 1843. Four years later, the Architectural Association was formed, as a club of the young and a place where teaching should go on outside the traditional system of the articled pupil being taught as much or as little as his master chose. For the Institute did not teach. Its object was professional respectability. When it established itself, Thomas Leverton Donaldson was made one of the two secretaries. In the obituary article which the *Transactions of the Royal Institute of British Architects* published,[25] he was called 'practically . . . the founder' of the Institute. The foundation is paralleled by the more or less contemporary foundations of the Institution of Civil Engineers (1818; incorporated 1828), the Chemical Society (1841) and the Institute of Actuaries (1848)—all bodies created to secure prestige and controls. Donaldson is the embodiment of the new architectural professionalism—positively and negatively.[26] He was born in 1795, son of an architect, and grand-nephew of Thomas Leverton, an architect who designed in a refined Adamesque style. He visited Italy and Greece in 1819 and remained throughout his life devoted to the classical, though not the Grecian ideal. *The Builder* in its obituary[27] called him 'the last of the old gods'. Yet his first building, Holy Trinity Kensington of 1826–9 was in a Commissioners' Gothic; and his best known, University Hall (now the Dr. Williams Library) in Gordon Square of 1848 in a domestic Tudor-Gothic [Pl. 32]. But the alterations to University College kept close to Wilkins's style; the house he built to a French architect's design for Thomas Hope's son Henry T. Hope in Piccadilly in 1849–51 was called by Henry Cole and Richard Redgrave's *Journal of Design and Manufactures*[28] 'in a somewhat new style more French than English',[29] the designs for the Royal Exchange are not too far from the Wrenian, and others such as those for a villa[30] are in an

---

[25] *Trans. R.I.B.A.*, New Ser., II, 1886, 89 ff.

[26] There is no adequate recent account of Donaldson's life, work and importance. Miss S. Blutman's article in the *RIBA Journal*, 3rd Ser., LXXIV, 1967, 542, does not go far. See therefore the *DNB* and the obituaries mentioned a little later.

[27] XLIX, 1885, 179.

[28] II, 1849–50. On Cole, his circle and the *Journal*, see below, p. 157 ff.

[29] The house is illustrated in Hitchcock's *Early Victorian Architecture*, 1954, and is not up to much.

[30] *Civil Eng. and A. J.*, V, 1842, 233.

Italianate Free Renaissance style—what Thomas Hope called *Cinque cento*. Donaldson had a great regard for the Parisian official style as represented for example by his friend Hittorff.[31] *The Builder* called it the 'peculiar French taste for grand . . . Classical compilation'.[32]

Donaldson was indeed an eclectic, and if he had not been, he could not have achieved what he did—professionally and in particular administratively. He brought out *A Collection of the most approved Examples of Doorways from ancient Buildings in Greece and Italy* (1833–6), a *Memoir of Sir John Soane* (1837), a *Handbook of Specifications* (1859), and innumerable contributions to the *Transactions* of the R.I.B.A. and the new professional journals. In 1841 he was made the first Professor of Architecture at University College.

That in itself is a characteristic fact too. Until 1840 the only professors of architecture had been those in the Royal Academy. But in 1840 King's College elected William Hosking, a very minor architect, to be Professor of the Arts of Construction, and in addition in 1841 to be Professor of the Principles and Practice of Architecture.[33] His first inaugural lecture (Jan. 1841) was addressed to the Class of Civil Engineering and Architecture. This and the second inaugural (Jan. 1842) do not tell us much. Only architecture and engineering together are 'strictly the complete practice of architecture, in its most extended sense';[34] hence all praise to Telford who was an architect as well as an engineer. If architects

[31] Hittorff's design for the Albert Memorial is dedicated 'à son ami Donaldson'—see *The Architectural Review*, CXLVI, 1969, 489.

[32] Ibid.

[33] Hosking (1800–61) was in fact an engineer. In 1838–9 he built the interesting railway, canal, and road crossing at Kensal Green in three tiers. But he also designed the buildings of the Abney Park Cemetery and an office building for Behrens & Co. in Cannon Street. In collaboration with Britton he published in 1842 his restoration of St Mary Redcliffe in Bristol (*Abstracts and Report by Messrs Britton and Hosking concerning the restoration of the Church of St Mary Redcliffe, Bristol*). In the Calendar for 1842–3 he announced two courses. One is called Arts of Construction in connection with Civil Engineering and Architecture and deals e.g. with draining and sewage, foundations, bridges, roads, railways, canals, and docks; and in addition Principles and Practice of Architecture which was to include the profession, the choice of a site, heating, lighting, and ventilation, economical planning, Elements of Beauty in Architectural Design and types of buildings, public and private. There were to be two lectures a week: Tuesdays and Fridays 4–5. Tuesdays and Fridays 3–4 was called Principles and Practice of Architecture and dealt with such matters as site, foundations, walls, floors, roofs etc., and also the Elements of Beauty in Architectural Design, the styles of the past (Egyptian, Grecian, Roman, Byzantine, Gothic, Italian, Moorish, Early Venetian, English and Continental varieties of Pointed), and building types (from churches and law courts to shops, farms, prisons, and factories).

[34] 1841, 12.

7

are not sufficiently appreciated this is due to laymen regarding them as mere draughtsmen or artists, 'scarcely as a profession for a gentleman'.[35]

Donaldson's Inaugural is more interesting, but to appreciate it one must see it against the whole panoply of his activities, jobs, and honours. In the Institute Donaldson became Secretary for Foreign Relations in 1839 and President in 1863–4. He had already been awarded the Royal Gold Medal in 1851. In 1863 he was made a Foreign Associate of the Institut de France. He was a corresponding member of the academies of Vienna, Berlin, Stockholm, Antwerp, Brussels, Ghent, Copenhagen, New York, and seven academies in Italy.[36] In the field of architectural publishing he was Treasurer of the Architectural Publication Society from 1848 to 1860.[37] He served on the building Committee for the Great Exhibition in 1850— the committee whose heavy design, in spite of incorporating a glass dome 200 ft in diameter, was ousted by Paxton's—and in 1860 was one of those advising the Committee on the future Albert Memorial.[38] In the end seven architects, including Donaldson, were asked to submit designs. Donaldson was once again unsuccessful and—as everyone knows—Scott's was chosen, for which Donaldson expressed admiration.

He was a generous and a fair-minded man; that is evident. When in 1847 a few very young architects—Robert Kerr, aged 24, foremost among them—created the Architectural Association, Donaldson, at the inaugural meeting, though over fifty then, said what would please the rising generation: 'The great question is, are we to have an architecture of our period, a distinct, individual, palpable style of the nineteenth century?'

But what did he mean by that? Evidently not the originality of the railway stations and the Crystal Palace nor indeed any originality, i.e. what we would call originality; for we know what his own mature designs were like, and so we must look in the first place

---

[35] Of course neither Hosking's nor Donaldson's courses were intended as a substitute for pupilage. The change from private to full academic tuition came only at the end of the century.

[36] Reciprocally, the Royal Institute elected as its first honorary and corresponding foreign Members, among others and in addition to Schinkel and Klenze, Percier, Fontaine, Le Bas, Gau, Hittorff, Poccianti (of the Leghorn *Cisternone*), Moller, Othmer, Gärtner, and also Bruloff of St Petersburg and Ithiel Town of New York. By 1838 Vaudoyer, Blouet, Laves, Zanth, Lassaulx, Hübsch, Förster, Nobile, Valadier, Canina, and Bianchi had been added to these.

[37] The Society's paramount publication is Papworth's *Dictionary of Architecture* (1853–92).

[38] See P. Ferriday, 'Syllabus in Stone', *The Architectural Review*, CXXXV, 1964, 423 ff.

for the theoretical counterpart to these. This we find in his *Preliminary Discourse* given on the occasion of the beginning of his lectures at University College.[39] There he first of all established himself as a Protestant (at that tense moment of Newman and Pugin, Pusey and the Cambridge Camden Society) by hitting out at the tyranny and 'the crafty arrangements' of priesthood. As regards architecture, like Hosking, he called the engineers 'to a certain degree identical' with the architects,[40] but that is only marginal. His credo is that no one style is preferable to any other. 'There is no style . . . which has not its peculiar beauties', and 'there is no fixed style now prevalent'. 'We are wandering in a labyrinth of experiments . . . trying by an amalgamation . . . to form a homogeneous whole.'[41]

Antiquity, the Middle Ages, the Italian and French sixteenth and seventeenth centuries are all studied. In Germany the Byzantine is the 'groundwork for their national style', as the Gothic is in England. Whewell and Willis are praised for their 'penetration and learning', but so are Barry's Houses of Parliament. In short, like Hope's, Donaldson's ideal is Eclecticism, and Eclecticism was almost bound to be the principle adopted by the new professional press. A journal needs variety, and hardly any in the nineteenth century could afford to stand up for one style exclusively. The *Annales Archéologiques*, as we shall see, are the exception.

Loudon's *Architectural Magazine* was certainly no exception. It was the sequel to his widely popular *Encyclopaedia of Cottage, Farm and Villa Architecture* of 1833 with its illustrations in all styles, the stress being on the one hand the Italian villa style, but on the other now the revived Elizabethan. For neo-Elizabethan was becoming popular just then as yet another alternative, especially after it had been sanctioned as officially as possible by being explicitly permitted in 1835 for competition designs for the Houses of Parliament. True, small-scale Elizabethan in accordance with existing real Elizabethan had already been done by Capability Brown at Burghley and Corsham, by Wyatville at Longleat and by D. Legg at Burghley, both the latter in 1801. But the fashion began on the most spectacular scale with Salvin and Burn's Harlaxton, begun in 1831, and Barry's

---

[39] Published in 1842.

[40] On p. 25 we read: 'Wherever construction is concerned, the Architect can only be worthy of his independent mission who possesses the science now sometimes considered to be exclusively appropriate to the Engineer.'

[41] Ibid., 28–30.

Highclere in 1837. On a more domestic scale both Burn and Salvin had already used it earlier.[42]

In the same years a flood of books came out of sumptuous, picturesque representations of Elizabethan and Jacobean mansions. The foremost are in chronological order: T. F. Hunt's *Exemplars of Tudor Architecture adapted to Modern Habitations* (1830), T. H. Clarke's *The Domestic Architecture of the Reigns of Queen Elizabeth and James I* (1833), J. Hakewill's *An Attempt to determine the exact Character of Elizabethan Architecture* (1835), C. J. Richardson's *Observations on the Architecture of England during the Reigns of Queen Elizabeth and King James I* (1837), and the same author's *Architectural Remains of the Reigns of Elizabeth and James I*, vol. I (1840) and *Studies from Old English Mansions* (1841), Henry Shaw's *Details of Elizabethan Architecture* (1839), and finally and most famous Joseph Nash's *The Mansions of England in the Olden Times* (1839–49).[43]

Not that there was anything like universal approval of the Elizabethan style and the Elizabethan Revival. Pugin called the latter 'a fashionable rage',[44] Bartholomew—on whom see the next chapter—branded the former as 'masses of trash',[45] and Scott in his more measured way as 'artistically imperfect and impure'.[46]

But Loudon to whom we can now return had no such hesitations. The *beau idéal* of the country house in his *Encyclopaedia* is Elizabethan. As has already been said, the *Encyclopaedia* was followed by the *Architectural Magazine*. It started after only one year, in 1834, and ran to five volumes. Loudon wrote much of it himself, in a philosophical vein and nearly always worth pondering.[47] The volumes from 1835 to the end contain long extracts from Hope's *Historical Essay*. In Volume Five Loudon states that 'the most striking architectural erections that have taken place throughout England in the last two years are, unquestionably, those connected with engineering.[48] This anticipates Hosking and Donaldson. Loudon also faces

---

[42] For early Burn, David Walker has a paper ready which the Victorian Society hopes to publish soon. For Salvin see e.g. Mamhead in Devon of 1827–33. Earlier still were Smirke's demolished Egmont Castle in Cumberland (1824) and Webster's Underley Hall in Westmorland (1827–7).

[43] On all these publications see now M. Girouard: 'Attitudes to Elizabethan Architecture', in *Concerning Architecture,* ed. Sir John Summerson (London, 1968).

[44] *True Principles,* 62.

[45] See below, p. 93.

[46] *Remarks,* 150.

[47] Another frequent author was W. H. Leeds (on whom see pp. 23, 40, 70 above). He also wrote under the pen-name Candidus.

[48] V, 1838, 530.

remarkably boldly the implications of iron as a building material. In an article signed 'M' the growing use of iron is recognized. 'Architects should qualify themselves, not less to adapt their designs to the new material, than the new material to their designs.' The author regards it as likely that iron will remain a material subsidiary to stone, but if whole buildings were in future to be erected of iron, then 'all habituated notions of . . . proportion . . . must, of course, be discarded'. That was said in 1837, fourteen years before the Crystal Palace.[49] But, like Donaldson, Loudon is in the *Magazine*, just as in the *Encyclopaedia*, predominantly eclectic. He illustrates a Norman villa, a thirteenth-century villa, and an Italianate villa (all three by Loudon's protégé E. B. Lamb), and he prints a paper by J. A. Picton of Liverpool on the 'Applicability of the Anglo-Norman Style to Modern Ecclesiastical Edifices'.[50]

The Civil Engineer and Architect's Journal whose first volume covers 1837–8 was a much more matter-of-fact affair. Little in the first five volumes is of interest: an article by James Thomson on Vanbrugh,[51] several contributions by George Godwin and several references to Alfred Bartholomew. Godwin (1815–88) had, in 1835, won the first essay prize ever given by the Institute of British Architects for an essay on concrete,[52] was one of the founders of the Art Union, and became the third editor of *The Builder* and without question the most influential architectural editor of his time. He was a man of fervent social interests in architecture. The first editor was Joseph Aloysius Hansom. He resigned after six months, in July 1843, and was replaced by Alfred Bartholomew. But Bartholomew died in 1845, and that gave Godwin the great chance of his life.[53] It is worth speculating on how Bartholomew would have directed the paper. Probably more wilfully and pugnaciously but less fairly and less circumspectly. This is at least what one would guess from his *magnum opus*, innocently called *Specifications*.

[49] IV, 1837, 277–87.
[50] I, 333; II, 257; III, 155; I, 288. Incidentally, Loudon also reprinted Anderson's papers of 1800 (see p. 17), which is interesting.
[51] III, 1840, 261.
[52] *Transactions*, 1835–6.
[53] On Godwin see A. King, 'Another Blow for Life', in *The Architectural Review*, CXXXVI, 1964, 448 ff. Also by the same: 'George Godwin and the Art Union of London', *Victorian Studies*, VIII, 1964, 101 ff.

CHAPTER XI

Bartholomew

ALFRED BARTHOLOMEW'S name appears in the fifth volume of
the *Civil Engineer and Architect's Journal* (1842, 324) with the description of a proposed church for Kentish Town. It must have been a
weird building indeed, or, as the reviewer writes 'one of the strangest
jumbles conceivable both as to style . . . and as to character'. The
style was 'decorated early English', in imitation of French cathedrals.
The plan was a rectangle with two pairs of short transepts. The east
end had an apse and two towers originally intended to rise to 130 ft.
The windows were partly lancets and partly traceried, but there were
also nine rose windows. The materials were white brick and terracotta dressings, in short a thoroughly debased and confused design.
There is in the *Civil Engineer* also some adverse criticism by Candidus,
i.e. Leeds, against Bartholomew's principal book,[1] and a proper
review of the same book[2]—the book to which this chapter is
dedicated. It is a book that roused feelings. Leeds hits out at
Bartholomew also in his introduction to the publication of the
Travellers' Club (p. 2), and *The Builder* in its second volume[3] used
the book as a stick to beat Pugin with.

Alfred Bartholomew was born in 1801. He was a cockney. He
had only enjoyed 'a moderate degree of education', was articled to
J. H. Good, a pupil of Soane, did during those years measured
drawings of the Bank of England, worked hard privately to read on
architecture and to learn languages, published in 1831 *Sacred Lyrics*,
a new version of the Psalms, 'applicable to parochial psalmody', and
built little and nothing of great importance.[4] His importance lies
entirely in one book.[5] Its title is *Specifications for practical Architects
preceded by an Essay on the Decline of Excellence in the Structure and in*

---

[1] III, 1840, 301.
[2] IV, 1841, 16.
[3] II, 1844, 165. Reprinted from the *Bristol and West of England Archaeological Magazine*.
[4] See G. G. Pace, *Arch. Rev.*, XCII, 1942, 99 ff. The above quotations are taken from the
obituary in *The Builder*, III, 1845, 29.
[5] Though he wrote another: *Hints relative to the Construction of Fire-Proof Buildings* (1839).

*the Science of modern English Buildings with the Proposal of Remedies for
those Defects*. It is dated in the foreword 1839 and came out in 1840.[6]
Half the book consists of commendably detailed sample specifications, but the other half, Part One, serves to vent the author's likes
and dislikes. This part starts with three mottoes, one from Humphrey
Clinker on the flimsiness of Bath stone, one from Serlio on unbonded
facing and one, quoted in Hebrew, from Ezekiel, on 'daubing with
untempered mortar'.

The bulk of Bartholomew's complaints is in fact structural. They
are voiced in the grand style of Victorian pulpit rhetoric, always
using four adjectives where two would have done, and they are
amazingly rude. Wyatt was 'slattern in business',[7] Soane's 'littleness
of architecture'[8] is slated, Decimus Burton's Hyde Park Corner
shows 'four-score settlements',[9] 'all the flat un-churchlike window-
heads below the galleries of St Mark's, Clerkenwell (by Chadwell
Mylne 1826–8) are broken,[10] and so are 1288 window-heads in
thirteen streets of London.[11] The Church Commissioners, 'a bank-
rupt commission of scarcely two shillings in the pound',[12] ought
to insist on fire-proof roofs and no external stucco, and they don't.[13]
Builders thrive on bad workmanship ('Some of the richest builders
of London have made their fortunes from . . . frauds').[14] But some
architects are praised, especially Sir Robert Smirke for holding out
against bad building,[15] Wilkins, 'the most learned literary architect
in the world',[16] Barry,[17] Henry Holland, 'one of the last of England's
real architects',[18] and Sir Robert Taylor who taught his pupils
honesty,[19] whereas Soane treated them as unpaid clerks and left
all the drudgery to them.[20]

Bartholomew's illustrations are as forthright—a metal ball with
a capital W means any weight pressing down, walls are bending out
and bending in excessively, a timber roof-truss becomes a pair of

---

[6] I have used the second edition of 1846.   [7] *Specifications*, §855.
[8] Ibid., §856.   [9] Ibid., §827.
[10] Ibid., §481.   [11] Ibid., §590.
[12] The Commissioners, it must be remembered, had under the first grant paid churches full-
up; under the second they gave on average about 10 per cent—see above p. 33.
[13] Ibid., §§715, 835.   [14] Ibid., §716.
[15] Ibid., §855. On Smirke the technician see J. M. Crook, *Arch. Rev.*, CXLII, 1967, 208 and
especially *Trans. Newcomen Soc.*, XXXVIII, 1965–6.
[16] Ibid., §666.   [17] Ibid., §481.
[18] Ibid., §703.   [19] Ibid., §854.
[20] In fact it was Soane who established the pupilage system, as the nineteenth century got to
know it in England (see B. Kaye: *The Development of the Architectural Profession in Britain*, London,
1960, 62).

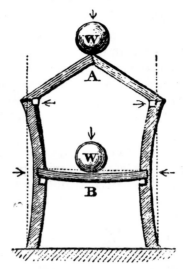

W, W, Weights.
A, An unrestrained roof, thrusting out the walls of a building.
B, A floor sunk by gravity drawing in the walls of a building.

FIG. I. Alfred Bartholomew, Diagram of Thrusts, from *Specifications for Practical Architecture*, 1846.

matching wrestlers, and so on [Figs. 1, 2, 3]; for it is in that light that he considers buildings and their parts. This is what made him take the line on Gothic architecture which according to *The Builder* inspired Pugin. It is hardly necessary to assume that, but Pugin's structural analyses of the elements of Gothic building are, as we shall see, indeed the same as Bartholomew's. 'The medieval builder put all the strength in the ribs', 'the panels between the ribs [are] a mere thin cuticle', and 'the active force [is conducted] down the ribs as easily as water'.[21] Counterbalance against the thrusts is by buttresses, flying buttresses, and their weighing down by pinnacles —'every particle [being] brought into active service'.[22]

A book which Bartholomew in his interpretation of the Gothic style makes much of is Dr. J. Robison's *System of Mechanical Philosophy*, published in Edinburgh in four volumes in 1822. Robison's

[21] *Specifications,* §469.   [22] Ibid., §470 ff.

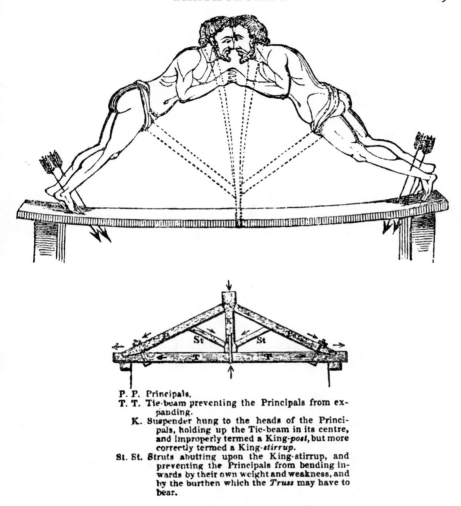

P. P. Principals.

T. T. Tie-beam preventing the Principals from expanding.

K. Suspender hung to the heads of the Principals, holding up the Tie-beam in its centre,
and improperly termed a King-*post*, but more
correctly termed a King-*stirrup*.

St. St. Struts abutting upon the King-stirrup, and
preventing the Principals from bending in-
wards by their own weight and weakness, and
by the burthen which the *Truss* may have to
bear.

FIG. 2. Alfred Bartholomew, Diagram of Roof-Trusses, from *Specifications for Practical
Architecture,* 1846.

sources were French treatises. When he writes: 'The Gothic architecture is perhaps entitled to the name of "*rational* architecture"', he
only repeats what the French had said from Delorme to Rondelet
and beyond.[23] Bartholomew, however crotchety his book, had read
a great deal to write it. §§83–259, nearly fifty pages, are an annotated
bibliography, including not only Alberti among Italians but e.g.

[23] Ibid., §§532–41. See R. Middleton's two papers quoted above, p. 4.

FIG. 3. Alfred Bartholomew, Diagram of Gothic Buttressing, from *Specifications for Practical Architecture*, 1846.

Frisi's *Saggio sopra l'architettura gotica* of 1761,[24] of Frenchmen of course Delorme and of course Rondelet, but also Gauthey's treatise on bridges,[25] of Germans only what existed in translation, i.e. Boisserée's Cologne Cathedral and Moller. As for English studies little is missing. Adam's *Spalatro* is the first item, Wren's *Parentalia* the last. John Britton gets high praise several times,[26] Hope's *Historical Essay* is 'an astonishing monument of amateur industry and ability', Whewell shows what 'gigantic strides . . . in an incredibly short time have been made'. Willis on the other hand is referred to without special enthusiasm.

And where in architecture as against architectural writing do his

---

[24] *Specifications,*, §501.
[25] But not Frézier, where he could have found his interpretation of Gothic structure.
[26] Ibid., §100 ff. 832.

enthusiasms lie? The answer is: with the Greek and with the Gothic builders, and with Wren. The compliments he pays to the Greeks sound less immediately felt than those to the others. Included is 'the beautiful church of St Matthew' in Lambeth, by Porden (1822), 'the only one of our modern Churches which has any high pretension to the title of pure Grecian'.[27] On the other hand he explicitly allows arches in Grecian buildings, because 'a people so shrewd and highly gifted' would have used them, had they known them.[28] Among the Neo-Grecians he seems to find the Germans superior to the others—which must mean Schinkel (whose *Sammlung architektonischer Entwürfe* of 1820–37 is not in his bibliography) and Klenze: 'The present German school of architecture . . . possess much grandeur of conception, much beauty of sculptural decoration . . . blended with considerable constructive science; we have in none of our own modern architecture, such exquisitely imaginative beauties.' But, he adds shrewdly, there is also 'a rudeness, which is totally surprising', a 'dash of Tedesco corruption' without which the buildings 'could be too soaring, too ethereal, to be human'. The corruption comes from 'a certain blending (with) the very worst principles of the very worst Gothic'.[29]

What, one wonders, did he think of? What in fact did he know? German Gothic buildings—'countless myriads' of them—he admires without qualification. 'Few, very few, very few indeed of them do not contain in a single edifice more variety . . . than all the race of Grecian, of Roman and of Egyptian buildings.' The steeple of Freiburg-im-Breisgau in gilt is on the binding of his book.[30]

But the most fervent superlatives are reserved for Wren. He 'had more science in his head and heart, than a thousand Sir John Soanes in their whole souls and bodies'. 'Science and humanity ennobled all Wren did', and St Paul's is 'the most scientific and successful work which was ever erected'.[31]

Included in Bartholomew's admiration and praise are also the engineers. No wonder, considering his emphasis on building science.

---

[27] Ibid., §697. It has the tower at the east end and hence a true portico without interference from the tower in the way Gibbs was originally responsible for. The order is Greek Doric.

[28] §692. He adds (§695) that the Greeks were not 'averse to curvilinear forms'—see the Lysicrates Monument. All the more surprising that in another place he explicitly excluded arches placed direct on columns (à la Spalato). He calls that a heresy and those who do it unscrupulous (§§604–5).

[29] Ibid., §705.   [30] At least of the second edition.

[31] Ibid., §384, 706, 367. Bartholomew incidentally illustrates the Ely Octagon with St Paul's, as its source of inspiration.

'Suspension bridges are so very beautiful, to a stranger so un-expectedly beautiful . . . that they form one of the noblest, most useful, and most successful inventions of man.' Stone bridges are no inferior. 'Were they the work of architects, [they] would, for their science and structure, almost make up for all the defects of modern architecture'.[32] But they are not, and so one of Bartholomew's demands is that we should return to the situation in the Middle Ages, when 'every architect was a civil engineer, and every civil engineer was an architect'.[33]

But this is a trifling demand compared with Bartholomew's grand demand which is the end of Part One of his book, the 'Proposal for the Foundation of a Great National College for the Study and Regulation of Architecture . . . for the Examination of Students and Professors of Architecture and Artificers in Building, for granting Honorary Degrees . . . and for the Conservation of Public Build-ings'.[34] Six years' study is to end with an examination and the grant-ing of the degree **m**, meaning Mason. The successful examinee will then be able to take up a paid job as an architectural clerk or as a clerk of work on a public building. After another four years a second examination, the degree **fm**, meaning Free Mason and the right to practise architecture. Yet another four years and yet another examina-tion make the patient student an **mm**, meaning a Master Mason and enabling him to hold a public office, design public buildings, and take in clerks and apprentices. By six more years—bringing the total up to twenty—and by a fourth examination you are an **mmm** or Mathematical Master Mason, i.e. scientific engineer-cum-architect allowed to construct public buildings and works. You must incidentally also be fully conversant with 'archaeologia'. There ought to be elaborate provisions to engrave or carve the names of all the higher grades on tablets of metal or stone—including the names of those whose buildings turn out to be 10 per cent or more above estimate and those who for dishonesty are removed from the register. Every nobleman of England is to be a president of the college, every M.P. a vice-president, the bishops and judges of England are to be on the Council. The Soane Museum, because of its library, is to be united with the college. Twenty-seven or more professors are to be appointed and seventeen master artificers—all

[32] At least of the second edition, §§406, 808.

[33] Ibid., §76. Hosking, as we have seen, was to say the same in 1841 (see p. 81) and Donaldson in 1842 (see p. 83).

[34] Ibid., §§ 925 ff.

these officers to be salaried, the funds coming from the fees charged for the various grades with their initials.

What is one to make of all this? The Institute of British Architects had only been founded a few years before. Could they take it seriously? Could anybody? Must it not have invalidated everything else Bartholomew had to say? Yet the book went into a second edition, and the author's views coincided sufficiently with those of others to form part of a pattern of informed opinion in the forties. So it is worth following his views yet a little further. The Italian Renaissance, emanating from 'the core of Popery' is 'an amalgamate of uncongenial forms', the Cinque cento (Hope's term) is corrupt, the Louis XIV is of course corrupt too, Italianate churches are 'the ghost of Wren's churches . . . mingled in the expenditure of some two or three thousand pounds . . . with the *contadinesse* of Italian farm buildings'.[35] The Elizabethan is yet worse. It is a 'gross corruption', 'masses of trash', 'puerile details', and if it is imitated today, our architects cannot even make it as impure as the originals were, because they know too much of classical detail. Only three or four architects submitted Elizabethan designs for the Houses of Parliament.[36]

As Bartholomew's Part One is called *On the Decline* one should perhaps not expect him to pronounce on what ought to be done today by architects—short of founding and trusting the Great National College. If one thumbs his pages for positive advice this is what one finds: When England was poor, the most magnificent buildings grew everywhere. 'Now that England has become a mighty empire—larger with its dependencies than was perhaps any former empire—now that it draws to its bosom the gold of all the earth', now that 'we have . . . steam engines, and rail-roads, and steam-vessels, and a thousand private comforts', 'almost everything of its modern architecture has become mean, weak, tasteless, crumbling . . . and an abortion of ugliness'.[37] One reason for this, we have seen, is bad execution, but the other now turns out to be the habit of copying the past. 'In almost every former age of the world, new wants, differences of habits, . . . peculiarities of climate and circumstances gave the architect the powers of new creation . . . But now, instead of fulfilling the wants of times altered . . . and then adding the perfection of the manual dexterity and the economy of the mechanisms of our times, we bind up our resources copying things ancient

35 Ibid., §§830, 922, 934.   36 Ibid., §§ 624–39.   37 Ibid., §§784–5.

without the views of the ancients.'[38] So we need a new style. But
can one be made, now that we have the knowledge of the older
styles? We are bound to 'find it almost impossible, really to invent
anything new in any style'.[39] Note—something new in any style. A
wholly new style Bartholomew does not even contemplate, in spite
of what he said about the suspension bridges. And so his final
answer is, like Hope's and Donaldson's, Eclecticism: 'Who says
that the architect of modern times has no resources left in taste?
Who says that he may not yet, in a thousand different ways . . . work
up the details of Egyptian, of Classical, of Pointed, or of any other
true and genuine style of architecture, taking care . . . that the stuff
on which he works shall be of the right quality for his purpose?'[40]

[38] At least of the second edition, §§646–7.
[39] Ibid., §663.   [40] Ibid., §915.

CHAPTER XII

Petit, Poole, and Freeman

How Eclecticism worked in the hands of a sensible and quite sensitive critic without any of the prestige of Hope, the professional competence of Donaldson, or the punch of Bartholomew one can see in the Revd J. L. Petit's *Remarks on Church Architecture*.

John Louis Petit (1801–68) was an amateur archaeologist, Secretary of the Lichfield Architectural Society, 'a non-high churchman',[1] designer of some churches,[2] and the author of a number of books.[3] The *Remarks* were published in 1841 and with their many deft sketches are in the tradition of picturesque travel. They may remind one at first of Gally Knight, but they have yet much less of a scholarly ambition. The first volume is at least loosely a survey by consecutive periods, the second is largely just strung-together notes on churches, and more than half of it is in the guise of a tour from England through the Netherlands, the Rhineland, Switzerland, parts of North Italy, the Riviera, and France back to England. The end: 'And here, reader, I bid you farewell',[4] is typical of the book. Much in volume two is advice to the sketching artist: 'The graceful costume of the inhabitants will give much character to his groups', or 'The artist who would devote a few days to the scenery of this romantic tract, will find fair accommodations at the small village of Ronco.'[5]

But most of the book is meant as direct or indirect advice to architects. One often finds remarks such as 'worthy of imitation' or 'furnishing an excellent suggestion to the architect of the present day'.[6] He needs it; for today one finds only too often either 'a capricious and unrestrained fancy' or 'a slavish submission to some

[1] *The Ecclesiologist*, X, 1850, 122.
[2] Mr. Howell has sent me a photograph of Petit's church at Caerdeon (Bentddu), Merionethshire, built in 1863. Petit is called in an inscription over the door the 'founder and benefactor' of the church.
[3] For an obituary see *Proc. Soc. of Ant.*, 2 Ser., IV, 1867–70. His principal book is *Architectural Studies in France* (1854), a briefer one is *Remarks on Architectural Character* (Oxford, 1846).
[4] *Remarks on Church Architecture*, II, 270.
[5] Ibid., II, 232, 221.   [6] Ibid., II, 72, 51.

arbitrary forms or maxims'.[7] This applies to new buildings as much as to the restoration and enlargement of old buildings. Some new ones Petit praises—e.g. Brereton in Staffordshire of 1837 by Thomas Trubshaw, the small St David's at Barmouth of 1839 by Edward Haycock, and Holy Trinity at Stanton near Bakewell of 1838[8]— but only a few. As a rule and especially in a whole chapter of volume two, called 'On Modern Repairs and Adaptations' he complains of the 'ignorant and presumptuous restorer', and of anyone who may be 'meddling rashly'.[9] Yet he has no doubt that interference with the old churches is 'absolutely demanded by necessity', and he can only plead that the restorer should 'follow the old work accurately' instead of doing his new work 'all indiscriminately to one standard'[10] What he means by this and what he pleads for is revealed right at the start of the chapter, where a poem is quoted in the tradition of Payne Knight's *The Landscape*. 'Handle with reverence each crumbling stone, Respect the very lichens o'er it grown'. The reverence, as a correspondence with George Gilbert Scott was soon to make clear (see p. 169), is extended to features of any style, including the 'debased' later ones, and the reverence is demanded for the sake of historical wholeness ('a link to bind the future with the past') and equally of picturesqueness. The building with all accretions is attractive because picturesque. How then is one to restore in actual cases? That, as we shall see, was Scott's question.

And indeed, here as in other arguments, Petit remains vague, and an amiable vagueness is in fact Petit's failing. Negatively, but also positively, he tries to be fair to all and never to be carried away. So he praises Renaissance as well (if not as much) as medieval churches: S. Maria delle Grazie in Milan of the Quattrocento, S. Maria di Carignano in Genoa of the Cinquecento, the Louvre and the Tuileries ('will be carefully examined by admirers of the Revival'), the dome of the Invalides ('perfect'), the exterior of the Madeleine ('unrivalled'), St Paul's ('a masterpiece of design, proportion, and composition').[11]

As for the Middle Ages, it is more remarkable that Petit gives high praise to the Romanesque than that he appreciates the Gothic; for, as we have already seen, with the former he joined that small minority which the Ecclesiologists found so objectionable. Petit's

---

[7] *Remarks on Church Architecture,*, I, VII.
[8] Ibid., II, 47–8, 143.
[9] Ibid., II, 129–30.
[10] Ibid., II, 130, 134, 140.
[11] Ibid., II, 219, 222, 257; I, 38, 25.

theory of the origin of the pointed arch is original. In the South of France you find pointed tunnel-vaults under comparatively high-pitched stone roofs. What more likely than that the profile of the vault would adapt itself to the profile of the roof![12] The structural explanation of the Gothic—the function of the ribs, of the buttresses, flying buttresses, and pinnacles—is accepted, but not made much of.[13] Historically Petit believes that Germany was the country of origin of the Gothic style, not England or France, and in this he followed Hope who had argued the German case in much greater detail.[14]

Hope also may have opened Petit's eyes to the Romanesque [Fig. 4]. The Italian, but even more the Rhenish, seemed to him to have great possibilities for today. On the Rhenish early thirteenth century—Whewell's preserve—he is in one respect even more perspicacious than Whewell; for he stresses that the style of Geln-hausen and the west end of Worms Cathedral [Fig. 5] ought to be seen less as a version of Early Gothic than of Late Romanesque ('a sequel to the preceding Romanesque', 'a modified Romanesque').[15] 'Might not a style be matured', Petit asks, 'upon the suggestions thrown out to us by those old buildings?'[16]

The end of volume one is Petit's great summing up of advice to church designers.[17] The Grecian is 'improper' for churches, because it cannot give a peculiar character to a sacred building. The Renaissance, 'though grounded on inconsistent principles, nevertheless offers some beauties and advantages unattainable in other styles and in towns will sometimes harmonize the best with surrounding buildings'. As regards the Romanesque, especially the German, 'if a pure round-arched style could be formed, it might, perhaps, be made to suit many kinds of arrangement to which no other is exactly adapted'. Norman and Transitional are 'incomplete styles, however interesting to the student'.[18] Early English should only be used where there are plenty of means. Otherwise it tends to meagreness. The Geometrical Decorated and the Flowing Decorated also are costly, the former for instance requires vaulting. That leaves the Perpendicular, and this 'allows the greatest latitude', and offers 'a wide field of improvement'.

Petit is not an eclectic in Hope's sense but in Donaldson's; he does

[12] Ibid., I, 114.
[13] Ibid., II, 6–10.
[14] Ibid., II, 80. For Hope see pp. 417–22.
[15] Ibid., I, 78, 142, 148.
[16] Ibid., I, 89.
[17] Ibid., I, 210 ff.
[18] Ibid., To Petit Norman 'is essentially Gothic'. I, 93.

FIG. 4. J. L. Petit, S. Michele, Pavia, from *Remarks on Church Architecture,* 1841.

not propose mixing, but he is an eclectic in tolerating all available
styles. Where he was taken most seriously was as a partisan of the
Romanesque which, as we have seen (pp. 66–7) was a vigorous fashion
of the forties. If *The Ecclesiologist*[19] devoted an exceptionally long
review to Petit's book, the object was of course to voice opposition
to a book so 'entirely opposed . . . to the authoritative commands

[19] *Remarks on Church Architecture,* I, 91 ff. On *The Ecclesiologist* and the Cambridge Camden
society see Chapter XIV, pp. 123 ff. Vol. XXIV, 1864 has a criticism of Petit's church at
Caerdeon (as Mr. Howell informs me).

FIG. 5. J. L. Petit, Cathedral at Worms, from *Remarks on Church Architecture,* 1841.

of our church' and in particular opposition to 'the Romanesque, or the Revived Roman, or Lombardic, or Italian styles' all of which 'can be of little use to English church builders'. Equally outspoken is *The Ecclesiologist's* criticism of Petit's recommendation of the Perpendicular style, but here the journal represented the new attitude, Petit the old, and *The Ecclesiologist* stood in a united front with Pugin and soon also with Ruskin to all of whom the Perpendicular was the style of the Gothic decline.

Contemporary buildings other than those in styles of the past are only once touched upon by Petit, and his two comments are worth noting. The one is as ready for a compromise as we expect Petit to be, but the other is totally unexpected. It is this. Present-day buildings, especially 'those connected with our railways'—and he points to bridges and viaducts—are 'the very perfection of mechanical beauty'. But he cannot have meant suspension bridges (as Bartholomew did and Scott was going to do) because in another place he says of the cast iron spire of Rouen Cathedral that 'the nature of its material deprives it of any claims to interest'.[20]

As a scholar Petit does not count. To say of St. Mary in Capitol at Cologne that 'parts . . . are supposed to be of great antiquity' and leave it at that, is not good enough, and his Gothic is a muddle of overlapping periods. He speaks, it is true, of Romanesque, Transition, Early Complete Gothic, and Late Complete Gothic, but between Romanesque and Transition is Late Romanesque or Norman which can only confuse, and the Katharinenkirche at Oppenheim for instance is discussed in the chapter on Transition, called there 'the most perfect Gothic', and given the dates 1262–1317. It comes again in Early Complete Gothic, and again in Late Complete Gothic as transitional between the two.[21]

Finally as a writer Petit cannot count either. His descriptions are weak. This is what he finds to say of Freiburg-im-Breisgau: 'Freiburg Cathedral has a lofty western octagonal tower, with a capping of pinnacles. The choir is without transepts, and somewhat deficient in length. The interior, however, is handsome, and has a triforium gallery . . . Its western door . . . is remarkable for its sculpture.'[22] Occasionally he goes into poetry.[23] This is as characteristic as anything. The *Remarks* is a pretty book, prettily written and prettily illustrated. It is neither of help to the scholar, nor has it a message to the architect of his own day.[24] The scholar went to Whewell and Willis, the architect went to the journals, and both went to the large fully illustrated books on English medieval architecture which now began to multiply: Pugin's earlier *Specimens*[25] were followed by the *Examples of Gothic Architecture* (3 vols., 1838–40), F. A. Paley's *Manual of Gothic Mouldings* (1845) and *Manual of Gothic Architecture* (1846), J. Raphael and J. A. Brandon's *An Analysis of Gothick Architecture* (1847), Edmund Sharpe's *Architectural Parallels* (1848),

[20] *Remarks*, II, 151 and 13.   [21] Ibid., I, 146, 167, 195–6.
[22] Ibid., I, 197.   [23] Ibid., II, 99, 115, 125, 140.
[24] Yet Henry van Brunt, that brilliant architectural critic, referred to Petit's *Architectural Studies in France* as late as 1886 (see *Architecture and Society; Selected Essays of Henry van Brunt*; ed. W. A. Coles, Harvard U.P. 1969, 176).
[25] See p. 25.

A Treatise on the Rise and Progress of Decorated Window Tracery in England (1849), and *The Seven Periods of English Architecture* (1851), Henry Bowman and J. S. Crowther's *The Churches of the Middle Ages*, (1845–53), R. W. Billings's *Illustrations of Geometrical Tracery* (1849), E. A. Freeman's *An Essay on the Origin and Development of Window Tracery in England* (1850–1), and J. Colling's *Gothic Ornaments* (1850) and *Details of Gothic Architecture* (1856).

One of these authors had written a book for reading as well, and both architects and laymen who were eager to read architectural history, if they wanted something less long and less heavy than Hope's *Historical Essay*, would turn to Freeman's *A History of Architecture*, published in 1849, if they did not prefer George Aycliffe Poole's *A History of Ecclesiastical Architecture in England* published one year before.

Poole was secretary of the Northamptonshire Architectural Society and a sensible man. His book is based on Willis, on Sharpe, on Paley, and on other recent scholars and contains much in the way of extracts from chronicles and documents, including the contracts for the Beauchamp Chapel at Warwick, for Catterick church, the Durham dormitory, and the Louth steeple. His descriptions of motifs are detailed, and he has valuable passages on the terminological confusion as to whether Geometrical ought to form part of Early English or of Decorated. The confusion was initially caused by Rickman and made worse by others. Poole's own taste is that of Pugin, the Cambridge Camden Society, and Scott. The late thirteenth century is 'a most exquisite style', 'perhaps the most perfect of all styles',[26] though the Decorated is 'the most fascinating style'. He nicely connects the character of the Decorated with the licence of the court of Edward II,[27] and he hits out at 'the barbarity' of the sculpture under Henry VIII and the 'monstrousness' of sculpture in churches since Henry VIII.[28] About today Poole is ambiguous. He warns against imitation—medieval architects 'did not imitate the parts of the building already erected'[29]—but he praises those who 'endeavour to restore a truly ecclesiastical style' and architects who build churches 'in the true spirit of the churchmen'.[30]

Freeman is much more radical in his judgements. E. A. Freeman (1823–92) is famous as the author of the great *History of the Norman*

---

[26] *A History of Ecclesiastical Architecture in England*, 237 ff.
[27] Ibid., 313–4. [28] Ibid., 260, 268.
[29] Ibid., 347. [30] Ibid., 406.

Conquest, but that only came out in 1867–76, and he was only made
Regius Professor of Modern History at Oxford in 1884. When he
was young, archaeology was his main interest. He joined the
Oxford Architectural and Historical Society which had been founded
in 1839 and to which we shall revert later (p. 123) and became its
secretary in 1845. In a lecture in that year he recommended the
Anglo-Norman style as 'suitable for the present time'[31] but calls in
his book 'on the whole Perpendicular . . . the best'.[32] This, as has
just been said, is in total contrast to the taste of e.g. the Ecclesiological movement, but Freeman all the same was much in sympathy
with it. Among scholars he prefers Hope and Petit to Whewell and
Willis, because of the more philosophical treatment of architecture
by the former two. The interest of Whewell and Willis he calls
'more mechanical'.[33] The most interesting pages of his book are
those at the end where he shows his hand, condemns the Renaissance
as corruption of the art of architecture, the Revived Grecian as
absurd, and the Revived Italian as worthless.

So Freeman does not belong to the eclectics. He was a medievalist,
even if with his appreciation of Norman, less confined and certainly
less passionately committed than the leading Gothicists of these
years. Their names are familiar. They are first Pugin, then Neale and
Webb, the founders of the Cambridge Camden Society, and then
Ruskin.[34] Pugin's *Contrasts* came out one year after Hope's *Historical
Essay*, and *True Principles*, his masterpiece, one year after Bartholomew's *Specifications* and in the same year as Petit's *Remarks*, and
Ruskin's *Seven Lamps* in the same year as Freeman's *History*.

---

[31] *The Ecclesiologist*, IV, 1845, 76.
[32] *A History of Architecture*, xiv.
[33] Ibid., xi–xiii.
[34] In 1846 the Cambridge Camden Society visited him in Oxford. Neale and Webb were of
the party. See W. R. W. Stephens (ed.), *The Life and Letters of E. A. Freeman*, 2 vols (London,
1895), 79–80.

CHAPTER XIII

Pugin

GOTHIC to Horace Walpole had been a sophisticated game, to Goethe a high flight of creative imagination, to Whewell and Willis a historical phenomenon to be investigated, to Hope and to Donaldson one of a variety of styles recommended according to circumstances—to Pugin it was a Christian duty.

Augustus Welby Northmore Pugin was born in 1812, the son of A. C. Pugin of the *Specimens*.[1] When still very young he designed furniture for Windsor Castle which had been commissioned from the firm of Morel and Seddon and subcontracted by them to A. C. Pugin. Still very young A. W. N. went into business on his own for Gothic decoration, did not succeed and had to go to his father to have his debts paid. That was in 1831, when he was nineteen. In the same year he married; but his wife died in 1832, and his parents died in 1832 and 1833. In 1833 he married again, and moved to Salisbury where he built St Marie's Grange for his wife and himself. 1834 is the key-date in his life. It marks his conversion to Catholicism. One reason for his conversion he himself gave as 'the study of ancient architecture'.[2] One year later he wrote *Contrasts*, his most challenging book, which came out in 1836. At about that time he received his first architectural commissions too. In 1837 he began at Scarisbrick Hall in Lancashire, his biggest domestic job, and in 1839 he already wrote that he had more work than he could well do.[3] His second wife died in 1844. He got engaged again twice, but in vain, but married a third time in 1848. However, 1846 is the year of his first mental

---

[1] On Pugin's life see B. Ferrey, *Recollections of A. N. Welby Pugin* (London, 1861) and M. Trappes-Lomax, *Pugin; a mediaeval Victorian* (London, 1932). Also D. Gwynn, *Lord Shrewsbury, Pugin and the Gothic Revival* (London, 1946) and much more briefly A. Gordon Clark's chapter in *Victorian Architecture*, ed. P. Ferriday (London, 1963). The London Ph.D. Thesis of 1950 by Mrs. Stanton is still in course of enlargement and revision. There seems no doubt that it will one day be the *magnum opus* on Pugin. Meanwhile Mrs. Stanton has published a smaller book of which I saw proofs only long after I had completed my book: *Pugin* (London, 1971). Unpublished so far is S. M. Coote, 'The Convent and Collegiate Architecture of A. Welby Pugin', B.A. Thesis, Reading University 1970. This also I read after completion of my book.

[2] Ferrey, *Recollections*, 103.   [3] Ibid., 95.

breakdown, and he died insane in 1852. He was slight, of dark complexion, a miraculously rapid and brilliant draughtsman, 'brusque and vehement in manner',[4] slovenly in dress, and had a passion for the sea almost as violent as his religious passion.[5] If many of his buildings look starved, this was due to the shortage of money available for Catholic church building so soon after the Catholic Emancipation Act (of 1829).

Pathetically he wrote late in his short life:[6] 'I have passed my life in thinking of fine things, studying fine things, designing fine things, and realizing very poor ones. I have never had the chance of producing a single fine ecclesiastical building, except my own church[7] . . . either for want of adequate funds or injudicious interference and control.'[8]

Pugin's *Contrasts* is a fighting book, and it is a picture book. Neither is a type of book we have met so far. Literature on Gothic architecture had been aesthetic defence or archaeological instruction. With Pugin to build Gothic becomes a responsibility of the very first order. It is Pugin the Catholic more than Pugin the architect who speaks in *Contrasts*. The book consists of an introduction and comparative pictures of certain architectural items in 1440 and 1840, culminating in a comparison of a whole town view added only for the second edition of 1841. The show starts with the contrast between the richly and intricately Gothic title-page and the frontispiece which is a 'Selection from the works of various celebrated British Architects'—all look as barren as does even the sans-serif typeface compared with the black-letter of the title pages: Wilkins's National Gallery, Nash's All Souls, Portland Place, Sir Robert Smirke's first Carlton Club, the Inwoods' Westminster Hospital are among them. Then follows a second frontispiece, the most entertaining of all the pictures. It is a page of mock advertisements 'dedicated without permission to The Trade' [Fig. 6]. Here are some samples:

New Church Open Competition. . . . A church to contain 8000 sittings. Estimates must not exceed £1500 and style plain. For the best Design Five Pounds.

---

[4] Ferrey, *Recollections*, 262.

[5] The obituary in the *Morning Chronicle,* reprinted in *The Ecclesiologist,* XIII, 1852, 354–7 is the most rewarding.

[6] *Some Remarks on the Articles . . . in the Rambler,* London, 1850, quoted here from *The Ecclesiologist,* X, 1850, 397.

[7] On this see below, p. 114.

[8] Sometimes, he continues, from 'a furious committee-man', sometimes 'a prejudiced ecclesiastic', sometimes 'a liberal benefactor'.

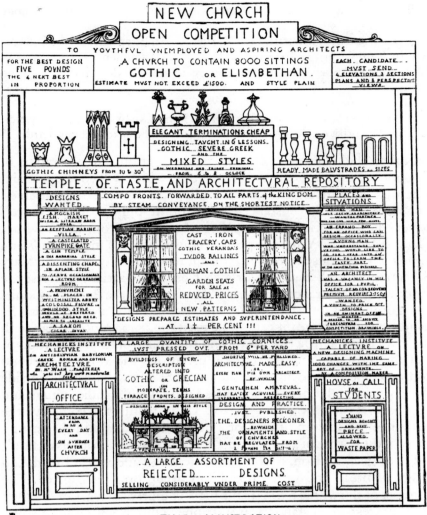

Fig. 6. A. W. N. Pugin, Mock Advertisement, from *Contrasts*, 1836.

Designing taught in 6 lessons, Gothic, Severe Greek and the Mixed Styles. Designs prepared, Estimates and Superintendance at $1\frac{1}{4}$ Per Cent!!! Mechanics' Institute. A Lecture on a new Designing Machine capable of making 1000 changes with the same Set of Ornaments.

Buildings of every Description altered into Gothic or Grecian on moderate Terms.
Designs Wanted. A Moorish Fish Market . . . An Egyptian Marine Villa . . . A Gin Temple in the Baronial style . . . A Monument to be placed in Westminster Abbey, A Colossal Figure in the Hindoo Style, A Saxon Cigar Divan.
Gothic Chimneys from 10 to 30s.
Compo fronts forwarded to all Parts of the Kingdom by Steam Conveyance.
A large Quantity of Gothic Cornices just pressed out for 6d per Yard.

Not all the jokes will be understandable at once to all readers of this book. But nearly all castigate matters which will come up again. There is no difficulty in understanding the Contrasts themselves. For town-halls for instance—to mention only a few—Dance's papery Gothick Guildhall façade in London is contrasted with a Flemish Hôtel de Ville, for private houses Soane's in Lincoln's Inn Fields with a house at Rouen, for churches the Inwoods' St Mary Somerstown with Bishop Skirlaw's Chapel at Skirlaugh. These are strictly architectural contrasts, but there are also the Public Conduits —a gorgeous Gothic structure stands for 1440, a pump with its handle chained so that it cannot be used for 1840. A policeman with top-hat chases a little boy away, and the Police Station is next door. But the most venomous are the illustrations added for the second edition. One is residences of the poor, St. Cross Hospital outside Winchester, and a new poor house with its eight radial wings and its observation centre like a gaol. Little pictures accompany the building: the solemn funeral of a deceased brother and the carting away of the corpse of a poor man, the coffin marked 'For Dissection'; a diet of beef, mutton, bacon, milk, ale, cider and wheat bread, and a diet of bread and gruel, bread and gruel, bread and gruel. The contrast of the whole towns is the most comprehensive. On the river bank nearest to us stands a proud abbey church with a high spire. This is now a ruin. A piece of waste land by the bridge approach has now become the New Jail. On the stone bridge used to be a chapel as at Wakefield; now there is an iron bridge. The tree-set river promenade (such as no English medieval town had) is now given over to high, bare warehouses. There were eleven churches; now there are five, but they are fortified by six non-conformist chapels and the Socialist Hall of Science.

Pugin's text fits the pictures. After a few introductory pages he goes straight into the blasting. In every case the die is loaded, in

every case Pugin—within his own terms—wins, and, to change the
metaphor, every one of his blows strikes home. Also the introduction
produces already most of the arguments on which a few years later
Pugin was to build a more considered system: 'That the former
Edifices appear to great advantage', that 'in comparing the Architectural Works of the present Century with those of the Middle Ages
the wonderful superiority of the latter' will be evident to everybody,
he takes for granted from the outset.[9] The reason to him is religious
at once: 'Such effects . . . can only be produced . . . by buildings, the
composition of which has emanated from men who were thoroughly
imbued with devotion for . . . the religion for whose worship they
were erected',[10] and consequently today also 'only by similar glorious feelings . . . similar glorious results can be obtained'.[11] Heresy,
schism, and avarice destroyed faith, and 'Architecture fell with the
religion to which it owed its birth'.[12] If Pugin in this context once
refers to the necessity of 'fitness to the purpose' as 'the great test of
Architectural beauty'[13] he means it in this way and does not yet go
with more intensity into the argument. A church today is just 'a
large room, well-aired, well-ventilated' with 'two or three tiers of
galleries by means of which a large auditory might be crammed into
a small space'.[14] Buckingham Palace, the National Gallery, the
British Museum are 'a national disgrace',[15] Westminster Abbey is
full of 'detestable monuments',[16] the 'brick and composition'
terraces in watering places, especially at Brighton, are 'abominable',[17]
and so on. In fact 'Were it not for the remains of the edifices produced
during the Middle Ages, the architectural monuments of this country
would be contemptible in the extreme.'[18] Then there is the indiscriminate imitation of a variety of styles.

We have Swiss cottages in a flat country; Italian villas in the coldest
situations; a Turkish kremlin for a royal residence; Greek temples in
crowded lanes; Egyptian auction rooms; and all kinds of absurdities and
incongruities; and not only are separate edifices erected in these inappropriate and unsuitable styles, but we have only to look into those nests of
monstrosities, the Regent's Park and Regent Street, where all kinds of
styles are jumbled together.[19]

9 *Contrasts,* iii–iv.   10 Ibid., 2.
11 Ibid., iii.   12 Ibid., 3.
13 Ibid., 1.   14 Ibid., 15.
15 Ibid., 31.   16 Ibid., 21.
17 Ibid., 31.   18 Ibid., 33.
19 Ibid., 30.

Mrs. Stanton has recently asked what were Pugin's sources in writing *Contrasts*.[20] She underrates Chateaubriand's *Génie du Christianisme* which had come out in 1802 and which Pugin could of course read in French. Chateaubriand, as we shall see later, had done for France what Friedrich Schlegel did for Germany. Both were Catholic and both saw art and architecture in the context of medieval religion. Otherwise Mrs. Stanton points to the recent English critics of the present, to John Stuart Mill's *Examiner* essays on 'The Spirit of the Age' of 1831, Carlyle's *Signs of the Times* of 1829, Southey's *Colloquies* of 1829–31 and Cobbett's *History of the Protestant Reformation* of 1824–7. But the chief source according to her—and she may well overestimate it—is Kenelm Digby's *The Broad Stone of Honour*[21] which was published in 1822 and again in 1823 and, enlarged to four volumes, in 1829. It was followed by *Mores Catholici* which began to come out in 1831 and finally finished with its eleventh volume in 1842. The third volume, published in 1833, contains a long discussion of medieval architecture. However, in that discussion Kenelm Digby does not seem specially attracted by English or French Gothic buildings, not even emotionally.[22] His sympathy lies evidently in Italy and includes the Baroque (p. 81 ff.) and even the Superga above Turin (p. 106). In fact most of what he prints is references to medieval sources. A great deal of learning has gone into this extensive anthology. Archaeologically Kenelm Digby knew less and evidently did not want to be informed in a scholarly way. For there is another passage not mentioned in Mrs. Stanton's paper, but known to her, as she drew my attention to it in a letter. It is in the Prologue to the 1823 edition of the *Broad Stone* (p. lii). To understand it, one must remember (see p. 45) that Digby who was born in 1796, and went up to Cambridge in 1815, had as his tutor Whewell and travelled with Whewell in Normandy and Picardy in 1823, the year of the passage in question. The passage is directed against those 'who make a separation between the heart and the head', who regard 'history, romance, poetry, painting, the beauties of nature and architecture, as fit for no other purpose but that of exercising the rational faculty . . . Speak to them of architecture, . . . they explain to you, even when surrounded by the

---

[20] *Concerning Architecture*, ed. Sir John Summerson (London, 1968), 120 ff.

[21] The curious title is a translation of Ehrenbreitstein, the name of the castle above Koblenz on the Rhine.

[22] Though he quotes Lamartine (p. 135) and also Victor Hugo's *Notre Dame* published only in 1831 (p. 80). See below, p. 196.

cathedral's gloom, all about the Norman and the pointed arch, the double centre,[23] and the intersection, the cross-ribs, the flowing tracery.' Poor Kenelm Digby, exposed to the searching scholarship of Whewell, but poor Whewell and Willis also, who were soon to find their clear world of scholarship clouded by the passions of Catholics and Anglo-Catholics and Anti-Catholics and Ruskin.

One example among the passionate rebuttals of *Contrasts* must suffice. Matthew Habershon, a minor architect working chiefly in the Midlands, used the opportunity of the publication of a book of totally different contents to reply. The book is *The Finest Existing Specimens of the Half-Timbered Houses of England* (1836), and Habershon first quite patiently proves how unfairly Pugin has chosen his contrasts and only gets up steam when he also turns from architecture to religion,[24] to the 'despotism' and 'tyranny' and the 'abominable crimes' of the Catholic Church and to 'Popish splendours . . . merely addressed to the senses'. Habershon writes as a Protestant, and we shall see that wherever in mid-nineteenth-century architectural writing that term is chosen to denominate the Church of England, there the Gothicists are likely to suffer.

Habershon had an easy task in attacking so aggressively challenging a book. In his next book Pugin was less the journalist. His task now was to build up a system of Gothic apology, and he made good use of the scholars to provide a solid substructure. This next book, his most influential statement, takes us once again to 1841. He called it *The True Principles of Pointed or Christian Architecture*, and the title is telling enough. In expounding its arguments it may be just as well to include those of his next two books *An Apology for the Revival of Christian Architecture* of 1843 and *The Present State of Ecclesiastical Architecture in England* [Pl. 33] of the same year. The *True Principles* were first developed as lectures at Oscott College in 1837–9, the *Present State* first came out in the *Dublin Review* in 1842.

The celebrated first sentence of the *True Principles* reads as follows: 'There should be no features about a building which are not necessary for convenience, construction or propriety.' That sounds like a functional credo of 1930, and has often been mistaken as such.[25]

---

[23] i.e. the two-centred arch.

[24] *The Finest Existing Specimens of the Half-Timbered Houses of England*, xxii.

[25] On the Functional Theory see E. D. De Zurko, *Origins of Functional Theory* (New York, 1957), and, more rewarding, A. Bøe: *From Gothic Revival to Functional Form* (Oslo, 1957) the latter with, among others, chapters on Pugin, Ruskin, and Morris. P. S. Manzoni, *Il Razionalismo*;

In fact it is developed straight from Pugin's reading of French architectural theory of the eighteenth century. *Convenance* is, says e.g. Blondel, that 'chaque pièce soit située selon son usage', construction needs no comment, but *propriété* is not so simple. It is really a term of architectural iconography—a building having to look proper for its purpose. Thus for instance a princely residence may have detached giant columns, a nobleman's attached, and so to the *bourgeois* who is not allowed even pilasters. But *propriété* also opens the door to an interpretation by which the Gothic style may become the only style proper to a church. This is what Pugin means. Nevertheless the sentence with which the *True Principles* start retains an emphasis on function and construction which must have come as a surprise to readers of *Contrasts*.

Nor is the sentence only an initial trumpet-blast; it remains a recurrent theme throughout the book. 'All really beautiful forms in architecture are based on the soundest principles of utility', one reads for instance on page 11. But propriety remains a counter-theme as well, and it is vigorously turned by Pugin in the direction of the equation which is in his title: Pointed or Christian. Christian first: 'I claim for Christian art a merit and perfection, which it was impossible to attain . . . in the errors of polytheism.'[26] And then at once Pointed: 'If we view pointed architecture in its true light as Christian Art, as the faith . . . is perfect, so are the principles on which it is founded.'[27] Why Gothic rather than Romanesque or Early Christian should be Christian, Pugin never argues out, and attacks were duly made by some intelligent critics, as will be shown later. On these two basic tenets a lofty structure is built. The Christian faith is true, so Christian art must be truthful: 'The severity of Christian architecture is opposed to all deception',[28] and so measured

l'architettura dell' Illuminismo alla Reazione neo-espressionista (Milan, 1966) contributes nothing new. Functional pronouncements by earlier nineteenth-century architects can be found here and there, most convincedly perhaps in the case of Charles Fowler: 'The proper excellence of architecture is that which results from its suitableness to the occasion. This leads to originality without affectation of novelty.' Loudon in the *Architectural Magazine*, IV, 1838 called Fowler 'one of the few modern architects who belong to the School of Reason and quotes as his principle 'Enough for security and not more than enough. Extravagance is waste.' See J. Taylor in *The Architectural Review*, CXXXV, 1964, 174 ff. and *Archit. History*, X, 1968, 61. Mr. Taylor also quotes David Laing, the original architect of the Custom House in the publication of this building in 1818 as writing: 'Fitness for the purposes intended controls every conception of beauty.' This may well remind one of A. J. Downing, the American landscape architect, and Horatio Greenough, the American sculptor. Downing wrote in 1842 of fitness as the 'beauty of utility', Horatio Greenough in the forties or about 1850 is so much of interest that he will be referred to in some detail in a later chapter.

[26] *An Apology*, 5.   [27] *True Principles*, 9.   [28] Ibid., 44.

by the criterion of truthfulness the Gothic Middle Ages win and the nineteenth century loses.[29] It is Contrasts once again, but fully argued this time at least on the Gothic side. The first paragraph is indeed nothing but the introduction to a treatment of Gothic architecture as functional architecture. We have seen convenience, construction, and propriety as the principles. Pugin goes on immediately to state that in pure architecture even the smallest detail 'should have a meaning or serve a purpose' so that construction for instance ought to 'vary with the material employed'. And the application follows at once: 'It is in pointed architecture alone that these great principles have been carried out.'[30]

In terms of materials Gothic architecture is conceived in stone; Greek architecture—the old theory which only Semper was to contradict—was initially conceived in wood. It is therefore 'a monstrous absurdity to hold Greek architecture up as an example.'[31] Altogether pointed architecture never conceals construction, 'but beautifies it', and as 'all ornament should consist of enrichment of the essential construction', Gothic again is right.[32] Buttresses and flying buttresses are used as examples of structure demonstrated, and Wren's flying buttresses at St Paul's hidden behind a sham upper-floor wall are held up to scorn.[33] Pinnacles also 'fulfil a useful end'—that of pressing down vertically on the buttresses,[34] and equally sound is the rib-vault, its cells filled by lighter, smaller stones—in contrast to Wren's dome whose inner as well as outer shape is structurally useless, because the brick core in between which no one sees does the carrying.[35]

Concerning propriety Pugin has less to say: 'The external and internal appearance of an edifice should be . . . in accordance with the purpose for which it is destined', and that in terms of churches means that 'they should be as good, as spacious, as rich and beautiful, as the means and numbers of those who are erecting them will permit' and certainly 'more vast and beautiful than the buildings in which they dwell'. This, needless to say, Pugin contrasts with the situation today, when 'a room full of seats at the least possible cost is the . . . idea of a church.'[36]

---

[29] It is amusing to see that as late as about 1858 young Thomas Garner, later of Bodley & Garner, said to young Thomas Graham Jackson of a hansom-cab: 'It is so truthful, so—so—so medieval.' (*Recollections of Sir Thomas Graham Jackson*, ed. B. H. Jackson, O.U.P., 1950.)

[30] *True Principles*, 1.

[31] Ibid., 3.   [32] Ibid., 3, 1.   [33] Ibid., 3, 5.

[34] Ibid., 10.   [35] Ibid., 6, 8.   [36] Ibid., 42–3.

With regard to convenience Gothic architecture is as exemplary. Here Pugin chooses secular architecture; and insists that, just as in ecclesiastic building, Gothic is as suitable for today as for its own centuries: 'It will not be difficult to show that the wants and purposes of Civic Buildings now are almost identical with those of our English forefathers. In the first place, climate, which necessarily regulates the pitch of roofs, warmth and internal arrangement, remains . . . precisely the same, [and] secondly we are governed by nearly the same laws and same system of political economy.'[37] That surely is open to argument, but Pugin then chooses as his example a building of which it is at least approximately true, a building incidentally designed by himself, the Bishop's House at Birmingham;[38] for *The Present State* was first published anonymously in *The Dublin Review*, and Pugin is not above praising 'Mr. Pugin's' designs. About the Bishop's House he says: 'It will be seen that convenience has dictated the design and that the elevation has been left in that natural irregularity produced by the internal arrangements.' In contrast to this the usual thing today, Pugin had written in the *True Principles*, is that 'the plans of buildings are designed to suit the elevation, instead of the elevation being made subservient to the plan'.[39]

Having put forward the case for Gothic today—even by the way on the score of cheapness[40]—the question now arises how it should be made use of. There Pugin is revolutionary. The following sentences establish a new principle, even if in practice it had already been followed by Essex, and occasionally by Rickman and others. 'We can never successfully deviate one tittle from the spirit and principles of pointed architecture. We must rest content, to follow, not to lead,'[41] and 'The only hope of reviving the perfect style is by strictly adhering to ancient authorities.'[42] Mr. Pugin again serves as the

---

[37] *True Principles*, 37.

[38] *Present State*, 102.

[39] *True Principles*, 63. But only one page before Pugin warns against making a building 'inconvenient for the sake of obtaining irregularity', an irregularity merely aimed at for the sake of picturesqueness. The result must be as ridiculous as an 'artificial waterfall or a made-up rock'.

[40] 'It is impossible to build substantially in any style so cheap as the pointed or Christian.' *Present State*, 103.

[41] *True Principles*, 9.

[42] *Present State*, 83. This is almost exactly what Winckelmann had said in 1754 in his *Gedanken über die Nachahmung der griechischen Werke*. The famous and familiar passage: 'There is but one way for the moderns to become great and perhaps unequalled; I mean by imitating the Ancients' (quoted from Fuseli's translation: *Reflexions on the Imitation of the Painting and Sculpture of the Greeks*, London, 1765)—a *non sequitur* if ever there was one.

model: 'Mr. Pugin, we believe, never claimed the least merit on the score of originality; nor does he profess to invent new combinations, but simply to revive, as far as circumstances and means will admit, the glorious . . . work of the Middle Ages.'[43]

A further question is what style of Gothic should be followed; for there is Early English, there is Decorated, and there is Perpendicular. Perpendicular had, as we have seen, been the favourite until now, although, as we have seen, Whittington, Gally Knight, Caumont, and others had preferred the thirteenth to the later centuries. Friedrich Schlegel incidentally was among the believers in the thirteenth century. He considered Cologne Cathedral the climax of Gothic architecture and Strasbourg, only one or two generations later, 'already arbitrary', with 'mere curlicues' instead of naturalistic foliage.[44] In any case, the thirteenth century had very rarely been used as the serious pattern of a neo-Gothic church. The best example is Theale in Berkshire of 1819, by Edward Garbett.

Pugin himself had, when he was young, sacrificed at the altar of Perpendicular. The external and internal details of the Houses of Parliament are the supreme proof. St Mary, Derby, of 1838–9 was still Perpendicular. But about 1840 Pugin changed to the style of the late thirteenth and early fourteenth centuries, the style of Westminster Abbey and the following decades, that is from the simplest geometrical tracery to the more complex, but not yet flowing. In the *True Principles* (p. 7) he states that as soon as the four-centred arch replaced the two-centred 'the spirit of Christian architecture was on the wane'. The stone pendants of Henry VII's Chapel are the 'commencement of bad taste'. The new allegiance appeared for the first time in Pugin's actual buildings at St. Oswald, Old Swan, a suburb of Liverpool, in 1840–2 [Pl. 34] and continued for instance at the cathedrals of Southwark (1841 ff.), Nottingham (1842 ff.) and Newcastle (1844 ff.).[45] With this Pugin broke new ground, and the Second or Middle Pointed, as it came to be called, became the unquestioned favourite of the ensuing decades. The reason is easy to see. Perpendicular was a style of close and relatively shallow surface decoration and in this is Early Victorian. The Second Pointed has stronger relief and larger, bolder motifs, which suited

---

[43] *Present State*, 113.

[44] *Krit. Ausg.*, IV, 1959, 192.

[45] Burges tells that Pugin's conversion from French Flamboyant to Middle Pointed was affected by Dr. Rock (*Art applied to Industry*, 1865; see below, p. 232).

the High Victorian taste. The most successful perhaps of Pugin's
churches are Cheadle of 1841–6 [Pl. 35], because the Earl of Shrewsbury of nearby Alton Towers made more money available than
usual for Catholic churches of these early years after the Emancipation, and St Augustine, Ramsgate, of 1846–51 [Pls. 36, 37], because
Pugin built it for himself close to his own house. A church like
Ramsgate has a solidity that makes the Commissioners' churches
look all papery,[46] and moreover its elements and details are so
expertly handled that here for the first time the neo-Gothic might be
mistaken for genuine Gothic—if not the whole building, at least
part of the building.

Much of Pugin's three later books are, like *Contrasts*, more than
an attack on architecture of his own day. Only the recent restoration
of the Temple church[47] and of Magdalen College Chapel[48] and of
course the Houses of Parliament escape his censures. The classical
quads of Oxford colleges—Queen's, Worcester and Peckwater at
Christ Church—'resemble sick hospitals or barracks . . . rather than
abodes of piety and learning'[49] and, as for an architect who would
build classically at Oxford or Cambridge now, Pugin's verdict is:
'A man who paganizes in the Universities deserves no quarter'.[50]
The new Royal Exchange by Tite, classical, turning Wrenian, as
we have seen, is 'another stale dish of ill-adapted classicisms—
heavy, dull and uninteresting'.[51] The new cemeteries are
no more than 'a marketable matter, a joint-stock concern,
an outlay of unemployed capital'.[52] And it is the same
everywhere:

Every good old inn is turned into an ugly hotel with a stuccoed portico
and a vulgar coffee room . . . with imitation scagliola columns, composition
glass frames . . . and twenty per cent added to the bill . . . Our good old St
Martin's, St John's, St Peter's and St Mary's streets, are becoming Belle-
Vue Places, Adelaide Rows, Apollo Terraces, Regent Squares, and Royal
Circuses . . . Government preaching houses, called churches, start up at
the cost of a few hundred each, by the side of Zion Chapels, Bethel

---

[46] Mrs. Stanton in her *The Gothic Revival and American Church Architecture* (Baltimore, 1968),
245 prints the atrocious pun of Robert Cary Long (*The Literary World,* 10 Feb. 1849) about 'Go-
thin alternating with Go-thick'. The terms fit the contrast of the Commissioners' and Pugin's
churches.

[47] By S. Smirke and J. Savage, 1840–2; *Present State,* 5. On this restoration see now J. M. Crook
in *Architectural History,* VIII, 1965, 39 ff.

[48] By Cottingham; Ferrey's *Recollections,* 9.

[49] *An Apology,* 32.

[50] Ibid., 3.

[51] Ibid., 18.

[52] *Present State,* 20.

Meetings, New Connexions, and Socialist Halls . . . Every linen-draper's
shop apes to be something after the palace of the Caesars, the mock stone
columns are fixed over a front of plate glass to exhibit the astounding
bargains.[53]

Only in the case of the railways has Pugin something positive
to contribute, and there it is Gothic again. Pugin had no objection
to the railways as such. In fact he calls 'the steam engine . . . a most
valuable power' and writes that 'the Christian architect should gladly
avail himself' of any mechanical improvements which our age has
produced and indeed any 'modern invention which conduces to
comfort, cleanliness, or durability'.[54] What is wrong with the railways is that the stations of the Great Western—we may think of the
original Temple Meads at Bristol still happily extant—'are . . . caricatures of pointed design, mock castellated work, huge tracery,
shields without bearings, ugly mouldings, no-meaning projections
. . . to make up a design at once costly, and offensive, and full of
pretension'. Instead the railways ought to have 'been naturally
treated'. They would then have 'afforded a fine scope for grand
massive architecture. Little more was required than buttresses,
weathering, and segmental arches, resistance to lateral and perpendicular pressure'. And he continues: 'I do not hesitate to say,
that, by merely following out the work that was required to its
natural conclusion, building exactly what was wanted in the
simplest. . . manner', something grand and durable could have been
produced.[55]

And yet, even in this passage, he speaks in fact of 'grand and
durable masses', of 'in the simplest and most substantial manner',
and hence he could not see that the new railway jobs called for a
new technique and new materials, that is for glass and iron. Pugin
hated the Crystal Palace. He called it in letters[56] the 'glass monster',
the 'crystal humbug', and 'as friendly as Salisbury plain'.[57] Pugin
himself was responsible for the Medieval Court in the Crystal Palace
which with its exhibits by Pugin and others was universally praised.
On design other than in the Gothic style by himself and his fellow-

[53] *True Principles,* 56.

[54] *An Apology,* 38–9.

[55] Ibid., 10–11.

[56] So Mrs. Stanton tells me. The letters are to John Hardman.

[57] This goes with Carlyle's 'this big Glass Soapbubble' *The Letters of Thomas Carlyle to his
Brother Alexander* ed. E. W. Marrs Jr. (Harvard University Press, 1968), 684. For abuse by
others see pp. 154, 230, 245, for praise pp. 127, 133, 160, 209, 228, 231.

Gothicists he is scathing everywhere: There is 'Brummagem Gothic',[58] named after 'that most detestable of all detestable places', Birmingham,[59] and there is 'Sheffield eternal', 'the madness of modern Sheffield castellated grates',[60] and Pugin assails them for good reasons well presented—the reasons indeed which eight and ten years later Henry Cole, Owen Jones, Matthew Digby Wyatt, and a few others were to take up.[61] At the bottom is 'the false notion of disguising instead of beautifying articles of utility . . . instead of seeking the most convenient form and then decorating it'. In wallpapers e.g. there is the 'absurdity of repeating a perspective over a large surface', in carpets the absurdity of 'reversed groining to walk upon, or highly relieved foliage', and in furniture 'all the ordinary articles . . . which require to be simple and convenient, are made . . . very uneasy'[62] so that e.g. anybody can consider himself fortunate 'who remains any length of time in a modern Gothic room and escapes without being wounded by some of its minutiae'.[63] On cast iron Pugin is especially illuminating: 'When viewed with reference to mechanical purposes it must be considered as a most valuable invention, but it can but rarely be applied to ornamental purposes.' The reason is that cast iron being so strong would require less thickness, and hence 'to be consistent the mullions of cast-iron tracery must be so reduced as to look painfully thin'.[64] So here again Gothic has precedence over any other consideration. Also—by its manufacturing properties—it is 'a source of continual repetition, subversive of the variety and inspiration exhibited in pointed design'. And finally and more sweepingly: 'Cast iron is a deception; it is

[58] *True Principles*, 24.

[59] Ferrey, *Recollections*, 86. Of Birmingham Benjamin Haydon had written only one year before (25 Nov., 1840): 'If ever any town needed a school of design . . . it is Birmingham.' See B. *Haydon's Diaries*, ed. W. B. Pope (Harvard University Press, 1963), 19.

[60] *True Principles*, 32, 23.

[61] See below, p. 157 ff., and my *Sir Matthew Digby Wyatt* (Cambridge, 1949) and *High Victorian Design* (London, 1951), both revised and reprinted in *Studies in Art, Architecture and Design*, vol. II (London, 1968).

[62] *True Principles*, 23, 26, 40.

[63] Ibid., 35.

[64] Cast iron tracery had of course been used quite freely in the early nineteenth century, especially in Shropshire, i.e. near the Coalbrookdale works, but also by Rickman in the two early churches referred to on p. 28. On this whole subject see e.g. John Gloag, *A History of Cast Iron in Architecture* (London, 1948) and a brief summary in my *Pioneers of Modern Design*. It may be worth a mention that Charles Garnier, the architect of the gorgeous neo-Baroque Paris Opera, used exactly the same argument against the use of iron in architecture as Pugin: Iron is incapable 'à donner des masses . . . suffisantes pour les yeux.' *Le Musée des Sciences*, No. 41, 11 Feb. 1857. Quoted from M. Steinhauser, *Der Architektur der Pariser Oper*, Munich 1969, 164. For buildings like hangars, stations, and markets he accepted iron, and he used it himself for the dome of the Opera though of course hidden (ibid., 31).

seldom . . . left as iron' but made to resemble stone, wood, or marble.[65]

After the consequences of the Gothic principles and forms on industrial design, those on education must now be examined and those on new Catholic architecture. Of education Pugin speaks in the *Apology*:

How is it possible for any good results to be achieved with the present principles of architectural education? Can we ever hope to see a Christian architect come forth from the Royal Academy itself, where deadly errors are instilled into the mind of the student . . . Pagan lectures, pagan designs, pagan casts and models, pagan medals, and, as a reward for proficiency in these matters, a pagan journey.[66]

More generally speaking Pugin of course objects to the newly founded University College in London which was to be non-denominational and which he likens to the 'factories of learning' on the Continent,[67] but his hottest hatred is against the new Mechanics' Institutes, those beneficial bodies established in 1823 by Dr. Birkbeck, first in Glasgow, then immediately in London.[68] They appear on the page of mock advertisements in *Contrasts*, and this is what Pugin has to say about them in the *True Principles*: 'Mechanics' institutes are a mere device of the day to poison the minds of the operatives with infidel and radical doctrines' (p. 33).

Only when one remembers this sentence can the whole impact be measured of a remark Pugin made to Newman, when they met in Rome in 1847. He implied, writes Newman to Lisle Phillipps in 1848 'that he would as soon build a mechanics' institute as an Oratory'.[69]

There is more from this letter that need be quoted but some preliminaries are necessary first in order fully to understand Pugin's remark. On Newman only a reminder is required. The *Tracts for the Times* had begun to be published in Oxford in 1833. Tract XC came

---

[65] *True Principles*, 29–30; also *An Apology*, 40–1, where Pugin says 'Had the old builders possessed our means of obtaining and working iron they would have availed themselves of it to a great extent.'

[66] p. 18. It will be remembered that C. R. Cockerell was the professor.

[67] *True Principles*, 54. We have seen that in the year of the *True Principles* the paganizing Donaldson was elected as the first Professor of Architecture.

[68] E. Delisle Burns, *A Short History of Birkbeck College* (London, 1924). The concept caught on immediately, and Mechanics' Institutes were started in 1824 at Aberdeen, Alnwick, Dundee, Lancaster, Leeds, and Newcastle, in 1825 at Ashton, Birmingham, Bolton, Davenport, Halifax, Lewes, Manchester, and Plymouth. In 1850 there were nearly 700. See for a recent brief account and a bibliography J. T. Lea in *Research in Librarianship*, II, Oct. 1968.

[69] *The Letters and Diaries of John Henry Newman*, ed. C. S. Dessain, XII (1962), 221.

out in 1841, W. G. Ward's *Ideal of a Christian Church* in 1845. Newman entered the Catholic church in the same year. He joined the Oratorians and was particularly anxious to create oratories in England. The hierarchy was re-established in 1851. Newman was finally made a cardinal in 1879. The Oratorians, it must be remembered, were founded by St Philip Neri in 1558, i.e. are a post-medieval order.

Pugin fought for medieval and English Catholicism, i.e. for Gothic buildings and for specific liturgical demands. His image of a Catholic church included the ritual, the customs, and the equipment of English medieval catholicism: plain chant and no orchestral flourishes, long choirs instead of the shallow ones of the Commissioners' churches, and screens and roods, English medieval vestments, no pews, and also strict orientation.[70] However, Bishop Walsh at the request of the 'Propaganda Fide' suspended all Gothic vestments, and at the opening of Pugin's St Mary at Derby in 1839 [Pl. 38] a crisis ensued. Lord Shrewsbury had presented a set of vestments of cloth of gold. Bishop Walsh was ready to wear them, but Pugin who was present with Lord Shrewsbury and Ambrose Lisle Phillipps was so shocked that instead of Gregorian chant and a surpliced choir there were to be 'lady sopranos and fiddlers' that he insisted on the vestments not being worn. So the Bishop performed the ceremony in 'a dingy set of French pattern', and Pugin, Shrewsbury, and Phillipps left in protest before the service began.[71]

So the meetings in Rome between Newman and Pugin were between a man whose Catholic fervour visualized gorgeous Italian churches and services and a man to whom Catholicism meant the English Middle Ages and could never mean anything else. The most enlightening letter is the one from which the foregoing quotation came:

... Mr. Pugin is a man of genius; I have the greatest admiration of his talents, and willingly acknowledge that Catholics owe him a great debt for what he has done in the revival of Gothic architecture among us. His zeal, his minute diligence, his resources, his invention, his imagination, his sagacity in research, are all of the highest order. It is impossible that any one, not scientifically qualified to judge of his merits, can feel a profounder reverence than I do, for the gift with which it has pleased the Author of all Truth and Beauty to endow him. But he has the great fault of a man of genius, as well as the merit. He is intolerant, and, if I might use a stronger word, a bigot. He sees nothing good in any school of Christian art except

[70] *Present State*, 24 ff., 18.   [71] Gwynn, op. cit., 72.

that of which he is himself so great an ornament. The canons of Gothic architecture are to him points of faith, and everyone is a heretic who would venture to question them.

Now something might be said in defence of this extreme view of the subject, had Gothic Architecture prevailed over the *whole* face of the Church, so that never had a rite been introduced, never a doctrine promulgated, but it came out in Gothic shape, and had been perpetuated under Gothic emblems. But this is notoriously not so . . . Nevertheless Mr. Pugin, with only half Christendom on his side, to say nothing of the Greek and Oriental bodies, rules that the other half is, what he calls reproachfully. *pagan.* But more than this, this pagan half happens to include in it the see of St Peter, which nevertheless does not escape that appellation. . . .

Nor is this even all—Something more might be said for his view of the subject, had there been an *uninterrupted tradition* of Gothic architecture from the time it was introduced till the present day; but this even is not the case. Mr. Pugin is notoriously engaged in a revival—he is disentombing what has been hidden for centuries amid corruptions; and, as, first one thing, then another is brought to light, he, like a true lover of the art, modifies his first views, yet he speaks as confidently and dogmatically about what is right and what is wrong, as if he had gained the truth from the purest and stillest founts of continuous tradition. But there is even more than this. . . . In order that any style of Architecture should exactly suit the living ritual of the 19th century, it should be the living architecture of the 19th century —it should never have died—else, while the ritual has changed, the architecture has not kept pace with it. This defect is actually found in the case of Gothic. Gothic is now like an old dress, which fitted a man well twenty years back but must be altered to fit him now. It was once the perfect expression of the Church's ritual in those places in which it was in use; it is not the perfect expression now. *It must be altered in detail* to become that expression. That is, it must be treated with a freedom which Mr. Pugin will not allow. I wish to wear it, but I wish to alter it, or rather I wish *him* to alter it; not that we do not feel the greatest admiration of the Gothic style, but that we will not allow details which were proper in England in the middle ages, to be points of faith now. Now for Oratorians, the birth of the 16th century, to assume the architecture simply and unconditionally of the 13th, would be as absurd as their putting on them the cowl of the Dominicans or adopting the tonsure of the Carthusians. We do not want a cloister or a chapter room but an Oratory . . .

Our Padre Ceremoniere tells me that the rigid observance of Gothic details is inconsistent with the Rubrics—that he must break the Rubrics if he would not break with Mr. Pugin; which is he to give up, Mr. Pugin or the Rubrics?[72]

[72] *Letters,* XII, 220–3.

So much for Newman. Pugin in the end saw that he was defeated and that Catholic architecture was becoming Romish architecture. His Gothic zeal was intemperable, and so at the end of his life he began to write 'An Apology for the Separated Church of England', an unfinished manuscript from which Ferrey quotes.[73] At the end of the Middle Ages, Pugin wrote, Leo X was the head of the neo-Pagan tendencies and English Catholic prelates were responsible for untold destruction. After that 'On the whole, our separation as a nation from the Communion of the so-called Catholic countries, in the sixteenth, seventeenth and eighteenth centuries, has been a great blessing. We have, by the mercy of God, preserved our liberties, and ancient legal constitution, and the great fundamental Christian doctrines.'

It is all humanly very sad, but also just a little ridiculous: Pugin, the Catholic, speaking of so-called Catholic countries which have abandoned the fundamental Christian doctrines, and the Cambridge Camden Society, a High Anglican society, to which we must presently turn, calling themselves Catholic, exclaiming about Pugin 'Utinam noster esses',[74] and calling him after his death 'the most eminent and original architectural genius of his time',[75] and Pugin saying of them that they 'are . . . doing immense service in the good cause'.[76]

However, before we can move on to the Cambridge Camden Society one postscript has to be inserted. In spite of all the opposition against Pugin, he never lacked recognition. Thomas Mozley reviewed *Contrasts* in *The British Critic* in April 1839, the journal which was then edited by Newman, and wrote[77] that Pugin was 'the first Gothic architect of the age', and *The Builder* (I, 69) in 1843 wrote 'Acknowledged or unacknowledged, Pugin is Pope in Gothic'. Also he appears among the great architects on the Albert Memorial. On the Continent appreciation began early too. The key document is *Die christlich-germanische Baunkunst* by August Reichensperger which was published in Trier in 1845.

Reichensperger was an interesting man.[78] He was born in 1808 and died in 1895. He lived in the Rhineland, developed his views and

73 *Recollections*, 438.
74 J. M. Neale and B. Webb, *William Durandus, The Symbolism of Churches*, (Leeds, 1843), XIX.
75 *The Ecclesiologist*, XIII, 1852, 352–3.
76 *Present State*, 56.
77 So Mrs Stanton tells me.
78 Leo von Pastor: *August Reichensperger*, 2 vols (Freiburg i. B, 1899).

political passions under the influence of Görres, founded the *Kölner Domblatt* in 1847, and was a member of the National Assembly of 1848, of the Prussian Parliament in 1850–63 and of the *Reichstag* in 1867–84, belonging to the *Zentrum*, i.e. the Catholic party. His dependence on Pugin is evident, even if it were not for the fact that he wrote a small book on him.[79] The *Christlich-Germanische* architecture is, needless to say, Gothic. We must cast out, he writes, any *Afterklassizismus*[80] and return to Gothic, our 'traditional, glorious, genuinely national art'.[81] And in praise of Gothic there are at once Pugin's arguments: there is 'no member which is not conditioned by the basic construction and fulfills a distinct purpose'. 'Without such rationality no beauty is conceivable'.[82] And then Gothic rationality is demonstrated in Pugin's terms: set-offs of buttresses, flying buttresses, pinnacles, rib-vaults with thin cells all serve a purpose.[83] This attitude incidentally did not prevent Reichensperger from praising Gothic buildings by comparing them with 'sacred groves'.[84] Nor is Pugin's *J'accuse* of building today left aside. The Grecian is 'a travesty of the Parthenon and the Propylaea',[85] the Cinquecento of the Uffizi, is 'chilly and boring'. Houses are designed by starting with a symmetrical facade, instead of from interior to exterior. Shops on the ground floor of glass and iron are 'against all static and aesthetic feeling.' The fault lies in the abandon of the apprenticeship system by a system leading to 'learned examination'[86] and in the abandon of craftsmanship by the use of machines: 'Amid the clanking and hissing of the machine art stands as a servant maid'. But 'utility is not the only need of our nature';[87] we need a deeper truth than that of usefulness. There can be no excuse for dishonesty to materials. Reichensperger anticipates Ruskin in writing that wood is painted to imitate bronze, iron to imitate stone, stone to imitate both—everywhere 'fake magnificence, anarchy and Babylonian confusion'.[88] As for the machine and architecture, Reichensperger was remarkably far-sighted. Parts of houses can be cast in quantity and assembled.[89]

The second half of the book takes up a number of notable

---

[79] *Augustus Welby Pugin, der Neubegründer der christlichen Kunst in England* (Freiburg i. B., 1877).
[80] Ibid., 7.   [81] Ibid., 5, 9.   [82] Ibid., 14–15.
[83] Ibid., 15.   [84] Ibid., 20.
[85] But Palladio and Schinkel are explicitly absolved, ibid., 24, 26.
[86] Ibid., 23–34.   [87] Ibid., 43, 40.   [88] Ibid., 44.
[89] His witness for this statement is J. B. Say's *Traité de'Economie politique*, published in 1803, translated into German in 1830 and into English in 1821. In 1841 the sixth French edition came out.

points. Antiquarian societies ought to be concerned as much with preservation as with history.[90] Studying is not enough, inventorizing is as important.[91] Most restoration work done today is vandalism. 'The best restoration is the one which is least noticeable'.[92] Work should not be commissioned under the rule of acceptance of the lowest tender.[93] A museum of Christian art ought to be created.[94]

One year after Reichensperger had brought out the *Christlich-Germanische Baukunst* he wrote from England that Pugin's buildings 'need not be afraid of any comparison with the creations of the most flourishing period of the Catholic style'.[95] So in this matter of quality the Catholic German and the Anglican high priests of Ecclesiology were in agreement.

[90] J. B. Say's *Traité de' Economie politique*, 72.
[91] Ibid., 73, also 102 where reference is made to the French Comité des arts et monuments.
[92] Ibid., 104.   [93] Ibid., 83.   [94] Ibid., 104.
[95] L. von Pastor: op. cit., I, 207.

CHAPTER XIV

The Cambridge Camden Society and the Ecclesiologists

THE programme of the Cambridge Camden Society was threefold: to re-introduce much of Catholic ritual into the Anglican church, to see to it that church buildings were decently kept and suitably restored, and to watch over the style in which new churches were to be built.

The society was founded by two Cambridge undergraduates in 1839. In the same year at Oxford the Oxford Society for Promoting the Study of Gothic Architecture was founded, soon to become the Oxford Architectural and Historical Society. It was in its beginnings closely connected with the Tractarian Movement;[1] among early members were James Mozley who became Regius Professor of Divinity,[2] John Rouse Bloxam of Magdalen College, friend of Newman and brother of Matthew Bloxam who had written *The Principles of Gothic Architecture* which between 1829 and 1859 went to ten editions, and E. A. Freeman whom we already know. Freeman was made secretary after the original secretary Thomas Combe, manager of the Clarendon Press, a friend of the Pre-Raphaelites, and the donor of the Anglo-Catholic church of St Barnabas. A member also was J. H. Parker, author of the famous *Glossary of Terms used in Grecian, Roman, Italian and Gothic Architecture* which first came out in 1836 and reached its tenth edition in 1900.

The founders of the Cambridge Camden Society were John Mason Neale (1818–66) who had gone to Trinity in 1836 and Benjamin Webb (1819–85) who had joined Trinity two years later.[3] In the year

[1] See S. L. Ollard, 'The Oxford Architectural and Historical Society and the Oxford Movement', *Oxoniensia*, V, 1940. No special monograph on the society has yet been compiled. It could be a worthwhile task.

[2] His brother Thomas married Newman's sister. Thomas, whose review of Pugin's *Contrasts* has just been referred to, followed Newman as editor of *The British Critic*, James was for a while editor of the *Christian Remembrancer*.

[3] The standard book on the Cambridge Camden Society is James F. White, *The Cambridge Movement* (CUP, 1962). I have made much use of this. See also A. G. Lough, *The Influence of John Mason Neale* (SPCK, 1962).

of the foundation they had thirty-eight members, in 1843 700, among them the Archbishops of Canterbury and Armagh, sixteen bishops, seven deans and chancellors of dioceses, twenty-one arch-deacons and rural deans, thirty-one peers and MPs. Among the first Honorary Members were Rickman and Salvin,[4] among the first Vice-Presidents were both Whewell and Willis, but Willis resigned in 1841 and published with some others a Remonstrance calling it 'in the highest degree improper' to 'convert the Society into an engine of polemical theology, instead of an instrument for promoting the study and practice of Ecclesiastical Architecture'.

But this is precisely what the society wanted to do and what has made it noteworthy, influential, and in the end fully successful. The Remonstrance came out in the first volume of *The Ecclesiologist*,[5] and a study of this and the following volumes leaves no doubt of the varied but always polemical intentions of Neale, Webb, and the others. Separate publications were brought out even before *The Ecclesiologist: A Few Words to Church Wardens* in 1839, *A Few Words to Church Builders* in 1841—Pugin praised this in *The Present State* in 1843[6]—*A Few Hints on the Practical Study of Ecclesiastical Antiquities* also in 1841.[7] and the remarkable *Church Schemes, or Blank Forms for the Description of a Church*.[8] These were forms to be filled in by the visitor to a church so as to record all its elements and motifs. The first edition, in 1839, listed fifty-eight items, the fourth, also still of 1839, 236. In 1841 the Society also embarked on the restoration of the church of the Holy Sepulchre at Cambridge. The architect was Salvin.

So far all seems archaeology. But ecclesiology means something different. It means 'liturgical science',[9] that is the science of how a church ought to be built or remodelled or re-equipped to make it fit the rubrics and the ritual of the Anglican church. In trying to define what these were the Ecclesiologists found that they were somewhat at variance with their passion for Gothic architecture, a passion they shared with Pugin and his predecessors and with

---

[4] But also Basevi and Cockerell—which should be noted.

[5] No. 2, Dec. 1841, pp. 25 and 29. In return *The Ecclesiologist* four years later, while granting Willis clearness, 'mechanical acumen almost unrivalled' and 'considerable powers of investigation and detection' denied that he had any 'comprehension of the spirit of the men of old' (IV, 1845, 220; VI, 1846, 217, 226).

[6] P. 61.

[7] This grew, until in 1847 it became the *Handbook of English Ecclesiology* with an excellent appendix of over 100 pages characterizing the church architecture of England county by county.

[8] White, op. cit., 54.   [9] *Ecclesiologist*, VII, 1847, 86.

Whewell and Willis. For to deal successfully with rubrics and ritual they had to turn not to the Catholic past but to the age of Andrewes, Bancroft, and Laud.[10] Yet Ecclesiologists called themselves Catholic and were so enamoured by this word that they introduced it wherever they could. Neale even in one place speaks of a 'grand Catholic oakwood',[11] and the use of Catholic in the form Anglo-Catholic has survived, although already in a pamphlet in 1844 Montalembert had called it 'unwarrantable' and 'the usurpation of a sacred name' and 'a wilful error' tantamount to 'a mortal sin'.[12] To insist on the term Catholic was a risky thing for Anglicans in those years of the Tracts and of Newman's conversion. To rhyme, however badly, as Neale did in *Hierologus, or the Church Tourists,* in 1843

> Oh the good old times of England! Ere, in her evil day,
> from their Holy Faith and their ancient rites the people fell away.[13]

meant asking for trouble, and Neale suffered bitterly for his Anglo-Catholic faith. As Warden of Sackville College, East Grinstead, he was inhibited by the Bishop of Chichester in 1849 and remained inhibited for sixteen years. The fact that the Catholic Pugin paid his tribute to the 'high Catholic view' of the Cambridge Camden Society, and that they paid tribute to him, did not make their position easier. However, Mrs. Stanton[14] has drawn attention to a more critical review of Pugin's works in *The Ecclesiologist* in 1846.[15] But by then the Society had been attacked so mercilessly that it had deemed it wise to separate (temporarily) *The Ecclesiologist* from the society, and in 1846 they changed their name to the Ecclesiological Society and their home to London.[16] These were indeed wise moves, considering the growing hatred of the Protestant against the Anglo-Catholic camp—what *The Ecclesiologist* still in 1850 called 'puritanical hatred against ceremonial worship.'[17]

[10] See especially *Hierurgia Anglicana* (London, 1848), 9.

[11] White, op. cit., 31.

[12] *A letter addressed to a Rev. Member of the Camden Society* [i.e. Mason Neale] *on the architectural, artistical, and archaeological movement of the Puseyites* (Liverpool, 1844), reprinted in *Oeuvres de M. le Comte de Montalembert*, VI, 1861, 366 ff. Also see Weale's *Quarterly Papers*, III, 1845, 9–10 which —very characteristically, as we shall see—took this up. Montalembert shared the Ecclesiologists' and Pugin's exclusive faith in Gothic architecture. See a letter to Pugin quoted in E. S. Purcell, *The Life and Letters of Ambrose Phillipps de Lisle* (London, 1900), II, 231 ff.

[13] *Hierologus*, 101.

[14] *The Gothic Revival and American Church Architecture* (Baltimore, 1968), 26.

[15] *E.*, v, 10–16.

[16] *E.*, IV, 1845, 216; V, 1846, V; also the Presidential Address of 1850 in which Archdeacon Thorp pronounces himself glad that the Society now carries on 'without making any noise' (*E.*, XI, 51).

[17] *E.*, XI, 352.

A more harmless side of ecclesiology, though this also was passionately objected to, was the investigation and the attempted restitution of the symbolism of the church building. As the *Rationale Divinorum Officiorum* of Durandus, a late-thirteenth-century book, was the standard book of the Middle Ages on such topics, Neale and Webb in 1843 published a translation of book one with a long introduction. The book had been known to Pugin already who mentions it in his *True Principles*.[18] It lists such examples as the allusion to the Trinity in a church having a nave and two aisles, or nave, chancel and apse, or a triplet window, and the allusion to the Atonement in cruciformity and the deviation of chancel to nave.[19] Symbolism, *The Ecclesiologist* summed up already in 1842, is a law of church building which 'ought not rashly to be broken, and cannot without great risk of a gross architectural impropriety'.[20]

Such remarks are a transition from the ritual to the architectural field. The architectural demands to achieve the 'sacramentality'[21] the Ecclesiologists fretted to re-introduce are long chancels for surpliced choirs,[22] no galleries, no organs, no pews,[23] but screens, because a 'distinction must exist between the Clergy and their flocks',[24] a proper altar, preferably of stone,[25] and a priest's doorway, simply because 'it is invariably found in ancient churches and ought therefore to be introduced in every modern design'.[26]

The 'therefore' is eminently characteristic. For *The Ecclesiologist*, just like Pugin, believed that everything in a church ought to be 'after some approved ancient model'[27] and that 'details . . . should be scrupulously correct';[28] for they say in another place that it is 'no sign of weakness to be content to copy acknowledged perfection'.[29] This is exactly Pugin. So is the passionate emphasis on 'truth' in

---

[18] J. Mason Neale and B. Webb, *William Durandus, The Symbolism of Churches* (Leeds, 1843). A French translation came out in 1846 (see *E.*, VI, 1846, 120). This is the parallel to the French translation of the *True Principles* (Bruges, 1850) noticed in *The Ecclesiologist*, XII, 1851.

[19] Neale and Webb, *Durandus*, lxxix.

[20] *E.*, II, 37. Poole (see p. 101) incidentally had already reached the same conclusion in 1841 and independently of the Cambridge Camden Society. He lectured on it at Leeds See *E.*, I, 1842, 125 and X, 1851, 123.

[21] For the word see e.g. *Durandus*, xxvi.

[22] *E.*, I, 45. In this W. F. Hook at St Peter's in Leeds (1837–41) had preceded the Ecclesiologists. They called the church 'perhaps the first really great undertaking of the present age' (*E.*, VII, 1847, 46). On St Peter see White, op. cit., 95–6, before White, G. W. O. Addleshaw and F. Etchell, *The Architectural Setting of Anglican Worship* (London, 1948), and after White, P. Stanton, *The Gothic Revival and American Church Architecture*.

[23] *E.*, III, 3.   [24] *E.*, II, 91.

[25] *E.*, III, 6.   [26] *E.*, III, 61.

[27] *E.*, I, 27.   [28] *A few Words to Church Builders*, 3rd ed. 1844, 3.

[29] *E.*, I, 134. Also: 'All we can expect to do is to copy carefully' (*E.*, V, 1846, 53).

architecture, also called 'reality'.[30] Reality meant truth and serious-
ness of purpose. Longfellow's 'Life is real, life is earnest' in the
Psalm of Life published in 1839 comes to mind at once. As for *The
Ecclesiologist*, it explains in 1846 'A real Swiss Cottage in Switzerland
is as characteristic as picturesque; for the simple reason because it is
real', and extends this identification of reality with truth and with
honesty even to the Crystal Palace: 'a reality of construction beyond
any praise'.[31] Similarly Gervase Wheeler of Philadelphia wrote of a
'timber cottage villa' he had designed in Maine: 'This is essentially
real', for it has 'simplicity and fitness of construction' and no 'inch
board finery',[32] and Street whom, as will be shown, the Ecclesiologists regarded as one of their allies wrote in his *Brick and Marble
Architecture in North Italy* in 1855 that the Gothic architects possessed
an 'intense love of nature grafted on an equally intense love of
reality and truth' (p. xii). Reality among the Ecclesiologists was
applied particularly to the use of materials, ('Let every material
employed be real'),[33] but it is at the same time a much broader moral
demand, and in the equation good man and good architect ('the
finest buildings were designed by the holiest bishops')[34] again Pugin
stood by their side. The ideal architect, *The Ecclesiologist* says[35] is
pictured 'pondering deeply over his duty to do his utmost for the
service of God's holy religion and obtaining by devout exercises of
mind a semi-inspiration', and the final result, 'the beautiful effect of
every building' is attributed to the architects' 'religious calling and
lives'.[36] But how few architects of the 1840s even approached this
ideal! One is reminded of *Contrasts* when one reads: 'Fresh from his
mechanics' institute'—there it is again—'his railway station, his
Socialist Hall, he has the presumption and arrogance to attempt a
church',[37] or: 'To think that any Churchman should allow himself
to build a conventicle',[38] or: church designs are 'manufactured' by
men who also do 'shop-fronts, club-houses, workhouses and sec-
tarian places of assembly'.[39] In short, church architects should build
churches only, and the architectural profession should be raised out
of its 'business-like spirit'.[40]

And the Ecclesiologists' implied criticism of current disrespect

[30] *Durandus*, xxx.   [31] *E.*, XII, 1851, 269–70.
[32] See A. J. Downing, *The Architecture of Country Houses* (New York, 1850), 300–1.
[33] *A Few Words to Church Builders*, 5.   [34] *Durandus*, xx.
[35] *E.*, IV, 277.   [36] *E.*, IV, 279.
[37] *E.*, I, 1842, 66.   [38] *Durandus*, xxii.
[39] *E.*, IV, 1845, 277.   [40] *Durandus*, xxii.

for the church as a building was indeed anything but mere combative journalism. It is hard for us today to believe how seemliness of manner in church had been abandoned, when the Tractarians and the Ecclesiologists set out to re-establish dignity. Professor White in his book refers to some cases, and so does Canon J. Stanley Leatherbarrow in his excellent *Victorian Period Piece* (SPCK, 1954) which, in spite of its title, is the full and serious history of a single church, Swinton in Lancashire. At Tong, so Neale tells, the squire in his pew regularly had the luncheon tray brought in, when the Commandments began. To put hats on the altar during service was customary in more than one church. At Moulton in Northampton-shire the font was a small mortar. At Fordingham christenings were done with the water supplied by the vicar spitting into his hand. In the same church no one ever received Holy Communion except the parson, the clerk and the sexton, and in another church a communi-cant, when given the Cup, said: 'Here's your good health, Sir.' The only other communicant must have felt that that was not quite in order; for he said: 'Here's the good health of our Lord Jesus Christ.'[41]

No wonder the Ecclesiologists wrote with passion and insisted on the most radical changes. When in 1844 Gilbert Scott won the competition for the Lutheran church of St Nicholas at Hamburg—the first international triumph for the English earnestness of Gothic Revival—*The Ecclesiologist* wrote: 'We are sure that the temporary gains of such a contract are a miserable substitute indeed for its unrealism, and we must say it—its sin,[42] and in at least one case an architect in sympathy with the Ecclesiologists refused to build a Unitarian chapel. The architect was Upjohn, the place Boston, the year 1846. He said that 'after having anxiously and prayerfully considered the matter, he had come to the conclusion that he could not conscientiously furnish a plan for a Unitarian church'.[43]

The Ecclesiologist besides dealing with matters of principle, pub-lished running criticisms of new churches and church restorations. That only Gothic could be recommended and receive praise, goes without saying. And yet, as in the case of Pugin, it should not. The

---

[41] Leatherbarrow, op. cit., 74.

[42] IV, 184. Lutheran worship is called on the same page 'the worship of one of the worst sections of a heretical sect'. Freeman agreed. In his *History of Architecture* (above, 452, see p. 101) he wrote: 'We behold . . . the noblest work that three ages have produced, the pile whose lofty spire would seem to call adoring crowds to the Church's most gorgeous worship . . . designed for a teaching alien to the fold.'

[43] Quoted from P. Stanton op. cit., 73.

Ecclesiologists, like Pugin (and like Ruskin later), had no better argument than their taste and the abuse of anything else. To state that the Gothic style 'is the one Christian style, to the exclusion of all others'[44] is no argument, even if it may be true that 'in pointed architecture Christian symbolism has found its most adequate exponent'.[45] To say that 'the greatest glory which Christian architecture has yet attained was reached in the early part of the Decorated style', i.e. 'between the years 1260 and 1360', and that therefore to the Decorated Style 'we ought to return . . . except for some very peculiar circumstances'[46] is a mere assertion.

Equally arbitrary is the abuse heaped on all other styles. Italian Romanesque is 'semi-pagan',[47] and Neo-Italian Romanesque 'mongrel architecture'[48] only employed by 'second-rate architects'.[49] Early English is 'only Romanesque improved'.[50] Perpendicular stands condemned for want of spirituality, for Erastian interference by the State and for 'worldly pomp,[51] and Georgian—needless to say—is 'the ne plus ultra of Wretchedness'.[52]

That all such statements are without adequate foundation anti-Anglo-Catholic architectural critics were quick to point out. The Roman-Catholic *Christian Remembrancer*[53] wrote in 1842, just as Newman was to write about Pugin: 'It is utterly absurd to assert, as Mr. Pugin has done, and as the Camden Society have re-echoed, that a style of architecture is exclusively Christian and catholic which was not introduced till twelve long ages of Christianity had lapsed', but the centre of attack was the group round John Weale's *Quarterly Papers on Architecture*.

John Weale (1791–1862) was a publisher and a fervent, aggressive Protestant, although it was he who published Pugin's *True Principles*. The *Quarterly Papers on Architecture* were issued in four volumes from 1843 till 1845. They almost burst with hatred of the Tractarians and the Camdenians. 'Impotent incipiency of bastard superstition', 'to

---

[44] *E.*, I, 1842, 111.   [45] *E.*, IV, 1845, 49–50.

[46] *A Few Words to Church Builders*. See also *Durandus*, xxiv and xxx ('the glorious architecture of the fourteenth century' and 'no other period can be chosen at which all conditions of beauty, of detail, of general effect, of truthfulness, of reality are so fully answered'. Also (ibid., xxxi) 'the finest development of Christian architecture which the world has yet seen'. No wonder that Lassus and Viollet-le-Duc were elected Honorary Members of the Society(*E.*, X, 1850, 349). For more on them and their connections with the Cambridge Camden Society see p. 197 n. 11.

[47] *E.*, I, 1842, 91 ff. in the long review of Petit's *Remarks*.

[48] *E.*, IV, 1845, 237 on Gärtner's Ludwigskirche in Munich.

[49] *A few Words to Church Builders*, 5.

[50] *E.*, V, 1845, 254.   [51] *Durandus*, cxxiv.

[52] *Durandus*, cxxvii.   [53] III, 356–7.

revive the power of Papacy', is their battle-cry.[54] What they set against it was not only put into words but also illustrated—by the Protestant cathedral designed by George Wightwick (1802–72) for his crotchety book *The Palace of Architecture* which had appeared in 1840. Wightwick had been a pupil of Lapidge and Soane's secretary and now was in practice at Plymouth.[55] *The Palace of Architecture* (not incidentally published by Weale) is a rather laboured 'educational pilgrimage' through the grounds of a fictitious Royal Palace which are full of buildings small and large in all styles: Indian, Chinese, Egyptian, Greek, Roman, Constantinal, Norman, Mohammedan, Gothic, Italian Pointed, Palladian, and so on down to Soanian. The Royal Palace itself is heavily classical, with a giant portico of ten columns and a dome, and the Protestant cathedral is a classical hybrid with a dome inspired by 'the matchless beauty and majesty of St Paul's',[56] but with walls not made dishonest by orders of pilasters. Nothing is taken from St Peter's because that building is 'replete with all vices', and the interior is a curiously weak Louis XVI with tunnel-vaults. The most original because demonstratively Protestant feature is the plan: a square centre, a short straight-ended choir, a short pronaos, two long transepts, and a portico and two west towers almost detached from the pronaos. But the last building in the palace grounds is 'our domestic abode',[57] the 'Anglo-Italian Villa' in which all features are explained functionally, for example, eaves against the wet, no parapet because of snow, sash-windows because they are less liable to leak, and so on. Wightwick adds that for other site conditions the Tudor might be preferable to the Italian.

In the third volume of the *Quarterly Papers*, as part of an article called 'Modern English Gothic Architecture', Wightwick presented a second Protestant cathedral, this in a rather fanciful Perpendicular [Fig. 7]. The plan is similar to the earlier one, but less radical, and the text proves in detail that such a plan is far more useful for Protestant church functions than the plan of St Mary Redcliffe in Bristol whose 'unfitness' Wightwick exposes. What Protestantism needs is for a church to be an Auditorium and at the same time a Spectatory. He has not changed his mind, however, about St Paul's, and if the Camdenians write about 'the faithless, and therefore disgraceful paganism of St Paul's', he counters that by 'the faithless and therefore disgustful Popery of the Camden churches'. This is

[54] II, 1844, 2.
[56] *The Palace of Architecture*, 183.
[55] On Wightwick see Colvin's *Dictionary*.
[57] Ibid., 200.

WESTERN ELEVATION

London John Weale 1845
Printed by Standidge & Cº

FIG. 7. George Wightwick, Design for a Protestant Cathedral, from *Modern English Gothic Architecture*, 1845.

the place where he also reprints with glee long passages from Montalembert's letter (see above, p. 125).

A second article, in the fourth volume of the *Quarterly Papers*, less aggressive because of the crisis in the Society, ends with the illustration and discussion of 'A Protestant church in the Anglo-Norman style', aisleless and also with long transepts. But neither the Anglo-Norman nor the English Perpendicular, in spite of a true 'feeling for the ancient ecclesiastic and domestic buildings of England',[58] must be imitated; for 'Fitness is the grand and imperative principle of architectural merit,'[59] and that means for churches fitness for Protestant worship, i.e. auditories,[60] and for secular architecture 'the adaptation of Greek and Italian details.'[61] So all praise to St Paul's, of which 'Protestant England has any right or reason to boast',[62] and praise also to 'the palatial architecture of modern Italy', the Travellers' and Reform Clubs—Leeds's book on the Travellers' had been published by Weale—and Cockerell's Sun Fire Office and Donaldson's design for the Royal Exchange.[63]

It is worth pointing out that nearly every time it is the Protestants who plead for the Italianate—after all the standard style of mid-nineteenth-century nonconformist chapels was Italianate, if it was not Latest Classical with a giant portico—and every time the Anglo-Catholics and the Roman Catholics who plead for the Gothic.

So between Weale's circle and Neale and Webb's circle no quarter could be given, and the Camdenians certainly could not complain about rudeness being used to them. They had used it and were using it to many others. The west front of Peterborough Cathedral is 'the most sublime . . . that ever entered into the human mind'[64] and the rest ought to be 'pulled down, if it could be replaced by a Middle-Pointed cathedral as good of its sort'.[65] So, when it came to new churches Rickman (who was dead by then) is accused of 'extreme ecclesiological ignorance',[66] Blore's church at Hoxton is 'truly contemptible',[67] Wild's Christ Church Streatham (as will be remembered, a paramount example of the Italian Romanesque of the forties) represents 'the spirit of a false religion'; 'we have seldom seen a more worthless design';[68] George Smith's St Thomas

---

[58] *Quarterly Papers*, II, 10. That feeling, incidentally, does not include 'the queer Lombardic drolleries' illustrated by Hope.

[59] Ibid., II, 3.

[61] Ibid., 15.

[63] Ibid., 7–9.

[65] This is Neale speaking. E., VII, 1847, 238.

[67] E., IV, 1845, 99.

[60] Ibid., 12–13.

[62] Ibid., 4.

[64] E., I, 11.

[66] E., VII, 91.

[68] E., VIII, 1848, 109.

Arbour Square, Stepney 'a most wretched specimen',[69] Roumieu and Gough's tower at St Peter's Islington is 'a complicated mass of Early English frippery',[70] John Wrey Mould's design for the Crimean Memorial Church at Constantinople has the details 'indescribable, and the arrangement monstrous',[71] and Dawkes's Holy Trinity Brompton, Kent is a building 'against which we have a special antipathy'.[72] The architects against whom the antipathy was specially violent were of course those of the classical school, indeed the very ones the *Quarterly Papers* praised and supported. Cockerell's admirable new Library at Cambridge is 'that monstrous, shop-front library with which he has disfigured this University',[73] and Donaldson and Tite are 'practitioners in heathen edifices'.[74] The reference in volume three of *The Ecclesiologist*[75] to 'paganizing professors' refers of course to Cockerell, Professor at the Royal Academy, and Donaldson, Professor at University College.

It is interesting to note that *The Ecclesiologist* is far more savage against the classical and Italianate schools than against so completely novel a building as the Crystal Palace. The journal[76] praises the way the building is adapted to the ends for which it was designed and declares itself 'lost in admiration at the unprecedented inner effects', but, in spite of that it is 'engineering of the highest merit and excellence, but not architecture'. The 'infinite multiplication of the same component parts [is] . . . destructive of its claim to high artistic merit'. So 'we need not expect an architecture of these new materials', and in the same volume a much more scathing assessment was reprinted from an article by Reichensperger in which he calls the Crystal Palace 'a hothouse on a colossal scale' with 'nothing grand, nothing original, nothing artistic'.[77] This is too bad—just as bad as Ruskin—and it shows up Neale and Webb as readier to recognize the 'real' even in a novel form. When it came to the differences between one brand of neo-Gothic and another they at once narrowed their field, and lusty intolerance prevails. In volume three of *The Ecclesiologist* they went indeed so far as to have in the Table of Contents a section 'Architects Condemned' and another 'Architects Approved'. Among the former are Barry, Blore, and Cottingham, among the latter Butterfield, Carpenter, Derick (of Pusey's St Saviour Leeds), Ferrey, and Sharpe.

---

[69] *E.*, I, 1842, 141.   [70] *E.*, I, 197.   [71] *E.*, XV, 1857, 116.
[72] *E.*, VII, 367.   [73] *E.*, II, 113.   [74] *E.*, VIII, 54.
[75] 122.   [76] *E.*, XII, 1851, 269 ff.   [77] *E.*, XII, 384 ff.

It is worth looking at the approvals, their form and their reasons. Littlemore, Newman's church of 1835 (still without the chancel and tower of 1848) is—another dangerous statement—'the most church-like of modern churches'[78] and 'thoroughly Catholic'[79] and indeed in simplicity and 'reality' anticipated Pugin's and the ecclesiological ideals,[80] Salvin's St Peter at Cambridge is 'beautiful and truly Ecclesiastical',[81] Scott's Hartshill, Newcastle-under-Lyme is 'magnificent',[82] so is his St Giles Camberwell [Pl. 39], though its chancel is too short,[83] and Scott for other churches also receives only qualified commendation,[84] Roehampton by Ferrey is 'one of the most praiseworthy buildings near London,[85] Street's early church at Treverbyn has 'a completely correct arrangement'[86] and is praised for 'unpretendingness' and 'a very substantial effect'[87] and so on. Among the Ecclesiologists' favourites were Carpenter, the purity of whose St Mary Magdalene, Munster Square of 1849 is indeed exceptional, and also Butterfield, in spite of his far from pure and far from imitative style, perhaps to a certain extent because of his Anglo-Catholicism and his collaboration with the Camden Society on such an enterprise as that pattern-book of church furnishings, the *Instrumenta Ecclesiastica* of 1847–8. Whatever the reason, the Camdenians' consistent support of Butterfield is much to their credit. To admirers of Carpenter appreciation of a style which Freeman in 1850 called 'absurd and ugly',[88] could not have come easily, and even *The Ecclesiologist* itself[89] in an article on All Saints, Margaret Street [Pl. 40] discovered the 'germ of the same dread of beauty' and 'the same deliberate preference of ugliness' as in the paintings of Millais (i.e. no doubt *The Carpenter's Shop*). Scott was probably referring to the same style when in his *Remarks on Secular and Domestic Architecture* of 1858 he spoke of 'that . . . artistic ugliness which some of our young architects labour to produce'.[90] On the other hand the article on All Saints in *The Ecclesiologist* praises certain qualities of the church liberally: the 'general force and power of the design', its 'manly' and 'austere' truthfulness, the 'honest originality'

---

[78] *E.*, I, 9.
[79] *E.*, I, 19.
[80] See J. Rothenstein in *Arch. Rev.*, XCVIII, 1945, 176 ff.
[81] *E.*, I, 81.
[82] *E.*, I, 58.
[83] *E.*, I, 68.
[84] *E.*, I, 56–8.
[85] *E.*, II, 95.
[86] *E.*, VIII, 1848, 368.
[87] *E.*, XI, 1850, 259.
[88] *E.*, XI, 209. The remark applies to St Matthew, Stoke Newington.
[89] *E.*, XX, 1859, 184–9.
[90] P. 275. Quoted from Collins, *Changing Ideals,* 245. But Butterfield was only eight years younger than Scott.

and the 'outspoken conventionalism' of the foliage and even its polychromy.

Another architect to whom the Camdenians permitted some liberties was Street. He contributed two articles to *The Ecclesiologist*, decidedly more individual than most of its run-of-the-mill material. The first, 'On the proper Characteristics of a Town Church',[91] was to become very influential, just because of its heretical recommendations. Street demanded that town churches should 'avoid rusticity', should use brick rather than rubble, and, if little money was available, should be 'conceived as grand shells'. Brooks received his inspiration from that passage. As regards style, Street recommends the use of Perpendicular in town (as against Middle-Pointed) and points out that Continental churches have much to teach us. The exclusive reliance on English Gothic was indeed waning. Webb himself in 1848 had brought out his *Sketches of Continental Ecclesiology, or Church Notes in Belgium, Germany and Italy*, in which he praised Pointed architecture, tolerated the Romanesque without any qualms and allows 'fine', 'gorgeous', and 'magnificent' even for Renaissance churches,[92] and of course very soon Ruskin's *Stones of Venice* was to appear.

The other remarkable article by Street is called 'The True Principles of Architecture and the Possibility of Development.'[93] It places truth as high as the Camdenians and Pugin and, as we shall see, Ruskin and Fergusson placed it, deprecates copying and faith in authorities, pleads with architects 'to think and to act . . . like men', and expresses his belief in the pointed arch as 'the greatest invention in construction . . . ever made', but admits explicitly that classic buildings also contain features worth studying, especially the *Cornicione*. He sums up: 'That architecture is best which best combines the verticality of Pointed with the repose of Classic architecture.'[94] Equally personal is Street's preference for abstract decorative motifs—dog-tooth, ballflower, diapers, polychromy,

[91] *E.*, XI, 1850, 227 ff.

[92] The Theatinerkirche in Munich is 'fine' (p. 139), St Michael in Munich is 'gorgeous' (p. 139), Santo Spirito in Florence is 'magnificent' (p. 343), the Pantheon in Rome 'leaves nothing to be desired' (p. 524), only Bramante's Tempietto of S. Pietro in Montorio is 'cold and heartless' (p. 540), and Michelangelo's Last Judgement 'most unfit for a Christian church' (p. 551). It is specially noteworthy that Webb can take the new Munich *Rundbogen* churches in his stride. The Allerheiligen Church is 'a kind of adaptation of a Byzantine style' (p. 142), the Ludwigskirche 'a sort of pseudo-Byzantine' (p. 143), the Basilica 'certainly resembles [a basilica] more than any other kind of church' (p. 143). No hard words.

[93] *E.*, XIII, 1852, 247 ff.

[94] Ibid., 253.

especially in stripes (i.e. Butterfield's and Ruskin's motif; see Pl. 41). Over-naturalistic decorative motifs, particularly in stained glass where stylization is essential, i.e. in art 'in the high sense', should not be aimed at. 'If you have any desire to have real art in the painting of glass, you desire, morally speaking, an impossibility.'

Once again, it is remarkable that Neale and Webb left so much freedom to Butterfield as a designer, to Street as a writer. For as a rule they were as demanding and as outspoken with the writers as they were with the architects. Hope's *Historical Essay* is 'a landmark of the first magnitude'[95] (which considering his Romanesque and Cinquecento leanings is a very strange judgment indeed), Petit's *Remarks* have no high standards and concern themselves too much with building abroad,[96] Poole's *History* is not ecclesiological enough, though he had taken an interest in ecclesiology as early as the very Society,[97] and the Oxford Architectural Society has no principle.[98] This from their point of view was true; for Freeman 'commended Norman as a form . . . suitable for the present time' and Parker 'would borrow features from the Italian Romanesque'.[99]

The battles which the Ecclesiologists fought in their early years were violent, but there can be no question that in the end they won a full victory. Already in 1847 they could say that 'the recognition of Middle-Pointed as the style to be studied and developed' is now achieved,[100] and over the fifties and sixties they achieved in fact much more. Looking at the Ecclesiologists from the viewpoint of today, it is obvious that the effect of their censures and praises is visible all over England, in the ritual arrangement of High and Late Victorian churches, the new long chancels added to Georgian and Early Victorian churches and the galleries ripped out of them, in the screens erected in medieval cathedrals, in the Minton floor tiles and the stained glass. But the most sweeping changes made under the influence of the Ecclesiologists concern restoration. There are very few churches in the country indeed which have not been restored on Camdenian principles between the forties and the time when Ruskin's and Morris's influence checked them.

What these principles were is stated in the society's publications unequivocally. 'A thorough and Catholick restoration' is a duty to

[95] *E.*, IX, 1849, 212.   [96] *E.*, I, 91 ff.
[97] *E.*, X, 1850, 120 ff.   [98] *Durandus*, xxxiii.
[99] *E.*, IV, 1845, 76.
[100] *E.*, VII, 203. Yet earlier Professor White tells of ninety-eight requests in 1842-3 for advice from the Society (p. 158).

be fulfilled 'fearlessly'.[101] This means the duty 'to recover the
original scheme of the edifice' and not to retain later work, except
for reasons of 'age and purity'.[102] Perpendicular clerestories in
particular ought to be removed so that the steep pitch of the earlier
roofs can be restored.[103] Tracery also can be remade where it is
no longer Middle-Pointed.[104] In *The Ecclesiologist* for 1847 a long
review appeared of a pamphlet by E. A. Freeman called *Principles
of Church Restoration* (London, 1846). In it Freeman distinguishes
three principles: the destructive, the conservative, and the eclectic,
i.e. for every age to build in its own style and to disregard what prior
ages had done, or to keep and restore every detail in whatever style
it may be, or to preserve some and to replace other features. Neale,
perhaps in a bantering mood, had—as we have seen (p. 132)—
pronounced himself in favour of the destructive principle using
Peterborough Cathedral as his example.[105] *The Ecclesiologist* at least
considered it too, and not without sympathy, saying that it was 'the
only system which offers the logical possibility of working a building
into a state of abstract perfection'. The conservative system is
turned down; for what would be the good of 'asserting one style of
Christian art as superior to others, if . . . we are not to employ it,
because it happens to have been removed'? So in the end, *The
Ecclesiologist* rather half-heartedly recommended the eclectic principle.[106] How this worked out, is seen e.g. in Scott's restoration of
Wren's St Michael Cornhill with its Venetian tracery inserted into
the Wren windows and its rose windows instead of Wren's circular
windows. This, *The Ecclesiologist* praised, as, to quote another, similar
case, 'conferring a religiosity of aspect and arrangement, above their
genuine nature' to such buildings.[107]

In fact the Ecclesiologists in these statements were more accommodating than some of their friends—no doubt because they were
as keen on new churches as on old. The best (and most entertaining)
example of a more preservationist attitude is F. A. Paley's *The
Church Restorers, a Tale* (London, 1844). Paley (1815–83), brother of
E. G. Paley of Paley & Austin, the best firm of Gothicists in the

[101] *E.*, II, 59.   [102] *E.*, I, 65.
[103] *E.*, IV, 104.   [104] *E.*, V, 77.
[105] Street, years later, called Neale's pronouncement a challenge, i.e. did not take it wholly
seriously (*E.*, XXVI, 246).
[106] *E.*, VII, 167 also VII, 238. The debate took place at the Eighth Anniversary Meeting of
the Society in 1847. Webb and Beresford Hope pronounced themselves eclectic, Street (240)
sat on the fence.
[107] *E.*, XVII, 107, and XXVIII, 231.

north of England, and grandson of Paley of the *Evidences*, is known to us as the author of learned books on Gothic buildings and Gothic mouldings. He was an original member of the Cambridge Camden Society and changed to the Roman Catholic faith in 1846, after which he had to earn a living as tutor to the Talbots, then the Throckmortons, then the Kenelm Digbys. The tale is that of the vicissitudes of Letherton church, a church in the style 'in use about the year 1200', with dog-tooth and foliage capitals. A Decorated window was later inserted marking 'the climax beyond which Christian art was never carried'.[108] Then the Reformation and despoliation passed, and finally the fox-hunting Parson Joliffe in 1770 alters the church, puts in a plaster ceiling and aisle windows with Venetian casements and uses a wine-cooler of red earthenware as a font. A little later yet the Evangelical Parson Holdworthy removes the screen, boards up the chancel, and puts in an iron stove of Birmingham Gothic design. So the moment of the tale itself is reached. The incumbent has secured plans for a restoration from Mr. Carter, 'a bustling little man' who had to his credit a hotel 'in no style at all', an Egyptian cemetery chapel, and a Swiss villa, but Francis, the incumbent's son, is at Oxford and has imbibed the new lessons of the Oxford Movement and the Cambridge Camden Society. He travels home and challenges Mr. Carter: 'That the same man shall erect a railroad bridge or station, a prison, a conventicle, a church is degrading'. To use Grecian for today's secular building is senseless, as all architecture is 'the expression . . . of the purpose of its use'. We know the argument, and Francis wins. Mr. Carter is replaced by Mr. Wilkins, a graduate of Oxford. We find him kneeling in the church where Mr. Carter had walked around whistling with hat on his head. So a restoration takes place which is mostly the recovery of half-effaced original features. However, a high-pitched roof is introduced afresh and encaustic floor-tiles are laid.

Paley appears thus far more opposed to restoration as against preservation than the Camdenians, but even he is nothing like as radical as Ruskin who five years later wrote: 'Restoration, so called, is the worst manner of Destruction . . . Take proper care of your monuments, and you will not need to restore them.'[109] In this though not in many other ways Ruskin represents the Late Victorian as against the Early and High Victorian attitude.

---

[108] *The Church Restorers, a Tale,* 53.   [109] *Seven Lamps,* Libr. Ed., VIII, 242.

CHAPTER XV

Ruskin

MUCH has been written about Ruskin.[1] In the context of this book it is not necessary to recapitulate more than a few significant facts about his life. He was born in 1819, the son of a wealthy wine merchant. His mother came of Scottish Puritan stock. He remained down to an uncommon time of life close to his parents. When he went to Oxford his mother took rooms for herself as well, and his decisive journeys right to 1859 were made with father and mother. When he was ten his father wrote to him: 'I must commence this letter by exclaiming wonderful, wonderful, wonderful . . . writing so like a classic author. You are blessed with a firm Capacity & even Genius & you owe it to the author of your Being . . . to cultivate your Powers . . . for the benefit of your fellow Creatures. You may be deemed to enlighten a People by your Wisdom . . .'[2] No wonder John Ruskin grew up to believe all this of himself. His first piece of writing was 'The Poetry of Architecture' published under the pseudonym Kata Phusin in Loudon's *Architectural Magazine* in 1837. It dealt chiefly with scenery. The books which made him famous and the ones from which nearly all the following quotations will be taken are *Modern Painters* I (1843), II (1846), III (1856), *The Seven Lamps of Architecture* (1849), *The Stones of Venice* I (1851), II (1853) and the *Lectures on Architecture and Art* given at Edinburgh in 1854. Of his disastrous marriage to Effie Gray—unconsummated—

[1] The briefest bibliography would have to include the following: E. J. Cook & A. Wedderburn, *The Works of John Ruskin*, 39 vols., 1903–12, the so-called Library Edition, here quoted L.E.; the brilliantly chosen and brilliantly annotated anthology by Lord Clark, *Ruskin To-day* (London, 1964; also Penguin Books) to which I am indebted for quite a number of my quotations, the equally brilliant catalogue of the Arts Council Exhibition *Ruskin and his Circle*, 1964, and of biographies Joan Evans 1954, Peter Quennell 1959 and the most recent and the most searching J. D. Rosenberg, *The darkening Glass* (New York, 1961; London, 1963). R. B. Stein, *John Ruskin and aesthetic thought in America* (Harvard U. P., 1967) remained unknown to me until it was too late, and G. P. Landow, *Aesthetic and critical Theories of John Ruskin* (Princeton U.P., 1971) arrived too late to be used. This is true also of H. Gill Viljoen, *The Froude-Ruskin Friendship* (New York, 1966) and the same (ed.) *Brantwood Diary* (Yale U.P., 1971). More specialized is H. L. Sussman: *Victorians and the Machine* (Cambridge, Mass., 1968), 76 ff.

[2] Quoted in the Arts Council catalogue, p. 13.

the less said the better, though the details reveal a warped character, and as a brilliant but warped being Ruskin must be understood. He married in 1848, and she left him in 1854. She was twelve when he met her, and he then wrote a story for her. Had she been older, he would not have fallen in love with her; for it was one of his aberrations only to be able to be attracted by adolescent or less than adolescent girls.[3] Adèle Domecq was fifteen, Rose La Touche nine. He illuminated a manuscript for Effie for her thirteenth birthday and wrote *Sesame and Lilies* for her when she was fifteen.

In 1855 he began to teach at the Working Men's College and continued till 1858. In 1857 he gave at the Manchester Exhibition the lectures on the Political Economy of Art which mark his turn to concentration on social problems. *Unto this Last*, published in the *Cornhill Magazine* in 1860 and as a book in 1862, and *Time and Tide* of 1867 are the most important documents. His father had died in 1864 leaving him £157,000. In 1874 he had his first nervous breakdown. Rose La Touche fell ill in that year and died in 1875. Madness showed itself first in 1878 and again in 1881–3. From 1889 to his death in 1900 he was insane.

Ruskin is a superb though a maddening writer and a confused thinker, though one with frequent flashes of genius. He was at the beginning deeply impressed by Carlyle, the author of *Signs of the Times* (1829), of *Chartism* (1839), and *Past and Present* (1843), who believed in the wisdom of the Middle Ages and vehemently queried the values of his own day; who had written—to put down just a few familiar quotations—: 'Cash payment is not the sole relation of human beings';[4] '"My starving workers?" says the rich Millowner "Did not I hire them fairly in the market? Did I not pay them to the last sixpence, the sum covenanted for? What have I to do with them more?"'[5] 'Not succeeding . . . not making money' is the only thing the modern English 'contemplate with entire despair',[6] and the liberty advocated by nineteenth-century liberalism is in fact 'liberty to die by starvation'.[7] However, Carlyle's remedy is not a development within the working class such as Chartism, though he preached that 'man is created to fight'[8] but a fancifully medieval relation of almost feudal trust between the ruling and the ruled class: 'the right of the ignorant man to be guided by the wiser, to be, gently or forcibly

---

[3] See especially Sir William James, *The Order of Release* (London, 1948).
[4] *Past and Present,* Book III, Ch. 2.   [5] Ibid.   [6] Ibid., Book III, Ch. 13.
[7] Ibid., Book III, Ch. 2.   [8] Ibid., Book III, Ch. 10.

held in the true course by him.'⁹ The employer, the manufacturer is accepted, it must be implied, among those with a duty to guide; for Carlyle combined in a surprising way enthusiasm for the Middle Ages with enthusiasm for what he called in *Sartor Resartus* 'industrialism' and in *Past and Present* 'captains of industry'.¹⁰ The humming of Manchester at 5.30 a.m. is 'sublime as a Niagara',¹¹ and John Bull's 'sea-moles, cotton-trades, railways, fleets and cities'¹² are as sublime. He also admired ours as the 'Mechanical Age', where 'nothing is . . . done directly, or by hand; all is by rule and calculated contrivance', though he recognized the danger of the doctrine that 'what cannot be investigated and understood mechanically, cannot be investigated and understood at all'.¹³ Carlyle's was a confused message,¹⁴ and some of it can only have enforced Ruskin's opposition, but the rest must have been drunk in by him, made doubly potent by Carlyle's dogmatic statement and his vehemence: 'Democracy is forever impossible! So much . . . with sure appeal to the Law of Nature . . . may be . . . asserted . . . The Noble in the high place, the Ignoble in the low, that is . . . in all countries, the Almighty Maker's Law.'¹⁵ This is how Ruskin was writing at the same time.

But on architecture Carlyle had nothing to give him. Here he was wholly influenced by Pugin; his hysterical denial proves it. He wrote: 'I glanced at Pugin's Contrasts once, in the Oxford architectural reading room, during an idle forenoon . . . I never read a word of any other of his works, not feeling, from the style of his architecture, the smallest interest in his opinion', and again: Pugin 'is not a great architect, but one of the smallest possible of conceivable architects'.¹⁶ Yet Pugin's message, as we shall see, is Ruskin's message; only Pugin's was single, whereas Ruskin has so many messages that they get entangled and tend to fight each other.

Two examples for many, and these taken from painting. All art is truth. Ruskin was thrilled by Turner; so Turner is truth. He disliked Constable; so Constable's truth must be wrong or inferior.¹⁷

⁹ I was unable to pin-point the source of this passage.
¹⁰ 'Industrialism' quoted from Raymond Williams, *Culture and Society, 1780–1950*, Penguin Books 1961, 90 'Captains of Industry' is the title of Book IV, Ch. IV of *Past and Present*.
¹¹ *Chartism*, Centenary Edn., XXIX, 182.   ¹² *Past and Present*, Book III, Ch. 5.
¹³ Again, alas, I could not trace this passage.
¹⁴ On his debt to Robert Owen, see below, p. 277.
¹⁵ *Latter-Day Pamphlets*, 1850, No. 1, *Works*, 1870 edition, XIX, 26–7.
¹⁶ L.E., V, 428 ff., IX, 436 ff.
¹⁷ See especially *Modern Painters*, III, L.E., V, 169 ff.

He also took to the Pre-Raphaelites and already in 1851 defended them,[18] so their truth must be reconciled with Turner's. And he fervently admired Tintoretto; so Tintoretto must find a place under the same umbrella.[19] Even more shameless, because the deception was recognized and thus condoned by him, is this footnote in *Frondes Agrestes* (1875):

> I knew nothing when I wrote this passage, of Luini, Filippo Lippi, or Sandro Botticelli, and had no capacity to enter into the deeper feeling even of the men whom I was chiefly studying—Tintoret and Fra Angelico. But the British public is at present as little acquainted with the greater Florentines as I was then, and the passage, for *them,* remains true.

This is advice not to worry about untrue statements as long as your readers won't find you out.

That is hard enough to accept; but Ruskin makes it harder by the arrogance with which he states what he states. It is the technique of the pulpit and the technique of many of his successful contemporaries 'Declaimers, not reasoners' is what W. R. Grig called them.[20] 'Rolling and thundering' the *Edinburgh Review* called Dr. Arnold's oratorial technique,[21] 'oracular arrogance' is Morley's comment on Macaulay's.[22] And as for Ruskin, Meredith characterized his style to perfection, calling it a 'monstrous assumption of wisdom' and 'preposterous priestly attitude'.[23] Ruskin knew it and defended it: 'I cannot write with a modesty I do not feel'[24] and 'Until people are ready to receive all I say about art as "unquestionable", . . . I don't consider myself to have any reputation at all worth caring about.'[25] The 'any—at all' is sermon technique; so are Ruskin's 'nay', 'fain', 'behold', his 'enough and to spare', and, to take a more extensive passage:

> Whatever can be measured and handled, dissected and demonstrated—in a word, whatever is of the body only,—that the schools of knowledge

---

[18] The Cambridge Camden Society in the same year expressed its 'great sympathy' for the Pre-Raphaelites' 'earnest endeavours' (*Ecclesiologist*, XII, 1851, 221). In the same year they also reviewed Ruskin's *Stones of Venice* and said that his attack on Pugin 'disfigures the book' (ibid., 275 ff., and 341 ff.). They had already written enthusiastically on the *Seven Lamps,* though they were hurt by his 'unreformed church' bias, 'as ungenerous as inconsistent' (ibid., X, 1850, 111 ff.).

[19] For appropriate quotations see the Index volume of the L.E.

[20] *Literary and Social Judgments,* 1868, I, 157, quoted from W. E. Houghton, *The Victorian Frame of Mind,* (Yale U.P., 1957), 151. Other examples 137, 139.

[21] Ibid., 206.   [22] Ibid., 137. Examples from Carlyle have just been given (p. 141).

[23] *Letters of George Meredith* (London, 1912), I, 200–2.

[24] *Pre-Raphaelitism,* L.E., XII, lii–liii.

[25] From a letter of 1854, L.E., XXVI, 169.

do resolutely and courageously possess themselves of, and portray. But whatever is immeasurable, intangible, indivisible, and of the spirit, that the schools of knowledge do as certainly lose . . . for whatever can be arrested, measured, and systematized . . .[26]

And so on, with the use of three or four words for one to fill in time or to intensify, with alliterations and all the other pulpit conventions, among them of course the always ready quotations from the Bible. Of them Lord Clark says nicely 'Whenever I have seen a biblical quotation in the offing, I have begun to lose interest, because I know that at this point Ruskin will cease to use his own powers of intelligent observation, and will rely on holy writ to save him further thought',[27] yet Ruskin was during the years which matter most a devout Christian—had there not been regular and prolonged bible-readings in his father's house?—an Evangelical Christian by the way, which helps to explain his vicious comments on Pugin.[28]

Yet as an intelligent observer, especially of nature, Ruskin could be so marvellous. Here as an example is the description of a spot above the village of Champagnole in the Jura:

It is a spot which has all the solemnity, with none of the savageness, of the Alps; where there is a sense of a great power beginning to be manifested in the earth, and of a deep and majestic concord in the rise of the long low lines of piny hills; the first utterance of those mighty mountain symphonies, soon to be more loudly lifted and wildly broken along the battlements of the Alps. But their strength is as yet restrained; and the far reaching ridges of pastoral mountain succeed each other, like the long and sighing swell which moves over quiet water from some far off stormy sea. And there is a deep tenderness pervading that vast monotony. The destructive forces and the stern expression of the central ranges are alike withdrawn. No frost-ploughed, dust-encumbered paths of ancient glacier fret the soft Jura pastures; no splintered heaps of ruin break the fair ranks of her forest; no pale, defiled, or furious rivers send their rude and changeful ways among her rocks. Patiently, eddy by eddy, the clear green streams wind along

---

[26] *Stones of Venice,* L.E., XI, 61.

[27] *Ruskin To-day,* xv. This is perhaps a little unfair to Ruskin, as nearly everybody used God as a means of elevating more common language. Thus, to give just one random example, the preface to the Official Catalogue of the Great Exhibition of 1851 ends with the assurance that 'glory and praise are due to God alone' (*Great Exhibition of the Works of Industry of all Nations. Descriptive Catalogue,* I, viii). On this and allied matters Professor Houghton's chapter Hypocrisy is required reading (op. cit., 394 ff.). His best piece is Kingsley's sermon with the passage: Seek 'the noble life, the pure life . . . the Godlike life' and 'the good things of this world, wealth, honour, power, and the rest . . . shall come to you of their own accord by the providence of your Father in heaven' (p. 406).

[28] And *The Ecclesiologist's* remark about 'unreformed church' (x, 1850, 112).

their well-known beds; and under the dark quietness of the undisturbed pines, there spring up, year by year, such company of joyful flowers as I know not the like of among all the blessings of the earth.[29]

Ruskin's drawings of nature have the same sensitivity and intensity. So have those of architecture [Pls. 42, 43]. But though what concerns the present book is his architectural theories they cannot be isolated from his theory of art, and his theory of art is bound up with ethics and with social history and theories of society.

'The first necessity for the doing of any good work in ideal art, is the looking upon all foulness with horror', and hence 'The art of any country is an exact exponent of its ethical life', or, to bring religion in, 'The great arts . . . can have but three principal directions of purpose:—first, that of enforcing the religion of men; secondly, that of perfecting their ethical state; thirdly, that of doing them material service.'[30] This, of course, is what Pugin and the Ecclesiologists had preached. The similarity is even more patent in the following passage: 'Great art is the expression of the mind of a great man, and mean art, that of the want of mind of a weak man.'[31] For Neale's Catholic oakwood, we have Ruskin's 'The Moral of Landscape'.[32] Or, to transfer it to architecture: 'A foolish person builds foolishly, and a wise one, sensibly; a virtuous one, beautifully; and a vicious one, basely.'[33] And briefer still: 'No rascal will ever build a pretty building.' This passage comes from the second edition of the *Seven Lamps*, and so is an addition of 1880.[34] But it only sums up the spirit and the theories of that epoch-making book. As it came out in 1849, it marks the moment of the mid-century, and it contains in fact as much that looks back to Pugin and the Ecclesiologists as it contains of matter determining the English attitude to architecture during the second half of the century.

Ruskin's Seven Lamps are the Lamps of Sacrifice, of Truth, of Power, of Beauty, of Life, of Memory, and of Obedience. It will be noticed at once that only one of them can possibly be concerned with the strictly aesthetic aspects of architecture. The others are all about life, about religion, about ethics, and Ruskin's influence on England has been indeed to deflect attention from art as art to all those other matters, admittedly an integral part of art but only one part. That the

---

[29] I have found it impossible to improve on Lord Clark's choice; *Ruskin To-day*, 95.
[30] *Lectures on Art* (Oxford, 1870); L.E., XX, 30, 39, 40.
[31] *The Queen of the Air*, 1865–6, L.E., XIX, 389.
[32] *Modern Painters*, III, pt. IV, Chap. 17; L.E.
[33] *The Queen of the Air*, L.E., XIX, 389.   [34] L.E., VIII, 48.

first lamp is a genuflection to God—only the best is fit for an offering to God—[35] goes without saying, and what Lord Clark wrote about Ruskin's references to God will be welcomed by any reader of the Lamp of Sacrifice: 'God is one and the same, and is pleased or displeased by the same things for ever, although one part of His pleasure may be expressed at one time rather than another, and although the mode in which His pleasure is to be consulted may be by Him graciously modified to the circumstances of men'.[36] Is that what we have come to Ruskin for?

The other lamps are more profitable. The second is the Lamp of Truth: 'Do not let us lie at all.'[37] And so, like Pugin, Ruskin is on to the deceits. There are according to him three. A structural deceit is 'the suggestion of a mode of structure or support other than the true one'.[38] A surface deceit is 'the painting of surfaces to represent some other material than that of which they actually consist'.[39] An operative deceit is 'the use of cast or machine-made ornaments of any kind'.[40] The list is typical Ruskin. The three deceits are not on the same plane logically, and besides Ruskin presses hard—a Ruskinian deceit—to show that the marble facing of a brick wall or indeed the gilding of an inferior material is permissible, while the marbling of wood is not. As for the operational deceit, there will be an opportunity a little later to discuss it.

The Lamp of Power deals with 'severe . . . mysterious majesty', with the sublime, with that which the human mind, by virtue of its innate power, can impress on a building.[41] The Lamp of Beauty needs no explanation. The Lamp of Life preaches that 'things in other respects alike . . . are noble or ignoble in proportion to the fulness of the life . . . of whose action they bear the evidence'.[42] The Lamps of Memory and Obedience can be inspected together. The Lamp of Memory tells that 'the . . . greatest glory of a building is not in its stones, nor in its gold. Its glory is its Age.'[43] 'It is in becoming memorial or monumental that a true perfection is attained

[35] Ibid., 34–9.   [36] Ibid., L.E., VIII, 3.
[37] Ibid., 56.   [38] Ibid., 60.
[39] Ibid., 60 and 72.   [40] Ibid., 60 and 81.
[41] Ibid., 101–2.   [42] Ibid., 190.
[43] Ibid., 233–4. Three years later and quite possibly independently, Theodor Fontane wrote this apropos St James's Palace in his *Ein Sommer in London* (14 June, 1852): 'An old tasteless building, but clothed in that interest which time and history bestow, and only they. America must therefore, in a certain way, be dull. One lock of Mary Queen of Scots, one old cloth petticoat of Anne Boleyn are more interesting than Buffalo and Milwaukee rolled together' (*Nymphenburger Ausgabe*, XVII, 523).

11

by civil and domestic buildings.' Hence they must be built stably—this is 'one of [the] moral duties', and hence they must be decorated in a way which conveys 'a metaphorical or historical meaning', an 'intellectual intention'.[44]

But in the event Ruskin does not leave it at this respect for all stable and intellectually decorated buildings of the past. Like Pugin and like the Ecclesiologists he turns out to be extremely selective. The Greeks are excluded, because their workmen were slaves and not free men as those of the Gothic centuries. Their ornament is therefore 'servile'.[45] The Romanesque and altogether early medieval is described as 'rude and ludicrous'—this on the sculpture of S. Ambrogio in Milan,[46] and blamed for 'meagre thinness'—this on Venetian mosaics.[47] The Renaissance is excluded as 'enervated sensuality'[48] and because it was evolved by 'the fallen Roman, in the utmost impotence of his luxury, and insolence of his guilt'.[49] Renaissance ornament is 'a wearisome exhibition of well-educated imbecility'.[50] The Coliseum is 'a public nuisance'. St Peter's is disgusting, 'the penny-room at Leamington, built bigger'.[51] The Georgian terraces of 'Harley Street, or Baker Street, or Gower Street' are the reduction of 'men's inventive and constructive faculties from the Grand Canal to . . . the square cavity in the brick wall'.[52] Gower Street after this became the whipping boy of the Gothicists and the Medievalists in general.[53] The Greek Revival, one need hardly add, is worse: 'I cannot conceive any architect insane enough to project the vulgarisation of Greek architecture.'[54]

---

[44] L.E., VIII, 225, 227, 230.
[45] *Stones of Venice*, 'Nature of Gothic', L.E., X, 188.
[46] *The Two Paths*, 1859, L.E., XVI, 277.
[47] *St Mark's Rest*, 1877–84, L.E., XXIV, 292.
[48] *Seven Lamps*, L.E., VIII, 98.
[49] 'Nature of Gothic', L.E., X, 185.   [50] Ibid., 189.
[51] Letter of 1840 and *Mornings in Florence*, 1875–6, quoted from Clark, *Ruskin To-day*, 30 and 251. After this St Peter baiting became quite a sport. Miss Metcalf quoted to me (from her yet unpublished thesis, 'The Rise of James Knowles, Victorian Architect and Editor', Ph.D., London, 1971) a note by James Knowles the Younger from his unpublished diary, under 6 April, 1854: 'St Peter is a dead swindle.'
[52] *Stones of Venice*, III, 1853, L.E., XI, 4.
[53] Disraeli in *Tancred* (1845) had already written of 'your Gloucester Places, and Baker Streets, and Harley Streets, and Wimpole Streets, and all those flat, dull, spiritless streets' (Book I, Chap. 10), and W. H. Leeds even before that of the 'wearisome succession of brick boxes' (quoted from J. Steegman, *Consort of Taste, 1830–1870* (London, 1950), 283). Wimpole Street also comes into Tennyson's *In Memoriam* as 'the bald street' (1850). Later comes Scott, in 1858 with 'the intolerable flatness of Baker Street and Gower Street (*Remarks*, 170) and yet later, in 1883, William Morris who finds much that went up in his day so bad that 'one is beginning to think with regard of the days of Gower Street' (*Coll. Works*, XXIII, 148).
[54] *Seven Lamps*, L.E., VIII, 258.

And, as we have seen with Pugin and the Ecclesiologists, even Gothic in its totality is not restricted enough. The Late Gothic is ignoble and uninventive,[55] the French Flamboyant all 'caricatures of form and eccentricities of treatment',[56] the English Perpendicular detestable,[57] and even King's College Chapel 'a piece of architectural juggling'.[58] No wonder that Tudor architecture altogether is 'impotent and ugly degradation',[59] and that the Houses of Parliament—Perpendicular Revival—are the object of his 'detestation' too.[60]

What then remains in the end? Ruskin says it with precision: '1. The Pisan Romanesque; 2. The early Gothic of the Western Italian Republics, advanced as far and as fast as our art would enable us to the Gothic of Giotto; 3. The Venetian Gothic in its purest development; 4. The English earliest decorated.'[61] In the event the Pisan Romanesque, which it was illogical to include anyway, dropped out, and the English of 1850 were left with the other three. As for number two, Ruskin's special love was the Campanile of Florence Cathedral by Giotto and others.[62] Number three means the Doge's Palace above all, 'a model of all perfection'.[63] This style became known as Ruskinian *par excellence* especially in the interpretation of Deane & Woodward—see e.g. the Meadow Building of Christ Church in Oxford. Finally, number four was to be the universal preference, especially in a form which Ruskin explicitly allowed: 'enriched by some mingling with decorative elements from the exquisite decorated Gothic of France' (e.g. Saint Urbain at Troyes).[64]

[55] 'Nature of Gothic', L.E., X, 261.

[56] *Seven Lamps*, L.E., VIII, 97. But Lord Clark prints a passage from *Praeterita* in which Ruskin, speaking of his early years, admits his 'preference of flamboyant to purer architecture' (p. 44). So that is the same development as Pugin's.

[57] *Seven Lamps*, L.E., VIII, 108.

[58] Ibid., 63. This was suppressed in the second edition, because of the 'many charming qualities' of the building.

[59] Ibid., 258.   [60] Ibid., 147 (addition of 1880).   [61] Ibid., 258.

[62] Ibid., 187. But Whewell called it rather an elegant piece of furniture than an edifice. See *Fraser's Magazine*, XLI, 1850, 151 ff. On this review of the *Seven Lamps* see more below.

[63] Ibid., 111.

[64] Ibid., 258. It is worth remembering that Webb, co-founder of the Cambridge Camden Society (see p. 123) had brought out in 1848 his *Church Notes in Belgium, Germany and Italy*, that already in 1846 E. A. Freeman had noticed and praised *The Ecclesiologist's* change from a narrow preference of the English Gothic to inclusion of the Continental (*The Eccles.*, V, 178), and that Street in 1850 had recommended a greater curiosity about the Continental Gothic. His *Brick and Marble Architecture in North Italy*, which came out five years later in 1855, praised Ruskin, acknowledged 'the revival of true principles within the last few years', and blamed the Renaissance for 'falseness of construction, . . . coarseness and bad grotesqueness of ornamentation' and 'contempt of simplicity, repose and delicacy' (Preface, ix–xi). The influence which Clutton

Having named these models, Ruskin tries by means of the last of his lamps, the Lamp of Obedience, to establish a dictatorship in their favour. This is what he says: 'Architecture never could flourish except when it was subjected to a national law as strict and as minutely regulative as the laws which regulate religion, policy, and social relations ... The architecture of a nation is great only when it is as universal and as established as its language', and 'our architecture will languish, . . . until . . . an universal system of form and workmanship be everywhere adopted and enforced'. Therefore, there is only one way: 'Choose a style, and . . . use it universally.'[65]

The introduction of workmanship must be noted; for it is Ruskin's fervent faith already in the *Seven Lamps* that 'so long as men work *as* men, putting their heart into what they do, and doing their best, it matters not how bad workmen they may be'.[66] Here is Ruskin's starting-point for the finest and deepest chapter he ever wrote, the chapter on 'The Nature of Gothic' in the second volume of *The Stones of Venice*, (1853). In 'The Nature of Gothic'. Ruskin's theory of architecture proves to be rooted in his theory of art.

Everything presented . . . in nature [Ruskin writes] has good and evil mingled in it: and artists, considered as searchers after truth, are . . . to be divided into three great classes, a right, a left, and a centre. Those on the right perceive, and pursue, the good, and leave the evil: those in the centre, the greatest, perceive and pursue the good and evil together, the whole thing as it verily is: those on the left perceive and pursue the evil, and leave the good.

The first class, I say, take the good and leave the evil. But of whatever is presented to them, they gather what it has of grace, and life, and light, and holiness, and leave all, or at least as much as possible, of the rest undrawn. The faces of their figures express no evil passions; the skies of their landscapes are without storm. The early Italian and Flemish painters, Angelico and Memling, Perugino, Francia, Raffaelle in his best time, John Bellini, and our own Stothard, belong eminently to this class.

The second, or greatest class, render all that they see in nature unhesitatingly, with a kind of divine grasp and governement of the whole, sympathizing with all the good, and yet confessing, permitting, and bringing good out of the evil also. Their subject is infinite as nature, their colour equally balanced between splendour and sadness, reaching occa-

---

and Burges's winning of the competition for Lille Cathedral had upon closer study of the Continental Gothic schools is well enough known. See C. L. Eastlake, *A History of the Gothic Revival* (London, 1872), Ch. XVIII and B. F. L. Clarke, *Church Builders of the Nineteenth Century* (London, 1938; paperback edn., 1970), Ch. VII.

[65] *Seven Lamps*, L.E., VIII, 251–2, 256.   [66] Ibid., 214.

sionally the highest degrees of both, and their chiaroscuro equally balanced between light and shade.

The principal men of this class are Michael Angelo, Leonardo, Giotto, Tintoret, and Turner. Raffaelle in his second time, Titian, and Rubens are transitional; the first inclining to the eclectic, and the last two to the impure class, Raffaelle rarely giving all the evil, Titian and Rubens rarely all the good.

The last class perceive and imitate evil only. They cannot draw the trunk of a tree without blasting and shattering it, nor a sky except covered with stormy clouds; they delight in the beggary and brutality of the human race; their colour is for the most part subdued or lurid, and the greater spaces of their pictures are occupied by darkness.

Happily the examples of this class are seldom seen in perfection. Salvator Rosa and Caravaggio are the most characteristic: the other men belonging to it approach towards the central rank by imperceptible gradations, as they perceive and represent more and more of good.

But Murillo, Zurbaran, Camillo Procaccini, Rembrandt, and Teniers, all belong naturally to this 'lower class'—Murillo, because of his 'repulsive and wicked children', Teniers, because, like most of the Dutch, he painted 'the besotted, vicious, vulgar human life'.[67] The first Ruskin calls the Purists, the second the Naturalists ('who contemplate with an equal mind the alternation of terror and of beauty'), the third the Sensualists. How different from Murillo's 'vicious vagrants' are the peasant boys of William Hunt, 'healthily coloured' and 'picturesquely dressed'! To show the soles of a poor man's feet (as e.g. Caravaggio does) is 'to thrust . . . degradation into the light'.

That is Ruskin's theory of art and ethics at its most dated. More worth serious argument is his theory of art and nature. 'All high art consists in the carving and painting natural objects.'[68] 'No great school [of art] ever yet existed which had not for primal aim the representation of some natural fact as truly as possible.'[69] 'All judgment of art . . . finally founds itself on knowledge of Nature.'[70] What in all such passages Nature means varies from the narrowest definition to one which includes the 'vital truth' of everything being in motion, of nothing standing still.[71]

---

[67] L.E., X, 221–2 and *The Cestus of Aglaia*, 1865–6, L.E., XIX, 49.
[68] *Seven Lamps*, Preface to the Second Edition (1855), L.E., VIII, 11.
[69] *The Two Paths*, 1858, L.E., XVI, 270.
[70] *The Elements of Drawing*, 1857, L.E., XV, 82.
[71] Ruskin's thought of, and feeling for, nature did not stand still either. Lord Clark emphasizes a development from a faith in beneficial and beautiful nature to a nature whose 'cruelty and

Now one of the messages of 'The Nature of Gothic', and the most baffling one, is that architecture also founds itself entirely on knowledge of nature: 'Whatever in architecture is fair, or beautiful is imitated from natural forms.' This he had said already in the Lamp of Power, and it means that the beauty of architecture is not architecture, but usually sculpture and always 'fine art'. Indeed to Ruskin 'sculpture and painting [are] . . . the entire masters of . . . architecture'[72] and architecture consequently is that which impresses on building 'certain characters venerable or beautiful, but otherwise unnecessary'.[73] Ruskin's illustration of this fact runs as follows: 'No one would call the laws architectural which determine the height of a breastwork or the position of a bastion. But if to the stone facing of that bastion he added an unnecessary feature, as a cable moulding, that is Architecture.'[74] All this is from the *Seven Lamps*. In 'The Nature of Gothic' he gives another illustration: 'The goodly building is the most glorious, when it is sculptured into the likeness of the leaves of Paradise.'[75] Paradise is a typical Ruskin touch. It means nothing; yet adds sublimity to the sentence.

'The Nature of Gothic' like the *Seven Lamps* is divided into categories. They are not quite so rigidly imposed, but they are more precise and less moralistic. They are savageness, imperfection, changefulness, redundance, and rigidity. Savageness, 'as wild and wayward as the northern sea', heaves 'into the darkened air the pile of iron buttress and rugged wall . . . creations of ungainly shape and rigid lines, but full of wolfish life',[76] imperfection belongs to all 'truly noble' architecture; for no great man can ever feel finally satisfied.[77] Changefulness is as essential; the 'perpetual variety of every feature' is the reward we reap, if we leave the workman his independence.[78] Redundance is 'the uncalculating bestowal of the wealth of . . . labour', and 'the sympathy with the fulness and wealth

---

ghastliness' horrifies him (Clark, *Ruskin To-day*, 119; letter of 1875), from the artist as a thrilled observer to the artist who is 'ruthless and selfish' who, if he sees a man die at his feet, does not help him but watches 'the colour of the lips' and who if he sees 'a woman embrace her destruction' does not save her, but 'watch how she bends her arms' (ibid., 184, from the MS. Appendix to *Modern Painters*, II, and L.E., IV, 388). Once, even such a desperate summing up of defeat appears early: 'I have never known a man who seemed altogether right and calm in faith, who seriously cared about art' (*Stones of Venice*, II, L.E., X, 125). This change is connected with two developments, the negative towards destruction of his own mind and the positive towards an insight into the connection of art with the facts of social life.

[72] *Seven Lamps*, Preface to the Second Edition (1855), L.E., VIII, 10.
[73] Ibid., 28.   [74] Ibid., 29.
[75] *The Stones of Venice*, 1853, L.E., X, 239.   [76] §8.
[77] §§22, 24.   [78] §26.

of the material universe'.[79] And finally rigidity is that stiffness which is 'analogous to that of the bones of a link, or fibres of a tree; an elastic tension and communication of force from part to part'.[80]

All this is beautifully put, and so is the final summing up of the criteria that make a building Gothic: 'First, see if it looks as if it had been built by strong men; if it has the sort of roughness, and largeness, and nonchalance, mixed in places with the exquisite tenderness, which seems always the sign manual of the broad vision'; for 'If the building has this character, it is much already in its favour; it will go hard but it proves a noble one'. 'Secondly, Observe if it be irregular, its different parts fitting themselves to different purposes, no one caring what becomes of them, so that they do their work. If one part always answers accurately to another part, it is sure to be a bad building.' 'Thirdly, observe if all the traceries, capitals, and other ornaments are of perpetually varied design. If not, the work is essentially bad. Lastly, *read* the sculpture', and when you read it, judge it on 'precisely the same principles as that of a book'.[81]

One important consequence of these theses and the only one which never, right down to the present moment, has lost its validity, is Ruskin's stand—already in the *Seven Lamps*—on the restoration of buildings. We have seen the ambiguity of Freeman's and the Ecclesiologists' attitude, and we shall soon see the more dangerously ambiguous attitude of Scott and Viollet-le-Duc. There is no ambiguity in Ruskin's attitude: 'Restoration . . . means the most total destruction which a building can suffer.' For the life of a building depends on 'that spirit which is given only by the hand and eye of the workman'.[82] Preservation therefore and not restoration. One of the reasons why Ruskin in 1874 refused the Gold Medal of the Royal Institute of British Architects was 'the destruction under the name of restoration brought about by architects.'[83]

The life of a building, Ruskin said, depends on the preservation of the actual surfaces as wrought by craftsmen. And his summing up of what constitutes Gothic confirms that ultimate criterion of life: 'Pointed arches do not constitute Gothic, nor vaulted roofs, nor flying buttresses, nor grotesque sculptures, but all or some of these things and many other things with them, when they come together

[79] §78.   [80] §73.   [81] §§111-4.
[82] *Seven Lamps*, L.E., VIII, 242.   [83] See p. 181.

so as to have life.'[84] The first part of the statement clearly aims at the Whewells and Willises. Yet Ruskin had read them carefully and many times quoted from Willis '(stump tracery',[85] discontinuous impost'[86]) and expressed gratitude to him. He 'taught me all my grammar of central Gothic'.[87] He also referred occasionally to Whewell[88] and stayed at his Master's Lodge in 1851, where he met Willis too and went with both of them to Ely.

No doubt he did not then know that Whewell was the author of a critical review of his *Seven Lamps* in *Fraser's Magazine*,[89] one of the most perspicacious reviews of any of Ruskin's writings. Whewell recognizes Ruskin's 'glowing and picturesque eloquence', but says that the Lamps give 'not so much light as splendour'; for they do not represent, as one would expect, 'exactly co-ordinated principles'. However, Whewell adds nicely, nor does Montesquieu's *Esprit des lois* nor Mme de Staël's *De l'Allemagne*. Also the principles as they are appear sometimes 'a little hard pressed in order that they might agree with [the author's] feeling'.[90] Yet, he sums up, the *Seven Lamps* are 'rich in refined criticism'.

Rich in refined criticism 'The Nature of Gothic' is too, and one can hardly decide whether to praise highest the diction or the sensitivity to medieval qualities or the recognition of the mutual dependence of these qualities and the status of the craftsman. Indeed it might well be argued that Ruskin's most important step forward from the position of Pugin, i.e. from Good-architecture-is-Catholic-architecture, is his Good-architecture-is-socially-healthy-architecture.

From here and from Ruskin's ever more absorbed criticism of the social system of his own day his attitude to the architecture of the nineteenth century can be guessed. 'It is the vainest of affectations to try and put beauty into shadows, while all the real things that cast them are left in deformity.'[91] Men are 'like fuel to feed the factory smoke', 'their souls withering in them'; 'there is slavery in our England', and division of labour is the wrong name for what is the division of men 'into small fragments'. 'The society [is] . . . made up

---

[84] §2.   [85] L.E., IX, 228.   [86] L.E., IX, 152.
[87] L.E., VIII, 95 ff. For more such passages see e.g. L.E., XX, 213; IX, 183.
[88] E.g., L.E., VIII, 65.   [89] XLI, 1850, 151 ff.
[90] On details of Whewell's criticism, that concerning Ruskin's view of King's College Chapel has already been referred to. He also disapproves of Ruskin's 'unmitigated admiration' of the Italian Gothic, pointing to the fact that 'the best architectural critics'—that means Willis of course—admit its incompleteness.
[91] I regret to confess yet once more that I cannot find this passage in the L.E.

of morbid thinkers, and miserable workers', whereas 'the workman ought often to be thinking, and the thinker often to be working, and both should be gentlemen in the best sense'. All this is from 'The Nature of Gothic[92] and so is Ruskin's answer to the question how, not the producer but we, the consumers, can help: Be determined to 'sacrifice ... such convenience, or beauty, or cheapness as is to be got only by the degradation of the workman' and be determined only to 'demand ... the products and results of healthy and ennobling labour'. That is: '1. Never encourage the manufacture of any article not absolutely necessary, in the production of which *Invention* has no share. 2. Never demand an exact finish for its own sake, but only for some practical or noble end. 3. Never encourage imitation or copying of any kind.'[93]

That Ruskin also, especially in the seventies, tried to help in the reform on the production side is familiar: the foundation of the St George's Guild in 1871,[94] the building of the Hinksey Road in 1874, the efforts to establish wool spinning at Laxey on the Isle of Man in 1876 and linen-weaving in Langdale in 1884. His social criticism could be as furious as his artistic: 'The worship of the Immaculate Virginity of Money ... is the Protestant form of Madonna worship.'[95] England should have 'the hyena instead of the lion upon her shield.'[96]

It was this fury that had initially driven Ruskin into the refuge of a Gothic Age whose buildings he had loved from the start. The social order which he subsequently attributed to the age is, we know now, not a true picture of what the age was really like, but Ruskin did recognize some essential contrasts between then and now. Only there was of course no hope of reforming an industrial society to go back to the crafts. The failure of the Guild left no doubt about that. On the other hand, in imposing an architectural style Ruskin as we have seen, was wholly successful. Due to him more than any other critic or theorist was the unshaken faith of the architects' clients in the continued use of styles of the past. Ruskin must have seen the danger to his position, if an original style of the century were to establish itself. The hysterical tone in which he refuses to consider any such style shows that he felt unsafe. This is what he writes in the Lamp of Obedience: 'A day never passes without our hearing our

92 §§13–16, 21.   93 §§16–17.
94 On the Guild see M. E. Spence, 'The Guild of St George', *Bulletin of the John Rylands Library*, XL, 1957–8.
95 *Val d'Arno*, 1874, quoted from Clark, *Ruskin To-day*, 299.
96 *Modern Painters*, V, 1860, L.E., VII, 425.

English architects called upon to be original, and to invent a new style . . . We want no new style of architecture . . . The forms of architecture already known are good enough for us, and far better than any of us; and it will be time enough to think of changing them for better when we can use them as they are.' Or, as he put it in another way: 'It does not matter one marble splinter whether we have an old or new architecture . . . A man who has the gift, will take up any style that is going, the style of his day and will work in that, and be great in that.'[97]

The latter assertion seems more ambiguous than the former. But Ruskin did not indend it to be read in that way. He had no doubt as to the loathsomeness of the innovations of his day. As a paramount example and one that occurs prominently in the writers before and after Ruskin we can take the architecture of iron and glass. Pugin had called the Crystal Palace the 'glass monster', the Ecclesiologists an example of engineering not architecture,[98] Reichensperger neither grand nor original,[99] Carlyle a soap-bubble.[100] This is what Ruskin said, with a highly characteristic, illogical twist: 'The quality of bodily industry which the Crystal Palace expresses, is very great. So far it is good. The quantity of thought it expresses is, I suppose, a single and admirable thought . . . that it might be possible to build a greenhouse larger than ever greenhouse was built before. This thought and some very ordinary algebra are as much as all that glass can represent of human intellect.'[101] So much of glass. And iron is 'perhaps the most fruitful source . . . of corruption which we have to guard against in modern times'. But the arguments following this statement are curiously involved and uncertain. Iron architecture cannot be architecture, because art has been practised until the early nineteenth century 'for the most part in clay, stone or wood', and because from this 'it has resulted that the sense of proportion and the laws of structure have been based on the employment of these materials'. 'The entire or principal employment of metallic framework would, therefore, be generally felt as a departure from the first principles of the art.' Yet, Ruskin adds, 'the time is probably near when a new system of architectural laws will be developed, adapted entirely to metallic

[97] *Seven Lamps,* L.E., VIII, 252–5.   [98] See p. 133.
[99] See p. 133.   [100] See p. 115, n. 57.
[101] L.E., IX, 450 ff., not III, 450 as I stated in my *High Victorian Design* and again in *Studies in Art, Architecture and Design,* II. Ruskin also wrote a whole pamphlet apropos the re-opening of the Crystal Palace at Sydenham in 1854. *The Opening of the Crystal Palace,* L.E., XII, 417 ff.

construction'.[102] A prophetic statement, but one in total contradiction to all that he was preaching and was to preach. Where for instance, he had an opportunity to see iron structure as in railway stations, his remarks are dictated by hatred not only against the stations but against the railways and 'the very doubtful advantage of the power of going fast from place to place'. 'No one would travel in that manner who could help it'. 'Better bury gold in the embankment, than to put it in ornament on the stations.'[103] And as a later footnote to the first sentence of the *Seven Lamps*, the sentence which defined architecture as 'the art which so disposes and adorns the edifices raised by man . . . that the sight of them may contribute to his mental health, power and pleasure', Ruskin added in 1880: 'This separates architecture from a wasp's nest, a rat hole and a railway station.'

There is much in Ruskin that infuriates, and while Whewell criticized only Ruskin's views of Gothic, others criticized more radically his stand on the possibility of an original architecture of the nineteenth century. The most intelligent of these was Matthew Digby Wyatt, Secretary to the Executive Committee of the 1851 Exhibition. He wrote in the *Journal of Design and Manufactures*,[104] and this is a summary of what he says: He calls the *Seven Lamps* a 'thoughtful and eloquent book', praises it for its 'denunciation of shams' and blames it for not paying 'a humble tribute to the truth and justice' of much that was written by Pugin. But, more important, he blames Ruskin for his 'half-views' on the topical problems of architecture and design: 'Instead of boldly recognizing the tendencies of the age, which are inevitable . . . instead of considering the means of improving these tendencies . . . he either puts up his back against their further development, or would attempt to bring back the world of art to what its course of action was four hundred years ago. 'Our course in this nineteenth century way may be hateful; if you please, denounce it, but as it *is* our course, wise men should recognize the fact.' By not doing that Ruskin, according to Wyatt,

[102] *Seven Lamps*, L.E., VIII, 66. The negative as well as the positive attitude is again remarkably similar to Pugin's (see p. 116). Street, on the other hand, agreed with Ruskin. He wrote of iron building in 1852: 'I do not believe that it is architecture at all.' (*Ecclesiologist*, XIII, 1852, 248). All-out defenders of iron architecture are rare before the fifties. Professor Peter Collins in his *Changing Ideals* has collected some examples (pp. 135 ff.), foremost the dotty William Vose Pickett with his patented *Metallurgic Architecture* of 1844. On him see Collins, *Arch. Rev.*, CXXX, 1961, 267.

[103] L.E., VIII, 264, 159–60.

[104] II, 1849–50, 72.

was bound to neglect any 'consistent theory of mechanical repetition as applied to art' and to arrive at a 'very lop-sided view of railways and railway-architecture'.

These are promising sentences indeed. Not every competent critic then looked at the mid-nineteenth-century with the disgust of Pugin and Ruskin. And we shall now see that Wyatt also recognized the virtues of the Crystal Palace. For the Crystal Palace has so often already been mentioned in passing, that it is time now to deal in more detail with it, with the Great Exhibition held in it, and the men to whose initiative it owed its realization, to Cole, Prince Albert, Wyatt, Owen Jones, Richard Redgrave.

CHAPTER XVI

The Cole Circle

SIR HENRY COLE was born in 1808, Owen Jones in 1809, Richard Redgrave in 1804, Sir Matthew Digby Wyatt in 1820. Cole[1] when still under twenty-five was a sub-commissioner in the Record Office, when thirty a Senior Assistant Keeper. In the same year he became Secretary of the Committee to introduce penny postage. Meanwhile Owen Jones had been a pupil of Lewis Vulliamy, had travelled to Paris and Italy (1830), to Greece, Egypt, and Turkey (1833), and twice to Granada. The outcome was his *Plans, Elevations, Sections and Details of the Alhambra*, published in London in 1842–6. This was followed in 1846 by a book on *The Polychromatic Ornament of Italy*, dealing with the sixteenth century. Ever since then it was decoration that absorbed him, and especially colour in decoration and equally especially decoration by abstract ornament.[2] Matthew Digby Wyatt had been a pupil of his much older brother Thomas Henry and published *Geometrical Mosaics of the Middle Ages* in 1848. Clearly his interests coincided with Jones's. Cole had also gone into the issuing of illustrated books, but his were children's books and also guide-books to Westminster Abbey and Hampton Court. They had begun to appear in 1841 and were called Felix Summerly's *Home Treasury*, Felix Summerly being Cole's pseudonym. A little later he tried his hand at designing. A tea-set won a Society of Arts prize in 1845, and in 1847 Felix Summerly's Art Manufactures was started, producing pieces of pottery, glass, metal, and wood, designed and often decorated with human figures and inscriptions by such accepted artists as John Bell, Daniel Maclise, and Richard Redgrave. Redgrave until then had painted subject pictures and shown them success-fully in the Royal Academy. What joined all four men was interest in design, decoration, and ornament and their improvement. Felix Summerly showed at the Society of Art's exhibitions of 1847, 1848,

---

[1] See *Fifty Years of Public Works of Sir Henry Cole*, 2 vols. (London, 1884).
[2] There is no book on Owen Jones yet—a serious gap in the historiography of Victorian design.

and 1849. 1849 is the year in which the Executive Committee for the Great Exhibition of 1851 was formed. Cole and Wyatt were members. And 1849 is also the year when Cole started the *Journal of Design and Manufactures*. Redgrave was editor. It lasted for only three years, but it did a remarkable job of criticism and propaganda in those years. As one turns over the pages of the first four volumes running from March 1849 to February 1851, one is struck by the freshness of presentation and the courageous criticism. Presentation included the sticking in of actual samples of textiles, criticism some-times is reminiscent of that of the young Cambridge Camden gra-duates ('a pure abomination', 'detestable', 'the workmanship is coarse . . . the design ugly').[3] But the *Journal's* rudeness is rudeness to good purpose, the programme formulated at the very beginning being the 'developing [of] sound principles of ornamental art'.[4] What are these principles? One is that 'ornament is not . . . principal; it must . . . be secondary to the thing decorated'. 'The best age is the simplest,—the decline is marked by the increase of ornament.'[5]

Redgrave in volume four wrote a special paper on 'Canons of Taste',[6] pleading for 'fitness in the ornament to the thing orna-mented' and illustrating this by insisting that a carpet should 'be treated as a flat surface and have none of those imitations of raised forms or architectural ornaments so often seen'. The 'shells and scrolls' of the French *Dix-huitième*, 'the tawdry *bouquets*', and 'land-scapes with palm-trees' are equally objectionable. Wallpaper is the background for furniture and pictures; it should therefore not 'grin and stare', and so on. Flatness of patterns for wallpapers had already been demanded in volumes one and two.[7] All this is straight Pugin (see p. 116), and Pugin is indeed praised for 'the truth and justice of many of his propositions'[8] (Wyatt) but attacked for his 'Gothicky' style as applied 'to articles of modern invention for which [it is] quite unsuitable'.[9] It need hardly be said that the *Journal* is against imitation of the past.[10]

But it also attacks the imitators of nature. In the first number three jugs are praised for their ornament being taken from nature, but 'mere imitation of nature is not ornamental design in its highest sense'.[11] And Redgrave went further. He recommended the use of native plants but in 'the spirit that animated the Greeks', i.e. by

[3] I, 87–8; II, 201; III, 52.   [4] I, 3.   [5] I, 56–7.
[6] IV, 14 ff.   [7] I, 79 ff.; II, 129 ff. and 171 ff.   [8] IV, 75.
[9] III, 88.   [10] II, 17.   [11] I, 16.

treating such motifs from nature with 'original thought'. Only thus can the designer avoid 'tiresome plagiarisms'.[12]

The most seriously considered statements in the *Journal* came from Wyatt—and these have already been presented—and from William Dyce, the Nazarene painter, who was keenly interested in the teaching of design for the benefit of manufacturers and had been superintendent of the Government Schools of Design from 1838 to 1843.[13] He wrote three articles in volume one. Students, he says, should look at ornament 'as ornament, suited to particular uses [and] situations . . . unbiassed by custom [and] by precedent'. Decisions should be guided by common-sense. One criterion is for instance the relation of ornament 'to the process by which a design is to be executed'. If execution is by machine, the designer must be 'perfectly conversant' with the technique.[14] Other papers give equally sound and practical advice. A class for the instruction of buyers would be of great value.[15] A manufacturer sent the *Journal* some 220 new patterns, 'at least two hundred more than there could be any reasonable necessity for at one season'.[16]

Wyatt's articles alone secure for the *Journal* a place of honour in the history with which this book is concerned. We have already[17] seen how brilliantly he criticized Ruskin's *Seven Lamps*, standing for the present as against the past. This is also the conviction of the others writing in the *Journal*: 'Since the period of the Reformation, we believe the prospects of Design . . . have never been so good as at the present time in England', it is stated in the opening address to volume four.[18] Wyatt is the most eloquent of the critical optimists. His two long articles deal with metalwork but go well beyond their limited scope.[19] Right at the start he distinguishes two types of users of iron: the Utilitarians who are 'careful cast-iron constructionists' and 'generally build railway-sheds *ad infinitum* and bridges *ad nauseam*' and the Idealists who

cover dog-kennels with crockets and finials, turn stoves and clocks into cathedral façades . . . and too often sacrifice comfort . . . to ornament and effect . . . No successful results can be obtained in the production of beautiful iron-work or beautiful anything else, until one of these things takes place:—either 1st, until the manufacturer and designer are one individual

[12] I, 149.
[13] Q. Bell, *The Schools of Design* (London, 1963). See also the catalogue of the Dyce Exhibition (Aberdeen and London, 1964).
[14] I, 91 ff.   [15] II, 87. It would still.   [16] IV, 49. This is also just as topical today.
[17] p. 155.   [18] p. 1.   [19] IV, 10 ff. and 74.

doubly gifted; or 2ndly, the manufacturer takes the pains to investigate and master so much of the elements of design as shall at least enable him to judiciously control the artist; or 3rdly, until the artist by a careful study of the material and its manufacture shall elaborate and employ a system of design in harmony with, and special to, the peculiarities so evolved.[20]

At present in iron the greatest works are done by engineers, the lesser by architects, 'but it is difficult to define where engineering ends and architecture begins'. What is only too obvious is that most of what the foundries turn out are 'monstrosities of form in every style of design', and that most architectural ornament made of iron is just as monstrous: 'the graceful honeysuckle of the Erechtheion shrunk into the atrophy of cast-iron' and 'the simply beautiful variations of the lotus ornament expanded into a lamp-post'.[21] But Wyatt has some praise too: Owen Jones's shop for Chappell's in Bond Street leaving 'the engineer's girder alone' and setting the charmingly decorated front back, the cast iron matching the heavy masonry of the Abney Park Cemetery,[22] and more enthusiastically 'those wonders of the world, Telford's Menai and Conway Bridges'[23] and Brunel's Hungerford Bridge 'lacking all meretricious and adventitious ornament'. And from the bridges Wyatt is carried away into prophesying: 'From such beginnings what future glories may be in reserve, when England has systematized a scale of form and proportion, and a vocabulary of its own in which to speak to the world the language of its power, and its future of thought and feeling, we may trust ourselves to dream, but we dare not predict.'[24] The reservation about a system of scale and proportion being still wanting ought to be noted; for like Pugin, Wyatt is worried by the thinness of structural iron members much as he must recommend it as a quality inherent in the use of iron. Iron columns, to separate the nave and aisles of a church, he writes, look inadequate 'to the eye of any person accustomed to the ordinary rules of ancient proportion.'[25]

The end of Wyatt's paper is a bow to the Crystal Palace which will no doubt 'accelerate the "consummation devoutly to be

---

[20] IV, 11.   [21] IV, 14.
[22] IV, 12–14.
[23] IV, 77. Here is the same appreciation coming from a very different quarter. Eduard Devrient the famous actor writing in a letter in July 1850: 'These bold adventures, the English bridges . . . will one day give a good testimonial to our time.' (*Briefwechsel zwischen Eduard und Therese Devrient*, Stuttgart, 1909, 190.)
[24] IV, 78.   [25] IV, 75.

wished"'. 'The novelty of its form and details will be likely to exercise a powerful influence upon national taste.'[26]

For by the time Wyatt wrote this, the Crystal Palace was going up. Illustrations had been inserted in the *Journal*[27] before the second article came out. What happened is familiar enough. Cole had remained the prime mover of the Great Exhibition. He stirred Prince Albert, and only Prince Albert could have made such a resounding success of so unprecedented a venture. Owen Jones became Superintendent of the Works in charge of the decoration of the palace, Wyatt Secretary to the Executive Committee. The Building Committee consisted of Barry, Cockerell and Donaldson, the architects,[28] Brunel and Stephenson, the engineers, and Cubitt the contractor. But six people cannot design a building, as the *Journal* wisely observed. So 'in steps a gentleman, neither engineer, nor architect', i.e. Paxton, 'and wins the prize'.[29]

The Crystal Palace generated violent reactions. We have noted them, although so far more negative than positive ones. But enthusiasm was not lacking. The Queen's diary represents the reactions of the common man accurately; so does *The Times* of 2 May 1851: 'A glittering arch, far more lofty . . . than the vaults of even our loftiest cathedrals.[30] . . . Some were most reminded of that day when all ages and climes shall be gathered round the throne of their MAKER.' Kingsley who as a parson must be regarded as more competent to sort the holy from the profane found his first visit to the Crystal Palace like 'going into a sacred place',[31] and Tennyson rhymed in raptures:

> A rare pavilion such as man
> Saw never since mankind began.

However, at present we are not yet concerned with the building but with the exhibits.[32] There the only passage of acclaim worth quoting here comes from an unexpected quarter, from Whewell who in a lecture given later in 1851 to the Society of Arts on the Great

---

[26] IV, 78. Wyatt also wrote factually 'On the Construction of the Building for the Exhibition' in the Official Catalogue and in *Proc. Inst. Civ. Eng.*, X, 1851.

[27] IV, 50–3.   [28] On the latter two see pp. 77–82.   [29] III, 190.

[30] A correspondent wrote shrewdly to *The Ecclesiologist* (XII, 1851, 271 ff.) that the vaulted part of the building, i.e. the transept, showed 'natural grandeur', but the unvaulted nave appeared 'dismally flat'.

[31] Charles Kingsley: *Letters and Memoirs*, 1877, I, 280–1.

[32] I have given a survey of them in *High Victorian Design* (London, 1951), reprinted in *Studies in Art, Architecture and Design* (London, 1968) II, 38 ff.

Exhibition[33] said this: 'What is it that we have seen? We saw all nations, but also all stages in the lives of nations'. The result is that 'man is by nature an artificer, an artisan, an artist . . . In savages how much practical knowledge [and] manual dexterity! In more developed countries [such as Persia, and India] . . . how much which we must admire, which we might envy, which, indeed, might drive us to despair.' But, Whewell continued, we have after all advanced beyond them. For in those countries the arts served only 'to gratify the tastes of the few', now 'we have machinery to produce in quantity'. Art now by means of the machine 'works for the poor no less' than for the rich. The manufacturer gives 'comfort and enjoyment to the public, whose servant he is'. Oh, naive scientist! The very makers of the exhibition saw deeper, because they could judge of aesthetic quality not as the scientist just of quantity.

Cole and his friends were disappointed, and, although it was their exhibition, they made no bones about it. The *Journal* itself led the chorus of critics with an article 'Gleanings from the Exhibition' by Owen Jones.[34] Christian architecture he says, received the death-blow at the Reformation. Attempts to revive the Gothic style have 'signally failed'; so have attempts at a revived Elizabethan, and the Italian revival 'must ultimately go with the rest . . . The universal thirst which now exists for an architecture in harmony with our institutions and modes of thought, must ultimately be satisfied.' If the ancients had had our materials and 'facilities of construction', our institutions and 'control of industrial processes', their architecture would have been very different. But the exhibition shows little of that. 'Novelty without beauty—beauty without intelligence, all work without faith'—that sums it up. Owen Jones then proceeds to lay down a few basic rules, the rules he was to elaborate five years later in his *Grammar of Ornament*. The most sweeping condemnation in the *Journal* appeared apropos an article in *The Times*. The *Journal* quoted from it: 'the absence of any fixed principles in ornamental design' and 'the negation of utility as paramount to ornament . . . The very best things at the exhibition are the least ornamented'.[35]

Richard Redgrave who edited the *Journal* and became Super-intendent of the Schools of Design in 1851 wrote a report on design at the exhibition, and this was published as one of the *Reports by the Juries* in 1852. This is what he says: Ornament is decoration of a

---

[33] *The General Bearing of the Great Exhibition on the Progress of Art and Science* (London, 1852).
[34] V, 89 ff.   [35] V, 1851, 158 ff.

thing constructed. Use must be primary, ornament secondary. The 'leading error' of the exhibition has been the tendency to 'reverse this rule'. 'Objects of absolute utility . . . where use is so paramount that ornament is repudiated' were the best in the exhibition. 'Those styles which are considered the purest . . . are those wherein constructive utility has been . . . most thoroughly attended to.' Thus High Gothic is better than Late Gothic, Tudor is 'debased from the Renaissance'. Equally degraded is Louis XIV. But it was the 'florid and gorgeous tinsel' of such late styles which prevailed in three fourths of the exhibition.

Two types of ornamental artist were represented, those who worship the past and those who go 'to the abundant sources of nature'. Both are wrong. The past ought to be studied for its principles not for imitation of its forms, and direct use of natural forms—carpets with 'water-lilies floating on their natural bed' or glass anemones and 'metal imitations of plants and flowers' are 'opposed to just principles'.[36] When such imitative designs are executed by machines they are doubly degraded.

Redgrave then reviews industry after industry. Wyatt is praised twice—for book-bindings and tiles. Other good tiles were designed by Pugin and Gruner. Pugin's Mediaeval Court is singled out for high praise too—'just principles . . . beautiful details . . . correct use of materials . . . excellent workmanship'.[37] The assertion which runs through the whole report is: 'There can be no doubt that half the ornament in the Great Exhibition . . . is in excess.'[38]

Redgrave became Inspector General for Art in 1857, Cole Secretary of the Department of Practical Art jointly with Playfair in 1852, solely in 1858. He received the Légion d'honneur in 1855, as did Redgrave, and Wyatt (for the British section of the Paris Exhibition of that year). Wyatt also received the Gold Medal of the Royal Institute of British Architects in 1865, having been Honorary Secretary of the Institute from 1855 to 1859. Owen Jones got the Gold Medal in 1857.[39]

In 1856 Jones's *Grammar of Ornament* had been published, a lavish folio of colour plates and a book still being printed in 1910.[40] Its Preface sets out briefly the scope of the book. It is to propose 'certain general rules'. The plates are not for copying; for no style

---

[36] *Reports by the Juries*, 708 ff.   [37] Ibid., 718.   [38] Ibid., 727.
[39] Cole incidentally never did, for reasons alluded to by Kerr in the paper reprinted on p. 291.
[40] Page numbers are quoted from that edition.

can be 'transplanted'. Instead students should 'search out the thoughts' behind the styles and apply them to the situation today. This calls for a 'return to nature' but again only in order to treat her as past styles have treated her. So after the preface, Owen Jones puts down at once thirty-seven Propositions. Here are a few of the most generally important ones:

I. The decorative Arts . . . should properly be attendant upon Architecture.
II. Architecture is the material expression of the wants, the faculties, and the sentiments, of the age in which it is erected. Architecture is the peculiar form that expression takes under the influence of climate and materials at command.
III. As Architecture, so all works of the Decorative Arts, should possess fitness, proportion, harmony, the result of all which is repose.
V. Construction should be decorated. Decoration should never be purposely constructed. That which is beautiful is true, that which is true must be beautiful.
XIII. Flowers or other natural objects should not be used as ornaments; but conventional representations founded upon them sufficiently suggestive to convey the intended image to the mind, without destroying the unity of the object they are employed to decorate.

The attitude is entirely that of Cole, Redgrave, and Wyatt. Wyatt in fact contributed two sections. Other propositions of Owen Jones deal with proportion and—altogether twenty-one—with colour. The last propositions are:

XXXV. Imitations, such as the graining of woods, and of the curious coloured marbles [are] allowable only when the employment of the thing imitated would not have been inconsistent.
XXXVI. The principles discernible in the works of the past belong to us; not so the results. It is taking the end for the means.
XXXVII. No improvement can take place in the Art of this present generation, until all classes, Artists, Manufacturers, and the Public, are better educated in Art, and the existence of general principles is more fully recognized.

The 111 colour-lithographed plates which follow start from the 'Savage Tribes' and go via Egypt, Assyria and so on to Greece and Rome and finally the eighteenth century. But the very last part is called 'Leaves and Flowers from Nature'. Two things are remarkable about Owen Jones's advice. Its catholicity and its emphasis on the East. Owen Jones was no partisan of any particular style of the past, certainly no Gothicist, but not an Italist either. His choice is truly eclectic. But if there is one preference, it is for Moorish—he calls it Moresque—Arabian, Turkish, Persian, and Indian; he pleads not for the architecture of these people but purely for the soundness of their way of treating ornament conventionally and not naturalistically. Nearly one-third of all his plates belong to the Near and Middle East. And the introductory texts to the chapters confirm what his choice indicates.

The system of decoration of the Alhambra is as great as that of the Parthenon. 'Every principle which one can derive from the study of the ornamental art of any other people is . . . ever present here.'[41] 'The mosques of Cairo are amongst the most beautiful buildings in the world',[42] and again he does not treat them as architecture at all. At the Exhibition the works of 'India and other Mohammedan countries', 'amid the general disorder, everywhere apparent in the application of Art to manufactures', amazed everyone by 'the presence of so much unity of design, so much skill and judgment in its application, with so much elegance and refinement in the execution'. It proved in total contrast to the Europeans' 'fruitless struggle for novelty, irrespective of fitness'.[43] Owen Jones recognizes that the fitness of the decoration of the East is that of the European thirteenth century too. So his Gothic is Pugin's and Ruskin's and that of the Ecclesiologists and, as will soon be shown, of Scott. 'Early English ornament is the most perfect', because (take the stiff-leaf motif) it conventionalizes nature. As soon as in the fourteenth century imitation of nature becomes the aim, the decline sets in. 'The more natural [the leaves] were made, the less artistic became the arrangement.'[44]

Wyatt's contributions to *The Grammar* are the long introductions to Renaissance Ornament and Italian Ornament. He praises, and Owen Jones had no objection, but he also warns the reader to 'eschew the extravagancies of the Renaissance style'. He illustrates Quattrocento and Cinquecento, calls Michelangelo too much concerned with novelty and Giulio Romano 'too egotistic'—and goes on without further discrimination to Lepautre and Berain. For his own day Wyatt—one can see that in his own architecture such as that of Paddington Station or the Courtyard of the India Office—preferred the Renaissance, a free Cinquecento, to all else, as Owen Jones preferred the Alhambra. 'Those styles', he writes, 'are noblest

[41] *The Grammar of Ornament*, 66.   [42] Ibid., 57.   [43] Ibid., 77.
[44] Ibid., 100-2. Street had said the same in 1852, see pp. 135-6.

richest and best adapted to the complicated requirements of a highly artificial social system, in which, as in the Renaissance, Architecture, Painting, Sculpture, and the highest technical excellence in Industry' are united.[45]

So that is Wyatt's answer to the nineteenth-century situation. Owen Jones's is different. In his last chapter he first re-iterates:

In the best periods of art ornament was rather based upon an observation of the principles which regulate the arrangement of forms in nature than on an attempt to imitate the absolute forms of these works ... In the present uncertain state ... there seems a general disposition ... to reproduce as faithfully as may be possible, natural forms as works of ornament ... We have ... in the floral carpets, floral papers, and floral carvings of the present day, sufficient evidence to show that no art can be produced by such means.

What then can we do? 'How is any new style ... to be invented or developed?' Owen Jones's final answer is to tell students that they will find new forms of beauty, if they are 'fully impressed with the law of the universal fitness of things in nature' and at the same time 'the wonderful variety of forms ... all arranged around some few fixed laws'.

This is straight William Morris, and he of course must have known *The Grammar of Ornament* like anybody else interested in design. The last chapter he must have read with particular care. For it is there that he could see how leaves and flowers can be made to look flat and become elements of true textile composition without losing their truth to nature. The plates in which *The Grammar* is particularly successful in that respect are Plate I, the chestnut leaves by Owen Jones [Pl. 45], and Plate VIII, the 'Plan and Elevation' of flowers contributed by Dr. Christopher Dresser.[46]

Owen Jones's influence on William Morris was belated, but in the event Morris made infinitely more of Owen Jones's theses than Jones had himself. Neither Jones nor anyone else of the Cole circle succeeded in purging taste. Their own tastes were too unsure; they were organizers in the first place—Cole of the South Kensington, now Victoria and Albert, Museum, and of art and design education. He was knighted in 1875, Wyatt in 1877.

But in our context here, i.e. as writers on architecture and design, their position is central. Without Cole there would have been no

[45] *The Grammar of Ornament*, 127, also 137 and 145.

[46] On Dresser see my paper in *The Architectural Review* LXXXI, 1937, and more recently Shirley Bury in *Apollo*, N.S. LXXVI, 1962, 766.

Great Exhibition and no Crystal Palace, and this event and this building are central in the nineteenth century not only by mere chronology—fifty years before, forty-nine after—but also by what they stood for. Reactions to the exhibits in the Great Exhibition are the touchstone of right or wrong in the principles of design, reactions to the Crystal Palace the touchstone of backward or forward looking.

But what was backward, what forward in the fifties? The answer is not simple. The case of Sir George Gilbert Scott demonstrates how complex it is.

CHAPTER XVII

Sir George Gilbert Scott

SIR GEORGE GILBERT SCOTT[1] was born in 1811, the son of a clergyman. He was articled to James Edmeston, architect of office buildings in the City and a man whose views on the style needed for the nineteenth century will be referred to later. In Edmeston's office he met W. B. Moffatt with whom he later went into partnership. But before that he gathered experience with Grissell & Peto, the big builders, Henry Roberts who later became the architect most interested in housing the working population, and Sampson Kempthorne who specialized in workhouses. Scott & Moffatt shrewdly took up the same speciality. In 1838 Scott designed his first church, a building he was not to be proud of. But in 1840 followed the Martyrs' Memorial (for which he 'obtained every drawing of old crosses [he] could lay hand on'[2]) and then immediately the Martyrs' Aisle of St Mary Magdalene at Oxford [Pl. 46], and these two are examples of Middle Pointed as archaeologically accurate as anything of the same date by Pugin. So, in spite of the fact that Scott later generously wrote: 'I was awakened from my slumber by the thunder of Pugin's writings' and 'I was from that moment a new man', and in spite of the fact that he called Pugin 'for all future ages the great reformer of architecture' and 'my guardian angel',[3] dates make it improbable that Scott's rise to this maturity of style should have been the result of inspiration from Pugin.[4]

[1] On Scott apart from his own *Recollections* (see below) there is an article by D. Cole in *Victorian Architecture,* ed. P. Ferriday (London, 1963). An elementary chart of Scott's work by H. V. Molesworth-Roberts appeared in *J.R.I.B.A.,* LXV, 1958, 207. See also the excellent article on the Albert Memorial by P. Ferriday, *Arch. Rev.,* CXXXV, 1964 and, as intimately connected with the subject matter of this chapter, P. Ferriday, 'The Revival: Stories Ancient and Modern,' *Arch. Rev.,* CXXI, 1957, 155 and P. Ferriday, 'The Church Restorers', *Arch. Rev.,* CXXXCI, 1964, 86.

[2] *Personal and Professional Recollections* (London, 1879), edited by G. G. Scott, jun., 89.

[3] Ibid., 241, 373. Scott met Pugin personally in 1852.

[4] Indeed the conversion to the Second or Middle Pointed was very rapid. Here are some more of the earliest dates. Theale (see p. 113) had been a special case; and so is Littlemore of 1835 (see p. 134) which *The Ecclesiologist* called 'the first unqualified step to better things that England had long witnessed' (IV, 1845, 33). Benjamin Ferrey (1810–80) who had been a fellow pupil with Pugin in Pugin Sen.'s office, built Compton Valence in Dorset in the Second Pointed in 1839–40,

Scott was also impressed by the Cambridge Camden Society[5] and became a reader of *The Ecclesiologist*, but he was not Anglo-Catholic —in views and style he may be called *juste milieu*[6]—and the Society, though praising some of his work, never forgave him the sin of winning the competition for the Lutheran St Nicholas in Hamburg. That was in 1844, and from then onward a steady stream of commissions for churches went through his growing office. Among the largest and most ambitious one might name the splendid Perpendicular parish church at Doncaster (1854–8) [Pls. 47, 48], the Middle Pointed St Giles Camberwell (1841–3) [Pl. 39] called 'a pretty church' by Ruskin,[7] and St Mary Abbots in Kensington (1869–71). These and many other Scott churches are handled extremely competently and with great self-confidence. Already in 1846 Petit wrote of the Camberwell church 'A work which may well bear comparison with any older building of its scale',[8] in 1848 Poole called Scott 'the greatest master of Gothic architecture in the present day',[9] and in 1849 Freeman called St Nicholas at Hamburg 'the noblest work, that these ages have produced'.[10]

Parallel with the stream of new buildings ran the torrent of restorations. The first cathedral was Ely, where he started in 1847. Two years later he became Surveyor to Westminster Abbey. Restoring, we have seen, posed a problem. The Cambridge Camden Society in 1847 and Ruskin in 1849 had pronounced, the one in favour of an eclectic course, the other radically against any restoration. Scott had laid down some principles briefly already in 1841 and 1843, and more fully in a book in 1850. The statement of 1841 was made in correspondence with Petit apropos his very first restoration, that of Stafford parish church, and it seemed important enough to Scott for him to reprint it in his *Recollections*.[11] It therefore deserves to be quoted here in full. Scott found the church full of galleries, with the pulpit near the west end. The nave was (and is)

Derick's St Saviour, Leeds, built at the expense of Dr. Pusey, was begun in 1842 (see G. G. Pace, *Arch. Rev.*, XCVIII, 1945, 178 ff.). Bellamy's St Anne, Highgate West Hill was proposed in 1841 (*Eccl.*, I, 19), though built only in 1852–3. The now demolished Christ Church Victoria Street by Ambrose Poynter dated from 1841–3 and Ferrey's well-known St Stephen, Rochester Row, Westminster dates from 1845–7.

5 'To whom the honour of our recovery from the odious bathos is mainly due'. *Recollections*, 86.
6 He called himself 'of the multitude'. Ibid., 112.
8 *Remarks on Architectural Character* (Oxford, 1846), 15.   7 L.E., XXXV, 382.
9 *A History of Ecclesiastical Architecture in England*, 1848, 326.
10 *A History of Architecture*, 1849, 452.
11 pp. 97 ff., 400 ff. The Correspondence with Petit was first printed in J. Masfen, jun., *Views of the Church of St Mary at Stafford* (London, 1852), 15 ff.

early Early English with a Perpendicular clerestory and roof, the chancel and transepts Early English too, but largely of a later phase, and with the upper parts of chancel and south transept of shortly after 1593. These parts 'wilfully mutilated in an age of degenerate taste', as Scott calls it, he wanted to restore on quite considerable evidence to the pristine Early English likeness. Petit objected: an architect 'ought to hesitate long, before he pronounces to be vile and worthless the works of those who lived [in an age] on the decline'. But Petit's practical suggestion then is to give these upper parts 'a Perpendicular appearance . . . clearing it of undoubted faults and imperfections'. This vague suggestion makes it easy for Scott to reply. Yet his replies are no more satisfactory. He wishes it to appear that this is a controversy 'between two conservatives', that Petit's is the right principle, and that his own arguments are 'for the exception, not against the rule'. That is typical Scott, as we shall see presently. Meanwhile, this is his summing up:

I do not wish to lay it down as a general rule that good taste requires that every alteration which from age to age has been made in our churches should be obliterated, and the whole reduced to its ancient uniformity of style. These varieties are indeed most valuable, as being the standing history of the edifice, from which the date of every alteration and repair may be read as clearly as if it had been verbally recorded; and in many cases the later additions are as valuable specimens of architecture as the remains of the original structure, and merit an equally careful preservation. I even think that if our churches were to be viewed like the ruins of Greece and Rome, only as original monuments from which ancient architecture is to be studied they would be more valuable in their present condition, however mutilated and decayed, than with any, even the slightest degree of restoration. But taking the more correct view of a church as a building erected for the glory of God and the use of Man (and which must therefore be kept in a proper state of repair), and finding it in such a state of dilapidation that the earlier and later parts—the authentic and the spurious—are alike decayed and all require renovation to render the edifice suitable to its purposes, I think we are then at liberty to exercise our best judgment upon the subject, and if the original parts are found to be 'precious' and the late insertions to be 'vile' I think we should be quite right in giving perpetuity to the one, and in removing the other.

It need hardly be pointed out that this is a statement full of ambiguities[12], and one turns with premature relief to the Statement of

[12] In the end, on Scott's suggestion, the case was submitted to the Oxford Architectural Society and the Cambridge Camden Society, and Scott won.

1843 which is a memorandum on the restoration needs of the church at Boston in Lincolnshire: 'There is no object on which an architect can be called upon to give an opinion which involves at once such deep interest and such serious responsibility as the restoration of an ancient church.' He then specifies: 'The object of every repair should be the faithful restoration of those features of the original building which yet remain, and their preservation from further injury . . ., and no alteration should be attempted which is not the renewal of some ancient feature which has been lost, or absolutely necessary for rendering the building suitable to the present wants of the parishioners; and this should be done in strict conformity with the character and intention of the building.'[13] However, the result in the event included a brand-new east window copied by Scott from Carlisle Cathedral.

So we are warned, when we turn to Scott's book of 1850 which is characteristically called *A Plea for the Faithful Restoration of our Ancient Churches*. Coming in 1850, it was clearly meant as a sensible, trustworthy man's answer to Ruskin, though the major part of it is a lecture Scott had given in 1848.[14] The book, Scott writes, is intended to hold up 'the torrent of destructiveness'[15] caused by unscrupulous restoration. 'It is a most lamentable fact, that there has been far more done to obliterate genuine examples of pointed architecture by the tampering caprices of well-meant restoration than . . . by centuries of mutilation and neglect.'[16] Once restoration has started, 'little by little, the conservative principle is departed from till the whole character and identity of the building is changed[17] and it has lost 'all its truthfulness.'[18] But what is the conservative principle whose 'champion' Scott calls himself? It is this: 'As a general rule, it is highly desirable to preserve those vestiges of the growth and history of the building which are indicated by the various styles and irregularities of its parts . . . Some vestige at least of the oldest portions should always be preserved.' On the other hand the removal of some later parts 'in some instances . . . may be desirable . . . particularly when the later portions are decayed, and the earlier may be restored with absolute certainty'. But as a rule 'an authentic feature, though late and poor, is more worthy than an earlier though

---

13 Pishey R. Thompson, *The History and Antiquities of Boston,* 1856, 167.
14 Scott expresses admiration for Ruskin (p. 8), but in an added note explicitly sets out in what way he differs from Ruskin (p. 120).
15 *A Plea for the Faithful Restoration of our Ancient Churches,* 2.
16 Ibid., 20.   17 Ibid., 6.   18 Ibid., 21.

finer part conjecturally restored,'[19] and this seems even meant to apply to 'reminiscences of the age of Elizabeth, of James or of the martyred Charles'.[20]

All this is not very precise, and when Scott assures us that, 'if he sees it expedient to restore an early form at the cost of removing a later one . . . [he] does so with pain',[21] we wonder what he felt when he gave Oxford Cathedral its completely new rose window in the style of the late twelfth century [Pls. 49, 50] and replaced at Nantwich in Cheshire the Decorated west doorway and the Perpendicular west window by a doorway and a window in Second Pointed.[22] At Cholmondeley, to stay in Cheshire, he proposed to pull down the mid-seventeenth-century chapel and rebuild it in harmony with the medieval chancel.[23] And there are more ominous remarks. 'An original detail . . . though partially decayed or mutilated, is infinitely more valuable than the most skilful attempt at its restoration.' Yes—and 'the true object of restoration' includes 'to replace features which have been actually destroyed by modern mutilation where they can be indisputably traced'. Yes—but where there is no clue for the replacement, 'let hints be searched for from churches of corresponding age in the same neighbourhood'.[24] This procedure Scott includes among what he calls 'raising the architectural character',[25] and he pleads that when the restorer has to follow the methods called by Freeman 'destructive' and 'eclectic' he should do so with 'warmth and feeling'.[26] And so, after all his assurances he approves of the destruction of the Norman north-west tower of Canterbury Cathedral to replace it by one matching the Gothic south-west tower;[27] for it would be intolerable 'that the metropolitan church of England should have an irregular, imperfect front' (with due 'lament' of the 'loss of the venerable Norman tower',[28]) and he equally approves of the replacement of the 'incipiently flamboyant' parts of the north-west tower of Cologne Cathedral by one in

[19] *A Plea for the Faithful Restoration of our Ancient Churches*, 29, 31.
[20] Ibid., 35.   [21] Ibid., 28.
[22] See *Journal of the Architectural, Archaeological and Historic Society for the County . . . of Chester* I, 1849–54 for Scott's report.
[23] *Journ. Chester & N.W. Archit., Archaeol. & Hist. Soc.*, XLIII, 1956, 45.
[24] *A Plea for the Faithful Restoration*, 126 and 31. Chester Cathedral affords the best insight into Scott's method. Much here was the result of careful study of original traces, but time and again hypothesis creeps in. See especially the strange east chapel of the south chancel aisle. Scott's report is reprinted in G. Ormerod: *The History of the County Palatine and City of Chester*, 2nd edn., 1882, I, 261–5.
[25] Ibid., 35.   [26] Ibid., 28.
[27] Ibid. This was done by George Austin in 1834–44.   [28] Ibid., 123.

harmony with the original plan which had been found in 1814.[29] So, on paper here and in practice throughout his life, Scott departed lustily from his egregious principles. Yet he may be over-blamed for this today. For one thing, people liked what the restorers did. Nathaniel Hawthorne[30] for example praised the 'great zeal' in England 'for the preservation and reverential re-edification' of churches, a zeal prizing 'the antique idea more than the ancient material' and resulting in old churches 'lovingly rebuilt'. And secondly many churches, even some of the grandest, were indeed in a desperate state when Scott appeared on the scene. In the chapter house of Westminster Abbey archive material was stored, with iron stairs and balconies,[31] and at St Albans a carriageway or cart-track actually went through the east chapels. Besides, it should never be forgotten that Scott was a scholar who knew his styles and his details.

But the book of 1850 is not on restoration exclusively; it also takes sides in the controversy over the possibility and desirability of an original style for the nineteenth century. Here again Ruskin's No had appeared in 1849. Scott sides with Ruskin, but again in a more accommodating way. He tells of a conversation he had in Germany with the Chevalier Bunsen, i.e. Baron Bunsen whom we already know (see pp. 66-7). Bunsen had called it inconsistent to endeavour to revive an old style, 'while every age but the present has had, in some degree at least, a style of its own'. Scott's answer was that, since 'the indigenous architecture of Christian Europe had fallen into decay', we have had three hundred years of 'mistaken paths'. So now we are without a style of our own, and the natural thing must be to 'find the point on the old path from which we have deviated'.[32] The deviation incidentally Scott resolutely blames on Rome and the Papacy; for despite his respect for Pugin, he is very outspokenly anti-Catholic. During the purest ages of Christianity no particularly Christian architecture was achieved because of the oppression of the church. This is why a style was used which had originated under Paganism.[33] So much to dispose of the defendants of the *Rundbogenstil*. But Christian architecture might have reached a climax earlier than it did, if it had not been 'weighed down by the

[29] Ibid., 123-4.
[30] *The English Notebooks*, ed. R. Stewart (New York and London, 1941) 568.
[31] Beresford Hope in a lecture of 1857 quoted in *The English Cathedral of the Nineteenth Century* 1861, 265 mentions the 'frightful presses'.
[32] *A Plea for the Faithful Restoration*, 76.   [33] Ibid., 14-15.

heresies and corruptions which invaded it',[34] and if the Romanists claim that the Gothic style arose 'at the eve of the most absolute sway' of the Papacy, Scott answers: 'rather in spite of, than as a consequence of that usurped domination' and 'not in the country of the usurpation', but among 'the nations who suffered from the usurpation'. In Rome on the contrary later on 'a Pagan standard' was set up,[35] and this Pagan style to Scott is a 'vacuum'. So back from the vacuum to Northern Gothic architecture we must move. That is all we can do. It would be 'hopeless for us to attempt to supply the vacuum by deliberate invention'. We must go to the very place where the ascent ended and the descent began. 'We should endeavour to profit by experience and to continue to advance on the ascent.' And where is that place? Not within the Romanesque, for that 'developed out of materials not exclusively Christian';[36] not within the Perpendicular, for that shows 'a want of religious feeling' and 'contained some essential principle of corruption';[37] nor even within the Decorated, i.e. the style of flowing tracery, for 'do we feel that elegance and luxurious beauty are the elements most needed for the architecture of a Christian temple?'[38] No—it must be the Middle Pointed. Scott joins forces with the Ecclesiologists and Ruskin. It is 'the highest development yet attained'[39] and also incidentally (as Willis had pointed out) the only one 'coincident in France, Germany and England' which is proof 'of its being the culminating point'.[40]

That leaves only one question unanswered: How should one set out to re-instate the Middle Pointed? First, after 'an interval of humble servility,[41] i.e. an apprenticeship in Middle Pointed, we can start with a perfect knowledge and appreciation of pointed architecture to achieve the 'adaptation of the pointed arch to the altered requirements of our own day'. This adaptation must involve the addition of 'such other and new features as are necessary to render it a genuine and living architecture'. And Scott goes surprisingly far in what he is ready to accept as new features. All he demands is that one should take the Middle Pointed 'as our nucleus of good work'. Once that is done he does not object to 'the engrafting on it of all the essential beauties of the earlier and later periods . . . and the fusing of the whole into a style essentially *one*, yet capable of greater variety

[34] *A Plea for the Faithful Restoration*, 14.   [35] Ibid., 40–3.
[36] Ibid., 79.   [37] Ibid., 93–4.
[38] Ibid., 97.   [39] Ibid., 72.
[40] Ibid., 89–90.   [41] Ibid., 110.

of expression than can be commanded . . . by any one development yet attained'.[42]

This is manifest eclecticism, and as eclecticism is an important quality of Victorian architecture—*the* most important one, the late Carroll Meeks argued[43]—and as moreover it is an ambiguous one, a little more must be said about it. We have already in the preceding chapters come across two different types of eclectics, both in opposition to the one-stylers such as Pugin and Ruskin on the Gothic side and Hübsch on the *Rundbogen* side.[44] We shall also very soon be able to add to these Alexander Thomson as a Grecian one-styler (see p. 183). The two types of eclectics are those who simply argue that 'there is no style which has not its peculiar beauties' (Donaldson 1842; see p. 83), and those who recommend the accumulation of stylistically discrepant motifs in one and the same building. Petit (1841) was one of the former praising St Paul's and even the Madeleine, Bartholomew another (1839), though Bartholomew saw the development in terms of three high-points: Greek, Gothic, and Wren. This catholic attitude was mirrored in for example the courts of the Crystal Palace at Sydenham. There were Egyptian, Greek, Roman, Assyrian, Alhambra, Byzantine and Romanesque, three Medieval, Renaissance, Elizabethan, and Italian Courts, all there to be studied and enjoyed. In fact this brand of eclecticism is simply one aspect of the general Historicism of the Victorian age. On the other hand Hope, as we have also seen, had suggested composing a new architecture by borrowing the best of every past style and adding to this amalgam whatever modern convenience demanded and new discoveries permitted (see p. 75).

Now Scott, for so vociferous a Gothicist, in the passage which caused this *excursus* on eclecticism comes very near Hope. After all he wants the Middle Pointed only as his nucleus and to graft on it earlier and later elements. What elements he was thinking of becomes clear only in his next book, the *Remarks on Secular and Domestic Architecture, Present and Future* which came out in 1858 and was dedicated to Beresford Hope. There he is willing to accept from the Italian Gothic the regularity of fenestration, the emphasis on the *cornicione*, structural polychromy, and the use of terracotta and of mosaic.[45] However, he ends his appendix on the Italian Gothic

---

[42] Ibid., 113–16.   [43] *The Railroad Station* (Yale Univ. Press, 1956).
[44] And Freeman pleading for medieval architecture in general. He liked, it will be remembered, Perpendicular best but was ready to allow even Norman.
[45] *Remarks*, 195 ff., 280 ff.

with a warning carefully to avoid 'the unbridled eclecticism of the day which leads every traveller to run wild after what he happens to have seen last'.[46] For—in spite of this tolerance in detail—the sole purpose of the *Remarks* was to prove that the Gothic style is not only a style for religious buildings but also eminently suited for public buildings and private houses. Why, he asks, that association of Gothic with religion? It amounts to limiting religious feeling to 'Sundays, and even then to the hours of service' and to suggesting 'a pagan style more befitting . . . private houses'.[47] But even apart from that, Gothic is also from the practical point of view the most suitable style. No other 'has so directly devised its characteristics from utility',[48] and it is 'pre-eminently free, comprehensive, and . . . ready to adjust itself to every change in the habits of society' without involving 'additional expense'.[49] A comparion between, say, Gower Street whose flatness Scott calls 'utterly intolerable'[50] and Scott's own houses of 1854 in Broad Sanctuary [Pl. 51] with their variety of fenestration, their gables and bay windows demonstrates what he wanted and why he wanted it. As he says in the book: 'The individualizing of the houses . . . giving . . . to each its own front marked out from those of its neighbours' is a most valuable element in street architecture.[51] That Broad Sanctuary is Middle Pointed, goes without saying; for, as eight years before, 'the best period of our national architecture was the latter half of the thirteenth and the beginning of the fourteenth centuries'.[52]

But in spite of this and of Broad Sanctuary he writes with great emphasis: 'I am no mediaevalist; I do not advocate the styles of the middle ages as such. If we had a distinctive architecture of our own day worthy of the greatness of our age, I should be content to follow it; but we have not'[53] and 'no age has ever deliberately

[46] *Remarks*, 290. The appendix was no doubt caused immediately by Street's *Brick and Marble Architecture in North Italy* which had been published in 1855. Street incidentally says there: 'The greatest danger to the progress of the true art [is] the eclectic spirit which the Italians never escaped from, and which, in our own day, leads men to design work in the style which they . . . fancy for the moment, and not in that which is the truest result of previous experience.' The *Building News* in 1858 (IV, 617) took a more positive view of eclecticism: 'Englishmen are the most eclectic of the human race . . . In their architecture . . . they receive elements from foreign sources . . . and, by purifying them from those constituents which are vicious and incongruous, fuse them into a homogeneous compact and national compound, as enduring, as distinct, and as capable of giving out clear fresh harmonies as bronze.' Scott must have been pleased when he read this.

[47] *Remarks*, 226.   [48] Ibid., 20.   [49] Ibid., vi–vii.
[50] Ibid., 171; on p. 174 the words used are 'abject insipidity'. For views on Gower Street see also p. 146 above.
[51] Ibid., 174.   [52] Ibid., 17.   [53] Ibid., 191.

invented a new style'; it is in fact 'morally impossible' to do.[54] And why is it impossible? Scott emerges again on the side of a broad eclecticism, but now with a much better stocked arsenal of arguments. In fact for his own time the arguments were incontrovertible. They deserve a long quotation.

In all periods of genuine art no one thought much of the past,—each devoted his energies wholly to the present. Their efforts were consequently *concentrated,* and none of their thoughts dissipated or diverted from the one object before them; and to this we mainly owe the perfection which each phase of art in its turn attained.

Facts, however, are stubborn things—and as we cannot, if we would, alter the conditions under which we have to work, let us (not—as I was going to say—submit to them, but) compel them to submit to us, and make them subservient to our own work . . .

It would be absurd to imagine that our knowledge of the whole history of art will be without its influence upon that which we ourselves generate,—it is impossible that it should be so. Influence it must exert,—it is for us to guide that influence by subjecting it to our intellect . . .

The first natural effect of working with this vivid *panorama* of the past placed constantly in our view, is to induce a capricious electicism—building now in this style, now in that—content to pluck the flowers of history without cultivating any of our own.[55] This is not, however, the part of wisdom. We have to lay down a plan for the future—to choose a distinct course and to follow it with determination, and, having fixed on the line we will take, to develope and enrich it with our utmost energy.[56]

The contrast between writing and performing is the same as in 1850, but it now becomes much more poignant by the story of the Government Offices, now the Foreign Office [Pl. 52]. The story has been told by Scott himself in great detail and more than once since. But as the paramount story of the conflict between styles and between convictions on style in one man, it must here be told again, and in Scott's own words.

---

[54] Ibid., 204.
[55] In a footnote Scott calls this 'manifestly vicious' and on another page (166) a 'sickly liberalism'.
[56] Ibid., 264–5. One such enrichment within the Middle Pointed is the use of polished granite for piers and columns which Scott recommends (*Remarks,* 97, 199), another the use of a wider variety of naturalistic foliage for capitals etc. than the thirteenth century had used (*Remarks,* 197, *Recollections,* 205). Miss Priscilla Metcalf, for her yet unpublished thesis on James Knowles has recently collected eight features on naturalistic foliage from the architectural journals of the one year 1858. As regards polished granite columns, Jacob Burckhardt in a letter of 4 Aug. 1879 wrote that nineteen years ago he had noticed them only in a few London Clubs (*Briefe an einen Architekten, 1870–89* (Munich, 1913), 89).

A competitition was held, but 'the judges, who knew amazingly little about their subject, were not well-disposed towards our style, and though they awarded premiums to all the best Gothic designs, they took care not to put any of them high enough to have much chance.' So the first prize went to someone else, and Scott only got third prize.

I did not fret myself at the disappointment, but when it was found, a few months later, that Lord Palmerston had coolly set aside the entire results of the competition, and was about to appoint Pennethorne, a non-competitor, I thought myself at liberty to stir. A meeting took place at Mr. Beresford Hope's, at which Charles Barry, myself, and Digby Wyatt were present; and, if I remember rightly, it was agreed to stir up the Institute of Architects . . .

The result was the appointment of a select committee to inquire into the subject. This committee had Mr. Beresford Hope for its chairman . . .

They reported in July, 1858, but no decision was come to till late in November, when I learned that I had been appointed . . .

Lord Palmerston, however, sent for me, and told me in a jaunty way that he could have nothing to do with this Gothic style, and that though he did not want to disturb my appointment, he must insist on my making a design in the Italian style, which he felt sure I could do quite as well as the other. That he heard I was so tremendously successful in the Gothic style, that if he let me alone I should Gothicize the whole country, &c, &c, &c . . .

This cold-heartedness was the greatest damper I had met with . . .

Shortly afterwards Lord Palmerston sent for me, and, seating himself down before me in the most easy, fatherly way, said, 'I want to talk to you quietly, Mr. Scott, about this business. I have been thinking a great deal about it, and I really think there was much force in what your friends said.' I was delighted at his supposed conversion. 'I really do think that there is a degree of inconsistency in compelling a Gothic architect to erect a classic building, and so I have been thinking of appointing you a coadjutor, who would in fact make the design!' I was thrown to the earth again . . .

Thus closed this stage of the business, and, being thoroughly knocked up (or down, as you may please to call it), I retired with Mrs. Scott and my family to Scarborough to recover. I was thoroughly out of health, through the badgering, anxiety, and bitter disappointment which I had gone through, and for the first time since commencing practice, twenty-four years before, I gave myself a quasi-holiday of two months, with sea air and a course of quinine . . .

The course I determined on was to prepare a design in a variety of Italian, as little inconsistent with my antecedents as possible. I had, in dealing with Lord Hill's chapel at Hawkstone, and with St Michael's church, Cornhill, attempted, by the use of a sort of early Basilican style, to give a tone to the existing classic architecture; and it struck me that not wholly alien to this was the Byzantine of the early Venetian palaces, and that the earliest renaissance of Venice contained a cognate element. I therefore conceived the idea of generating what would be strictly an Italian style out of these two sets of examples; Byzantine, in fact, toned into a more modern and usable form, by reference to those examples of the renaissance which had been influenced by the presence of Byzantine works. To the study of this I devoted myself while at Scarborough. . . .

I was sent for to Lord Palmerston on September 8th, 1860, when he told me that he did not wish to disturb my position, but that he would have nothing to do with Gothic; and as to the style of my recent design, it was 'neither one thing nor t'other—a regular mongrel affair—and he would have nothing to do with it either:' that he must insist on my making a design in the ordinary Italian, and that, though he had no wish to displace me, he nevertheless, if I refused, must cancel my appointment . . .

I came away thunderstruck and in sore perplexity, thinking whether I must resign or swallow the bitter pill, when whom should I meet in Pall Mall but my friend Mr. Hunt . . . He urged the claims of my family, whom I had no right to deprive of what had become their property as much as my own, for a mere individual preference on a question of taste, &c., &c. I saw Mr. Digby Wyatt shortly afterwards, who, very disinterestedly, urged strongly the same view—I say disinterestedly, for had I resigned he would beyond a doubt have had the whole design of the India Office, instead of a half of it, committed to his hands. I was in a terrible state of mental perturbation, but I made up my mind, went straight in for Digby Wyatt's view; bought some costly books on Italian architecture, and set vigorously to work to rub up what, though I had once understood pretty intimately, I had allowed to grow rusty by twenty years' neglect.

I devoted the autumn to the new designs, and, as I think, met with great success. I went to Paris and studied the Louvre and most of the important buildings, and really recovered some of my lost feelings for the style, though I fell, ever and anon, into fits of desperate lamentation and annoyance . . .[57]

We are struck by the hypocrisy of this story;[58] yet it contains much serious matter to meditate over. There is for instance Scott's unquestioning conviction of his own worth—the same arrogance as

[57] *Recollections*, 178 ff.
[58] Once again Professor Houghton's chapter on hypocrisy would be corroborative reading. Also see e.g., to give one additional example, Spurgeon saying in a lecture in 1862: 'In these days men are strongly tempted to believe that to look like a Christian will certainly be as useful as to be a Christian.' (*Lectures delivered before the Young Men's Christian Association in Exeter Hall*, Nov. 1861–Feb. 1862, 340.)

Ruskin's. Doncaster parish church 'stands very high amongst the works of the revival',[59] the competition design for the Town Hall for Hamburg 'would have been a very noble structure',[60] the competition design for the Law Courts was 'fully as good as any recent work I know of by any other architect'[61] and so on. Then there is the baffling fact that the Foreign Office after Broad Sanctuary and before St Pancras [Pl. 53] is exactly what Scott told architects they must not do: build now in this style, now in that, that Scott did not refuse what was so blatantly a sin against his principles, and that in the end he sinned so superbly. For the Foreign Office, no more than thoroughly competent towards Whitehall, is an outstanding composition to the park [Pl. 51], outstandingly detailed—in fact as a demonstration of Scott's principle of variety far superior to Broad Sanctuary.[62]

Finally to complicate matters further Scott in his *Remarks* also comments favourably on the 'massive utilitarianism' of town warehouses, and on iron architecture. Warehouses to him have a beauty which results 'from carrying out the obvious requirements and conditions of the case in the most genuine and natural manner—making no attempt to give the building a character other than its own—making parts which have the same functions uniform and alike . . . and reserving the architectural touches to a few special points, as the doorways or the eaves-cornice'.[63] So warehouses are beautiful but not architectural and Scott designed none.

How now about iron architecture? 'The peculiarity of modern ironwork is that, whether cast or wrought, it is unlimited in the extent of its application—not only forming roofs of a width unequalled in other material, but bridges spanning wide rivers, or even arms of the sea. It is self-evident that this triumph of modern metallic construction opens out a perfectly new field for architectural development.' Moreover, 'it is true that some of these wonderful constructions have an inherent beauty of their own which renders them architectural . . . A simple . . . cast-iron bridge has almost always a certain degree of beauty; a suspension bridge would puzzle

[59] *Recollections*, 172.   [60] Ibid., 174.   [61] Ibid., 274.

[62] In praising this particular view it should however not be forgotten that Scott in his *Recollections* acknowledged that 'the idea as to the grouping and outline' of the park side of the building was suggested to him 'by a sketch of M. D. Wyatt'. In fact, Kerr in 1891 wrote more sweepingly that to Sir Matthew Digby Wyatt should go 'the credit of the cortile and the grouping towards the Park' (Kerr's third edition of Fergusson's *History of the Modern Styles of Architecture*, 139).

[63] *Remarks*, 220, 216.

the most ingenious blunderer to render it unpleasing . . .[64] There are, however, some other pieces of metal construction which are always ugly, unless artistically treated; such for instance as beams . . . The only at all successful instance of architecturalizing cast-iron beams, is in Mr. Butterfield's Gothic building in Margaret Street', and indeed the principles of iron bridges and iron roofs are 'more allied to mediaeval timber construction, than to any works we know of classic antiquity'.[65] What a muddle! Iron can be beautiful, iron is akin to a medieval technique, but iron can be made architectural only by some 'architecturalizing'—which incidentally can hardly be said of Butterfields' priest's house of All Saints. And if iron roofs are beautiful, why did Scott do everything in his power to hide Barlow's iron roof of St Pancras Station [Pl. 54], which was the largest span ever to that time achieved by man? It is true that inside his station terminus there are decorated girders in the great Coffee Room and the splendid ornamented work of the main staircase [Pl. 55], that inside the Government Offices there is (rather Hittorffish) ironwork too, and that the Gothic Brill's Baths at Brighton had over the plunge bath an iron dome,[66] but this amounts to little in comparison with his recognition of 'a perfectly new field of architectural development'. Still, it is more than Ruskin's one remark contradicting all his others, and it is no less than Matthew Digby Wyatt's.

Scott's *Recollections* written at the end of his life add nothing to the corpus of his theories and convictions. His last years were evidently made unhappy by the gathering strength of the anti-restoration movement. Scott died in 1878; in 1877 Morris had started the Anti-Scrape, the Society for the Protection of Ancient Buildings. Protection, not restoration; that was Ruskin's programme. Moreover, as has been referred to before, already in 1874 Ruskin had refused the Gold Medal of the Institute, partly because of the misdeeds of the restorers. Scott had written to defend the architects and finally made a courteous speech.[67] Three years later, i.e. also in 1877, J. J. Stevenson, except for Nesfield the earliest protagonist of the so-called Queen Anne, really a mid- to later-seventeenth-century revival, much more elegant and much less demanding than the Middle

---

[64] Bartholomew's and Wyatt's praise of suspension bridges will be remembered and Petit's of viaducts—see pp. 92, 100, 160.

[65] *Remarks*, 109–11.

[66] *Civil Engineer and Architect's Journal*, XXIX, 1866, 313 and plates 37–8. See S. Muthesius, 'The "iron problem" in the 1850s', *Architectural History*, XIII, 1970.

[67] Ruskin, L.E., XXXIV, 513 ff.; reprinted *J.R.I.B.A.*, 3rd Ser. LXX, April 1963, 165 ff.

Pointed, had attacked Scott as a restorer in a very outspoken address at the R.I.B.A.[68] He had said: 'It is a delusion of restorers that their new work, because it is correctly mediaeval in style, is of any historical value', and decried the examples of the clearing out of box-pews and galleries, the removing of plaster from the walls, the replacement of low-pitched Perpendicular by high-pitched roofs and the destruction of the old buildings at Balliol. Retorts to the address were furious. Beresford Hope called it intellectual barbarism, Ferrey concurred, and Scott complained that Stevenson's initial description of the typical unrestored church was unjustifiably *couleur de rose*.

But the stigma remained, and so, at the end of his *Recollections*, partly put in by Scott's son, there are long and repetitive defences of the Gothic, and a stab at the neo-Queen Anne as 'a vexatious disturber of the Gothic movement'.[69] Scott, we read, had always been a conservative restorer, but what should be done in churches where eighteenth-century box pews hide the medieval piers or where plaster and glass partitions shut off the chancel or transept? He likes to preserve three-decker pulpits, but there are 'the prejudices of my clients',[70] and 'we may be weak, and open to intimidation'.[71] Besides, it is all right for Stevenson to describe an unrestored church poetically, but in reality such churches may be unstable and sordid. It is all rather pathetic. Still—we should perhaps not worry too much. Scott left £130,000 when he died.

---

[68] *Sessional Papers,* R.I.B.A., 1876–7, 219–35.

[70] Ibid., 410.

[69] *Recollections,* 372.

[71] Ibid., 419.

CHAPTER XVIII

Thomson

ONE of Scott's most ambitious secular Gothic buildings is Glasgow University [Pl. 56]. Scott was commissioned in 1866 without a competition having been held. That stung into action a Glasgow man who hardly ever publicized his thoughts, who was a greater architect than Scott, and who was the most violent of anti-Gothicists. That man, needless to say, was Alexander Thomson, Greek Thomson.[1]

Thomson was born in 1817, and when one looks over his *œuvre*, one should, in spite of the purely Schinkelesque terraces of houses he designed—Moray Place of 1859, Northpark Terrace of 1866, Great Western Terrace of 1869—not call him a Grecian. For he was a rationalist first and foremost in his domestic and commercial buildings, and in his three grandiose churches he was overpoweringly original. They are (or were) the Caledonia Road Church of 1856 ff. [Pl. 57][2] the St Vincent Street Church of 1859 ff. and the Queen's Park Church of 1869 ff.[3] They have Schinkelesque motifs, but also frankly Egyptian motifs and in addition whole passages such as the tower tops of all three which depart entirely from period precedent. So do such commercial premises as Grosvenor Building of 1859 ff. and the Egyptian Halls of 1871 ff. For the purposes of office buildings Thomson accepted iron as naturally as the non-Grecian Glasgow and London architects of the fifties. So he was not a historicist, strictly speaking, and that is one of the things which emerge from a reading of his 'Enquiry into the Appropriateness of the Gothic Style for the proposed Buildings for the University of Glasgow', a paper read to the Glasgow Architectural Society, of which a fair copy survives in the Mitchell Library.[4]

[1] On Greek Thomson see Chapter VI of A. Gomme and D. Walker, *Architecture of Glasgow* (London, 1968), and also still Graham Law 'Greek Thomson', in *Arch. Rev.*, CXV, 1954, 307–16.
[2] Largely destroyed by fire in 1965.
[3] Destroyed by fire in 1942.
[4] Dr. Law refers to this paper which has never been printed, and Mr. Ronald McFadzean kindly provided me with a xerox copy. Mr. McFadzean is preparing a thesis on Thomson.

The paper is only about 12,000 words long and is throughout an attack on Scott and the University authorities, as uninhibited as Stevenson's attack on Scott was to be ten years later. The very start leaves one in no doubt that here an architect is speaking who is aggrieved not to have had a chance to compete for so vast and splendidly situated a building. 'It may be supposed that the Professors of the University are the truest representatives of wisdom and learning amongst us'; so they should have 'sympathized with the local professional men' of Glasgow such as Thomson himself who were naturally anxious to prove 'whether there were not some men amongst ourselves . . . capable of undertaking the erection of those buildings in a style creditable to the institution'. Only if no such man could be found, would 'the professors, as promoters of social progress and intellectual culture 'have had the duty 'to search for a properly qualified architect wherever he could be found'.[5] But no, they went straight to 'the "celebrated architect, Mr. G. Gilbert Scott, of London"'. By doing that the professors 'relinquished all claims to the possession of any degree of knowledge or regard for the interest of art superior to the vulgar public'; for 'everybody knows that [Mr. Scott's] is the most fashionable establishment in the great metropolis, and that his business is so enormous that, to expect him to bestow more than the most casual consideration upon the work which passes through the office, is altogether unreasonable.' So what they should have done is to turn 'from a workshop like this with disgust and indignation' and to select one of those architects 'who would have devoted their whole energies of heart and soul to a work of this kind'.[6]

The reader of these pages today does not know whether to be more amazed at so blatant a self-advertisement or at so direct and sweeping an attack of one established architect against another. But Thomson had not done yet. He now proceeded to attack not the architect but the style. 'The pleasures which we derive from objects of sight derive partly from the association which they suggest, and partly from their own inherent beauty. It is difficult to see anything in the association of the Gothic style that should recommend its adoption as the proper architectural exponent of learning and mental cultivation. It had its origin in what are termed the dark ages', a period of many centuries in which very little was done 'for the advancement of knowledge and civilisation'. In fact, 'a great part

⁵ Pages B and C.   ⁶ D to F.

of the work of the last two or three centuries has consisted in rectifying the errors of the mediaeval system'.[7]

And if 'the Gothic revivalists' claim theirs as 'the national style' they are no nearer the truth. The Gothic style 'certainly had not a national origin' and if it was adopted here and indeed 'assumed national and local peculiarities', the same would be true of 'the Classic styles'.[8] The Gothicists also tell us that Gothic is the Christian style, but this is a 'most impudent assertion' and should never have been accepted 'by earnest and intelligent Protestants'.[9] So Gothic is neither specially national nor specially Christian; nor is it structurally specially commendable. 'Can anything be more absurd than to rear a fabric with the very agents of destruction?' Gothic, and indeed all styles employing the arch, are a fight against 'the law of gravitation', and the result is that the arcuated styles altogether have 'strewed Europe with ruins, whilst in Egypt and Greece we have lintelled structures which have stood the test of thousands of years without showing an open joint or any other symptom of decay . . . Stonehenge is really more scientifically constructed than York Minster.'[10]

So much against Gothic structure. Now for the artistic merits of the style. The organization of the higher animals is symmetrical, of the lower forms of life 'such as trees, rocks, and hills' asymmetrical. Gothic is asymmetrical; hence Gothic is picturesque, which 'may be a source of pure delight'[11] but is 'manifestly inferior in ideal qualities'.[12] In its earlier forms it 'seems to embody the spirit of the words—not the outward semblance, as some say, but the . . . character . . . A kind of forest life pervades the old grey piles . . . as if it had taken a long time to grow but might grow a long while yet . . . The light streaming through the stained glass is suggestive of leaves and flowers, while the gloom is associated with lurking terrors of wolves and hobgoblins.'[13] So Gothic building is 'rather interesting than excellent'. Moreover, it lacks 'fixed harmonies' in proportion, it springs out of the earth instead of standing upon the earth like the Greek building, it seeks 'for diversity rather than . . . unity'. Similar things are never allowed to be 'exactly alike', because 'the individual workman' had been allowed 'considerable latitude'.[14]

[7] G and H.   [8] H.   [9] I.
[10] J to M.   [11] Thomson's churches are boldly asymmetrical.   [12] M.
[13] Q to R. In fact Thomson later recalls with relish Ruskin's remark in 'The Nature of Gothic' that good Gothic must have something 'wolfish' in it (page 418; see above, p. 150).
[14] R to U.

In the end we are left with 'an impression of multitudinousness and incomprehensibility' and if we are pleased, it is because 'the softening influences of decay cover many of the defects inherent in the style'.[15]

All this has little of applicability to Glasgow University, but now Thomson advanced to fire at closer range:

The Gothic is altogether unsuitable for buildings of a great extent [he now means secular buildings], because when it assumes the horizontal form its different parts cease to have an apparent relationship to each other, and become more like a little town than a great building. In a colonnade . . . the element of length is developed . . . and it will be readily perceived that there is no single building or combination of buildings, however great in extent, to which this element does not apply.

Praise therefore to John Martin's architectural phantasies, and praise to Turner and Roberts for showing in their paintings 'the mysterious power of the horizontal . . . in carrying the mind away into space'.[16] Look at Egyptian architecture with its repose, its 'expression of quietly waiting till all the bustle is over'. Or, better still, look at the Greek style. The 'modern Italian' is not a substitute for it. 'Its loose composition, its gross mouldings, and its barrel-bulged columns are fitly associated with corpulent cherubs, with festoons of . . . blown out forms, and with tangled and weedy spandrils.'[17] True, Gothic may 'admite [sic] of the greatest latitude' and flexibility, but is not 'prudent cautious self-control' preferable?[18]

So now at last to the Glasgow job. 'Unquestionably the two finest [recent] buildings in the kingdom' are the Edinburgh High School and St George's Hall in Liverpool.[19] There is not one recent Gothic building 'that anyone cares a straw about'. If it ever became the fashion, that was due to 'the aid of literary men'. So Gothic, to sum up all the general arguments put forward so far 'is most unfit to express the character and purpose of the University'.[20] And if Mr. Scott admits that 'he had devoted his attention chiefly to the very humble business of concocting the plans and dealing out to each of the professors the exact kind and amount of accommodation which the business of his class required—at the same time keeping in view with the tail of his eye the refinement of society and the resuscitation

---

[15] V and W.   [16] Z to B2.   [17] C3 to D4.   [18] F6.

[19] Thomson's design for the Natural History Museum in London, illustrated in Dr. Law's paper, is in fact evidently inspired by Hamilton's High School.

[20] L12 to N14.

of Scottish architecture', he has not succeeded in that either. The
motif of two inner courts has only the effect of 'needlessly excluding
air and light',[21] the total composition is really not Gothic but classic,
'that is to say, it assumes a horizontal form with the larger features
uniform and regularly disposed' and only 'the minor features are
Gothic'—of the fourteenth century in France. What little of diversity
is in the composition is only 'introduced to baffle the mind and
evade comprehension'.[22] Examples of this element of deliberate
confusion are the fact that on the west side of the tower there are
four bays on each side of the entrance to the court, on the east side
four in one, five in the other case, the fact that some windows are
of two lights and others of three or of four, and the fact that the
buttresses are irregularly placed. The result of 'these vagaries' is
that the building will look like 'the side of a street' in spite of its
detached place on a hill.[23] The last sentence of the paper is: 'Upon
the whole, I think that the less the professors say about the artistic
merits of these designs the better, and certainly the local architects
have nothing to fear from this invasion from the South'.[24]

[21] O15 to P16. [22] R18 to U21.
[23] U21 to Aa. [24] Ff.

CHAPTER XIX

Greenough and Garbett

GREEK THOMSON'S *Enquiry* has never been printed; Edward L. Garbett's *Rudimentary Treatise on the Principles of Design in Architecture* has, but it seems to be known to very few in spite of that, and in spite of the fact that the most famous American functionalist before Sullivan, the sculptor Horatio Greenough (1805–52) in one place explicitly refers to it.[1] Greenough is a baffling phenomenon. As a sculptor he belongs to the neo-Classical school—see his semi-nude *George Washington* in the Washington Museum of History and Technology. He lived in Italy from 1829 to his death, and he wrote on architecture, but totally differently from his Italian contemporaries.[2] The dates of his articles seem to lie between 1843, when *American Architecture* came out, and shortly after 1850, the year of the publication of Garbett's *Rudimentary Treatise*. Greenough has been quoted often enough. So he will here be treated briefly and more or less by way of an introduction to Garbett.

Greek Thomson's *Enquiry* is the most comprehensive contribution to the battle of the Styles, and the last one in which Grecian, not Italian, is set against Gothic. Greenough, though earlier and though devoted to the classical ideal in sculpture, does not concern himself in any of his articles with specific styles. His arguments deal with principles, and the all-pervading principle is 'the organic' which is what we call function. 'In all remarks upon important public edifices there is a twofold subject under contemplation: first, the organic structure of the works, second, their monumentality. To plant a building firmly on the ground, to give it the light that may, the air that must, be needed; to apportion the spaces for convenience, decide their size, and model their shapes for their functions—these acts organize a building.' Architects ought to 'make organization

---

[1] On Greenough see the book quoted in note on page 189. His writings are collected as *Form and Function; Remarks on Art by Horatio Greenough,* ed. H. A. Small (Univ. of Calif. Press, 1947; also as a paperback).

[2] Though it is just possible that he knew the functionalism of the Abbate Lodoli through Memmo's edition of his talks published in 1786.

the basis of their design, instead of a predetermined fruit'.[3] In 'American Architecture' in 1843 he had already made the same distinction between organic and monumental, and he had added that organic buildings 'may be called machines'.[4] In other places in the same paper, he speaks of 'the compact, effective, and beautiful engine', and he also compares the way organic buildings are organized with 'the skeletons and skins of animals', the war clubs of 'the savages of the South Sea Islands', and—of course—ships.[5] That he knew Hogarth's *Analysis of Beauty* is more than likely; for there on the very first page of the first chapter, called 'Of Fitness', we read: 'When a vessel sails well, the sailors always call her a beauty; the two ideas have such a connexion.' Pugin, of course, in the *True Principles*, published two years before Greenough's *American Architecture*, had also started his first chapter with a plea for fitness, but he had then proceeded to fight for one particular style. This is just what Greenough refuses to do. He defines memorably 'Beauty as the promise of Function' and goes on: 'Action as the Presence of Function; Character as the Record of Function'.[6] Thus 'the most beautiful chairs' are not those puzzling you by their carving but those which 'invite you by a promise of ease',[7] and if anyone objected that 'such a system ... would produce *nakedness*', he is ready to accept the challenge. 'In nakedness I behold the majesty of the essential instead of the trappings of pretension.'[8]

These are the most advanced statements of architectural theory of the whole mid-nineteenth century, except for those contained in 'Mr. Garbett's learned and able treatise'.[9] Greenough's remarks on beauty as the promise of function, and on nakedness were made after he had read Garbett—that must be remembered. Edward Lacy Garbett's *Rudimentary Treatise on the Principles of Design in Architecture* came out in 1850, i.e. one year after the *Seven Lamps*. It is a small, unassuming book, but it is the only one of its date in England to face fully what architectural theory ought to involve. It is in its setting of problems much more like textbooks on architectural design today than like any of the writings so far examined. We do not know who Edward Lacy Garbett was, perhaps the son of William, surveyor of Winchester Cathedral, or of Edward Garbett, designer of the remarkable church of 1819 at Theale which

---

[3] *Form and Function, Remarks on Art by Horatio Greenough*, ed. H. A. Small, Berkeley & Los Angeles 1947, 20–2.

[4] Ibid., 65.   [5] Ibid., 57, 59–60.   [6] Ibid., 71.

[7] Ibid., 122.   [8] Ibid., 75.   [9] Ibid., 78.

took Salisbury Cathedral as its model. Our Garbett later in life turned away from architectural writing and published instead pamphlets with such titles as *God's View of our Babylon shown in slaying Alford, beginner of the Bible Revision* (1885), *Huxley's Mendacity* (1891), and *England's God the Bible's Baal* (1892). The publisher of the *Rudimentary Treatise* was John Weale whom we are familiar with (see p. 129). It was a successful book. Bond in his *Gothic Architecture* of 1906 quotes the seventh edition, 1891.

Chapter one defines as the objects of architecture not only convenience and stability but also beauty. 'Purely utilitarian buildings are always ugly', and they are because of their 'selfishness'.[10] Such buildings are about everywhere, yet they are detrimental to 'mental health'.[11] 'Selfish rudeness' must be corrected by 'politeness'.[12] But that is only the lowest class of aesthetic requirement. 'It needs refinement into beauty.'[13] However, beauty, referring to aesthetic qualities only, still lacks one quality: expression. But even this 'though almost forgotten . . . in modern English architecture . . . is yet not the highest aim'.[14] That is poetry, and so poetry is tentatively defined. The next chapter discusses 'the lowest class of beauties': colour, repetition and uniformity, unity and variety, gradation and contrast, curvature. Chapter three includes thoughts on the sublime and the picturesque, an old juxtaposition, going back to the Uvedale Price and Payne Knight generation, but freshly argued by Garbett.[15] The 'Higher Beauties' of chapter four are Imitation of Nature and, firmly based on Reynolds, the Imitation of Masters, Honesty as against Deception,[16] and especially Constructive Truth. These side by side with Constructive Unity, 'are the two most important principles to be borne in mind, in tracing the history of architecture' and in understanding 'the two standard systems which the world has hitherto seen'—the Greek and the Gothic.

---

[10] *Rudimentary Treatise,* 5. 'The selfish and even cruel aspect [of] great mechanical works' is a quotation from Ralph Waldo Emerson. Garbett knew his work and thought, and conversely Emerson told Greenough in a letter in 1852 that he preferred Garbett even to Ruskin. See R. W. Winter, 'Fergusson and Garbett in American Architectural Theory', *Journal of the Society of Architectural Historians,* XVII, Dec. 1958, 25–30.

[11] Ibid., 11.   [12] Ibid., 7.   [13] Ibid., 12.   [14] Ibid., 30.

[15] And incidentally, as is true of the whole book, argued with recognition of such recent books as the *Seven Lamps* and Fergusson's *Principles of Beauty* which will have half a chapter to itself (see p. 238). Ruskin published his answer to Garbett's criticism of the *Seven Lamps* as an appendix to *Stones of Venice* I, 1851 (L.E., IX, 450 ff.). The pages are worth reading as a summing-up of Ruskin's views. It is at the end of this answer incidentally that the famous diatribe against the Crystal Palace occurs.

[16] Ibid., 123.

'Constructive Truth requires that a building shall never appear to be constructed on different statical principles from those really employed.'[17] Constructive Unity is the consistent aesthetic expression of the structural principle underlying a building, and that principle is of necessity one of pressures. There are three systems of reacting to pressures.[18] The Greek is the system of exclusive vertical pressure. 'Every oblique pressure is excluded.' The second is the Gothic or 'compressive system'. 'Throughout the visible construction there was no portion of matter subjected, as far as the eye could judge, to any other force than simple compression.' But Gothic timber roofs are 'a tensile construction'. However, they were invisible. When 'the Gothic system gradually declined', tensile construction increased. 'In the compressible system all apertures and spaces were covered on the arch principle, and the oblique pressures thus occasioned were transmitted down to the ground by . . . buttresses or abutments. But this is not the most economical mode of treating the said pressures when we have materials of great length and strong in tension, as timber and iron.' So one arrives at the various kinds of truss, where 'no part [is] subjected to cross-strain, but every part either to direct compression or direct tension'. But, so Garbett ends his first part, 'though there are three styles of construction, there have been only two systems of architecture . . . possessing constructive unity . . . The third . . . has yet to be elaborated into a system. . . . The two systems are past and dead. The third is the destined architecture of the future.'[19]

Following this view of architecture past and present Part Two examines first the Greek in detail, then in a few paragraphs the Roman and the Romanesque, then, again in detail, the Gothic system, and finally in a mere twenty-odd pages 'Post-Gothic Architecture'. The Italian Renaissance is divided into three schools, Florence, Rome, and Venice, and these are nicely compared in character with Doric, Ionic, and Corinthian.[20] Garbett appreciates all three, as he appreciates Inigo Jones, Wren, the 'exceptional genius' of Vanbrugh, and Chambers whom he calls 'the last earnest truth-seeker'.[21] After that novelty won over truth. How can we get back to truth? Garbett had already given one answer at the end

---

[17] Ibid., 130.

[18] One is at once reminded of Leopold Eidlitz's categorical: 'All architecture [is] . . . conditioned by strain and its resistance', but that was said in 1897 (*J.R.I.B.A.*, 3rd Ser., V, 1897, 213–7) and even then was still received with anger.

[19] Ibid., 130–5.   [20] Ibid., 243 ff.   [21] Ibid., 247–8.

of Part One. Another, and a surprising and eminently Victorian answer is given now, intelligently argued, as everything is in Garbett's book: Italy 'has never attained a system of constructive unity' or even 'the appearance of constructive unity'. It is a country of 'mixed construction'. This 'affords more scope for variety in general arrangement than . . . the pure systems . . . It possesses a pliancy that may be bent to all . . . purposes.' Therefore 'we may safely predict the continued preference of this architecture among the thinking.'[22] So Garbett sides with Hope (see p. 74) and the Barry of the clubs and of Trentham Park. The end of the treatise is as follows:

If you imitate the archless style, your building must be archless, or a huge lie.[23] If you imitate the beamless style, it must be beamless, and every unvaulted building, . . . that apes this style, is an . . . unmeaning sham. Not less preposterous than the attempt to revive dead styles,[24] is the requirement to invent, for ordinary buildings, a new one. As long as we have no new style in construction, we can have none in architecture; but if we call the mixed construction a new kind, we have a new style adapted to it— a modern, a living style . . . But while no inventive architect would *wish* for a new style, convinced that there is far more scope for variety and new combination in one already enriched with the accumulated genius of three centuries; it is certain that, in another point of view, a new style is indispensable. There *is* a class of buildings tending towards a new style of construction,—becoming less mixed in this respect,—and approaching a consistent use of *tensile* covering to the exclusion of every other. To this third system of constructive unity, there is no old style adapted. . . . Let us not mistake what we have to do. It is that which has been done only twice before; in the time of Dorus, and in the thirteenth century. . . . Let us not deceive ourselves: a style never grew of itself; it never will. It *must* be sought, and sought the right way. We may blunder on in a wrong path for ever, and get no nearer the goal. . . . A new style requires the generalized imitation of nature and of *many* previous styles; and a new system requires, in addition to this (as Professor Whewell has remarked), the binding of all together by a new *principle of unity,* clearly understood, agreed upon, and kept constantly in view. Constructive statics affords three such principles,— the DEPRESSILE, the COMPRESSILE, and the TENSILE methods,— the *beam,*—the *arch*—the *truss*; of which the two former have been made the bases of past systems: the third is ours, to be used in the same manner.

[22] *J.R.I.B.A.,* 3rd Ser., V, 1897, 260.
[23] Garbett adds a footnote, starting: 'What are called classic churches . . . are, for the most part, mere anti-art.'
[24] The *British Critic* had written in 1839: 'Architecture is become a language. We learn a number of styles as we learn a dead language.' Quoted from B. F. L. Clarke's *Church Builders of the Nineteenth Century* (London, 1938; now also as a paperback), 32.

Such I believe to be the problem Truth propounds to the architects of the present time.

Garbett is of great importance in the context of this book for two reasons. He is the most intelligent, the most rational, the most-far-seeing of the prophets of an original style of the future, and he is among historicists the ablest of all defenders of the Italianate, at least in England. In Germany Semper provides a parallel, as we shall see later, and in France, in some ways, Hittorff[25] provides another.

But Hittorff did not write on architectural theory. What he did, however, was to practise what Garbett recommended.[26] He was a defender of Antiquity from the time of his journey to Sicily (1823) where he discovered the polychromy of Greek architecture for which he then battled for decades against Raoul-Rochette and others. Hittorff remained on the Grecian side, but in reality, from 1825 onwards, he used freely modified Cinquecento forms, and these about 1850 and after became more and more frequent. But he also believed in constructive truth, and his Gare du Nord of 1859–62 [Pl. 58] reveals its function as much as King's Cross, which did not yet exist when Hittorff visited England in 1851, and Duquesney's old Gare de l'Est which had been built in 1847–52 [Fig. 8]. He saw the Crystal Palace and designed for the Paris Exhibition of 1855 a building of glass and iron. But before that he had already used iron prominently in the Panorama of 1838–9 in the Champs Élysées,[27] i.e. before Labrouste's Bibliothèque Ste Geneviève which impressed Viollet-le-Duc so much. Hittorff and Viollet-le-Duc were not friends. Their attitudes in and towards the Académie des Beaux-Arts are a reflection of the English Battle of the Styles. Scott[28] had suggested that the Royal Academy should have two professorships of architecture, 'the one for classic, the other for Gothic architecture'. That compromise was not acceptable to Hittorff. He stood stubbornly for the Classical, as Viollet stood for the Gothic. In 1861 Hittorff attacked Viollet in the Academy,[29] and he objected to the separation between the École des Beaux-Arts and the Academy which Viollet regarded as absolutely necessary for a regeneration of the school. Viollet won, the reform was carried through, but Viollet did not profit from it as he had hoped.

[25] See p. 214.
[26] On Hittorff see Karl Hammer, *Jakob Ignaz Hittorff, ein Pariser Baumeister, 1792–1867* (Stuttgart, 1968).
[27] For this building Hittorff also visited England; see Hammer, op. cit., 177. Hittorff in 1842 published a book on the Panorama.
[28] *Recollections,* 176.   [29] Hammer, op. cit., 232.

14

CHAPTER XX

Viollet-le-Duc and Reynaud

VIOLLET-LE-DUC was the Gilbert Scott of France, Scott the Viollet-le-Duc of England. Both were the leading restorers of their time and nation, both believed in the Gothic of the thirteenth century as the best style of all ages, and both were scholars and thinkers as well as practising architects. As an architect Scott was superior in volume and quality, as a thinker Viollet-le-Duc towers above Scott.

Eugène Emmanuel Viollet-le-Duc was born in 1814, three years after Scott.[1] He came of wealthy parents, his father being Conservateur des Résidences royales and a book collector, his uncle, E. J. Delécluze, a pupil of David, art critic of the *Journal des Débats*, and a passionate liberal. Young Viollet-le-Duc went to the Lycée Condorcet, helped to build barricades in 1830, refused to go to the École des Beaux-Arts for his training, travelled in France in 1831, 1832, and 1833, began to teach at what is now the École des Arts décoratifs in 1834, visited Italy in 1836-7 (where he found Palladio, Sansovino, and Vignola 'plus qu'ennuyeux'),[2] began to supply picturesque drawings—221 in seven years—for Taylor and Nodier's *Voyages Pittoresques* (see p. 22) in 1838, and in the same year entered

---

[1] See P. Gout, *Viollet-le-Duc* (Paris, 1914); V. Sauvageot, *Viollet-le-Duc et son œuvre dessiné* (Paris, 1880); *Compositions et Dessins de Viollet-le-Duc* (Paris, 1884); *Lettres inédites de Viollet-le-Duc, recueillies et annotées par son fils* (Paris, 1902). The best recent works are Dr. Robin Middleton's Cambridge Ph.D. thesis, 'Viollet-le-Duc and the rational Gothic tradition' (1958), a work which covers the Gothic survival and revival in France from Delorme to Viollet-le-Duc, and *Viollet-le-Duc*, catalogue of an exhibition held in 1965 and published by the Caisse nationale des Monuments historiques. The latter is now indispensable. There is also an excellent paper, by Maurice Besset, 'Viollet-le-Duc, seine Stellung zur Geschichte', in *Historismus und bildende Kunst*, ed. L. Grote (Munich, 1965). J. P. Paquet and others, in *Les Monuments historiques de la France*, N.S. XI, 1965, 1 ff. I saw only after this chapter had been written. Lastly some Italian contributions: C. Bricarelli, *Eugenio Viollet-le-Duc e il rifioramento degli studi medioevali nel secolo XIX* (Rome, 1915); A. Nava, 'Le teorie di Viollet-le-Duc e l'architettura funzionale', in *Critica d'Arte*, VIII, 1949. The first chapter of R. De Fusco, *L'Idea dell'Architettura*; *Storia della Critica da Viollet-le-Duc a Persico* (Milan, 1964) is called 'Viollet-le-Duc e Ruskin', but no comparisons are made, as I have endeavoured to do in *Ruskin and Viollet-le-Duc* (First Neurath Lecture at Birkbeck College, London, 1969).

[2] Catalogue, p. 34.

the Conseil des Bâtiments Civils. Guizot, as Minister of the Interior, had created the post of Inspecteur Général des Monuments in 1830, and as Minister of Education in 1837 the Commission des Monuments historiques to which the Conseil des Bâtiments belonged. The first Inspecteur Général was Ludovic Vitet. He was followed in 1835 by Mérimée, when Vitet became president of the Conseil. Among members of the commission incidentally were Taylor and Le Prévost, and also the architects Duban, who designed the classical library of the École des Beaux-Arts, and Caristie who designed the classical Law Courts at Reims.[3] In 1840 Mérimée asked Viollet-le-Duc to report on the state of the abbey church of Vézelay. This was the beginning of a career in church restoration unparalleled in France.

The creation of the Commission des Monuments historiques was the direct outcome of the activities of Arcisse de Caumont, first for Normandy, then for the whole of France. Viollet-le-Duc paid tribute to him (and his English predecessors) in the introduction to his great *Dictionnaire*. This is what he wrote: 'Les premiers travaux de M. de Caumont faisaient ressortir des caractères bien tranchés entre les differentes époques de l'architecture française du nord.'[4] Caumont on the other hand lived long enough to place the whole *Dictionnaire* in the bibliography to his *Archéologie des écoles primaires* (Caen, 1868).

We have so far only looked at France with the eyes of Caumont. But, although the romantic approach to the Middle Ages and to Gothic architecture in particular was a German speciality, it was by no means absent in France. Chateaubriand's *Génie du Christianisme* was published in 1802 and contains a chapter 'Des églises gothiques'.[5] He speaks of the 'frissonnement' on entering a Gothic church; of the magic wrought by the distance in time of the buildings, of the majesty of Reims, of Ossian of course, and of the beauty of Christian ruins (the most beautiful ones being those of England 'au bord du lac de Cumberland' and 'dans les montagnes d'Écosse'), and repeats the derivation of Gothic architecture from the trees of forests: 'The forests of Gaul have continued . . . in the temples of our forefathers . . . the freshness of the vaults, the darkness of the sanctuary, the obscurity of the aisles—all reminds one of woods.'

But the real, indigenously French Romantic Movement dates from

[3] See P. Léon; *La vie des monuments français*, (Paris, 1950) also *Congrès Archéologiques*, CXVII (Paris, 1934) I, 53 ff.

[4] *Dictionnaire raisonné de l'architecture française du XIe au XVIe siècle* (Paris 1854–68), I, ii.

[5] Book I, Part III, chap. 8; also Book V, Part IV, chap. 2.

Victor Hugo, from *Hernani* and then *Notre Dame de Paris*.[6] The cathedral to Victor Hugo is 'a vast symphony in stone . . . the gigantic work of both a man and a people . . . complex like the Iliad and the *romanzeros* whose sister the cathedral is . . . powerful and fertile like the divine creation from which it has taken its double character of variety and eternity'. And so to the 'anarchic and splendid deviations of the Renaissance', and the 'more and more grotesque and silly fashions . . . which have followed each other in the unavoidable decadence of architecture'. The eighteenth century is 'ignoble, quand il n'est pas ridicule' and 'ridicule quand il n'est pas hideux', the Panthéon is 'le plus beau gâteau de Savoie qu'on ait jamais fait en pierre' and the Halle au Blé 'une casquette de jockey anglais',[7] and finally came the 'mutilations, amputations, dislocations' at the hands of the restorers.[8]

Two years after *Notre Dame* Montalembert whom we have already come across exposing the false use of the term Catholic by the Cambridge Camden Society dedicated a short book *Du Vandalisme en France* to Victor Hugo.[9] It was published in 1839, and at its start Montalembert declares his 'passion . . . profonde . . . pour l'architecture du moyen-âge'. He then proceeds in great detail to list examples of vandalism to buildings committed by Government, municipalities, owners, parish councils, and parsons. Vandalism, he adds, again in detail, need not be destruction; it can be restoration. 'Expulsons les barbares', is the end.[9a]

Now to return to Viollet-le-Duc, it was, as we have seen, as a restorer that he began his career. But he too, before 1840, had experienced Gothic the romantic way, and letters such as one written

[6] 1831. See now J. Mallion, *Victor Hugo et l'art architectural*, (Paris, 1962), a thesis (Publications de la Faculté des Lettres et Sciences humaines, XXVIII) and hence very long. The most important chapter of *Notre Dame* for us is Book III, chap. 1. But the most interesting, though marginally only for the present book, is Book V, chaps I and 2, where Claude Frollo foretells that the book will kill the church, the book being cheaper and going further, a democratic as against a theocratic manifestation. 'Architecture is dead, beyond recall.'

[7] These three quotations are taken from Mallion, op. cit., 624 and 629.

[8] Hugo incidentally considers Notre Dame a transitional building, neither as massive as Tournus nor as light and multiform as Bourges, neither—he writes—pure Romanesque nor 'of pure Arab race'. So the old Evelyn-Wren tag still survives. Hugo incidentally calls St Germain-des-Prés Carolingian and Notre Dame Saxon.

[9] See Léon op. cit., also L. Réau, *Histoire du Vandalisme. Les Monuments détruits de l'art français* (Paris, 1959), II, 117 ff.

[9a] Schinkel had written in his memorandum on Cologne Cathedral in 1816: 'We have been assiduously working for half a century at the annihilation (of our heritage) and we have done this with so barbarous a system that we have left far behind the unsystematic barbarity of Attila's time.' (Schinkel's *Bericht über den baulichen Zustand des Kölner Doms*, September 3, 1816). Quoted from Reichensperger: *Christlich-germanische Baukunst*, p. 113.

from Chartres in 1835 describe the 'douceur inexprimable' of the building, the sculpture which 'fait vibrer le coeur', the 'lumière sombre' and so forth.[10] Immediately after Vézelay, still in 1840, followed his appointment as Inspector (with Lassus) for the Sainte Chapelle, under Duban. In 1844 Viollet and Lassus were chosen for the restoration of Notre Dame.[11]

The forties were years of battles of styles in France, earlier and more ferocious than those in England.[12] The two protagonists were at first César Daly (1809–93), founder in 1840 of the *Revue Générale de l'Architecture*, and A.-N. Didron (1806–67), founder in 1844 of the *Annales Archéologiques*. Viollet-le-Duc wrote in the *Annales Archéologiques* from the beginning.[13] They stood for what he stood for. The *Revue Générale* had different concerns. Daly was a friend of Donaldson;[14] that places him. So does—perhaps a little unfairly—the ideal church by A. J. Magne which Daly illustrated in 1848 [Pls. 59, 60].[15] But whatever the differences and hence public quarrels between the two journals, they were united against the Academy and the École des Beaux-Arts.[16] France is of course the country *par excellence* of academies. In one sense they are a French invention. Colbert was their begetter, and when they had been smashed by the Revolution, they were almost at once re-erected. The organization now was that the Institut de France, established in 1795, had a section for the fine arts, that this in 1816 became the Académie Royale des Beaux-Arts, and that the Academy ran the École des Beaux-Arts. Permanent secretary of the Academy was A. C. Quatremère de Quincy (1755–1849),[17] upholder of academic discipline, and of Antiquity as the sole pattern, and a passionate hater of the Gothic as 'un mélange fortuit' and 'une compilation incohérente de tout ce qui lui avait pu transmettre le goût dégénéré du Bas-Empire'. Words like 'désordre', 'abus', 'décadence', are used

[10] Gout, op. cit., 33.

[11] Lassus reported on the Sainte Chapelle and Viollet-le-Duc on Notre Dame in *The Ecclesiologist*, X, 1850, 297 and XI, 1850, 95. Viollet-le-Duc had been referred to already in 1846 (VI, 81 ff.) because of his controversy with Raoul-Rochette, on which see later. Lassus reappeared in *The Ecclesiologist* in 1852 (XIII, 46) with a criticism of new buildings in London. He deprecates the Houses of Parliament as conceived more in a classical than a Gothic mood and ends—much in the spirit of Viollet-le-Duc—in an attack on the 'radically vicious' teaching of architecture at the École des Beaux-Arts.

[12] On the mid-century situation in French architectural writing Professor Collins's *Changing Ideals* provides indispensable documentation.

[13] So incidentally did Viollet-le-Duc père: II, 261; III, 201.

[14] *Rev. Gén.*, III, 1842, 80.   [15] Ibid., VIII, 64 ff.

[16] On all this there is plenty in Hautecoeur, *l'Architecture classique en France*, vol. VI.

[17] See R. Schneider, *Quatremère de Quincy et son intervention dans les arts* (Paris, 1910).

in other places to characterize the Gothic. Even in Gothic rib-vaulting he refused to accept any merits. To him they show 'une intelligence fort ordinaire' and 'la simple économie de peines et dépenses'.[18]

When he retired in 1836, Raoul-Rochette (1790–1854) succeeded him. Raoul-Rochette was also Quatremère's successor as the holder of a chair of archeology. Raoul-Rochette was no more tolerant than Quatremère, though academic taste was now moving from neo-classicism towards that grand Italianate style which one calls Beaux-Arts. Typical examples are the three ornate railway stations, Est (Strasbourg) by Duquesney (1847–52) [Fig. 8], Montparnasse by Lenoir (1848–52) and Nord by Hittorff (1861–5) [Pl. 58].[19] They are typical also as showing in their façade the existence behind of the glass and iron vault of the train-shed; for the Beaux-Arts men called themselves rationalist and believed they were. Henri Labrouste's Bibliothèque Ste Geneviève, begun in 1842, has a façade of very pure monumental Italian Renaissance character—one of the finest anywhere—but inside the long reading room iron columns and iron roof are proudly displayed [Pl. 61]. This situation is reflected in the *Revue Générale* and the *Annales,* and they will therefore now be followed year by year through the forties.

In the very first volume of the *Revue*[20] railway stations are discussed, and in the second[21] the teaching of the École—very adversely of course. Louis-Pierre Baltard, architect of the Palais de Justice at Lyons with its long even façade of giant Corinthian columns and its series of domes over the Salle des Pas Perdus had ruled out for his programme anything in the Bas-Empire style or a medieval style.[22] Raoul-Rochette in his obituary for Percier attacked the neo-Renaissance: 'Vouloir fair de la Renaissance dans un temps tel que le nôtre, c'est prouver qu'on ne comprend pas la Renaissance et qu'on connaît mal notre siècle.'[23] Daly agrees up to a point, but prefers as the rule to be followed that one should go to whatever

---

[18] *Dictionnaire historique de l'Architecture* (Paris, 1832), II, 320, 670–9. Earlier, in his *Histoire de la Vie et des Ouvrages des plus célèbres Architectes du XIe. siècle jusqu'à la fin du XVIIIe. siècle* (Paris, 1830), he had spoken of Gothic architecture as an art of 'ignorance complète' of 'la vanité de la hardiesse' and 'la forfanterie de la légèreté', of disorder, confusion and 'bizarrerie' (I, 45), of Giotto in contrast to the preceding 'puériles découpures' of Gothic ornament (I, 32) and of Arnolfo di Cambio as the man 'qui annonce l'abandon des . . . erreurs du goût gothique' (I, 20).

[19] See p. 193. Also Carroll Meeks, *The Railroad Station* (Yale University Press, 1956).

[20] *Revue,* I, 1840, 513 ff., 733 ff., also II, 129.

[21] Ibid., II, 1841, 634 ff.

[22] Hautecoeur, VI, 335 quotes Baltard in 1843 on the 'impuissance de l'art de bâtir' and the 'mauvais goût' of the 'œuvres barbares' of the Middle Ages.

[23] *Revue,* II, 36.

epoch did a particular job best—Renaissance for Palaces, Gothic for churches.[24] So there was then no Gothic animosity, and in fact in volume four (1843) Willis's paper on vaults was translated by Daly who incidentally in the same volume explicitly mentions Donaldson's *Preliminary Discourse*.[25] One year later Daly could report that he had been made an honorary member of the Royal Institute of British Architects. The letter informing him was of course signed by Donaldson.[26]

But 1844 is also the year of the first number of the *Annales Archéologiques*, and in the first volume Didron reports at once a controversy in the *Revue Générale*.[27] Raoul-Rochette had published a book on Pirro Ligorio's Villa Pia in the Vatican Gardens (see p. 71, n. 40). He had praised its architecture and said it would be 'ignorance' and 'faux zèle' to be shocked by it. An uncalled-for attack on Gothic churches as bare and barren followed. M. de Calonne had answered in the *Revue* and said that a pagan style was surely unsuitable for a villa for the Pope and that Gothic churches were bare only because Raoul-Rochette's favourites and predecessors had mutilated them. Didron, needless to say, agreed with Calonne.

1845 saw a more serious quarrel break out between the two editors and finally divide the two journals sharply. The quarrel was over a matter of relatively minor significance. In St Ouen at Rouen, that superb church of the fourteenth century, was a wrought iron Rococo screen. Ought it to be thrown out as in conflict with the Gothic building or kept as of aesthetic value in itself? Curiously enough it was the *Revue* that wanted the screen removed, the *Annales* that wanted it kept. Their argument was that all beauty goes together, while Daly (or rather M. H. Janniard who had written the paper on St Ouen), although strongly stating 'Nous approuvons . . . tous les styles devenus historiques . . . tous sans exception', yet wished the styles to be kept separate.[28]

So far the fronts seem confused, but when it comes to the attitudes towards Gothic and the nineteenth century they appear in all clarity. In the *Annales* in February 1845 Lassus (of Notre Dame) had defended against the Academy the use of the Gothic style for today.

---

[24] Ibid., II, 36.
[25] Ibid., IV, 1843, 123. Viollet-le-Duc in volume nine of the *Dictionnaire* also pays his tribute to Willis's 'Vaults' (525).
[26] Ibid., V, 1844, 96.   [27] *Ann. Arch.*, I, 1844, 133 and *Rev. Gén.*, V, 1844, 15.
[28] In 1847–8 the quarrel got worse. It was now over some alleged misrepresenting, and Daly wrote: 'La Vérité ou la Guerre!', VII, 427.

True, as the academies say, our habits are not those of the thirteenth century, but they are yet more distant from Antiquity, and Gothic is at least 'notre art national', born on our soil.[29] But, Lassus continued in June, there are not only the academies who were responsible for buildings like the Madeleine, and ourselves, the Gothicists, there is a third group calling themselves wrongly the rationalists, but in fact being eclectics. They believe that one should 'borrow forms from all countries and all epochs, and even invent forms, and then combine them in an amalgam and thus create a new art'. This Lassus regards as impossible. Instead 'one ought to take as one's point of departure the *plus belle époque* of our national art', i.e. the early thirteenth century, and then not copy it but by combining it with all new resources transform the Gothic into art of our time.[30] Viollet-le-Duc (Lassus's colleague as restorer of Notre Dame) joined in[31] without saying anything new. The predecessors of the Academy have mutilated and destroyed our heritage for four hundred years. Antiquity will not do for today. Gothic is 'dicté par le bon sens', and it is ours.

This was too much for the *Revue* and also for the Academy. In the *Revue* no more happened at first than a letter by 'X' saying that our churches ought to be in the same style as our houses and our factories. Art must follow society; men ought not to be forced 'de se façonner pour les édifices'.[32] One year later L. Gounod wrote that all these proposed medieval examples 'kill invention'. One should not copy anyway, but study all styles of the past, 'grouper habilement' and 'd'une façon neuve'. Footnote by Daly: 'in order to create new expressions'.[33]

But by then a major event had shaken both journals. The Academy had taken a most unusual step. In 1846 Raoul-Rochette published official *Considérations sur la question de savoir s'il est convenable, au XIXe siécle, de bâtir des églises en style gothique*.[34] The answer of course was No. Praise is freely given to the surviving Gothic buildings, but to build new ones would mean 'rétrograder'. It would be tantamount to an endeavour to give to our society the habits of the twelfth century—an obvious 'anachronisme', 'une bizarrerie'. The buildings would be in a 'contraste éloquent' with everything

---

[29] *Annales*, II, 69 ff.

[30] Ibid., II, 1844–5, 197 ff. and more 329 ff. Had Scott read this, when he wrote his *Remarks* (see pp. 173–6)?

[31] Ibid., 303 ff.

[32] *Revue*, VI, 383.

[33] Ibid., VII, 28 ff.

[34] Reprinted *Ann. Arch.*, IV, 1846, 326 ff.

around. Gothic architecture is by no means 'l'art chrétien par excellence'; on the contrary it never penetrated properly into Rome, 'la ville chrétienne par excellence'. Christianity appears at all times, in all styles. But, however that may be, one should never try to 'ressusciter un art qui a cessé d'exister'. It would of necessity mean 'méconnaître la nature de la société, qui tend sans cesse au progrès'. Besides, Gothic has severe structural faults and Gothic sculpture fails for lack of 'imitation de la nature'.

The last pages are a summing-up. The arts must always be 'de leur temps'. They must make use of all available elements of civilization. If we want to be original, 'n'avons-nous pas l'exemple de la renaissance, pour nous apprendre comment on peut être original?' —It is the familiar collapse. We must be original, but our original style must yet be historicist. So Raoul-Rochette ends by evoking Alberti, Brunelleschi, Bramante, San Gallo, Peruzzi, Palladio, and Vignola, and also Bullant, Delorme, Lescot. Our architects ought to 'faire de même' and build churches both Christian and 'de notre société'. This is what reason prescribes and the interests of art demand, and this is also what our schools teach—'not to copy the Greeks and Romans, but to imitate them, by taking, like them, from art and nature all that lends itself to the convenience of all societies and the needs of all epochs'.

It was too bad. The archaeologists and the Gothicists rose as one man. In the *Bulletin Monumental*[35] Villers wrote calling the Madeleine and Notre Dame de Lorette 'coquet', and lacking in religious character and praising Notre Dame de Bon Secours at Blosseville near Rouen, a recent church by Barthélemy in the thirteenth-century style. Didron published a special pamphlet of retort by Lassus:[36] What the Academy recommends is anarchy. It used to defend Classical Antiquity. That has at least the recommendation of a style of unity. Raoul-Rochette instead prefers 'accouplements monstrueux'.[37] On his own programme he ought to plead for 'un art entièrement nouveau et complètement indépendant des arts précédents'. But to do that he has not the courage. So his would still be an art 'of the future, inspired . . . by an art chosen from the past'— and besides an alien, not a national art.

Viollet-le-Duc's answer to Raoul-Rochette was published in the

[35] XII, 1846, 564–5.
[36] *Réaction de l'Académie contre l'art gothique* (Didron, Paris, June 1846).
[37] Ibid., 11.

Annales the very same month.[38] He is more aggressive than Lassus: 'The Academy has nothing in common with the gods of the past it loves so much, except being wrapped in the clouds.' Raoul-Rochette praising the Villa Pia declares himself for the alien and the pagan. We want a national and a Christian art, and we want unity. Raoul-Rochette wants eclecticism. If we get what Raoul-Rochette recommends, it will be 'ce que nous avons depuis vingt ans, du désordre'. Besides, the Renaissance is 'sometimes attractive', but 'always a bastard art', and as for Raoul-Rochette's attacks on Gothic construction and on Gothic decoration Viollet-le-Duc could of course invalidate them without effort.[39] Thirteenth-century ornament is 'une des créations les plus originales, les plus spontanées . . . de l'esprit humain' and moreover inspired by 'the vegetation of our forests and fields'—is the École blind to all this? There it is, 'mélant tous les styles et tous les âges', and teaching not one but 'ten architectures'—and all of them in fact impossible to imitate, because made for a different climate and particular manners.[40] What we demand is a logical art instead and a beautiful art, and one grown 'sur notre sol'.[41] This is what the art of the thirteenth century is. Besides, it is easy to make it fit the needs of our churches today, as the cult has not changed. Is it not characteristic that even French sixteenth- and seventeenth-century architects have kept to plan and structure of the Gothic period?

What else ought we to demand? 'Un art nouveau'? To have that 'il faut une civilisation nouvelle, et nous ne sommes pas dans ce cas'.[42] So let us start again from the moment before 'the types were corrupted'. It will be easy to apply 'the modifications necessary for our needs'. 'In the middle of modern industry, progress will not keep us waiting.' But, Viollet adds: 'Nous n'en sommes pas encore à savoir quelles sont les modifications que le génie moderne apporterait.'[43]

Later he thought he knew. The radicalism of his conviction grew, his experience also grew, and in spite of his radicalism his recognition grew. Gradually the appointments to restore Amiens, Chartres,

[38] *Annales*, III, 1846, 333 ff.   [39] Ibid., 339 ff.   [40] Ibid., 347.
[41] Ibid., 349.   [42] Ibid., 351.
[43] It is interesting that Vitet, the first Inspecteur Général, in the same year made a far more radical speech. It was given to the Antiquaires de Normandie and reported in the *Revue Générale* (VII, 1847–8, 392 ff.). He said that 'never in the world has art produced the same thing twice' and that 'any architecture which fits the needs of an age, has a physiognomy which is tantamount to a certain kind of beauty'. Honour therefore 'to those who don't despair of being able to invent a new architecture'.

Reims, Saint Sernin at Toulouse, Clermont-Ferrand, and also the château of Pierrefonds and the walls of Carcassonne fell to him.[44] Légion d'honneur 1849, Inspecteur Général des Edifices Diocésans 1853, R.I.B.A. Gold Medal 1864. The *Dictionnaire raisonné de l'Architecture* began to come out in 1854 and was finished in ten volumes in 1868. It was followed by the *Dictionnaire raisonné du Mobilier français* in six volumes (1858–75) and numerous other books, including one on the geology of Mont Blanc (1876). For Viollet-le-Duc was a great mountaineer, and the story of his fall into a crevasse and his two and a half hours abandoned in it makes thrilling reading.

But before Viollet-le-Duc's theories and views of the years after 1850 can be presented, a work must be introduced in some detail which began to come out in that year and remains the most substantial French mid-nineteenth-century manual of architectural theory. It is Léonce Reynaud's *Traité d'Architecture*. It appeared in 1850–8 in two volumes of text with three volumes of plates. Léonce Reynaud[45] was born in 1803, i.e. he was older than Viollet-le-Duc. He went to study first at the École Polytechnique which he left soon for political reasons and then at the École des Beaux-Arts. He took his engineering diploma in 1835 and began to teach at the École Polytechnique in 1837 and at the École des Ponts et Chaussées in 1840. From 1853 to 1857 he was one of the Inspectors of Diocesan Monuments (like Viollet-le-Duc) and became Inspecteur Général des Ponts et Chaussées in 1856 and Director of the École des Ponts et Chaussées in 1869. He had received the Légion d'Honneur already in 1839 and became Officier in 1834 and Commandeur in 1864. In short, a highly successful professional and official career, undisturbed by any of the violent opposition which time and again propelled Viollet-le-Duc.

The *Traité d'Architecture*[46] is, so Reynaud tells us, an enlarged version of his teaching course. Such general, systematic courses and treatises are French rather than English. England has produced none that could be compared with Reynaud or the later one of Guadet. Reynaud divides his into two volumes, the first dealing

---

[44] A typical Viollet-le-Duc restoration report has recently been published. It was written in 1864 as a piece of detailed advice concerning the restoration of Roermond Minster by Cuypers, the most important Dutch architect of his time. See *Opus Musivum* (Een bundel studies aangeboden aan Prof. Dr. M. D. Ozinga, Assen 1964), 106–11.

[45] F. de Dartein: *Léonce Reynaud, sa vie, ses œuvres* (Paris, 1885). Mr. A. H. Wasencraft kindly helped me with some biographical details.

[46] In English Professor Peter Collins alone, in his *Changing Ideals*, has made some use of the *Traité*.

with materials and the elements of building—foundations, walls, the orders of columns, arcading, doorways and windows, attics, cornices, pediments, floors and ceilings, vaults, staircases. All these are elements of building in stone. Building in wood follows with its elements, and finally building in iron. Of this we shall hear more. Volume two is devoted to composition, i.e. to types of buildings: churches, schools, libraries, museums, and so on to railway stations, lighthouses, and bridges, and to houses and towns.

It will be noticed that there is no history of styles and no philosophy. All that is done for the history of style is about 100 pages on the development of church building and of course analyses of individual buildings of the past. What Reynaud has to say of a general nature is condensed into an introduction of no more than sixteen pages. Reynaud's principles are simple. Architecture is 'l'art des convenances et du beau dans les constructions'. The relation between the first two is that 'rien n'est beau que ce qui est convenable'.[47] Commodity must come first; for 'l'architecture . . . est née de besoins matériels' and so 'l'utile est son premier but'.[48] But that is not all. Within the limitations of the functional, many solutions are possible. Which are the beautiful ones? Taste must decide, and 'notre goût n'accepte pas tout ce dont notre intelligence se conduite'.[49] By what criteria should we choose then? Reynaud, like many before him, pleads for 'order and simplicity'[50] and for harmony.[51] After these aesthetic qualities to be achieved in the building itself, follows decoration, an 'accession importante', but an accessory, i.e. not something indispensable to architectural Beauty.[52] The final summary is this: 'l'Architecture est un art éminemment rationnel, mais elle demande beaucoup à notre imagination.'[53] Every age, from Egypt onwards, has found its own solution. We must study them, but what we must look out for, is 'moins la forme que l'esprit'.[54] The only thing to be imitated is 'l'accord des moyens avec le but'.[55] Yet Reynaud has his preferences. They are clearly not on the medieval side: Gothic flying buttresses 'sont d'un pauvre effet'. They embarrass the building, and moreover

[47] Traité d'Architecture, I, 1.
[48] Ibid., I, 2.
[49] I am unable to trace this reference.
[50] Traité d'Architecture, I, 3.
[51] Ibid., I, 4.
[52] Ibid., 1, 7–8.
[53] Ibid., I, 15.
[54] Charles Garnier formulated it nicely in his À travers les arts in 1869: 'L'eclecticisme doit être repoussé complètement, quand il s'agit de produire; il faut être eclectique pour admirer.' Quoted from M. Steinhauser, Die Architektur der Pariser Oper (Munich, 1969), 176.
[55] Traité d'Architecture, I, 16.

'il y a . . . quelque chose de vicieux' in a building having to be propped up like that.[56] Hence the Renaissance gave up this system to return to Roman construction. Reynaud evidently welcomes that, but he at once states his conviction that we ourselves are 'en progrès à la fois sur les Romains et sur nos pères'. Proof of that is that we can obtain results with less effort, i.e. less weight of materials, than any age before,[57] and this is due to progress in science and industry.[58] So Reynaud proclaims himself at once as an optimist, like Donaldson in England.

The most significant parts of the *Traité* in our context are those dealing with iron, and we must look at them before we can return to Viollet-le-Duc. Labrouste, it must be remembered, had already in the forties proudly exposed iron in the Bibliothèque Sainte-Geneviève. Now, Reynaud says, iron is used more and more; for its advantages are obvious. It allows 'plus de légèreté et de hardiesse' than stone or timber, more widely spaced and slenderer supports.[59] Moreover, it offers an answer to the ever repeated demand for a new system of architecture. Iron calls for new forms and new proportions. 'Ce qui convenait à la pierre ne saurait, sous aucun rapport, convenir au fer.' Hence if not a 'rénovation complète' at least new elements and considerable developments must be expected, and we would see more of them already now, if architecture did not need, apart from architects, 'une opinion publique disposée à les apprécier'. The new proportions must enter into the 'sentiment de l'époque'.[60]

So much of general considerations. It will be agreed that they are both progressive and reasonable. There follows the difference between wrought iron (fer forgé) and cast iron (fonte) and then jointing, and, as in the parts dealing with stone, paragraphs on walls, columns, floors and ceilings, roofs, and so on. Polonceau's binder is discussed,[61] and railway stations offer the most frequent references including Reynaud's own Gare du Nord[62] so soon to be replaced by Hittorff's on which Reynaud was the engineer.[63] Of other buildings included the most important by far is of course the Bibliothèque Sainte-Geneviève.[64] The description ends: 'Cette remarkquable construction est due à M. H. Labrouste . . . un des hommes de

[56] Ibid., I, 12.   [57] Ibid., I, 13.   [58] Ibid., I, 14.
[59] Ibid., I, 446.   [60] Ibid., I, 447–8.   [61] Ibid., I, 470.
[62] Ibid., I, 469, 478.
[63] Hittorff's Cirque des Champs-Élysées of 1838–9 is also referred to. See p. 193.
[64] Ibid., I, 461–4.

l'époque chez lesquels le sentiment de la forme est le plus développé.'[65]

The second volume of the *Traité* came out in 1858. It reinforces what the first volume had stated; and this Reynaud may well have found necessary; for the battles between Gothicists and Anti-Gothicists, between Historicists and defenders of the nineteenth century raged on in the fifties, mostly now conducted by or apropos Viollet-le-Duc. On iron and its uses, Reynaud found, no confirmation was needed. In fact, although among the building types which Reynaud reviews, railway stations and market halls have chapters to themselves, little is said in defence of iron, and iron bridges are, oddly enough, not referred to at all.

The philosophical aspects on the other hand are expanded beyond the short introduction of volume one. The start of the chapter on Composition is the traditional Vitruvian one of commodity, firmness, and delight. Delight, i.e. *beauté*, is least easy to discuss; truth, simplicity, order, symmetry all do not help much.[66] Nor does the division into the *beau rationnel* and the *beau idéal*, which latter changes from epoch to epoch.[67] Thirty inconclusive pages on decoration follow.

Among the most interesting are the pages on style, the term not used in the general sense of Semper's *Der Stil*, but simply as the style of an epoch. What Reynaud says is that there are epochs 'qui ont foi en elles-mêmes' and others 'où les esprits flottent irresolus dans toutes les directions . . . Ils sont tristes pour l'art et n'ont point de style qui leur soit propre . . . Tantôt on veut tel style du passé, tantôt tel autre.' So architects must study all these styles, as they must in their designs avoid mixing them; for 'les compositions hybrides sont toujours vicieuses'.[68] There is no final flourish of hope for the future as there had been in the Introduction of 1850.

Another difference between 1858 and 1850 is the treatment of the Gothic style. What had been a few sentences, is now blown up into five pages.[69] Amiens receives its due praises[70] but decadence set in in the second half of the thirteenth century, and the fifteenth was a century of total decay. The decline was in fact bound to come; for 'le point de départ était erroné'. For reasons admittedly spiritual the

[65] On Labrouste see *Labrouste*, Catalogue of an Exhibition held at the Bibliothèque Nationale in 1953. This has a bibliography including the privately printed *Henri Labrouste, Souvenirs, notes receuillées et classées par ses enfants*, Paris, 1928, which I have not seen.

[66] *Traité d'Architecture*, II, 17, etc.   [67] Ibid., II, 25.   [68] Ibid., II, 90.

[69] Ibid., II, 295–9.   [70] Ibid., II, 247, 287.

Gothic mason denied the laws of matter and scorned reality. The result was a system of vaults and their supports contrary to what 'accepte une saine théorie de l'art'. No proof is given of this, but praise of Michelangelo's St Peter's and also, with a view to what might be done today, praise of the Basilica of Constantine (i.e. of Maxentius), of S. Maria degli Angeli in the Baths of Diocletian, of St Sophia, and of the east end of Florence Cathedral.[71] So in this direction of classical monumentality Reynaud visualized a worth-while future for architecture. And he adds: Verticalism as in Gothic cathedrals, yes; mysterious perspectives, yes, but with them 'toutes les ressources que . . . présentent l'art, la science et l'industrie'.[72]

With this we are ready to return to Viollet-le-Duc and to follow him into the fifties and sixties. Viollet-le-Duc, like Victor Hugo, had always been an enemy of academies. But he liked teaching. At the École des Arts décoratifs his teaching had come to an end in 1850. So when in 1856 Labrouste whom he highly respected—for reasons which will be obvious later—closed his teaching studio, Labrouste's pupils led by Anatole de Baudot asked Viollet to open a studio. This he did, but it lasted only for a few months. Partly inspired by Viollet's writing in the *Gazette des beaux-arts* in 1862–3, in 1863–4 the École des Beaux Arts itself was re-organized and so Viollet joined at last. However, after only seven lectures he gave up against the hostility of staff and students. The outcome of his pedagogic passion before he joined the École, and of his lectures given and not given was the *Entretiens sur l'architecture*, his most important book from our point of view. It appeared in two volumes, in 1863 and 1872, with two albums of 1863 and 1864. There are twenty *Entretiens* in all, numbers one to ten datable to 1856–63, numbers eleven to the end to 1863–72, the Atlas of plates to 1863.[73]

To appreciate Viollet-le-Duc's views one should go principally to the *Entretiens*, but also, of earlier writings, to the introduction to the *Dictionnaire*, dated 1854, and of course to sundry articles in the *Dictionnaire*. In the Introduction to the *Dictionnaire*, one year after Ruskin's 'Nature of Gothic', Viollet stated for the first time his mature principles. His aim, he writes, is to make known not only the forms of architecture, but their *raisons d'être*, and the customs and ideas behind them; for complete harmony exists between the art and the spirit of the peoples in the Middle Ages. The aim of studying medieval architecture should not be 'to make artists walk backward',

[71] Ibid., II, 316–7.   [72] Ibid., II, 315.   [73] English edition, 1877–81.

'to repeat what others have said', and 'to erect in our country today houses and palaces of the thirteenth century'. If the architect does that, he is merely 'the costumier who dresses us up according to our fancies'. Instead he ought to learn the medieval principles, because they are useful in expressing one's thoughts. For the principles of the twelfth and thirteenth centuries 'can bear fruit today as they did then' and may indeed lead to 'a happy revolution'.

But, in contrast to Ruskin, today remains emphatically today. 'Never have so many resources been offered to the architects.' This is one topical point; the other is political: artists were free down to the Age of Louis XIV. In Gothic reliefs you can see Kings led into Hell and never see Kings in the clouds. 'The arts belonged to the people and . . . no-one dreamt of directing them.' As soon as art left the abbeys, ideas of 'intellectual liberty' evolved. The free craftsman is a conception Viollet-le-Duc shared with Ruskin, but he meant it differently, as the *Entretiens* prove.

The *Entretiens* start with a fighting preface. His lectures had been attacked as dangerous by a Professor of the École, because they drew attention to an art which in fact belongs to us, as Greek architecture belonged to the Greeks and Roman art to the Romans.[74] What he intended instead and what he intends by the publication now, is 'to enquire into the reason of every form—for every architectural form has its reason; to point out the origin of the various principles that underlie them . . . and to call attention to the application which can be made of the principles of ancient art to the requirements of the present day'. So it is history, and the needs of the nineteenth century Viollet promises to treat of, and the first volume indeed deals with primitive building; Greek and Roman architecture; Byzantine and Romanesque architecture; The principles of Western architecture in the Middle Ages, culminating in those of Gothic architecture; the decline, i.e. the Renaissance; and so to the last lecture called 'Architecture of the Nineteenth Century'.

Greece and Rome in the *Entretiens* receive an objective treatment; it is in the Gothic lecture that Viollet-le-Duc departs from objectivity, though he still avoids appearing as a partisan of the Gothic Revival. His thesis is that 'laymen alone . . . organized in guilds' designed the Gothic buildings and that therefore alone the buildings 'manifested the special genius of the French'. Viollet goes on pointedly to call the Gothic 'the lay school of France',[75] and he had to do so being a

---

[74] He means of course Raoul-Rochette.   [75] *Entretiens,* I, 265.

liberal and an agnostic. Gout quotes him as writing: 'It is as ridiculous to pretend that there is a god as it is impertinent to maintain that there isn't.'[76] And in the lecture he insists that 'in the thirteenth century . . . art was essentially democratic'.[77] Thus by a legerdemain he succeeded in secularizing the great French cathedrals. Even 'hatred of injustice and oppression' as felt by artists is dragged in.[78] But once that is done, Viollet's analysis of Gothic principles is as admirable in the *Entretiens* as it was in the same years and in so much more detail in the *Dictionnaire*. The Gothic builders succeeded in creating equilibrium by means of a very complex construction [Pl. 62]. And anticipating what was to come, Viollet continues by saying that the principles underlying Gothic architecture are far more applicable to today's needs than those of Greece and Rome. In fact he uses at once the possibilities of iron in this context. 'It is impossible to erect a Greek or Roman building with certain materials provided by modern appliances—iron for instance—whereas the principles and methods introduced by the lay architects of the late twelfth century adapt themselves, without effort, to the use of these new materials.' Viollet goes even so far as to speak of their 'having anticipated the industrial progress' of a later age.[79] Let us therefore, he concludes the lecture, adhere to their principles 'which are eternally true, applicable and vital'.

Lecture Six has as its centre a consideration of what the word Style should mean. Style is 'inspiration subjected to the laws of reason.'[80] It is 'one of the essential elements of beauty, but does not of itself alone constitute beauty'.[81] All animals have style, but not all men; for men may be 'artificial or vulgar'.[82] Elementary vessels on the other hand all have style; for they are the most natural form for their purpose. We may speak of the style of Louis XV, but the period's 'contempt of appropriate form'[83] proves that it had no style. That does not, however, mean that 'a very advanced civilization necessarily precludes style'.[84] For the hundred-gun sailing vessel has style, since its forms are 'so perfectly adapted to their purpose that they appear beautiful'. But 'naval engineers in building a steam-ship and machinists in making a locomotive', if they reproduced 'the

---

[76] Gout, *Viollet-le-Duc*, 133.   [77] *Entretiens*, I, 304.   [78] Ibid., I, 274.

[79] Ibid., I, 274. The same thought was put more neatly by an American in 1864. The Crystal Palace, A. W. Colgate wrote, in the *Continental Monthly*, vol. V, 'in iron is what is Gothic in stone' (quoted from R. W. Winter, *J.S.A.H.*, XVII, Dec. 1958, 28).

[80] *Entretiens*, I, 179.   [81] Ibid., I, 180.   [82] Ibid., I, 181.

[83] Ibid., I, 183.   [84] Ibid., I, 184.

15

forms of the sailing vessel of the time of Louis XIV, or of a stage-coach' would forfeit style. But they don't do that, they

conform to the novel principles with which they have to deal, and then produce works which . . . have . . . style. The locomotive, for example, has a special physiognomy which all can appreciate, and which renders it a distinct creation. Nothing can better express force under control than these ponderous rolling machines; their motions are gentle or terrible; they advance with terrific impetuosity, or seem to pant impatiently under the restraining hand of the diminutive creature who starts or stops them at will. The locomotive is almost a living being, and its external form is the simple expression of its strength. A locomotive therefore has style. Some will call it an ugly machine. Buy why ugly? Does it not exhibit the true expression of the brute energy which it embodies? Is it not appreciable by all as a thing complete, organized, possessing a special character, as does a piece of artillery or a gun? There is no style but that which is appropriate to the object. . . . A gun has style, but a gun made to resemble a crossbow will have none. Now we architects have for a long time been making guns while endeavouring to give them as much as possible the appearance of crossbows.[85]

The message is clear enough, Viollet never doubted its validity. Years later, in a comment on the International Exhibition in Paris of 1867 he wrote in the *Gazette des beaux-arts*:

L'observation vraie de la qualité et de la force des matériaux en oeuvre donne des formes originales toujours . . . Je pousserai la barbarie jusqu'à avouer que ces machines dont chaque pièce est si parfaitement combinée en raison de son emploi, où rien n'est sacrifié à des formes traditionelles transmises par un 'grand siècle' quelconque, me ravissent . . . par les beautés des formes qui ne sont telles à mon sens que parce qu'elles sont l'expression rigoureusement exacte d'une necessité.[86]

The theme is never far from the *Entretiens*. Lecture Eight for instance deals with the false principles of the sixteenth and seventeenth centuries not 'based on any of the principles recognized during the great periods of art.'[87] Yet Viollet analyses the sixteenth-century Renaissance well, better than the age of Louis XIV. Here he is obviously partisan. This is the age that made architecture autocratic and whose architects cared not for suitability, require-

---

[85] *Entretiens*, I, 186–7.
[86] Quoted from F. Welch, *Das Gebäude der Pariser Weltausstellung 1867* (Diss., Karlsruhe, 1967), 208–9.
[87] *Entretiens*, I, 323.

ments, and arrangement of rooms for the sake of convenience.[88] Why should—this is added in Lecture Ten—all houses in a square be identical, why should façades have all the windows identical, why should the façade of a town hall be the same as the façade of a church, why indeed porticoes which no one ever uses.[89] Later on in *Habitations Modernes*[90] he sums the argument up neatly. 'Pour faire une boite, il est bon de connaître ce qu'elle doit contenir.' Against enforced symmetry Viollet sets asymmetry as a natural and desirable quality, the rule of Gothic secular architecture and hence—or for reasons of the *Zeitgeist*—the rule of Viollet's own house façades [Pl. 63]. Yet, like Pugin, he warns[91] against being 'irregular for the love of irregularity'. He was certainly sensitive to the charms of asymmetry, as an excellent 'townscape' comment in a letter of his shows.[92] He says there, apropos the axial view newly contrived for Amiens Cathedral, 'the geometrical point is unique, the others are infinite in number. One should therefore not build with a view to the unique point but with a view to the multiple others.' Lecture Eight, as many of the others of Volume One, contains apart from the historical theme much that is general and much that is topical. As for the topical, the historical treatment of the French Renaissance and the French Classical of the seventeenth century already mentioned calls for a warning against what Viollet-le-Duc calls 'the eclectic school' of his own time, the school of those 'of a more liberal order' who would 'give a welcome to all the forms that have been recognized, from classic times down to our own day'. He wants to have nothing to do with them. They forget that there are 'invariable principles'. Their language of form must therefore be 'a *macaronic* language . . . whose meaning no-one can decipher.'[93]

So to Lecture Ten and the real programme for the nineteenth century. The lecture starts with the question which had troubled Ruskin and Scott and, as we shall see, troubled others: 'Is the nineteenth century condemned to end without having possessed an architecture of its own? Is it to transmit to posterity nothing but

---

[88] *Entretiens,* I, 384. On Gabriel's Place de la Concorde on the other hand he is fair and appreciative, II, 199.

[89] Ibid., I, 482.

[90] 1875, 2 vols., I, 2. The *Habitations Modernes* include several English buildings, e.g. Waterhouse's Master's Lodge for Pembroke College, Cambridge of 1871–3, Col. Edis's Boscombe Spa Hotel at Bournemouth of 1873, and also Norman Shaw's Grimsdyke at Harrow Weald of 1872. In the eighth of his *Entretiens* he had incidentally used the story of Scott's Government Offices as an example of wrongheaded 'doctrines exclusives' (VIII, 328).

[91] *Entretiens,* II, 279.   [92] *Lettres,* 106.   [93] *Entretiens,* I, 338.

pastiches and hybrids?'[94] Viollet's answer is a No, as convinced as Matthew Digby Wyatt's, and for similar reasons.[95] Architecture must never be 'hors de la vérité'. We must be 'true to the programme, true to the processes of construction'. We must 'fulfil exactly, scrupulously the conditions which needs impose'. We must 'employ materials according to their qualities and properties'.[96] So far so good, but 'once the programme is fulfilled, once the structure is there, that is not enough to produce a work of art; form is needed as well.'[97] So the next question is: 'Which is the most suitable form today, for our civilization'? The answer is foreseeable: the precedents needed are neither Greek nor Roman, but in the lay-school of the Middle Ages. That school alone 'has foreseen the resources which industry, mechanics, and the ease of transport provide us with'.[98] 'Let stone appear stone, iron iron, wood wood.'[99] And as an example just like the Renaissancist Reynaud, he quotes the Bibliothèque Sainte-Geneviève and as a second example Saulnier's factories[100] of which the best-known today is that for Chocolat Menier. Moreover, in the second part of the Atlas to the *Entretiens*, published in 1864, Viollet illustrates public spaces spanned by stone rib-vaults on iron shafts.[101] It is clumsy architecture, not as accomplished as Labrouste's is, nor as original as it seems; for Louis-Auguste Boileau had already built the church of Saint Eugène in Paris with iron ribs as well as piers in 1854–5 [Pl. 64]. And of course, what Viollet presented in the Atlas was never built.

Still, the boldness of his statements and the logic of his system remain. The second volume of the *Entretiens* re-states them, and iron is the dominant theme. Iron for supporting wide spans, iron for private houses,[102] iron for staircases, iron for floral capitals,[103] iron for all the advantages of prefabrication—'the parts executed in factories . . . and taken to the building ready to be . . . raised into position',[104] and iron of course for bridges. The bridges are engineering work, and Viollet several times goes out of his way to praise the engineer and warn the architect. In their bridges for instance 'our

[94] *Entretiens*, I, 450.

[95] Incidentally, a letter exists from Wyatt to Viollet written on 17 March, 1855. In it Wyatt proclaims himself interested in a translation of the *Dictionary* and promises to try and interest 'nos meilleurs éditeurs'. Quoted from the catalogue of the Viollet exhibition of 1965, 233.

[96] Ibid., I, 455–6.   [97] Ibid., I, 465.

[98] Ibid., I, 465.   [99] Ibid., I, 472.

[100] II, 334.   [101] The text to go with them is in the eleventh lecture.

[102] Lectures XVII and XVIII.   [103] *Entretiens*, II, 126, 130.

[104] Ibid., II, 95.

engineers have struck out a new path; but our architects have up to now not ventured further than a timid adaptation of the new techniques to old forms'.[105] There is a danger in this for the whole profession. The engineers 'who have made locomotives, have not dreamt of copying horse-drawn coaches'.[106] 'If then the architects of our time don't want to watch the decline of the profession or even the annihilation of the art of architecture, they must become . . . able constructors, ready to take advantage of all the resources which our social situation provides.'

But did Viollet-le-Duc himself heed that warning? As so often before, there is a gulf between what he discoursed on and what he did. His teaching is the superiority of the late twelfth and thirteenth centuries over all other architecture, its suitability for today, ecclesiastically as well as secularly, and the necessity of a nineteenth-century style founded on Gothic principles. What we find in reality is competent Gothic Revival churches—foremost St Denis-de-l'Estrée of 1860–5—and mediocre houses, fanciful rather than logical and ill-fitting together.[107] And in addition the enormous volume of restoration work, profiting from his unparalleled scholarship, but lacking in the respect one would have imagined as a matter of course in the author of the *Dictionnaire*. What in fact restoration meant to him is summed up in the eighth volume of the *Dictionnaire* (1866), where his very first sentence is that restoration of a building is 'not just to preserve it, to repair it and remodel it, [but] to reinstate it in the complete state, such as it may never have been in at any one moment'. A few pages further on he provides chapter and verse. Whether, if a building was altered at a later date, one ought to restore both periods or return to the 'unité de style dérangée' must depend on the circumstances. If e.g. a vaulted twelfth-century building has now a later vault one ought to restore the twelfth-century vault. If piers in a secular great hall were re-done at different dates, one should restore them to the original shape, or else one might sometimes leave them in order to 'éclaircir un point de l'histoire de l'art'.[108] What such advice was to look like in reality can be seen at the cathedral of Clermont-Ferrand which has a nave of the mid-fourteenth century and was, when lengthened to the west by Viollet, given a totally new façade in the thirteenth-century

[105] Ibid., II, 90.   [106] Ibid., II, 64.
[107] The American critic Russell Sturgis stated that Viollet's own buildings show 'scarcely any edividence of artistic design' (*The Nation*, XXIX, 220).
[108] *Dictionnaire*, VIII, 23–5.

style [Pl. 65], exactly what Scott would have done—the Middle Pointed for ever.

Viollet-le-Duc—this has already been said at the beginning of this chapter—has much in common with Scott, and the chapter will also have proved that the battle of the styles, Gothic or Classical, i.e. Italianate or Cinquecento or Mixed Renaissance has also much in common in both countries. On the whole it must however be said that the intellectual level of the combatants' argumentation was higher in France. Also the battle was conducted much more fiercely. This is due no doubt to national differences. The French are intellectually more radical, and also they believe more in powerful central organizations. Without the power of the Académie des Beaux-Arts and its stranglehold over the École des Beaux-Arts there would have been less need of ferocity among attackers as well as defenders. The Academy called the Gothic Revival an anachronism, the Gothicists called the eclecticism of mixed motifs 'accouplements monstrueux'. That far English parallels could easily be pointed out.

But where the situation in France differs from that in England and is very French indeed is that both parties are proud to call themselves rationalists and that both are ready to come to terms with iron in architecture—on the one hand Viollet on paper and Boileau in reality, on the other Reynaud on paper and Labrouste and Hittorff in reality.

One postscript to Hittorff and Viollet-le-Duc before we leave France for good. It is concerned with 1861 and the part of the Prix Bordin for the best book on the arts published in the preceding two years, which Viollet received in that year. The book was the volumes of the *Dictionnaire* published by then.[109] On 17 August the Bordin Commission considered Courdaveaux's *Du beau dans la nature et dans l'art*, Chenavard's *Voyage en Grèce*, Sanzey's *Études sur le quatuor*, Rio's *L'art chrétien*, Charles Blanc's *Histoire des Peintres*, Lerègne's *Science du beau*, Grinzère's *Les Loges et les Stances de Raphael* and Viollet-le-Duc's *Dictionnaire*. During discussion Reynaud's *Traité* was added, and Alexandre Lenoir's works. It was Hittorff who proposed Reynaud. The result was a division of the prize into three parts: for Reynaud, Blanc, and Lenoir. Félix Duban (architect of the river front of the École des Beaux-Arts and the Hôtel Pourtalès

---

[109] David Stewart ready as always to help, copied the following for me from the Procès-Verbaux of the Académie des Beaux-Arts (Institut de France). The Prix Bordin was founded in 1852 and still exists.

and closely connected with Viollet's early restorations) then regretted that Viollet should have been left out, for the 'richesse des matériaux', the 'exactitude des dessins' and for 'science' and 'érudition' of the *Dictionnaire*, which is up to date 'the most complete history of Gothic Art'.[110] Hittorff answered recognizing the qualities of the *Dictionnaire*, but 'l'amour de son sujet a entrainé l'auteur à des exagérations, et lui a fait émettre des doctrines très contestables, d'après lesquelles l'art gothique devrait être préféré même à l'art grec.' Hence he was to vote against the proposal. M. de Nieuwekerke (shortly to be made Surintendant des Beaux-Arts) agreed with Duban and praised Viollet for 'la conservation de nos temples du moyen-âge'. Hittorff added that Viollet was wrong in making the Gothic style a French affair. It flourished at the same time in France, Germany, and England. M. Lemaire considered the *Dictionnaire* and Reynaud's *Traité* as 'sur la même ligne'; this Gilbert, the architect, denied; for Reynaud's work was didactic and intended for teaching purposes, Viollet's may have its exaggerations, but what does that matter to 'un homme dont les opinions sont faites'? The richness of documentation, the drawings, the research remain.

No result was obtained, and the discussion continued on 24 August. It started with Duban saying that Hittorff had accused Viollet of placing Gothic above Greek art. That was not true; Viollet had not. Hittorff however was not there, and had written a letter to the President of the Academy to say that for personal reasons he had to stay away. This letter exists, and in it Hittorff points out that in the most recent instalments of the *Dictionnaire* there were 'déclamations banales contre notre compagnie' and also 'une attaque personelle contre moi'. This, Hittorff thinks, must be, because he had recently praised Ancient above Gothic art, or because of Viollet's wounded pride in not having won the competition for the Opera in which Hittorff was one of the twelve-man jury.[111]

---

[110] Viollet-le-Duc's erudition is indeed impressive. A sign of it is his Library which was sold in auction in May 1880. David Stewart kindly arranged for me to have a xerox copy made of the *Catalogue des livres qui composent la bibliothèque de feu M.E. Viollet-le-Duc*. Under architecture and *beaux-arts* are 802 items. They include, apart from matters and buildings of the French Middle Ages, Delorme, Ducerceau, Derand's *Voûtes*, Laugier, Durand's *Recueil*, Reynaud's *Traité*, Willis on Canterbury, Winchester, and the Holy Sepulchre, Willis's translation of Villard de Honnecourt, Rickman's *Attempt* in an edition of 1862, Scott's *Gleanings*, Beresford Hope's *Cathedral of the Nineteenth Century* (see p. 229), Hittorff and Zanth on Sicily (see p. 67), Percier and Fontaine on Roman Renaissance palaces (see p. 71, n. 40), and Owen Jones's *Alhambra*.

[111] Viollet's is indeed a decidedly weak design. On this design see J. Corday, 'Viollet-le-Duc et l'Opéra', *Bull. de la Societe de l'histoire de l'art Français*, 1941–4, 77 ff., and more recently M. Steinhauser, *Die Architektur des Pariser Oper* (Munich, 1969).

In the end the Prix Bordin was divided not among three but five: Reynaud, Viollet, Lenoir, Blanc, and Lerègne. In the end? If we take a longer view, in the very end Reynaud and Hittorff won, and Viollet and the Gothicists lost. For, whereas in England the Great Domestic Revival of the late nineteenth and twentieth century stemmed from Morris who stemmed from Ruskin, who both stemmed from the English medievalists, in France instead in the same years the style triumphed which we call Beaux-Arts after the Académie and the École and which is an amalgam of Roman Antiquity, Renaissance, and Rationalism.

CHAPTER XXI

Young Robert Kerr

IT may be refreshing after Viollet-le-Duc, after Scott, after Ruskin, after the Cambridge Camden Society, and after Pugin to come to an architect who in 1846 called the antiquarian 'the scientific man in Rubbish'. This iconoclast was Robert Kerr, then aged twenty-three and later to become Professor of Construction at King's College London. Robert Kerr was a lively and entertaining writer, an extremely competent planner of houses and a mediocre eclectic—macaronic—architect. He was born in 1823 at Aberdeen, visited the United States when very young, was—like many others—dissatisfied with the way aspirants were taught, became one of the founders of the Architectural Association and in 1847 its first president.[1] The Association was intended to be a club and a school. The Institute of British Architects, we must remember, had been founded in 1835.[2] Kerr, it will be seen, was not its friend any more than he was the friend of the antiquarians, and at the first official meeting of the Architectural Association when Professor Donaldson asked the momentous question: 'Are we to have an architecture of our period, a distinct style of the nineteenth century?'[3] young Robert Kerr had already given his answer; for *The Newleafe Discourses on the Fine Art Architecture* had been published by John Weale, the publisher of the *Quarterly Papers* (see p. 129), in 1846.

The Newleafe Discourses take place between Mr. Heavyith'heel, Fellow of the Institute of British Architects, Mr. Newleafe, a thoughtful gentleman, and Mr. Verditurus the Librarian who says 'thine' for 'your', and 'he designeth' for 'he designs', and the discourses are about 'The Fine Art Architecture'. For architecture is not about foundations, drains, stone, brick and mortar, slating etc.—that is building. It is not about 'looking after scoundrel builders'. It is not about the five Orders—that is Fiddlededee and Fiddlededum.

[1] See the brief but brilliant *The Architectural Association, 1847–1947*, by Sir John Summerson (London, 1947).
[2] See p. 24.   [3] See p. 82.

It is not about 'The Camden Society sort of thing', as that is archae-ology. It is not about the Greek style, the 'Roman; Egyptian; Italian; Byzantine; Gothic; . . . Norman, Early English, Decorated, and Perpendicular; Tudor, Elizabethan, Castellated; Cottage Swiss; Sir John Soane's style; and so forth'. 'That may be Architecture, but Architecture is not that.'[4] If architecture is not the imitation of old styles, should there then be a new stlye? 'I have not', says Mr. Newleafe, in spite of his name, 'pretended to be able intellectually to invent a new style; perhaps I might be able, perhaps I might not.'[5] In the event Kerr-Newleafe was not. All one ought to be able to do is to test architecture 'by principles of Nature and Reason', and the witness is the great Professor Cockerell himself who in a lecture in that very year 1846 had said: 'He who would really become an Architect must leave the special discussion of styles, and steadily look to the true end and aim of his Art.'

Then Kerr introduces one by one the false architects. First 'Alderman Beefeater, Architect and Engineer, Surveyor, House-Agent and Appraiser', 'brought up to the architectural business', then 'Mr. Scamozzi Brunelleschi Brick' who believes in 'purity of style . . . the pure orders, pure Gothic, pure Elizabethan, pure every-thing else'.[6] Next an aside against those who vehemently urge 'the doctrine . . . that Construction is Architecture'. No, Kerr says: they are two things, 'and there is no need for putting the one in antagonism against the other', the construction-man (that is, the builder rather than the engineer) concerning himself with 'pipe castings . . . nuts, bolts, washers; air-traps, stink-traps . . . five-coat-work and four-coat-work' and so on.[7] On 'the Antiquarian—the scientific man in Rubbish' Kerr speaks with special glee. He is the Revd. Bluebottle Crape, D.D., L.L.D., F.R.S., F.S.A. etc. etc. etc.', an 'utter enemy of Art by nature'.[8] Kerr is not fair to him, nor quite logical in his arguments. He does not want to blame him wholly for his research into the past; he is anxious to get on quickly to 'the absurd notion that we ought to imitate the ancients'.[9] Why should we, especially if the past is the Middle Ages, the age of 'the blood-thirsty beef-eating barons'?[10] And so Kerr can now hold forth on 'the dethronement of a tyranny' and on 'the liberation of enslaved Thought', and then on to 'the hideous monstrosities of the sculptors

[4] *The Newleafe Discourses*, 2–4.   [5] Ibid., 16.   [6] Ibid., 20–1, 45.
[7] Ibid., 48.   [8] Ibid., 54–5.   [9] Ibid., 58.
[10] Ibid., 76.

and painters of the dark ages', the 'ugly old brasses'.[11] No, the Middle Ages have nothing to teach us that could be of value today. We are in advance over the past, we are older, because the world has grown older. 'We are the biggest boys now.' If I want to admire the past in religion I may look at 'the closet where Luther pondered and resolved' or at a cathedral too, but when I do that 'I read History'.[12] Professor Willis is mentioned as the type of the archaeological scholar, without rudeness but also without enthusiasm,[13] though later his 'perspicacity in discovery' is acknowledged.[14]

Kerr's conception of history is interesting, because it anticipates Viollet-le-Duc's. In the eleventh century 'civil liberty began . . . to dawn', though 'monkery ruled unchecked' still. Rome was still 'the fountain-head of wicked thraldom', but the Freemasons—to be understood as free masons—ranged over Europe.[15] But then, in the fifteenth century, Copyism began to appear and became the bane of architecture, though Kerr does not deny the talents of Palladio, of Jones, of Wren, and so on,[16] and even admits that the Grecian mode was an improvement over the 'old mode'.[17]

And so to today, to the architecture suited to us 'railway-travelling Reform-bill people'.[18] The combination of liberal politics with the railway is typical of the mid-nineteenth century. Even Newman in his *Apologia* could say: 'Virtue is the child of Knowledge, Vice of Ignorance: therefore free education, periodical literature, railroad travelling . . . serve to make a population moral and happy.'[19] Kerr's answer to the quest for a nineteenth-century architecture is this: 'Beneath a surface of seeming quiet and smooth prosperity is concealed a secret smouldering volcano. Greek and Goth, two giant powers, divide the world . . . itching for war.' But 'the Genius of the Art [is] watching . . . with an eager smile . . . Between your two stools the soulless system . . . may haply tumble to the ground.' Then perhaps architects will at last determine to think for themselves. 'We have the greatest abstract skill ever attained; . . . we have the

11 Ibid., 75. 12 Ibid., 54–69. 13 Ibid., 69.
14 Ibid., 136. 15 Ibid., 93–4, 106–7. 16 Ibid., 114, 122.
17 Ibid., 125. 18 Ibid., 76.
19 Quoted from G. M. Young, *Portrait of an Age* (OUP, 1936), 7. G. M. Young on that page also quotes the prospectus of the Rochdale Pioneers: 'The objects of this Society are the moral and intellectual advancement of its members. It provides them with groceries, butcher's meat, drapery goods, clothes and clogs.' As for the railway Thomas Hardy in *Jude the Obscure*, i.e. as late as 1896, lets Jude ask Sue: 'Shall we go and sit in the cathedral?' and receive the answer: 'I think I'd rather sit in the railway station . . . That's the centre of the town life now. The cathedral has had its day.' (Wessex Ed., 1912–31, 160).

greatest variety of demands ever made; . . . we have the greatest
wealth ever had; we have the greatest command of materials ever
had', and so 'might [we] not hope for great things?'[20] This question-
mark remains the end. If even Professor Cockerell, with his 'Artist-
mind' remains 'chained down by the creed', and 'with the best will
. . . and the clearest vision . . . can't see in the dark',[21] how can Kerr
be expected to say more than he said in his preface?

The *Newleafe Discourses* end with three chapters in the nature of
appendices. The first is a special attack on Ecclesiologism represented
by the Revd. Mr. Coeur-de-lion Mwffe, Catholic but not Roman
Catholic, and with wild notions of symbolism in church architecture. They cannot be of any consequence to ordinary people.

Oy zay Hob!

Whoat, Beell?

Thee doant know whoat thim poasts be vor, thee doant.

Poasts? Whoat poasts?

Thim voar poasts?

Whoy thim? Whoat does thee take Oy vor? Thim be vor a-bearin'
the roof, to be zure.

No thim beant, Hob.

Thim beant? Thim be.

Oy tell thee thim beant.

Whoat be thim vor, thin?

Thim be vor the voar vangelisters, Hob.

Coom, noon of thoy gammonin' of Oy; Oy'll give thee a whackin'.

Will thee? Oy'd loyke to zee thoy whackin'.

Doant gammon Oy, thin.

I beant, Hob. Parson toald measter, measter toald missis,
missis toald Oy, and Oy be a-tellin' of thee;
thim poasts be vor the voar vangelisters.

And whoat be the vangelisters?

Whoy, doant thee know?

No, I doant.

Thim be whoat the parson speaks about; doant thee know?

No, I doant; whoat do thim be?

Whoy, I doant know noyther, I doant, But thim poasts be vor 'em.[22]

And then, a little repetitive, more on 'the disgusting filthy-minded
monks' and on 'hideous hell figures'.[23] What difference between

[20] *The Newleafe Discourses*, 128–9.   [21] Ibid., 132–3.
[22] Ibid., 145–6.   [23] Ibid., 152.

'the queer flat saints with such a world of half-inch lead work'[24] and the 'grace and beauty of an Eve or an Angel of the modern studios'![25]

The following chapter castigates architectural study. Mr. Smug has a son who draws well, but to be a painter seems to Mr. Smug 'a poor trade'. So 'a sort of compromise' is effected, and young Smug is articled to one of our crack Architects. He draws 'the primitive hut . . . and the Corinthian maiden', he attends the talks at the Institute, and he learns to abuse 'all the Architects of London—except Mr. Barry and the Guv'nor' and to talk about 'nice little bits of Italian' and 'fine old Elizabethan', and after the end of his articles travels and becomes a 'Michael Angelo-Raphael-Palladio-Rome - Florence - Venice - Acropolis - Byzantine - Laocoon - Apollo Belvidere-Titian-da Vinci-Munich-Berlin-Paris sort of person', but never explores England.[26] Anyway, that is not what study should be. It should be determined by nature and reason. 'The Requirements in a Building must be made fundamental in the arrangement of it.' 'Construction must be a fundamental principle.' What appears 'at variance with the facts of construction cannot be excused'. In addition there are 'principles of fitness and propriety'—the *True Principles* were only five years old in 1846—but there are also 'principles of pictorial Effect' which will help 'to command the feelings and awaken the sympathies of the spectator'[27] In these two last clauses one hears the later Kerr and indeed a later attitude to style.

Finally eighteen pages on the 'Royal Institute'. It is blamed for everything—a false doctrine, a false constitution, and an 'irresponsible and despotic Council'. And the twenty-three-year-old Robert Kerr ends by pleading for 'the broader basis . . . the freer Liberty' and for art instead of professionalism.[28] Forty-six years later Norman Shaw and T. G. Jackson edited a closely argued book of attack on The Institute, and they called it *Architecture, a Profession or an Art?* At that time Kerr was still alive, an old gentleman of nearly seventy, he had written and was still going to write on a variety of subjects ending with a brilliant obituary of Ruskin.[29] We shall hear more of him in the next chapter.

[24] Ibid., 74. [25] Ibid., 161.
[26] Ibid., 164–9. [27] Ibid., 176–9.
[28] Ibid., 204–7. [29] *J.R.I.B.A.*, 3rd ser., VII, 1900, 181–8.

CHAPTER XXII

The Battling Builder: Copyism v. Originality

IN England the years from 1845 to 1850 had been years as busy in the field of architectural theory as in France. The *Newleafe Discourses* had come out in 1846, the *Seven Lamps* in 1849, Fergusson's *True Principles of Beauty in Art* which will be discussed in the next chapter also in 1849, Scott's book on restoration in 1850, and Garbett's *Rudimentary Treatise* also in 1850. *The Builder*, itself young, and now under the brilliant editorship of George Godwin,[1] at once took up the various views and joined the fray by publishing leaders (in which incidentally Godwin reveals himself as a firm Protestant[2]), but mostly by opening its columns to writers of letters. That Kerr was one of these need hardly be said. The story[3] begins with a leader on the retort Pugin had sent to *The Rambler* complaining of the way in which lack of money spoils the execution of initially valuable designs.[4] An answer came from Fergusson. He calls his contribution 'Of the Want of Reality in the Works of modern Architects'.[5] He denies what Pugin says: The public would pay for what it wants. But 'copying of dead . . . styles' is not what they can want. Nor can anybody want imitations. 'All contain falsehoods and deformities.' The whole situation today is a 'struggle between archaeology and common sense'. We can do carpentry to make buttressing unnecessary, we can do thin walls, we can do brick arches. We can do a sensible job inexpensively. Why not do it?[6] Before Pugin had time to answer another leader came out, this one a review of Garbett's book.[7] It is praised as of 'much ability' though with 'some vagaries', and it is much quoted. But also quoted are the *Newleafe Discourses* 'first published in our pages', and we know that that also implies an attitude of common sense, Protestantism, and anti-archaeology.

[1] See p. 85.
[2] e.g. the review of Pugin's book on screens: IX, 1851, 399.
[3] Dr. Stefan Muthesius some years ago first drew my attention to this whole series of articles.
[4] *The Builder*, VIII, 1850, 109. See above, p. 104.   [5] On 'reality' see p. 127.
[6] *The Builder*, VIII, 1850, 122.   [7] Ibid., 133.

Pugin's answer[8] is indignant—'We pointed men have pointed tools.' Churches ought not to be treated in so utilitarian a fashion. How can anybody recommend roofing a church like 'a station or a fish-market'? Back comes Fergusson:[9] 'I, as a Protestant' can only think in terms of 'places of Protestant worship', although no good modern ones yet exist. They can't, as long as the 'servile doctrine of copying' survives. Pugin must be admitted to be 'the most truthful of copyists', but his truth is not mine, says Fergusson. Fergusson defines as truth in a building that which represents 'faithfully the wants and feelings of the people who use it'. The imitation of the thirteenth century can only amuse 'a few amateurs of mediaeval antiquities'. The spirit of the nineteenth century is a changed spirit. Pugin did not answer back, but Scott did:[10] The revival of pointed architecture is not copyism. Scott wishes that critics would rather spend their time to 'invent or discover' the new style they preach. Only as long as one has to learn the language does one copy. Later one can use the language 'spontaneously', reproducing the Gothic style 'liberally, with any variation of which it is capable'. We know the argument. Fergusson will not have it.[11] Architects should forget their archaeology and 'act as thinking and reasoning men'. The letter marks no progress in the debate. Nor does Scott's next.[12] except that—Scott being Scott—it is more conciliatory. We don't differ all that much. The medievalists want to develop a new style from the point in history where deviation began. This argument we also know already. You, says Scott, have not even a starting point. The last of this group of letters is Fergusson's again:[13] This and this only is how the architect ought to work. He ought to 'design a building wholly and solely for the purpose for which it is to be used, without the least reference to any bygone age'. He ought to construct in the best available materials according to their properties. And he ought to decorate the building, dressing, not concealing the structure and with ornament 'in whatever manner [he] can conceive most appropriate and most elegant'. It is this last remark which was, as we shall see, to lead Fergusson back to a style well within nineteenth-century historicism. If you want to see sensible houses, you can find them in Paris, Berlin, Hamburg more than in London.

A little later *The Builder*[14] reported a lecture given to the R.I.B.A.

---

[8] Ibid., 134.　　　　[9] Ibid., 147–8.　　　　[10] Ibid., 169.
[11] Ibid., 183.　　　　[12] Ibid., 197.　　　　[13] Ibid., 209.
[14] Ibid., 253, 266, 278.

by James Knowles, the architect father of James Knowles Jun. who designed the Grosvenor Hotel at Victoria Station and edited *The Nineteenth Century*. Knowles had demanded that efforts should now be directed 'to investigation which may result in the production of novelty, beauty, fitness . . . and greater economy'. Let no one be taken in by 'a small and non-professional party' (Ruskin?) which wishes 'to introduce a movement of retrogression to the styles and fashions of a former age'. Instead the 'discoveries of science' ought to be made use of.

After that was a break. But later in the same year Kerr carried on with an article called 'Originality in Architecture':[15] If we young architects 'denounce non-originality', it is not fair to demand from any architect that he should 'at once [make] all things new'. The new style may well be only 'accomplished by his children'.[16] A further article by Kerr is a reprint by *The Builder* of a lecture given at the Architectural Association.[17] It is once more called 'Copyism in Architecture'. Kerr here refers to the time he spent in Donaldson's office and then in America—a country of liberty and 'go-ahead-ism'. Scott is all wrong in denying that we have a style of our own. 'I can see very clearly that we have a style of our own . . . and one which cannot fail to triumph ultimately.' As an example the 'glass palace' is already mentioned—in November 1850. Other examples are non-conformist chapels. These comfortable preaching-houses to which Pugin so much objects, 'by the common-sense judgment of plain men' make the new Gothic churches and the Houses of Parliament 'sink . . . into disrepute'. Or walk along ordinary streets in England or America. Don't you see a style, where houses are built without the expense of 'the styles'? Architecture, Kerr reiterates, is based on requirements and construction. 'A natural style of architecture is such as can accomplish the wants of the circumstances . . . in the most suitable and economical manner with the full command of all the materials and . . . appliances at command.' Such a natural style—

[15] *The Builder*, VII, 1850, 401.

[16] Very much the same was said five years earlier by the Viennese architect Eduard von der Null, architect with Sicard von Sicardsburg of the Vienna Opera. Von der Null wrote in 1845: 'New construction is bound to produce new characteristics, and we believe that on the strength of this all the younger talents might get nearer each other and come to an agreement so that in the end, after many decades, the characteristics of new modes of construction will be ennobled by art and will give an opportunity to later descendants to arrive at a really original national style.' (*Österreichische Blätter für Literatur und Kunst*, II, 1845, 401 ff. and 411 ff. Quoted from H. C. Hoffmann, 'Notizen zu Eduard von der Null und August Sicard von Sicardsburg', in *Darmstädter Schriften*, XXII, 1968, 48.)

[17] Ibid., 541, etc.

here again is the loophole—must 'of necessity be very . . . varied for the variety of subjects'.

Two letters followed this up. In the first 'F.', i.e. Fergusson, asks more pressingly: 'Which is the fit kind [of architecture] for us Englishmen of the nineteenth century?' It must be wrong to suggest one style for one kind of building and another for another. 'That which is not suitable for every sort of architectural building does not deserve the name of architecture.' He then runs through Classical, Mediaeval and the Revived Classical from the point of view of form and of expression and turns down all three. Greek suits the Mediterranean with its strong sunlight, Gothic is aspiring and reached its climax at Cologne Cathedral. The later Gothic—including Henry VII's Chapel is 'square tasteless shapes, incrusted with unmeaning decoration'. The Revived Classical is 'more really beautiful' but relies too much on ornamental and figural carving for our climate with little sun and much soot. So Fergusson in the end leaves it all wide open.[18]

One week later Garbett joined the fray. He attacked Kerr. It is nonsense to say that England and America possess a 'natural style'. A new style may indeed be there, but it is 'not a style of *architecture*, nor even capable of becoming one'. For it is not pure construction; it is 'sham construction . . . from the sham plinth that is not a foundation, to the sham coping that is not the covering'. Down to the Edwardian era there was 'ever more truth', since then 'continually increasing falsehood'. And that does not exclude the 'conventicles' either which Kerr had held up for approval. So Garbett is no more positive here than Fergusson. With this we reach the end of 1850.

In 1851–2 Kerr contributed a whole series of articles to *The Builder*. They are typical Kerr in that they are easy to read and tend to be funny. But compared with the *Newleafe Discourses* they are markedly more accommodating—Kerr settling down and getting ready for his successes in the sixties. They are called 'Architecturus to his Son' and set up Seven Lamps other than Ruskin's. 'The practical architect must be well grounded in seven separate things': artistic design, delineative language, scientific construction, practical house building, learning and teaching, and the transaction of his business.[19] So Mr. Beefeater is accepted in the fold, and he who knows about sink-traps. Moreover, on restoration also, in a separate

<hr>

[18] Ibid., 555. [19] Ibid., IX, 701.

final (and again humorous) article,[20] Kerr is ready for compromises. 'Everything has a scientific system.' So let us have one here. The ancient building can have six values: serviceable, monumental (commemorating a hero of today), patriotical (associated with past history), artistical, art-historical, and archaeological. Only on the last-named is Kerr still aggressive ('fashionable and dogmatical'). There are also four forms of restoration: preservation, passive repair, total renovation when in ruins, and improving by altering and adding. If you apply these four forms to the six values, the result is that all four ways have to be applied where the value is serviceable or monumental. Where it is patriotical, apply only preservation and repair. Artistical value on the other hand may make all four desirable—Kerr, like Scott, never doubts that new improvements can increase the aesthetic value of an old building— art-historical value of course forbids improvements, and archae- ological value does not even allow repair. But of this Kerr does not approve.

This report of matters published in *The Builder* has taken us to 1852.[21] Five years later *The Builder* embarked on regular reports of the lectures Sydney Smirke gave at the Royal Academy of which he had been made Professor of Architecture in 1857 as the successor to Cockerell. In the volumes for 1857 to 1862 twenty-three instalments were printed, in 1863–5 only another six. By then the editor must have become bored by the dulness from which we still suffer in reading the reports from their very beginning. Sydney Smirke, the much younger brother of Sir Robert, and the architect of the excel- lent classical Oxford and Cambridge Club of 1835, the equally excellent Venetian-Cinquecento Carlton Club of 1846–7, and the Reading Room of the British Museum of 1857 was a man of crush- ingly *juste milieu* views.[22] Beauty 'begins where utility ends', but beauty must not offend 'the sense of usefulness'. Fitness alone is all right for engineers, but 'as artists . . . we desire . . . something more'.

[20] Ibid., X, 226–7.

[21] In fact there is more in the later fifties, e.g. Alfred Bailey in 1853, p. 713 (with a hope that soon the 'party-spirit' between Gothic and Classic will be 'amalgamated . . . so as to produce a national style'), J. K. Colling in 1858, p. 81 ('Let us regard ancient styles only as insignificant parts of modern character') and a leader on Scott's *Remarks* in 1858, p. 1, where *The Builder* votes for 'the true basis . . . ever [to be] the actual and the present', but the method of achieving modern architecture to go to 'many sources . . . without neglecting any line, or passing by any beautiful form wheresoever found'—i.e. the very eclecticism for which Kerr was to stand in the sixties, as we shall see presently.

[22] See J. M. Crook: 'Sydney Smirke', to be published in a book on some Victorian architects sponsored by the Victorian Society. It should come out in 1972.

And as for the aesthetics of architecture, neither Classic nor Gothic
holds a monopoly. Both are still evocative, even if both are structurally outdated. Do we need a new style then? Yes—but no new
style can be invented. 'It is useless to deny that aesthetics generally
have not kept pace . . . with the exact sciences.' To find a new style,
you ought to 'seek it in the application of some *material,* or in the
invention of some new *system of construction*'. But that would not be a
matter of architecture; for architecture is a *fine art,* and the Academy
lectures are concerned with taste. So 'seek rather for that which is
good, than for that which is *new,* and in this search you may perchance
fall in with something *new* which is *good*'. Anyway, imitation of past
styles is not the answer. 'To feed upon the réchauffées of the past
is . . . mischievous' and must be 'stigmatised as eclectic or lati-
tudinarian'. Sydney Smirke goes no further, and if in the end he
sums up: 'Such a course . . . would afford us the best chance to
ultimately arrive . . . at a sound, consistent and original style, worthy
of the genius and civilisation of the nineteenth century', we do not
know at all what 'such a course' could really be.

But some others in England by 1865 thought they knew.
Thomas Harris should stand as the beginning, and Kerr again
will be at the end. In addition Fergusson will have a chapter to
himself.

Thomas Harris (1830–1900), an architect of minor achievements
and of the type Goodhart-Rendel called rogue architects, comes into
this story by a pamphlet which he published in 1860 and boldly
called *Victorian Architecture*[23] and by contributions to a monthly of
which only one volume came out and which equally boldly called
itself *Examples of the Architecture of the Victorian Age.* The volume
is dated 1862.[24]

Victorian Architecture is against historicism: 'The works of past
ages . . . must and ever will claim the admiration of every thoughtful
mind, but . . . a reproduction of any will not suffice. No remodelling
or adapting will do.' We need 'an indigenous style of our own'. The
study of past buildings can be recommended, but only for principles,
never for 'stereotype copying'. 'The fundamental principles of [all]
true art in Architecture [are] . . . the natural characters of the

[23] The term incidentally was used two years earlier by *The Building News* (18 June 1858, 617).

[24] P. F. R. Donner, 'A Thomas Harris Florilegium', *Architectural Review,* XCIII, 1943, and
Dudley Harbron, 'Thomas Harris', ibid., XCII, 1942. The volume is not mentioned by F.
Jenkins, 'Nineteenth Century Architectural Periodicals', in *Concerning Architecture,* ed. Sir John
Summerson (London, 1968).

materials at command, and their strict applications to the requirements of the time.' Thus stone, wood, and wrought iron ought to
display their natural, brick, cast iron, and plastic materials their
manufactured character. That is reminiscent of Wyatt; Harris's plea
that one material should not be painted to represent another, on the
other hand, comes from Ruskin. By adhering to such principles a
style may perhaps be found for our age, 'an age of new creations . . .
Steam power and electric communications [are] entirely new revolu-
tionizing influences. So must it be in Architecture. We must . . .
chisel out for ourselves new expressions, being content with simple
and, it may be, rude achievements at the outset.'

Examples of the Architecture of the Victorian Age is bolder. Like
Kerr, Harris separates 'mechanical construction' from 'high art'.
'The architectural vice of the present day . . . is the want of high art.'
But then the most stimulating passages deal not with art, but with
construction. At Euston Station for instance the great hall had an
iron roof with arched ribs. It looked beautiful when visible, but it
was hidden by 'a sham covering of the most flimsy kind'.[25] 'One of
the great requirements of the day is to cover large areas, at the most
moderate cost, and probably for a temporary purpose only. This
problem has been satisfactorily solved in the numerous magnificent
railway stations.' The same principles were applied to the Crystal
Palace, 'where a new style of architecture, as remarkable as any . . .
may be considered to have been inaugurated. We consider that iron
and glass in conjunction have succeeded in giving a distinct and
marked character to the future of architecture.' Prophetic words,
and equally prophetic is the modest rider: 'The architecture of the
nineteenth century . . . cannot be expected to reach its full development in our time, but the future of that style, the Victorian style, . . .
is assured.'[26]

The crux of the architecture of his day Harris incidentally saw
just like Kerr in the presence of 'two spectres . . . Grecian and Gothic;
who will deliver us from them?'[27] It is alas a rhetorical question;
for Harris's own buildings are Gothic, and of a peculiarly wild and
undisciplined kind [Pls. 66, 67] That was his conscious solution;
for he ends one of his papers by pointing out that 'the most popular
of our rising architects in the mediaeval style are those who evince
most boldness in deviating from ancient models.'[28]

[25] *Examples of the Architecture of the Victorian Age*, 78.   [26] Ibid., 57–8.
[27] Ibid., 79.   [28] Ibid., 58.

One year before the *Examples* had come out, a very distinguished amateur, President of the R.I.B.A. in 1865, appeared with a book called challengingly *The English Cathedral of the Nineteenth Century*. The author was A. J. B. Beresford Hope, son of Thomas Hope, and he had been connected from early on with the Cambridge Camden and the Oxford Architectural Societies. He was rich and had been the patron for whom in the small church of Kilndown in Kent Salvin had provided a stone altar, Carpenter a screen, and Butterfield a brass lectern and two brass *coronas*. So here, in 1840 or 1841, Beresford Hope had assembled the three favourites of the Camdenians. In 1849 Hope embarked on a far more ambitious scheme, an Ecclesiologist model church in the west end of London: All Saints, Margaret Street, by Butterfield [Pl. 40] with wall paintings by Dyce. The church cost £70,000 of which a substantial part came from Beresford Hope. It was not completed until 1859. We have heard what *The Ecclesiologist* had to say about it (p. 134).

Beresford Hope's *The English Cathedral of the Nineteenth Century* is about the necessity, due to the fast growing population of England, of creating more cathedrals. Places are discussed where existing churches might be converted, others where new cathedrals might be built. How should new cathedrals be designed? What accommodation does an Anglican cathedral need? Beresford Hope is a great believer in choral services. If the chapel of the Primitive Methodists can make 'the glen re-echo to their stentorial psalmody'[29] why should not the Anglican cathedral? Having set down what is needed, formulated it in terms of plans and tested it by a description of nineteenth-century cathedrals in Britain (e.g. Perth and Inverness) and the colonies, he asks after style. There he turns out to be an out-and-out Middle Pointed man. He was a Conservative M.P. and became a determined adversary of the Second Reform Bill. What he now defends the Middle Pointed against is—characteristically for the sixties—no longer only the 'basilican' type, because it is not English and would take us back to 'a past state of society',[30] but the Early French Gothic which was, it will be remembered, the new fashion since the Lille Cathedral competition of 1855.[31] So his choice is what he calls Edwardian England, though he does slip in a proviso that the style 'may, in the course of time, become very different from the old Gothic'.[32] But how different? It is remarkable

[29] *The English Cathedral of the Nineteenth Century*, 117.   [30] Ibid., 182–3.
[31] Ibid., 56.   [32] Ibid., 66.

that Beresford Hope allows himself a page or two on iron and glass.[33] Could iron be used in his future cathedrals, as in the Oxford Museum, or even as at Sydenham? Indeed 'iron may be used more extensively, and to more advantage', but it will not 'revolutionize . . . the architecture inherited from the good old days', and 'as to the Crystal Cathedral, I must humbly say that I cannot grasp so novel an idea'.

After so hesitant a consideration of a possible new style it comes as a complete surprise to find Cardinal Wiseman in a lecture in 1864[34] praise the new warehouses of London as 'splendid efforts made by private enterprise' and express his conviction that 'they are an indication of a new spirit which may become national . . . because they are characteristic . . . of our social conditions.'[35] It is a curious lecture, leisurely in construction, starting off with a bit of excavating around Rome and ending in a strong plea to railway companies not merely to destroy but to build beautifully. This includes a passing compliment to railway viaducts, as beautiful in their simplicity as the Roman aqueducts.[36] But while the warehouses as such receive all his praise, he is unhappy about the fact that buildings today, including the warehouses, appear in all styles, Norman, Pointed, Byzantine, Venetian, and Renaissance in 'a miscellaneous combination'. The Renaissance, he finds, is 'steadily gaining ground',[37] and he raises no objections to that.

In the same year in which the Cardinal extolled London's warehouses, an architect whose speciality was just such warehouses gave a lecture too, to the R.I.B.A. The title was 'Iron as a Building Material', and the lecturer was George Aitchison[38] whose 59–61 Mark Lane of that very same year is essentially of iron construction. So he asks aggressively why architects shut their eyes to the possibilities of iron. Are they not aware of its possibilities 'for the NEW STYLE, about which so much has been said . . . and so little has been done'? Needless to say, Aitchison is anti-Gothic. 'A Protestant church of this age has very different requirements from a church of the middle ages.' How can the architects of our age of science and machinery turn to 'the architecture of an age in which science was in its infancy'. It makes them mere triflers. The new race of architects is the engineers. Admittedly they commit 'monstrosities', but let no

---

[33] *The English Cathedral of the Nineteenth Century*, 66–7.

[34] *Judging from the Past and Present, what are the Prospects for Good Architecture in London* (London, 1864). The lecture was given in the South Kensington Museum on 12 April 1864.

[35] Ibid., 16–17.   [36] Ibid., 3.

[37] Ibid., 21.   [38] *Sessional Papers 1863–4*, 1864, 97–107.

architect attempt to put an 'ugly construction into an ornamental box'. No, the thing itself ought to be made 'graceful and elegant'. What is needed is 'purity of outline and elegance of proportion, with an almost total absence of ornament' and this is what should be applied to 'everything from our buildings to our tea-spoons'.

This was too much for the historicists, and so a particularly intelligent Gothicist answered back the very next year: William White (1825–1900)[39] who started with extremely simple, sensible, small Gothic churches, schools, and parsonages in Cornwall, but later also built the grand church at Lyndhurst in the New Forest, one of the most robust and ornate churches of the sixties (1858–70), and wrote much and always reasonably. In a lecture to the R.I.B.A.[40] he protested against Aitchison, though without naming him. He insisted that he himself had long been interested in the use of iron and its 'artistic treatment'. But if some people say that iron should be used for all purposes, for girders and columns, for walls, roofs and floors, they may be right, but 'So far as I am concerned, it may predominate in Utopia.' Iron ought to remain 'a servant to architecture'; for it 'cannot express bulk . . . upon which the proportion of all true architecture . . . materially depends'. It is the old Pugin argument. Iron allows architectural members to be thin, but if they are thin, the result cannot be architecture. So in his lecture White proceeds to discuss the decorative uses of iron, first wrought then cast.

Yet White was more open-minded than Ruskin, because he was not insensitive to the needs of providing cheaply for the masses. He appreciated the Crystal Palace and the train sheds, but as monuments of science, not of art. He had already some years earlier written on the Crystal Palace[41] that, 'as a piece of constructional engineering in iron and glass on a grand scale, whose object is not the production of a "work of art", but only the covering of a vast area for a specific purpose, with the most available means in a short space of time . . . it is a noble as well as successful work . . . so far as it is capable of being noble.' White even suggests that the architect should co-operate with the engineer, but the two must yet remain distinct. And White also appreciated machinery for quantity production of

[39] P. Thompson, 'The Writings of William White', in *Concerning Architecture*, ed. Sir John Summerson (London, 1968).

[40] *Trans. R.I.B.A.*, 1865–6, 15–30.

[41] *The Palace; an Artistic Sketch* (London, 1854), quoted in *The Ecclesiologist*, XVI, 1855, 162–3.

objects for everyday use: 'A vast population must have vast supplies at a reasonable cost.' What should they be like?

In manufacturing for the million, we do not want the highest class of art, or a cheap and nasty reproduction of . . . that which ought to be costly . . . We want the best of its kind . . . If iron or pewter spoons are wanted for our cottages . . . we do not require them to aim at ornate patterns . . . We want a handle for holding. It must not bristle with ornament so as to cut our fingers . . . Simplicity is wedded for ever with utility.

Such a message is surprising enough coming from a man like White, but that William Burges (1827–81), the most fanciful, the most robust and florid of all the English High Victorian Gothicists, should, at least once, have backed this message is almost beyond belief. Yet in a lecture Burges gave in 1865 he said:[42] There is no 'distinctive architecture' of our day. All other periods had a style. Today in the streets of London we see 'half-a-dozen sorts of architecture'. Students must learn them all, but there is no time for that, and so they don't know any well enough. The most frequently seen at present are 'a very impure and bastard Italian'—we have heard plenty of that—and 'a variety of the architecture of the thirteenth century, often . . . not much purer'. We must hope that 'in course of time one or both of them will disappear' (and with them 'all . . . books on architecture'). Only then we 'may get something of our own of which we need not be ashamed'. This may take place as late as the twentieth century, he adds, prophetically. After this introduction follow chapters on glass, pottery, metal work, furniture, and textiles. They are mostly historical and not specially interesting. Burges's love of decoration by human figures comes out in various places. Other topical remarks are rare and mostly do not point in any particularly profitable direction. He castigates 'the enormities, inconveniences and extra-vagaries of our modern upholsterers[43] and the 'starved' woodwork of new churches,[44] and for cast iron he speculates how the Middle Ages would have made locomotives to look like dragons and funnels of boats like castellated towers— a typical Burges dream.[45] However, at least in one sentence he pleads for 'better forms for cheaper articles'.[46] Interesting from a different point of view is the last chapter called 'The Modern

---

[42] *Art applied to Industry,* The Carter Lectures (Oxford, 1865). The book is dedicated to Beresford Hope. On Burges see C. Handley-Read in *Victorian Architecture,* ed. P. Ferriday (London, 1963).

[43] Ibid., 69.   [44] Ibid., 82.   [45] Ibid., 31–2.   [46] Ibid., 39, 49.

Development of Mediaeval Art'.[47] Burges had already before said that we have not only no architecture, but 'we have not even settled the *point de départ*'.[48] However, it seems to him 'now to be almost generally recognized that some architecture founded upon that of the Middle Ages is the most suitable for our climate'. Burges reviews the pioneers, especially Rickman, Blore ('one of the most minute and beautiful architectural draughtsmen the world has ever beheld'), Pugin whose *True Principles* 'did immeasurable good', and Ruskin with whose tenet of the importance for architecture of painting and sculpture he agrees. He then criticizes some 'crying defects of modern Mediaeval art, such as the overdoing of chamfers and of notches, of marble inside churches and of too much 'piebald' colour altogether. And that is the end.

Thoughts similar to Burges's and White's and even more Aitchison's and Harris's were turned over in the nimble mind of Robert Kerr, when he wrote that long and essentially practical book of advice to potential clients and competing colleagues: *The Gentleman's House*. It came out in 1864, and a second edition followed almost at once, in 1865, and this was called *The English Gentleman's House*.[49] Its greatest merit is that it is an entirely 'real' manual of how to plan houses. It tells you what you can get for £1,250, £2,500, £5,000, and so on to £40,000 and more, how you plan so that at the entrance 'the visitors [do not] rub shoulders with the tradespeople', and how you plan inside the house so that 'the walks of the family shall not be open to view from the Servants' Department', how in a large mansion the butler's and the housekeeper's domains must be separate ('with the Kitchen the butler may be said to have no intercourse whatever'), how the nursery can be located so as to provide the mother with a 'certain facility of access' and how in the elevation the W.C. must be placed so as 'not too much to provoke identification'.[50] It tells you of ice-houses but already mentions the refrigerator,[51] of dry larder and wet larder and game larder,[52] and of a food lift.[53]

All this is outside the scope of the present book, but parts at the

[47] Ibid., 109 ff.   [48] Ibid., 91.

[49] Precisely in 1864 the Royal Commission on Public Schools had defined as their function: 'moulding the character of an English Gentleman'—by governing others, but controlling oneself by the combination of freedom and order, by manliness and healthy sport. See G. Kitson Clark: *The Making of Victorian England* (London, 1962), 271. That Dr. Arnold stands behind this ideal hardly needs saying.

[50] *The English Gentleman's House*, 75, 221, 246–7, 139, 171.   [51] Ibid., 273–5.
[52] Ibid., 238.   [53] Ibid., 108.

beginning and the end are well within. Here Kerr has two important contributions to make. At the beginning[54] he describes how in the nineteenth century Palladianism, 'long the Vernacular of Europe' changed into 'the fastidious Greek', then became involved in 'the romantic Gothic', spared some attention 'for the dainty Elizabethan' and gave 'greater share' to the non-Palladian Italian—the architects 'avowing the more or less novel but striking doctrine of Eclecticism'. Eclecticism seems indeed Kerr's credo. It had been Scott's a few years before, but in a much less comprehensive sense. Also Scott's 'ground work' was Gothic, Kerr's is what Redgrave and Wornum, the critics of the 1851 exhibition, called the 'free or mixed Renaissance'.[55] This is made plain for all to see in his remarkable recommendation of 'the modern adaptation of Classicism (primarily Italian) received . . . through a French channel' but with a 'treatment throughout English, massive and bold, picturesque even when required, substantial and unaffected'—macaronic in fact, to use the term of Viollet-le-Duc.[56]

And this is the perfect definition of the style of Kerr's *chef-d'œuvre*, Bearwood near Reading, built in 1861–8 [Pl. 68], very large, very sensibly planned but externally an ill-disciplined mixture of English Jacobean mansion and French Loire château.[57]

However, and here comes the greatest surprise of the book, Kerr has yet another answer, and one which seems to contradict everything else he has said about style. It appears on pages 356–7.

In what style of Architecture shall you build your house?' . . . The architect will generally put this query to his client at the outset of their intercourse; and if the client be unlearned in such matters, he may be somewhat astonished to discover what he is invited to do. By the exercise of some instinct . . . he is expected to make a choice from amongst half-a-dozen prevailing styles all more or less antagonistic to each other . . . The bewildered gentleman ventures to suggest that he wants only a simple, comfortable house, in no style at all but the comfortable style, if there be

[54] *The English Gentleman's House,* 58 ff.

[55] N. Pevsner, *Studies in Art, Architecture and Design* (London, 1968), II, 60–2.

[56] *The English Gentleman's House,* 379, 381. An exact parallel from America has come my way very recently. Bruce Price (1845–1903) wrote about a house of his at S. Mateo in California: 'It would answer equally the assertion that "it is French in feeling", "Romanesque in its handling", or "Dutch in its mass"; still it is an American house, planned for American uses'. (From *Modern Architecture and Practice,* I, New York 1887, preface. Reprinted in H. D. Kalman, 'The Railway Hotels and the Development of the Château style in Canada', *Studies in Architectural History* (University of Victoria, B.C., Maltwood Museum), I, 1969, 29.)

[57] See M. Girouard, *The Victorian Country House* (Oxford, 1971) 121–4; also *Country Life,* CXLIV, 1968, 964 ff. and 1060 ff.

one. The architect of course agrees; but there are so many comfortable styles,—they are all comfortable. Sir, you are paymaster, and must therefore be pattern-master; you choose the style of your house just as you choose the build of your hat; you can have Classical; either columnar or non-columnar, either arcuated or trabeated, either rural or civic, or indeed palatial; you can have Elizabethan in equal variety; Renaissance ditto; or (not to notice minor modes) Medieval—the Gothic which is now so much the rage—in any one of its multifarious forms—of the eleventh century, twelfth century, thirteenth, fourteenth, whichever you please,—feudalistic, monastic, scholastic, ecclesiastic, archaeologistic, ecclesiologistic, and so on.

But really, I would much rather not. I want a plain, substantial, comfortable Gentleman's House; and, I beg leave to repeat, I don't want any style at all. I really would very much rather not have any; I daresay it would cost a great deal of money, and I should very probably not like it. Look at myself; I am a man of very plain tastes: I am neither Classical nor Elizabethan—I believe I am not Renaissance, and I am sure I am not Medieval. . . . I am very sorry, but if you will kindly take me as I am, and build my house in my own style.[58]

It could be Lethaby or even more Baillie Scott, that is 1900 rather than 1865, and it is by no means the only profoundly surprising thing that Kerr wrote or rather lectured on in the sixties and after. There is for example a paper 'On the Problems of Providing Dwellings for the Poor in Towns',[59] where Kerr realistically proposes blocks of flats with one-room dwellings, instead of the more spacious accommodation provided in the designs of Henry Roberts and those of the Improved Industrial Dwellings Company which were indeed proved to be too expensive for the class for which they were meant. A system of publicly subsidized housing was not then yet being considered at all. Kerr's dwellings would have been deplorable, but they would have been an improvement on the ghastly slums described by Chadwick, Kay Shuttleworth, and others and illustrated by Godwin in *The Builder*. Kerr also lectured on Ancient Lights,[60] on artificial stone,[61] on architectural competitions—critically of course,[62] on arbitrations,[63] and on English Architecture

[58] *The English Gentleman's House*, 356 ff.

[59] *Trans. R.I.B.A.*, XVII, 1866–7. See my paper on this subject in *Studies in Art, Architecture and Design*, II, 1968, and much more thoroughly J. N. Tarn 'Housing in Urban Areas', Ph.D. Thesis, Cambridge 1962. I am glad to see that this in a suitably changed form will now be published. Meanwhile the briefer but equally authoritative *Working Class Housing in Nineteenth-Century Britain* (Architectural Association Papers 7), (London, 1971).

[60] *The Builder*, XVI, 1865–6.   [61] Ibid., XIII, 1862–3.
[62] Ibid., XXI, 1870–1.   [63] Ibid., 3 ser., IV, 197.

thirty years hence, in fact on English architecture from the foundation of the Institute to about 1880,[64] i.e. to the time of the mature
Philip Webb, Norman Shaw, and William Morris. This lecture is
an amazing performance, outspoken to a degree unimaginable
within the walls of the Institute now, and very shrewd though very
biased—so shrewd indeed that, as a companion piece to William
Morris's only lecture on architecture, it is reprinted *in toto* as an
appendix to this book. Nor was this Kerr's last word; for yet later,
in 1891 he edited, after Fergusson's death, the third edition of
Fergusson's *Modern Styles of Architecture*. Much here is the same as
in the R.I.B.A. lecture, but in much also Kerr went further still.
The most interesting part is the thirty pages on America, ending in
the recognition of Richardson's virile muscularity as the 'backbone
of a novel national style'.[65]

But that goes beyond the limits of this book and certainly this
chapter. We must return to the sixties. However, before passing on
to Fergusson's first edition a question must be asked seriously
which has one way or another come up in the preceding chapters
from Rickman to Scott and Thomas Harris and William White.
Why is there time and again that discrepancy between an architect's
thought and the same architect's performance?

The answer is that the Victorian Age is full of contradictions—
Professor Houghton arranges his chapters in antinomies: Optimism/
Anxiety; Radical Criticism/Wish to believe; Commercial Spirit/
Enthusiasm; Worship of Force/Family Love, and so on—is not
enough. There must be something more specific. Now in painting
the split which runs through the century between welcome and
unwelcome art is familiar, Salon art, and Courbet or Manet. In
architecture unwelcome art is impossible. The painter can starve
and paint, the architect can only build if he has a client. If his performance consistently displeases clients, there will be no buildings.
Hence it may well be that the young man of aesthetic talents who
is totally radical by nature and convictions will not choose an
architectural career. The radical themes propounded by Victorian
architects are then an expiation of major and minor compromises.
This is one explanation.

Another is this: Georgian architects had been conventional and
refused to consider drastic changes. Victorian architects were not

[64] *The Builder,*, XXXIV, 1883–4.
[65] *Modern Styles of Architecture*, 374. Van Brunt had of course preceded Kerr in this estimate.

different, except that the doctrine of one pattern style only which all followed in a well-mannered cortège was no longer believed. As more and more styles were used as patterns at the same time, doubts increased as to the validity of historicism altogether. But while this succeeded in producing radicalism on paper, the effort to realize what thought dictated was too great. After all, it must be remembered that Europe had had more than four hundred years of an architecture operating with motifs and elements of the past. To break that convention required men of exceptional calibre, and even they could only win after Morris and his followers had softened the defences. In the decades with which we are dealing, architects and architectural critics grew frightened as soon as they actually saw what their radical theories would look like in brick and mortar, or rather iron and glass. The habit of seeing buildings as ornamental façades was too deeply ingrained. To demonstrate this, there is no better example than the leading English architectural historian of these years, James Fergusson.

CHAPTER XXIII

James Fergusson

JAMES FERGUSSON was born in 1808.[1] In his early manhood he was a manufacturer of indigo in India. After ten years he was able to retire and live in London. The outcome of his Indian years were two books on Indian architecture which he published in 1845 and 1847–8.[2] In 1849, the year of the *Seven Lamps*, followed *An Historical Enquiry into the True Principles of Beauty in Art, more especially with Reference to Architecture*, and in 1855 the *Illustrated Handbook of Architecture* in two volumes. After that, in 1862, came his most important book: *A History of the Modern Styles in Architecture*. This and the *Handbook* were finally, in 1865–7, issued together as *A History of Architecture* in three volumes. In 1871 Fergusson received the Gold Medal of the R.I.B.A. In 1886 Schliemann dedicated his *Excavations of Tiryns* to him. In the same year he died. *The Builder* wrote:[3] 'He is as important a writer on architecture in the modern world as Vitruvius was in the ancient world.' It is almost beyond belief.[4] Among his books his own favourite was the *True Principles*.[5]

The *True Principles* are the very opposite of Pugin's. Fergusson is not moved by religion nor is he really interested in this book in the art and architecture of the past. His passion is system-building, and never before had art and architecture been pressed so hard to fit a system. In rudeness to his own day on the other hand he is a match for Pugin and also for Ruskin, and in arrogance he occasionally even surpasses Ruskin.

[1] A book on Fergusson would be well worth while. For the moment we have only Maurice Craig in *Concerning Architecture*, ed. Sir John Summerson (London, 1968).

[2] *Illustrations of the Rock-cut Temples of India* and *Picturesque Illustrations of Ancient Architecture in Hindostan*. The first of the two books was impressive enough for John Weale to dedicate volume two of the *Quarterly Papers* to Fergusson 'as a testimony of respect for his devotion to architectural science'.

[3] *The Builder*, L, 1886, 113.

[4] And *The Ecclesiologist* (XI, 1850, 43) was indeed of a different opinion. In the Royal Academy Fergusson had exhibited a design for rebuilding the National Gallery, and *The Ecclesiologist* calls it 'outré' and 'the production of an amateur genius, the well known Mr. J. Fergusson'.

[5] See *British Architect*, XXV, 1886, 48, reprinted from *The Times*.

Fergusson's great indictment of contemporary architecture we have already seen formulated in the letters he wrote a year after the *True Principles* to *The Builder* in participation in the controversy over copyism *v.* originality (p. 222). To put it now in the words of the preface to the book: he promises to fight for 'common sense' and for 'honest Protestant Christianity' and against 'the monkey styles of modern Europe'.[6] Also he is an aggressive liberal pronouncing the easy belief of the High Victorian manufacturers who resented social legislation beyond items like sanitation. 'All men are equal . . . in power to enjoy, improve, or deteriorate their own condition', and 'Poverty and misfortune cannot long oppress the well trained and virtuous man.' Let him pursue knowledge, and he will succeed.[7]

Immediately after that the system begins in all its rigours with a passion for classifications (and praise on that score of Bacon, d'Alembert, Bentham, Ampère, and also Whewell's *Philosophy of Inductive Sciences*) and a crazy delight in new terms: Etherics, Biotics, Thermatics, Nosology, Amativeness, Eumorphics[8]—enough to warm the heart of any American scholar today. It is fortunate that the theory as such need not be explained in the context of the present book. There are also ingenious tables in which all arts find their place, including Gastronomy, Upholstery, and De-odorizing. The arts are primarily divided into Politic—Medicine, Morals and Religion; and Anthropic—Technic, Aesthetic and Phonetic, denoting the use of tools, our senses, and speech. Aesthetic thus is not what is usually so called. As soon as beauty comes in, it should be cal-aesthetic. Now in this field of cal-aesthetics, i.e. beauty in art, further categories are introduced. We speak of the beauty of a ship or a machine, but that is only technical beauty.[9] Higher are the sensuous beauties, but highest the phonetic, i.e. the intellectual, beauties. Thus a chart and a graph become possible.[10] It looks like this, with technical beauty counting one per unit, aesthetic two, phonetic three.

	TECHN.	AESTH.	PHON.	TOTAL
Heating, Ventilation etc.	11	1	0	$=13$
Gastronomy	7	5	$0 \ (=7+2 \times 5)$	$=17$
Gardening	4	6	$2 \ (=4+2 \times 6+3 \times 2)$	$=22$
Architecture	4	4	$4 \ (=4+2 \times 4+3 \times 4)$	$=24$
Painting	3	3	$6 \ (=3+2 \times 3+3 \times 6)$	$=27$
Poetry	0	2	$10 \ (=0+2 \times 2+3 \times 10)$	$=34$
Eloquence	0	1	$11 \ (=0+2+3 \times 11)$	$=35$

[6] *True Principles,* xiii–xvi.   [7] Ibid., 4, 6.   [8] Ibid., 27, 37, 58, 104.
[9] One will remember Hogarth, Greenough and Viollet-le-Duc (see pp. 189, 209).
[10] Ibid., 140–3.

So much of the system. Now the views delivered in its name. 'All the common and useful things', Fergusson writes, 'may be refined into objects of beauty.'[11] But by refining he means not the maximum fitness, but a desirable 'pretension to high art' which is impossible at present only, because such things are 'in the hands of shop-keepers'.[12] That fitness is not enough comes out in Fergusson's comments on the architecture of warehouses and common dwellings. They are merely utilitarian today. 'How much ornament and what change in disposition' would be necessary to raise them to a higher class?[13] The book of 1862 contains the answer. In the case of engineer buildings, such as bridges and stations, Fergusson is even more explicit. They are 'standing before us naked and cold', and yet 'a very small modicum of taste would have draped [them] with beauty'.[14]

These comments and the chart prepare for a definition of architecture which is almost identical with Ruskin's and, given the year of Fergusson's book, must be independent of his. Painting and sculpture belong with speech and writing to his phonetic arts, because they 'attempt poetry or elevation of sentiment' or, in other words, 'some intellectual form of utterance'. So they share in Fergusson's definition of the value of a work of art. 'A work of art is valuable in the direct ratio of the quantity and quality of the thought it contains.' That is Ruskin again, though it is also Reynolds.[15] By thought Fergusson clearly means matters of content not of composition, let alone planning for convenience. Architecture can become phonetic only by the addition of painting and sculpture.[16] Where then in the light of such a definition does architecture stand today, and how should it be directed into the future?

The great enemy for Fergusson, as his articles in *The Builder* had already made clear, is copyism. Copyism Fergusson now explains very interestingly out of the association of ideas, 'the lowest and most unreasoning source of beauty'. For reasons of association architects and their clients choose styles for buildings, and 'the same architect [may be] forced at the same moment to build correct

  11 Ibid., 96.
  12 Ibid., 100–1.   13 Ibid., 102.
  14 Ibid., 105. Incidentally, in connection with technological progress Fergusson mentions electricity as 'an infant power' (83) and especially the telegraph (118).
  15 There is in fact a good deal from Reynolds's *Discourses* in Fergusson's *True Principles*.
  16 Ibid., 119–21.

buildings in all the styles, thus contradicting himself every hour'.[17]
Such a remark ought to imply that architects instead should work in
one style only, and once that were said, Fergusson would have to
come down either for Grecian or Gothic or Italianate, or for a new
style for the century. But there he fails us, as all others so far have
failed us. What is certain to Fergusson is that architecture must 'give
up all imitation of past styles'. This is the only way by which
'progressive vitality' can be secured. Progress has always existed,
for example from 'the rude and heavy Norman pier' to the 'clustered
shaft of the late Gothic'; from the 'rude waggon-vault' to the 'fairy
roof of tracery'. Let architects today do as scientists, as ship-
builders, as manufacturers do: build on all the accumulated knowledge. Thus progress would be made on a broad front. A Watt or
an Arkwright will spring up only rarely.[18] If architects behaved like
that, they might be able to progress beyond anything built so far.
For instance they might ask in an unprejudiced way what would be
'the best possible edifice for the performance of the Anglican-
Protestant form of worship'. If they then did their best, defects would
still be found—in height, in lighting, in acoustics, or 'the cornices
[might be] too heavy, the ornaments inappropriate', but the best
solution would in the end be realized.[19]

It will be noticed that Fergusson mixes objective and subjective
criteria, and we shall see later how subjective criteria play havoc
with his assessment of buildings of the past. As for today, Fergusson
is certain that to go on building in 'fossil and exotic styles' will only
present us with 'dried specimens', but if you ask him what we should
substitute, he says: 'The answer is simple . . . I do not know',[20] and
the only specific recommendations do not help: 'Sordid minds
cannot express elevation'. 'A higher class of blood' ought to get into
the profession, but there should be less personal ambition. The
greatest works of architecture have always been anonymous, 'a
nation's labour'. 'No man of gentlemanly feelings should expose
himself to the unfairness of competitions', and so on—a mixed bag.[21]

How out of that, one asks oneself, could a history of architecture
be made which became an accepted textbook for a generation? The
foundation given at the end of the *True Principles* is shaky: Good
architecture comes about, when the architect entrusts himself to 'the
guidance of commonsense for the disposition, and of discriminating

---

[17] Ibid., 144–5.   [18] Ibid., 156–8.   [19] Ibid., 160.
[20] Ibid., 164, 161.   [21] Ibid., 164–5.

17

taste for the decoration' of his buildings.[22] So that is what we shall have to look for in the *History of the Modern Styles of Architecture*.

When this book was published in 1862, Ruskin's *Stones of Venice* and Scott's *Remarks* were available, the Crystal Palace was there for all to see, and so were Barry and Pugin's Houses of Parliament. The Modern Styles of Fergusson are the styles from the end of the Gothic to the present day. What made him write the book? The reply is odd. The *raison d'être* of these fully illustrated 500 pages is negative. In his preface he calls his story 'a critical essay on the history of the aberration of the art'. The Introduction makes it clear what that means; the Conclusion sums it up. The villain in the piece of course is 'the Copying Styles of Architectural Art'. Both St. Peter's and St. Paul's are untruthful. Imitative work 'can never appeal to our higher intellectual faculties', and it is they that should operate. Architects should always consider what is 'most convenient and appropriate' and how a building can be made 'most ornamental with the least sacrifice of convenience'. We know the theses, and Fergusson indeed returns at once to his Technic, Aesthetic and Phonetic Forms of Art.[23] The crushing end of the introduction must be quoted in full.

We have got to deal with an art which is not conducted on truthful or constructive principles, but on imitative attempts to reproduce something which has no real affinity with the building in hand; with an architecture which occupies itself almost exclusively with the meaner objects of domestic and civil wants, instead of the more elevated aims of templar or ecclesiastical buildings; with a style of building where the interior and the internal arrangements are almost everything and the exterior, which is the true place for architectural display, may be anything, and consequently generally it is a sham; with an art whose utterances, whether Classic or Gothic, are the products of the leisure of single minds, not always of the highest class, instead of with an art which is the result of the earnest thinking of thousands of minds, spread over hundreds of years, and acting in unison with the national voice which called it into existence; we are describing an art which is essentially Technic in all its forms, but which is now conducted on principles which are only applicable to the Phonetic arts.[24]

Cautioned in this way the reader now embarks on Fergusson's voyage through the countries from Italy to Russia, India, and

---

[22] This again comes straight from Reynolds.
[23] *History of the Modern Styles of Architecture*, 2, 9–10, 17.
[24] Ibid., 37.

America. Unfortunately Fergusson is not a good guide, partly because so many countries and buildings were not seen by him,[25] and partly because he does not describe well. 'A general simplicity and elegance of the design which [has a] most pleasing effect' is not good enough for Mansart's building at Blois.[26] The epithets, 'elegant' and 'in good taste' are repeated time and again, for instance of Alberti's façade of S. Francesco at Rimini and Galilei's of S. Giovanni in Laterano.[27] And there are other failings.

One of them is the universal High Victorian failing, Ruskin's and Scott's and Macaulay's: excessive self-confidence and hence arrogance of pronouncements. Examples are plentiful. If he blames Michelangelo for 'dreadful vulgarities' and Michelangelo's windows of St Peter's for being 'in the most obtrusive and worst taste',[28] that had been done before, by Milizia and others. Giulio Romano is vulgar too, Borromini is absurd, the Escorial has 'no human interest',[29] and Wren is blamed for his 'want of knowledge of the artistic principles of design'[30]. In fact Fergusson goes further. He takes St Paul's and tells Wren what he ought to have done to make a better job of it. The following is only a sample of a much longer criticism.

The great defect of the lower part of the design arose from Wren not accepting frankly the Medieval arrangement of a clerestory and side aisles. If his aisle had projected beyond the line of the upper storey, there would at once have been an obvious and imperative reason for the adoption of two Orders, one over the other, which has been so much criticized. Supposing it were even now determined to fill up the interval between the propylaea and the transept, as shown by the dotted lines on the plan at A, the whole would be reduced to harmony; it would hide the windows in the pedestals of the upper niches, which are one of the great blots in the design; and, by giving greater simplicity and breadth to the lower storey, the whole would obtain that repose in which it is somewhat deficient.[31]

Chambers's Somerset House does not fare better:

The river front . . . was Chambers's great opportunity, but it unfortunately shows how little he was equal to the task he had undertaken. To treat a southern façade nearly 600 ft. in extent in the same manner he had treated a northern one only 132 ft. long, would have been about as great a blunder

---

[25] Freeman in his *History of Architecture* incidentally also admits to having had to work partly from illustrations (p. x).

[26] *History of the Modern Styles of Architecture*, 207.   [27] Ibid., 43, 67.   [28] Ibid., 103, 62.
[29] Ibid., 124, 132.   [30] Ibid., 280.   [31] Ibid., 273.

as an architect ever made. In order to produce the same harmony of effect, he ought to have exaggerated the size of the parts in something like the same proportion; but instead of this, both the basement and the Order are between one third and one fourth less than those of the Strand front, though so similar as to deceive the eye. As if to make this capital defect even more apparent than it would otherwise have been, he placed a terrace 46 ft. wide, and of about two-thirds of the height of his main building in front of it! No wonder that it looks hardly as high, and is not more dignified than a terrace of private houses in the Regent's Park or elsewhere. This is the more inexcusable, as he had 100 ft. of elevation available from the water's edge, without adding one inch to the height of his buildings, which was more than sufficient for architectural effect, if he had known how to use it.[32]

Nor, to go abroad and into the nineteenth century, does the Bauakademie in Berlin, the masterpiece of Schinkel's last and most independent years, fare much better. Here, admittedly, Fergusson is more appreciative, and one gets a faint idea of what he is going to like. Still, carping follows the praise.

The design of this edifice is extremely simple. It is exactly square in plan, measuring 150 ft. each way, and is 70 ft. in height throughout. The lower storey is devoted to shops; the two next to the purposes of the institution; and above this is an attic in the roof, which latter is not, however, seen externally, as it slopes backwards to a courtyard in the centre. The ornamentation depends wholly on the construction, consisting only of piers between the windows, string-cornices marking the floors, a slight cornice, and the dressings of the windows and doors. All of these are elegant, and so far nothing can be more truthful or appropriate, the whole being of brick, which is visible everywhere. Notwithstanding all this, the Bauschule cannot be considered as entirely successful, in consequence of its architect not taking sufficiently into consideration the nature of the material he was about to employ in deciding on its general characteristics. Its simple outline would have been admirably suited to a Florentine or Roman palace built of large blocks of stone, or to a granite edifice anywhere; but it was a mistake to adopt so severe an outline in an edifice to be constructed of such small materials as bricks. Had Schinkel brought forward the angles of his building and made them more solid in appearance, he would have improved it to a great extent. This would have been easy, as much less window space is required at the angles, where the rooms can be lighted from both sides, while the accentuation of what is now the weakest place would have given the building that monumental character which elsewhere is obtained from massiveness of material.[33]

[32] *History of the Modern Styles of Architecture*, 291–2.   [33] Ibid., 355–6.

Examples of this kind of self-confidence can be multiplied. Even St Sophia 'could easily be improved'.[34] In the Crystal Palace Paxton ought to have used brick and terracotta, because, as it is, it lacks solidity,[35] and so on. However, perhaps we are too timid today and too much awed by buildings of the past. And it must be admitted that Fergusson criticized on the strength of certain principles, though their application often surprises. Even so, there cannot be an excuse for sweeping statements about whole nations of whose buildings he knew few or none. Germany has not in three hundred years produced one architect of whom the country could be proud. After the Hohenstaufen the Germans have produced 'nothing great or original', because they 'have no real feeling for the refinements of Art'.[36] Nor incidentally have they any 'real appreciation of the beauty of Nature'.[37] North-western Europe, that is Belgium, Holland, Denmark, Sweden, and Norway 'have done very little in the way of artistic building'.[38] The Belgians are 'not essentially an artistic people'; as for the Danes, 'it need hardly be said that Architecture, as a fine art, has not existed among them', and the Swedes and Norwegians again 'are not an artistic people'.[39] The Russians 'are not an artistic race', and in the United States one could not find 'a single building . . . worthy . . . of being mentioned'.[40]

Such arrogance ill befits a man who prints Palazzo Valmarina and a house called 'the Griefswald', and the piazzi as a plural, and the Sposalizia as a singular. But the book, impudent and irritating as it is, has its redeeming features. Occasionally Fergusson formulates well, as for example when he says of Colen Campbell: 'His design is elegant, but no one cares to look at it a second time.'[41] And, to repeat it and now to demonstrate it, he judges individual buildings according to principles.

His criteria, foreseeable after having looked at the earlier book, are these. Truth first. 'One of the first rules [is] . . . that whatever is not seen must be accounted for.' If not, we don't know 'if the building is truly and honestly constructed'.[42] But, he later contradicts this by saying that not 'every engineering or domestic exigence [ought to be] thrust forward . . . exactly where it may be the most

---

[34] Ibid., 407. [35] Ibid., 483–4. [36] Ibid., 330–1.
[37] Ibid., 365. [38] Ibid., 368. [39] Ibid., 369, 374, 377.
[40] Ibid., 381, 436. [41] Ibid., 287.
[42] Ibid., 213.—Pugin of course must not be accepted as truthful. He is a man of the theatre, and he taught us 'the value of absolute falsehood' (318, 406–8). This is clearly the Protestant speaking.

conveniently situated'.[43] In fact Fergusson is ambiguous on the engineers and their works. Like Scott he praises bridges, but unlike Scott only bridges of stone or brick. A viaduct is 'so beautiful an object in itself that it is difficult to injure it'.[44] More generally speaking, Fergusson pleads that the engineers should not be divided from the architects. As long as they are divided, 'the one great hope [is that] the engineers may become so influential as to force the architects to adopt their principles'.[45] But again there is at once a contradiction; for the architect, 'properly so called' should still remain 'the artist who attended to the ornamental distribution of buildings, and their decoration when erected'.[46] So the engineer, it seems, provides the truth, the architect applies the art. Truth without applied art is not enough. The aim must be 'to elaborate Building with truth into Architecture'.[47] Now how is that done? Of course not by any dressing up in the garments of the past. In fact the hunt for period and imitation goes on in full cry. No quotations need be given; the *True Principles* were already full of them.[48] The best now is the remark on the Oxford Museum that they should have in the library Darwin's *Origin of Species* 'in black letter and illuminated'.[49]

What then is Fergusson's recipe for making Architecture out of Building? We have heard it. It is the applying of art, that is the decorating of façades. London Bridge is 'scarcely sufficiently ornamental to become architecture'. King's Cross is 'entirely truthful', and if more money had been 'employed in ornament, a more architectural façade might have been attained'. That was done in the Gare de l'Est [Fig. 8], and for that reason, for 'its higher degree of ornamentation' it has become 'really an object of Architectural Art'. Finally the Crystal Palace; for this is 'not ornamental to such an extent as to elevate it into the class of Fine Arts'.[50]

All this is of course essentially Victorian; it corresponds to Ruskin's stress on painting and sculpture converting building into architecture. But Fergusson's answer to the question what ornamentation ought to be used, is diametrically opposed to Ruskin's. We can approach it by examining more of his judgements on buildings of the past. He admires the Florentine *palazzi* of the fifteenth

---

[43] *History of the Modern Styles of Architecture*, 325.   [44] Ibid., 476.

[45] This was written before Viollet-le-Duc's *Entretiens* had been published.

[46] Ibid., 474.   [47] Ibid., 491.

[48] In the *Modern Styles*, see e.g. 321 ('the degrading trammels of imitation'), 322 ('one of these forgeries'), 342 ('dried specimens').

[49] *History of the Modern Styles of Architecture*, 328.   [50] Ibid., 476, 478, 480, 483.

FIG. 8. James Fergusson, Gare de l'Est, Paris, by Duquesney, from *A History of the Modern Styles in Architecture*, 1862.

century for their 'manly energy'. 'No palace of Europe [can compare with the Pitti Palace] for grandeur.'[51] But Venice he admires even more, though not Ruskin's Gothic Venice. 'No other city possesses such a school of Architectural Art as applied to domestic purposes.'[52] From Venice also hints for the present can be taken. 'If we must look for types from which to originate a style suitable to our modern wants, it is among the Venetian examples of the early sixteenth century that we shall probably find what is best suited.'[53] But, curiously enough, of Wollaton also—that is the pattern for Baron de Rothschild's Mentmore of 1852–4—Fergusson says that it 'would be good for today', if its details were made purer.[54] So Elizabethan is permitted. The only thing in fact which Fergusson excludes furiously is 'the Gothic mania, which is proving . . . fatal to real progress in art'.[55]

Progress is, if one tries to sum it up, seen by Fergusson in two directions. One is the elevation of Building to Art by ornamentation. The other comes out in what he says about the Louvre. The Colonnade is criticized as being only a screen, but the north side of the

[51] Ibid., 82, 85.   [52] Ibid., 100.   [53] Ibid., 100.
[54] Ibid., 251.   [55] Ibid., 129.

FIG. 9. James Fergusson, Rouen Custom House, from *A History of the Modern Styles in Architecture*, 1862.

Louvre is 'singularly plain' with 'practically no ornament', and, though a little more would have helped, if the French 'had . . . persevered in cultivating' this style, they might have reached a 'true style of the age'. Towards the end of the book he generalizes thus: 'It is far better that we should be content with plain, honest, solid, but useful erections, than that our buildings should be adorned on mistaken principles.'[56] Plain applies to appearance, solidity to construction, but honesty to the intention. And on this mental and moral attitude behind buildings Fergusson has more to say. Common sense is always an attribute of praise. It is bestowed on the Italian Renaissance, 'the common-sense style' to him and incidentally a style 'never having attained the completeness which debars all further progress'.[57] So according to him the Custom-house at Rouen [Fig. 9] is Renaissance fitting the function of today.

[56] *History of the Modern Styles of Architecture*, 482.
[57] Ibid., 329. This argument of being 'développable'—to use a term of Antoine Pevsner, the sculptor (Colonne développable de la victoire)—had already been used by Hübsch and was, as the next chapter will show, also used by Semper. Fergusson incidentally owned Hübsch's *Die altrichristlichen Kirchen*, 1862, as he also used Bunsen's *Basilikas*, Hittorff and Zanth's *Architecture moderne de la Sicile*, Gally Knight's *Ecclesiastic Architecture of Italy* of 1842–4, Puttrich's *Baukunst*

'The new Custom-house at Rouen is another . . . favourable specimen of the mould in which the French architects of the present day design the minor class of public edifices. Neither the dimensions nor the purposes of such a building admitted of very great grandeur or richness being obtained. It is, however, sufficiently magnificent for the custom-house of a provincial city, and it expresses its purposes with clearness, while no useful element is sacrificed for the sake of effect, and no ornament added which in any way interferes with utilitarian purposes. The ordinary receipt for such a design, especially in this country, would have been a portico of four or six pillars, darkening some and obstructing the light of other windows, besides necessitating the building being—in appearance at least— only two storeys in height. It is an immense gain when architects can be induced to apply the amount of thought that is found here; and with a little more care in the details; and a little more variety in the arrangement of the parts, this might have become a more beauti- ful design than it is, though few of its class can, on the whole, be called more satisfactory'.[58]

Much less is said about Labrouste's Sainte-Geneviève Library: 'A promise of common sense' is held out by the building, but there is no specific praise of the nobility of the façade nor is there a word about Labrouste's use of exposed iron.[59] And 'the man of common sense' will also be happy with Wyatville's parts of Windsor Castle, because they show at once that this is 'a Royal residence of the nine- teenth century'.[60] So buildings ought to tell their function—be *architecture parlante*, in fact. Hence the praise of Newgate Prison, of Schinkel's Neue Wache which 'speaks of resistance and security', of the Vienna Arsenal and the Federal Palace at Berne [Fig. 10].[61]

des Mittelatters in Sachsen, of 1836–44, Gruner's *Terracotta Architecture of North Italy*, of 1867, Boisserée on Cologne, Street on Spain, Vogüé on Syria, Percier and Fontaine's *Maisons de Plaisance de Rome* of 1809, Letarouilly's *Edifices de Rome Moderne* of 1840–57, Durand's *Recueil*, and Klenze's *Entwürfe*—besides Voltaire's Works in 70 volumes, and Rousseau's, Wieland's, Goethe's, and Schiller's works. See the Catalogue of the sale, 22–24 June, 1886 at Sotheby's. It is in the British Museum.

[58] Ibid., 230.   [59] Ibid., 229.   [60] Ibid., 313.

[61] Ibid., 296, 355, 362, 366. Schinkel wrote more generally in 1834: 'The ideal in architecture is reached only, when a building entirely and in all its parts corresponds physically and spiritually with its purpose' (A. Freiherr von Wolzogen: *Aus Schinkel's Nachlass*, 4 vols. (1862–4) III, 333). To return to Fergusson, he holds up the Federal Palace as an example of what ought to have been done in the case of the Houses of Parliament. The Federal Palace to him is 'perhaps the best specimen of the Florentine style that has yet been attempted', and he then imagines in London 'a block like the centre of the Bernese Federal Palace placed at either end . . . between these a central block, more ornate, but of the same height as the wings . . . and then these joined by curtains four stories in height . . . Which would have been the nobler building?' Poor Fergusson; no one today would not have his answer ready. Only Gwilt agreed. Among the

FIG. 10. James Fergusson, The Federal Palace at Berne, from *A History of the Modern Styles in Architecture,* 1862.

Where Fergusson uses 'appropriate' he means it in this sense too. The Palais Bourbon for example with its giant Corinthian portico is 'inappropriate and does not tell its own story'. But the use of Gothic forms for churches is appropriate; so are Elizabethan mansions; so is Inigo Jones's Wilton House; but Holkham is not, because the façade makes us think that 'the noble host and hostess sleep in a bedroom 40 ft high' or in a garret.[62]

Fergusson's book ends with four pages of Conclusions.

... what is to be the style of the future?

To give a distinct and categorical answer to such a question is of course, impossible, as it would be equivalent to attempting to foresee what has not been invented, and to describe what does not yet exist. It would have been as reasonable to have asked Watt to describe the engines of the 'Warrior' or Stephenson to sketch the appearance of the Great Western

---

many disagreeing, Waterhouse of the Gothic Manchester Assize Courts and Town Hall and the Gothic Prudential, may serve as an example. He called the Federal Palace at Berne 'a disappointment in everything except the ceiling and wall paintings'. The remark comes from an unpublished diary of 1857 to which Dr. Stuart A. Smith refers in his Ph.D. Thesis on Waterhouse (London University, 1970).

[62] *History of the Modern Styles of Architecture,* 319, 223, 255, 263, 295.

express train at the time when he had started the 'Experiment' on the Stockton and Darlington line. If the style is to be a true style, it will take many years to elaborate, and many minds must be employed in the task; . . . In the mean while, however, it is easy to reply negatively that it certainly will not be Gothic . . . [which] must remain only a fragment of the past, utterly strange and uncongenial to our habits and our feelings—an amusement to the learned, but taking no root among the masses nor ever being an essential part of our civilization.

. . . The same is true of the pure Classical styles, from which we are separated by even a longer interval of time and also by a geographical barrier which renders them unsuitable for our climate. But it is not quite correct to say that our sympathies are not equally engaged by them . . . It need hardly be added that all this is even more true as regards the Saracenic, the Indian, the Chinese, or Mexican; but there is yet one other style within whose limits progress still seems possible. The Renaissance Italian is by no means worked out or perfected, and, from the causes pointed out in the preceding pages, has hardly yet had even a fair trial of its merits . . . Within the limits of such a style as this progress seems possible; and if it is, the problem is of easy solution. It does not require a man or set of men, as some have supposed, to invent a new style; the great want now is self-control and self-negation. What we require is that architects shall have the moral courage to refrain from borrowing, and be content to think, to work, and to improve bit by bit what they have got. . . . The demand, however, must arise with the public, and cannot come from the profession. We have no right to ask that an architect shall starve because he refuses to erect Gothic churches, Grecian temples, or Chinese summer-houses, feeling that he can do better. The public must say to those it employs, you shall arrange your design according to the dictates of common sense, you shall elaborate it by thought, and you shall apply ornament with taste to what you have thus worked out; but beyond these three postulates you shall not go. When this is done we shall again know what the art means. If we ask for anything else we may get something which may be very beautiful, but it will not be Architecture.[63]

[63] Ibid., 488–90.

CHAPTER XXIV

Semper

FERGUSSON'S position in the pattern which this book tries to trace is clear. He stands close to Kerr, that is for truth, for the importance of recognizable construction, for the engineers, for *architecture parlante*, for common sense, but also for the adding to all this of applied enrichment in the Italian style. But as against Kerr he respects a certain purity of Italian where Kerr pleads for a rather wild mixture.

In his respect for the Renaissance Gottfried Semper agreed with Fergusson; indeed Semper was the greatest Central-European representative of the neo-Renaissance. He was born at Hamburg in 1803, studied first mathematics at Göttingen and then architecture with Gärtner (of the Ludwigskirche in Munich and other *Rundbogen* buildings), lived twice for a while in Paris, in 1826–7 and 1829–30, where he worked with Gau, the Gothicist, and got to know Hittorff, and he travelled in Italy, Sicily, and Greece in 1833. Two years later he was appointed Professor at the Dresden Academy. In 1848—to quote from the obituary by Donaldson who calls him 'an intimate friend'[1]—he 'allowed an irrepressible political and democratic feeling against kingly rule to overpower his better judgment', that is he joined the revolution. The revolution, as is known, miscarried, and Semper had to flee. He first went to Paris and then to London, where he stayed from 1851 to 1855. He was responsible for the display of some of the sections of the 1851 Exhibition and later taught the technology of metals in Henry Cole's newly founded Department of Practical Art. At least once he wrote a brief article for Cole's *Journal of Design and Manufactures* too.[2] In 1855 he went to Zürich as Professor at the Polytechnic, and in 1871 was made Imperial *Baurat* in Vienna. He died in 1879.[3] He does not seem to have been a happy

---

[1] *Trans. R.I.B.A.*, 1879, 233 ff.   [2] V, 1851–2, 112.

[3] The two big monographs on Semper are H. Semper, *Gottfried Semper* (1880) and C. Lipsius, *Gottfried Semper in seiner Bedeutung als Architekt* (1880). In 1881 *Bauten, Entwürfe und Skizzen* were published posthumously, in 1884 *Kleine Schriften* containing a number of his London lectures. Some of these together with *Wissenschaft, Industrie und Kunst* (see below) have recently been

man. Eduard Devrient, the actor, met him in London in 1854 and again in Switzerland in 1857. The first time he writes home: 'He is of course still our old *raisonneur*'; the second time: he is 'through and through peevish (vergrämelt) with his hatred of the world and mankind always on his tongue—but always perspicacious.'[3a]

Semper's foremost works of architecture were the first and the second opera houses at Dresden (1838–41 and 1871–8) [Pls. 69, 70], the Oppenheim Palais at Dresden (1845–8), the Dresden Gallery (1847–54) [Pl. 71], the Zürich Polytechnic (1859–64) and, in collaboration with Hasenauer, the Museums and the Burgtheater in Vienna (1872 ff.). The development from a restrained to a freer and more Baroque Cinquecento is evident and corresponds to the general European development. Foremost among Semper's numerous writings is the brief *Wissenschaft, Industrie und Kunst* (Braunschweig, 1852), a report on the 1851 exhibition, and the far from brief *Der Stil*, 1860–3, in two volumes, with a third never completed.

As *Der Stil* makes painfully clear, Semper, like Fergusson, was a system-builder and categorizer. However, he had a philosophical mind, and that resulted in a system not as naïve as Fergusson's. Semper had read his Schiller and Schinkel, and his system is one of a rather involved idealism. He had also read Kant, and the result of that is a literary style which can be terrible. One passage must suffice, and it must be left in German for obvious reasons: 'Letztere sucht alle Eigenschaften oder Bedingungen des Rein-Schönen in der Form aus letzterem heraus, als nur für sich bestehend und sich selbst erklärend, zu entwickeln'.

reprinted with an introduction by H. M. Wingler (Neue Bauhausbücher, Mainz and Berlin, 1966). On Semper's theories see E. Stockmeyer, *Gottfried Sempers Kunsttheorie* (Zürich and Leipzig, 1939), and H. Quitzsch, *Die aesthetischen Anschauungen Gottfried Sempers* (Berlin, 1962). In English there is just one recent paper: L. Ettlinger, 'On Science, Industry and Art; some Theories of Gottfried Semper', *Architectural Review*, CXXXVI, 1964, 57 ff., and a letter from O. Hornbostel, ibid., 241. In the later eighties on the other hand, there seems to have existed some Anglo-American interest in Semper—see Lawrence Harvey: 'Semper's Theory of Evolution in Architectural Ornament, *Trans. R.I.B.A.* n.s., I, 1885, 29 etc. and John Welborn Root, 'Development of Architectural Style', *Inland Architect and News Record,* XIV–XV, 1889–90. I owe the first of these two references to Mr D. Stewart, the second to Professor David Gebhard. Lawrence Harvey's first sentence is: 'Perhaps many of my British colleagues have never heard of Semper'. Maybeck, the brilliant Californian architect, planned a translation of *Der Stil* in 1891. Mrs. Elizabeth Sussman and Mrs. Leslie Freudenheim told me about this. The reference they gave me is this: *The Architectural News,* San Francisco, (January, 1891) No. 3, Vol. I, 23. 'We have in preparation a translation of *Der Stil* by Semper, of which there is no English version to our knowledge. We believe particular mention of the great value of this work to be unnecessary.' A German thesis on Semper, by C. Zoege von Manteuffel, I have not seen: Freiburg i. B., Ph.D. 1952, 326 pages. Nor do I know the contents of a lecture called *Semper und das Gesamtkunstwerk* given at the Deutsche Kunsthist. Tagung, Cologne, 1970.

[3a] *Briefwechsel zwischen Eduard und Therese Devrient* (Stuttgart, 1909), 213 and 283.

Semper's first book dealt with Polychromy in Greek architecture. It was published in 1834. Hittorff,[4] who was eleven years older than Semper and like Gau came from Cologne, had made his discovery in Sicily in 1823–4 and begun to speak and write about it immediately after his return to Paris, though his final publication had to wait until 1851. The violent controversy over this subject does not concern us here,[5] though Semper's and Hittorff's liking for strong polychromy is the Classical parallel to the contemporary fight of Butterfield and other English architects for polychromy in neo-Gothic buildings.[6] But in the foreword Semper makes some points already which are of importance for his later and more comprehensive writings.

The disciple runs all over the world, crams into his book of pressed leaves well pasted-on tracings of all kinds and returns home happy, cheerfully expecting that pretty soon he will be asked to do a Valhalla à la Parthenon, a basilica à la Monreale, a *boudoir* à la Pompeii, a palace à la Pitti, a Byzantine church, or may be even a bazaar in a Turkish taste.[7]

The barbs are directed against Klenze in Munich whose Walhalla had been completed in the year of Semper's book and whose All Saints, and somewhat Pitti-like range of the Royal Palace had been begun in 1826 and 1825. A few pages later Semper adds to the list, as the most recent source of imitation, the Rococo of Louis XV, and his comment on the quick succession of patterns is the expression of his hope 'that the nuisance will soon be at an end'.[8] Semper's hostile attitude to this kind of historicism is of course the same as Hübsch's whose *In welchem Style sollen wir bauen?* had come out in 1828.

In the same foreword, however, Semper also states two positive principles. One is 'Let materials have their own say, undisguised,' in the shape, the proportions, most suited to them by experience and science . . . Wood should appear wood, iron iron.'[9] The other

[4] See K. Hammer *Jakob Ignaz Hittorff* (Stuttgart 1968).

[5] Among the opponents was Bartholomew who wrote of 'the fevered small-minded pursuit of "Polychromy"', of 'Poly-gewgawery' and other insults, (*Specifications*, l. cit., p. lxxxiv).

[6] In *Die vier Elemente der Baukunst* (Braunschweig, 1851) Semper tells that Donaldson had already observed colour in Greek buildings in 1820 and that in 1837 a Committee met in London to examine remains of colour on the Elgin Marbles. Present were both Donaldson and Hittorff. Semper, while in London, must have been specially friendly with Owen Jones. They shared a passion not only for polychromy but also, as will be seen presently, for principles of ornament.

[7] *Kleine Schriften* (Berlin and Stuttgart, 1883) 216–17.   [8] Ibid., 220.

[9] Ibid., 219. Viollet-le-Duc (who by the way owned Semper's *Der Stil*—see his library sale catalogue of 1880, No. 1009) wrote almost exactly the same: 'Il faut que la pierre paraisse bien être de la pierre; le fer du fer; le bois du bois' (*Entretiens*, I, 472). For the sale catalogue of which

principle sounds even more categorical: 'Art has only one master—needs. It degenerates where it follows the whims of an artist or, worse still, where it obeys powerful patrons.'[10] But Semper does not mean needs in a utilitarian sense only. 'Religion has at all times been the nurse of art' and 'the fire of liberty and the political self-confidence' of the Greeks, their 'fight for freedom against tyrants' explains the greatness of Greek art which is 'liberty tamed by taste'.[11] No wonder Semper was on the side of the revolution in 1848.

A yet earlier opportunity for Semper to state his convictions had come about, when in 1845 he had been given first prize by a jury for his design for St Nicholas at Hamburg [Fig. 11] and a second jury had ousted it and chosen Scott's design. With Scott's design we are already familiar. It was Middle Pointed in that archaeologically accurate and at the same time powerful manner of which in the 1840s only England was capable. Semper's design was not Gothic; nor was it Renaissance as his earlier Dresden Opera. It was in an indefinite mixture of Romanesque and Byzantine with a dome derived from Brunelleschi. Any jury preferring purity would prefer Scott, but Scott would also be the choice of any jury preferring an accepted plan and elevation to an untried. For Semper had provided an essentially central though in fact elongated plan and seating on the auditorium principle. Auditorium is Latin and comes from *audire*. Semper actually uses the term *Hörsaal* (which is the German for the university lecture theatre) in a short publication of his design and the ideas behind it, written in answer to a pamphlet published anonymously by one F. Stöter which had defended Scott's design and the Gothic style for St Nicholas.[12]

Stöter's defence was essentially associational. Gothic—we know these arguments from England as well as France—has the greatest *Christlichkeit* and is moreover the *deutsche Bauweise*. The Gothic spire is a true 'sursum corda'; it expresses 'the yearning for what is above', whereas the dome, though 'it reaches out towards the sky

David Stewart first told me, see p. 215. August Reichensperger in 1845 said the same negatively: 'Wood is painted to simulate bronze, iron to simulate stone, stone to simulate both' (*Die christlich-germanische Baukunst,* (Trier, 1845) 44).

10 Ibid., 217.

11 Ibid., 226, 228.

12 Semper's *Über den Bau evangelischer Kirchen* (Leipzig, 1845) was reprinted in *Kleine Schriften,* 443–67. The anonymous pamphlet is called *Andeutungen über die Aufgabe der evangelischen Kirchenbaukunst* (Hamburg, 1845). Stöter answered Semper: *Erwiderung auf Herrn Profesor Semper's Schrift über den Bau . . .* (Hamburg, 1845). On all this see K. E. O. Fritsch, *Der Kirchenbau des Protestantismus . . .* (Berlin, 1893), 221 ff., and very recently M. Bringmann, *Studien zur neuromanischen Architektur in Deutschland* (Diss. Heidelberg, 1968), 159 ff.

FIG. 11. Gottfried Semper, Design for St. Nicholas, Hamburg, from *Über den Bau evangelischer Kirchen*, 1845.

yet returns to earth'. The cathedral plan with aisles and radiating east chapels even Stöter cannot prove to be useful, but he argues that aisles are 'for evangelical service neither useless nor damaging';

so why sacrifice the whole style in order to eliminate them? And as for the radiating chapels, they can be used for vestries, sacristies, etc. Semper's answer is functional in the first place, but stylistic, i.e. anti-Gothic, as well. Semper not only contradicts Stöter but also Stöter's principal witness, Bunsen, whose work on the basilicas of Christian Rome, as we have seen,[13] had ended with a recommendation of the Gothic style, 'the so-called German vaulting style'. But Bunsen also ended with a warning that 'nothing old can be revived literally'. Stöter agrees with the first, Semper only with the second of Bunsen's statements. We have incidentally also heard of Scott's conversation with Bunsen as reported in Scott's book of 1850.[14] Bunsen, Scott tells us, had asked him whether there should not be an original style of the nineteenth century. Now Semper's answer to this question is Yes. He blames the 'confusion in our time', 'caused by erudition' and insists that 'our churches must be churches of the nineteenth century'. But once that is said the quandary results which we have met so often. Semper deprecates 'the attempts made in a spirit of an opposition trying to be utterly original' and instead, after having demonstrated that his plan is functionally adapted to protestant worship, defends his Byzantino-Romanesque style with much less rational arguments. First it reaches back to the *Urtypus* of the Christian church, secondly, 'as the Nibelungen Saga is nearer to us than Parsival, Titurel, Vigalois and all the fantastical romances of the thirteenth century, so the *Rundbogen* is closer to our time than the pointed arch'. Thirdly, the Romanesque style 'whose genuinely national development was disturbed by the super-added element of the pointed arch, has never outlived itself as did the Gothic style and is hence more capable of further evolution besides being supple and less exclusive'.

These are questionable arguments, but Semper's functional arguments are sound, and as English defenders of Protestantism pointed back with approval to Wren, so Semper can praise the Frauenkirche at Dresden, where he lived, a centrally planned building with galleries, dating back to 1726–38. Poor Scott! While the Ecclesiologists disapproved of him for agreeing to build a Lutheran church, Semper disapproved of him for not being Protestant enough.

Before leaving St Nicholas a paragraph must be added to draw attention to an almost entirely overlooked book of about 100 pages, published in Hamburg in 1845 and called *Von welchen Prinzipien soll*

[13] p. 67, n. 19.   [14] p. 173.

18

die Wahl des Baustyls, imbesonderen des Kirchenbaustyls geleitet werden?
The author is called G. Palm. He begins by saying that there are
two schools of thought, those who say that all styles have something
notable, and those who start from materials, technical experience,
climate, needs, etc. Palm pleads for choosing a style so as to harmonize
with the character of each building.[15] The Greek, the Roman, the
Gothic style have achieved identity of character and form; we must
be able to do likewise. True, we are Germans of the nineteenth
century, but what we are, we owe to the past. So the determining
elements of our style should be Graeco-Roman, Gothic, and
modern,[16] Graeco-Roman for theatres, concert halls, museums,
libraries, grammar schools and the like, modern e.g. for poly-
technics and railway stations,[17] but emphatically Gothic for churches.
And like Stöter, Palm uses Bunsen in his arguments, and also
incidentally Thomas Hope and his conviction of a German origin of
the Gothic style.[18] The *Rundbogenstil* is heavy and lacks spirituality.
The round arch rises, but falls again, whereas Gothic is 'himmel-
anstrebend'.[19] Why then not continue from the climax instead of
returning to an earlier stage? Byzantine is even less suited—and
here Palm refers by name to St Nicholas. Domes are not German;
they are passive and don't point upward, and their use in such
Protestant churches as St Michael at Hamburg only shows up that
they go with a type of Christianity no longer ours.[20] No—Gothic it
must be for churches, and if long choirs and aisles are not strictly
needed for Protestant worship, they can at least be accommodated.[21]

Palm was a conservative. His classical is still Graeco-Roman and
not Italian, and for the buildings with a modern function he can do
no more than recommend that they should have an independent
style of 'Wahrheit, Reinheit, und charaktervolle organische
Gestaltung'[22]—easier said than done. Pure brick, as so excellently
used by Schinkel, round arches, Florentine *palazzi*—it takes us
nowhere, and iron is not mentioned.

Semper had written as early as 1834 that iron should appear iron.
Fifteen years later he returned to iron in a paper on conservatories,
written apropos the Jardin d'Hiver in Paris, where he had gone after
the Revolution, and again he contradicted himself at once. Conservatories of course mean the use of exposed iron in architecture,

---

[15] *Von welchen Prinzipien,* 9–12. [16] Ibid., 13–15.   [17] Ibid., 15–20.
[18] Ibid., 72–4.   [19] Ibid., 76–7; 42.   [20] Ibid., 78–80.
[21] Ibid., 49 ff.   [22] Ibid., 92.

'naked iron'. As yet, there was no Crystal Palace, but Labrouste's
Sainte-Geneviève Library was complete and open. Semper mentions
that building and calls the visible iron roof construction unfortunate.
His argument, interesting enough, is exactly that of Pugin and
William White. Iron according to its nature calls for thin forms;
architecture needs 'effects of mass', and iron can therefore only be
used for 'light accompaniment'.[23] And as for the Jardin d'Hiver,
that is just 'an enormous glass box on a rather shapeless plan'.[24]

Even in his earliest writings Semper had evidently been interested
in the crafts as much as architecture. So it was understandable that,
living in London in 1851, he was asked—like Redgrave, like
Wornum—to put on paper his thoughts on the Great Exhibition.
The request may well have come from Prince Albert. Anyway it
came from what Semper called 'a private source', and the pamphlet
was published in German at Braunschweig in 1852. Semper called
it *Wissenschaft, Industrie und Kunst*. Much of the pamphlet is of no
great relevance to the present book, but a few passages may profitably
be quoted as a preface to *Der Stil*. Style to Semper is 'the basic idea
[of a work] raised to artistic significance', not the total of the elements
and forms used by one period as against another, i.e. for instance of
the Renaissance as against the Baroque. But, Semper goes on,
Style is modified by materials and tools, and also by place, climate,
age, customs.[25] These definitions are of importance to Semper in
the context of the exhibition, because the problem arises how our
new means of production are influencing our basic ideas. The topical
aspects are very well seen: devaluation of materials ('the hardest
stone can be cut like cheese and bread')[26] and devaluation of labour,
and also devaluation of place and time. Everything can be made
everywhere, and it is made by machine and not by hand.[27] 'Even
whole houses can be bought ready-made in the market', and in the
United States, so Semper reports from what an informant had told
him, mechanization of the house is more frequent than in Europe.
Finally there is the speculator instead of the patron. The artist
becomes 'the slave of the employer and of the fashion of the day'.[28]
Artistic quality suffers from this new situation.

23 *Kleine Schriften*, 484–5. Semper says the same again in *Der Stil*, II, 263–4: construction of
metal framing is 'infinitely . . . distant from monumental art'. The ideal of metal construction
would be 'an invisible architecture'.

24 *Kleine Schriften*, 488.   25 *Wissenschaft, Industrie und Kunst*, 15–16.   26 Ibid., 18.

27 Semper asks: 'Are not the new Houses of Parliament made unpalatable by the machine'?
(p. 19)—which is not doing justice to Pugin and his craftsmen.

28 Ibid., 20, 24.

But Semper, like Matthew Digby Wyatt and, as we have seen, Whewell, is an optimist and a believer in *laisser-faire*, both for producers and consumers. As for production he foretells that the present symptoms 'will sooner or later be developed for the benefit and the honour of society',[29] and as for the public, it is absolutely essential that it keeps

the right to decide . . . also in matters of taste . . . Hence no proposals for a jury of artists and institutions to act as the guardian of public taste, no dualism of high art and industrial art, no aesthetic police . . . To raise public taste is necessary, but the public itself must do it. It is much better that for a time it should still go in for nonsense than that it agrees to having taste dictated . . . If it is found necessary to reform conditions more systematically, then the remedy is a suitable teaching of taste, as general as possible.

And for that, what is needed is teaching studios in art schools and public collections.[30] This is what Semper is leading up to, and indeed the South Kensington Museum was erected and the Government Schools of Design were reformed.[31] For a year the new collection even included a Chamber of Horrors.[32]

While in London Semper lectured on a number of subjects connected with architecture and design, and the origins and categories of style. When at Braunschweig, in 1851, another short book by Semper was published called *Die vier Elemente der Baukunst* this was a result of his lecturing in London. Others of his London lectures were reprinted in his *Kleine Schriften*. The lectures must have puzzled his English audiences greatly. They were profound rather than practical and just a little cranky. As far as one can see, they had no effect; for where Semper's views come close to those of Cole and his circle, it must be remembered that Cole's *Journal of Design* had put them forward ever since 1849. Style and styles are Semper's principal subject, and they are treated systematically as well as historically. For classification as such Semper takes Cuvier as his principal example. For style he has now a revised definition: Style is 'a certain degree of perfection', achieved by the artistically just use of the available means and the observation of those limitations which modify the final solution. These limitations are partly inherent in the task, partly due to concomitant circumstances; in the former case they are based on the laws of nature or on function, and Semper

---

[29] Ibid., 10.
[30] Ibid., 61–2.   [31] See Q. Bell, *The Schools of Design* (London, 1963).
[32] *Der Stil*, I, 42–3.

rather confusingly also calls them motifs or types—a bowl for drinking from, for example, is a type valid in all places and at all times, though high civilization tends to dim the sense of the right choice of forms. In architecture the 'type' of partition wall is the mat or rug.[33] Much more will be found on this in *Der Stil*. It is interesting to see already here—for that also is one of the basic concepts of *Der Stil*—that Semper derives architectural elements from those of the applied arts: 'The principles of architectural aesthetics were first used in objects of industry, and the division between architecture and high art and art industry, as we have it now, is one of the main causes of the decline of art industry.'[34]

So once again, but in other words, types are 'basic forms pre-scribed by needs'. They are modified by materials, but the types over-ride. Different materials for one purpose assume the same forms, and the same material for different purposes develops different treat-ments. According to the combination of purposes and materials Semper decrees four classes: clothing (i.e. basic textiles), ceramics, wood construction, stone construction. Metal is left outside, because the types, he states, were already in existence when metal came in. Architecture is a combination of the four classes, and so must be divisible into four categories as well. They are the hearth as the centre of the family and hence the *Ur*-house, to develop in more advanced civilizations into the altar. And as this is where vessels are needed, the hearth means ceramics. The walls, as we have seen, were initially mats; that accounts for textiles. Wood construction is the roof, stone construction the sub-structure.[35]

So far Semper's exposition is entirely on the material side. But in another of the London lectures he goes deeper: 'The . . . charac-teristics of the different systems of architecture will remain obscure to us as long as we have no idea of the social, political, and religious conditions of those nations and ages to which these styles of archi-tecture belonged. Monuments of architecture are in fact nothing but the aesthetic expression of social, political, and religious institutions.'[36]

But that is not enough either. Yet another London lecture, called 'On Architectural Symbols', establishes a third approach. Archi-tecture becomes architecture only by means of poetic qualities, and

[33] *Kleine Schriften*, 267–70. Semper was evidently thinking of Goethe's *Urformen*.
[34] Ibid., 266.
[35] *Die vier Elemente*, 32 ff.; *cf.* also *Kleine Schriften*, 283–8.
[36] *Kleine Schriften*, 351.

these express themselves in the painting or carving of the naked parts of the structure. Here, it need hardly be pointed out, Semper joins hands with Ruskin and Fergusson. The required poetic language—and in this Semper is original—architecture could take over from the applied arts which, as we have seen developed earlier than architecture. Semper demonstrates this poetic language by referring to Greek architecture and decoration; for their principles are perfect. Hence incidentally they cannot die, and a Greek 'resurrection' became possible. And Semper takes the claws of chair legs, and such motifs as the egg and dart, and the cyma, to demonstrate how the part stands for the whole—the claw for the carrying animal etc.—where the part is enough to convey the idea.[37]

The London lectures were a trial run for *Der Stil*, Semper's *magnum opus* and a book that was still read and debated in the Otto Wagner circle in Vienna round about 1900. Yet it is long, it is incomplete, and it is far from lucid. Moreover, from the point of view of the present book, what is missing is the most important part; for volume one is on the Textile Arts, volume two on the Ceramic Arts, and volume three was to be 'on the Styles of Architecture'.[38]

However, architectural matters arise throughout the work, and besides there are thirty-eight pages of Prolegomena. At the start of these Semper states at once his topical purpose. We are 'in the middle of a crisis'. There are signs of 'general decay' or at least 'temporary confusion'.[39] If art has lost its propelling force, education is largely to blame which makes experts not men. In the Middle Ages 'every craftsman was in his way an artist'.[40] Now that is no longer so. Manufacturers create demands and insist on novelty. They interfere with artistic creation from the one side, the 'academic hierarchy' interferes from the other. The architect is no more than the unimportant man who adds the taste, the 'Geschmacksrath'. What we need is first of all humanist elementary schools and then workshops to teach skills.[41]

Semper then reviews the existing attitudes of the architects, who fall into three classes: Materialists, Historicists, and Purists. The Materialists wrongly believe that forms are produced exclusively

---

[37] *Kleine Schriften*, 293–301.

[38] *Der Stil*, II, 371. But at the very end of volume two Semper had clearly given up hope of a third volume.

[39] Ibid., I, v.   [40] Can we not hear Morris some twenty years later? See p. 280.

[41] Ibid., viii–xiii.

by material and construction, whereas matter serves ideas. The Historicists aim at 'imitating the art of long past periods or alien peoples as entirely accurately as possible' instead of 'solving freely a task according to its own premisses as the present sets them'. But this very sentence continues: 'taking into consideration those traditional forms which over the centuries have proved themselves to be unshakably true expression of types'.[42] We know what Semper means by types, but even so this proviso will have to be watched.

On the Gothic Revival Semper is interesting. For the initial phases garden pavilions as well as Goethe and the Romantics are referred to. But the style also recommended itself because of its consistent structural principles and because, at least in England, it was not really dead, when the Revival began. The Gothicists are fighters. They regard Europe as pagan and to be conquered. In France, Semper says, they wisely take their inspiration from the early phase, from which development is still possible, whereas in Germany and England they try to proceed from its 'petrified form'.[43] He must be thinking of the Houses of Parliament and not have been aware of the universal English preference for the Middle Pointed, which is odd.

Altogether the Classical Revival is more hopeful. One reason for this is that we know so much less of classical Antiquity and hence there is more scope for the artist's 'divinatory sense'. This is what made the 'unsurpassed Cinquecento' possible which has the advantage in addition of 'not being complete in itself'.[44] Here is Semper's justification for the style of his own buildings, a style much purer and much more disciplined than that advocated by Fergusson, let alone that used by Kerr.

What Semper calls the Purists he also labels Schematists, and, actually, Futurists ('Zukünftler'). But he does not seem to think of those who regarded the Crystal Palace as an earnest for the future. He merely means the Gärtner school in Munich, who at the command of King Maximilian of Bavaria were to create a new style. Semper spoke about that in a late paper 'On Styles in Architecture'.[45] The Maximilian style, 'as our civilization is mixed', was bound to turn out to be 'a mixture of the styles of all times and peoples'.

After this topical survey Semper is off on to his classifications.

[42] Ibid., xv.   [43] Ibid., xvi–xvii.   [44] Fergusson said exactly the same—see p. 248.
[45] *Kleine Schriften*, 399 ff. On the Maximilianstil see A. Hahn in *Hundert Jahre Maximilianeum* ed. H. Gollwitzer (Munich, 1952).

Most of them we know already, but some of them are over and above
those of the London lectures. There are for instance symmetry,
proportionality, and direction co-ordinated with height, breadth
and depth. But all this is only by way of an introduction. The bulk
of the two volumes is a learned survey of the textile and the ceramic
arts, with plenty of Latin and Greek quotations[46] and with ample
references to primitive peoples. The survey in a very stimulating
way mixes the technical with the historical, though on Semper's
postulated earliest stages of developments one would do well to
remember Jakob Burckhardt's *Weltgeschichtliche Betrachtungen*, where
he writes in the Introduction: 'Everywhere in our studies we may
start with the beginnings, except in history. Our images of the
beginnings are usually mere constructions.' A typical case in point
is Semper's basic thesis that the technical arts precede architecture.
The argument in favour is that in all the surveying of traces of early
society the same basic types of art occur. The types must therefore
be older than the societies.[47]

Throughout the survey Semper also gives topical advice. The
whole book has as its sub-title: *Practical Aesthetics*. So the educational
aspects must not be neglected, and phrases such as 'the law one has
to follow is . . .', 'It is a fault to . . .', 'permitted are . . .', 'more suitable
is . . .', 'it is against good taste . . .' are plentiful.[48] Sometimes the
advice becomes a command: fruit, shells etc. are 'to be condemned
absolutely' on floor coverings.[49]

The most curious feature of Semper's theory is that architecture
does not evolve from the structural skeleton, i.e. the hut of tree-
trunks from which Laugier had started, but from the surfaces in
between, i.e. the clothing of the skeleton. The clothing, originally of
basketry, then of woven mats, defines space. This is why the textile
arts are Semper's Volume One. Weaving precedes architecture, and
the principle of clothing goes on and becomes the stucco patterns
on walls, metal cladding, ashlar cladding and the Greek painted
polychromy.[50]

But Semper's high admiration of Greece brings in a new complica-
tion. It is the old theory that the temple represents in stone the
elements of prior wooden buildings. How can this be justified in
Semper's terms? It needed some involved arguing, and it brings in

[46] E.g. I, 279, 341, 405, 519.   [47] *Der Stil*, I, 5–6; cf. I, 276.
[48] Ibid., I, 46; II, 218, 219.   [49] Ibid., I, 43. Pugin said that before Semper.
[50] Ibid., 227–8, 368, 409.

the term 'structural symbolism'. Classic Greek architecture is the
'emancipation of the form from the material and the naked need'.
The resulting form is what he had earlier called the poetic form.
Just as polychromy is 'the most subtle, the least corporeal clothing',
so real structure is now hidden but expressed symbolically.[51] The
most enlightening statement of this theory is as follows: 'Annihilation of reality, of material matters is necessary, if form is intended to
appear as significant symbol, as an autonomous creation of man.
We are meant to forget the means which have to be used to achieve
the intended artistic impression instead of blurting out the real
means and thereby spoiling the game',[52]—the game being the
creation of 'ideelle Gebilde'.[53] Semper has often been branded as a
materialist, and many of the basic statements seem to confirm this.
But not only has he denied it himself categorically ('the author is
in fundamental opposition to modern materialism in art'),[54] but by
placing the Greek fifth century at the apex of his pyramid of values,
he has proclaimed in favour of these 'ideelle Gebilde'. Reading
Goethe must have encouraged him; for Goethe in his *Baukunst*
(1795) had defined the art of architecture as 'the transfer of qualities
of one material to a semblance of another' and had called that 'poetic
fiction'.[55] It was not easy for Semper to maintain this theory. He
cannot help admitting that the Greeks are 'an example of frankly
carried-on inconsistency'[56] and that the ancient authors like to
praise precious building materials and never refer to what Semper
calls their function of 'clothing'. They don't, says Semper, because
to them it was 'a matter of course, as it were'.[57]

So the Greeks must be secure as the climax. Yet Semper as an
architect does not make them his pattern, as during the same years
Glasgow Thomson did.[58] But like Thomson, Semper was hostile to
the Gothic style and its nineteenth-century revival. Semper argues
that if a building is vaulted, the eye demands information on the
supports. If, as in Gothic buildings, they are outside, while the vault
is inside, 'the . . . eye must feel anxiety'. Semper, moreover, denies
that Gothic architecture can be called organic. The Greek column
is organic, Gothic piers are merely structure. Semper, the liberal
politician, is called in too, and it is entertaining to see how Viollet-
le-Duc, the older liberal and former active revolutionary, uses

[51] Ibid., I, 443–5.   [52] Ibid., 216–17; also I, 232.   [53] Ibid., II, 347.
[54] Ibid., II, 249.   [55] Weimar Edition, XXXXVII, 69.   [56] *Der Stil*, II, 246.
[57] Ibid., I, 448.   [58] See p. 183 ff.

similar political arguments for the opposite end. Semper with
passion denies that Giotto was a Goth or Dante a Goth.[59] Dante was
in protest 'against the system' all his life. The perfect Gothic ruled
at the time of the bloody crusades against heretics. The Italians
never felt Gothic. Gothic is French, and it is familiar what sinister
meaning organization has in France. That is your organic Gothic.
Gothic is rigid. Anyway, furnishings have never fully accepted the
system. They show 'a spirit of resistance against the domination of
architecture'. From the twelfth century onward they are 'anti-
Gothic', 'a kind of Pre-Renaissance'.[60] And Renaissance is what
Semper wants to put forward for his own century. So, of course,
'the indefatigable zeal of the medieval propaganda' receives a
passing swish[61] and the neo-Greek simply disappears from the
deliberations.

The Renaissance borrowed from Antiquity, true, but it was
'animated by a wonderful creative spirit all its own' and so created
works 'new and never emulated'. The Renaissance architects used
no polychromy, true, but they used deep shadows instead. Bramante
may still have been meagre, and Bernini was 'coloratura to excess',
but between them lies 'that period in art which alone, save for the
period of Phidias, can be considered totally emancipated from
barbarity'.[62] These are the last words of volume one, and in volume
two the same conviction is re-iterated apropos furniture and even
extended beyond the Renaissance into the Baroque: Renaissance
furniture was a return 'to the true principles of structural symbolism'
treated in 'the most spirited, freest and most tasteful way', and
Renaissance decoration is 'original, serene and at the same time
thoughtful and gaily elegant'. Jakob Burckhardt's 'forthcoming'
History of the Renaissance is referred to and incidentally called 'caviar
for the masses' and 'not bread-and-butter' for those who are 'too
lazy to think'.[63] Semper is even ready to say of the so-called Northern
Renaissance—what corresponds to the Elizabethan in England—
that it is 'charmingly arbitrary', of the Rococo that it is 'spiritedly
gay' and of the Louis XVI that it is 'very amiable'. But the Italian
Cinquecento remains his favourite. He now says that it has a
'superiority . . . over all that preceded it, including even the highest
art of the Greeks' and he says in its favour moreover, as he had done

---

[59] This is in opposition to Didron's *Annales Archéologiques*, XIV, 341, XV, 51, 171 ff., where
Rome is called more Gothic than Rouen, Siena more Gothic than Bourges.
[60] *Der Stil*, II, 328–33.   [61] Ibid., I, 507–9.   [62] Ibid., I, 510.
[63] Ibid., II, 336. Burckhardt's *Geschichte der Renaissance in Italien* was published in 1867.

FIG. 12. Gottfried Semper, Design for Punch-bowl, from *Der Stil*, 1860–3.

before, that 'it has not reached the goal yet, but is probably only halfway along its course on which, owing to unfavourable times, it was overtaken by its sister-art, music, and left behind at a miserable distance'.[64] And so, when Semper includes in volume two one object designed by himself, it is in that Free Cinquecento style which we have seen praised in contemporary England as well [Fig. 12].

Burckhardt, fifteen years younger than Semper (1818–97), agreed with him. This is what he wrote in 1867 on centrally planned churches, the climax of Renaissance architecture and a climax of Burckhardt's inspired writing.[65]

The Renaissance has brought near to perfection and handed on as its testament to religion of the future the central plan for churches, the highest of architectural forms, essentially superior to all that is Gothic. As the Greek temple is the first in the field of absolute architectural form, so the centrally planned church is the ultimate. Its possibilities are by no means exhausted. There may be intermediate periods such as the major part of the nineteenth century, which had as it were to repeat by heart the thirteenth-century

[64] *Der Stil*, II, 457.   [65] *Geschichte der Renaissance in Italien*, para. 62.

lesson. But time and again the great task will appear, and the endeavours of the Renaissance will then re-enter splendidly as the indispensable pattern.

Alas, looking at the situation of architecture in the sixties, when Burckhardt wrote, no one could say that his Renaissance—Alberti's and Bramante's—was re-entering splendidly. The most prominent and most impressive public buildings were Garnier's Opéra in Paris, begun in 1861 and the Law Courts in Brussels begun in 1866. They are splendid no doubt, but they are of the most ornate Baroque and not of Burckhardt's noble Renaissance, exuberant the one, overpowering the other. And if we return to England and examine the fate of the neo-Renaissance, what do we find? The palazzo style was disappearing under surfaces of mixed Cinquecento and other vaguely Italianate details. The Italian villa style had disappeared. The Wren Revival, so promising in the hands of Cockerell about 1840, had also gone, to be re-awakened for official purposes only towards the end of the century. The most serious architects of Burckhardt's generation worked in the Gothic style and did it supremely well—Scott, Street, Burges, Pearson, Bodley, and in a more personal, energetically rationalized mode, Waterhouse. The Gothicists also were the most serious writers, but they were conservative in their convictions. If you wanted adventurous writing you had to go to Kerr, and he practiced a shamelessly mixed style in which the Italian jostled the French Renaissance and the English Tudor and Jacobean.

But in the sixties a new generation was already coming to the fore, a generation which believed in the intimate and the serviceable. These new qualities were handled most elegantly and resourcefully by Nesfield and Norman Shaw, most thoughtfully and radically by Philip Webb. The earliest dates are Nesfield's lodge of 1866 in Kew Gardens, where the so-called Queen Anne, really an Anglo-Dutch mid-century style, begins, Thackeray's house of 1861 in Kensington Palace Gardens, where the real neo-Queen Anne begins; and of course, yet earlier, Webb's Red House designed in 1858. It was designed, as everybody knows, for William Morris.

CHAPTER XXV

Morris

AT the beginning of this closing chapter a look back is called for. Semper, though an architect, had written more on craft and design than on architecture. Pugin's theory had its application in design as much as buildings. To Ruskin carving and painting make architecture architecture. Only Viollet-le-Duc, Kerr, and Fergusson kept to architecture strictly, only Cole and his circle to design strictly.

All of them in dealing with history wrote for the day as well, and it can be said, with one exception, that those who mainly attacked their own age were the Gothicists—Pugin and Ruskin—whereas those who were happy in their own age and optimistic for the future were the Eclectics, the adherents of the Free or Mixed Renaissance, Cinquecentists broadly speaking—Kerr, Fergusson, Semper.

The exception was Viollet-le-Duc whose very Gothicism led him to the belief in a fitting style for the nineteenth century. But there is a second exception: William Morris who had a faith in the Middle Ages as fervent as Ruskin's and attacked his own age as violently as Pugin, but who not only showed the possibility of a fitting style for his century on paper, as Viollet did, but ceaselessly worked towards tomorrow. This concentration on practical work of a kind directed to the future distinguishes Morris from all others recorded in this book and is the justification for devoting its last chapter to him.[1] William Morris was born at Walthamstow in 1834. His father

---

[1] The standard biography of William Morris is still J. W. Mackail, *The Life of William Morris*, 2 vols., originally 1899, also in The World's Classics. I am quoting from the edition of 1950. Mackail whom I knew a little was the son-in-law of Burne-Jones. Of recent books three can be highly recommended: E. P. Thompson, *William Morris, Romantic to Revolutionary* (London, 1955), especially for Morris's political views; Paul Thompson, *The Work of William Morris* (London, 1968) which is as good on the politics as it is on the poetry, the prose, and the designs; and Philip Henderson, *William Morris, his Life, Work and Friends* (London, 1968) which is a straightforward biography going beyond Mackail in the use of biographical material not accessible to him. Mr. Henderson has also edited *The Letters of William Morris to his Family and Friends* (London, 1950). *The Collected Works of William Morris* were published in twenty-four volumes, London 1910–15. They were edited by Morris's daughter, May Morris, and May Morris added two volumes called *William Morris, Artist, Writer, Socialist* (Oxford, 1936). Much minor material will be found in the *Journal of the William Morris Society* (editor R. C. H. Briggs)

was a wealthy bondbroker, having grown rich by his holding of over a quarter of the shares in the Great Consol Mine in Devon, and, when the son came of age in 1855, he had £900 a year at his disposal. Walthamstow was then 'a suburban village on the edge of Epping Forest', but—Morris added in the letter of 1884 from which this is quoted—it is now 'terribly cocknified and choked up by the jerry-builder'.[2] The boy rode about the forest on his pony, and it is in those years that he acquired his intense love and wide knowledge of nature. A passage in his late *News from Nowhere* recalls that 'The roses were rolling over one another with that delicious super-abundance of small well-tended gardens which at first sight takes away all thought from the beholder save that of beauty. The black-birds were singing at their loudest, the doves were cooing on the roof-ridge, the rooks in the high elm-trees beyond were garrulous among the young leaves, and the swifts wheeled whining about the gables.'[3]

In 1848 he went to Marlborough, one of the many new mid-century public schools, and in 1852 to Oxford. He was at Exeter College, where he made friends for life with Burne-Jones. They read theology, but this satisfied neither. Morris later described the Church of England as 'that curious bundle of subterfuges and com-promises',[4] and himself as 'careless of metaphysics and religion',[5] and he prophesied that in the new order of things . . . social morality . . . will . . . take the place of theological morality'.[6]

Undergraduates have an itch to found societies; it is characteristic of Morris at even this early date that he wanted to create a kind of secular monastery or guild instead.[7] Where precisely the inspiration came from, we don't know. He read Ruskin avidly,[8] but Ruskin then

and in the lectures given to that society and published by it. Mr. Briggs also prepared for them *A Handlist of the Public Addresses of William Morris*, 1961, and the excellent catalogue *The Typo-graphical Adventure of William Morris*, 1957. On Morris and the machine there is a chapter in H. L. Sussman: *Victorians and the Machine* (Cambridge, Mass., 1968), 134 ff. On Morris's designs, especially those for textiles, the late Peter Floud wrote three essential articles: 'William Morris as an artist, a New View', and 'The Inconsistencies of William Morris' (*Listener,* 7 Oct. and 14 Oct. 1954) and 'Dating Morris Patterns' (*The Architectural Review,* CXXVI, 1959). For the stained glass Mr. A. C. Sewter has ready for the press a complete catalogue. It will, I hope, be published soon. After this chapter had been written the indispensable Morrisiana were enriched by E. D. Lemire, *The unpublished lectures of William Morris* (Wayne State University Press, Detroit, 1969).

    [2] Henderson, *Letters,* 184.
    [3] Quoted from A. R. Dufty, *Kelmscott, an Illustrated Guide* (London, 1969), 28.
    [4] Lemire, *Unpublished Lectures,* 203 (1887).   [5] *Coll. W.,* XXIII, 280.
    [6] Ibid., 112.   [7] Mackail, *Life,* I, 64.
    [8] 'The books of John Ruskin . . . were at the time a sort of revelation to me' (Henderson, *Letters,* 185).

had not turned to such ideas yet. The Pre-Raphaelite Brotherhood
on the other hand must have impressed Morris and his friends.
Mackail suggests that Newman's community at Littlemore may have
acted as a stimulus, but he also points to a scheme of about 1848
which the architect Street had in his mind, and this would have
combined 'the character of a college, a monastery, and a workshop',
and it was Street's office that Morris joined when he had taken his
degree. So he decided that architecture was to be his job. But he
was soon disappointed again. Philip Webb whom he met in Street's
office and who became his close friend, said that Morris 'was out of
place in an office'.[9] But Street was a convinced Gothicist and a
brilliant draughtsman, especially of furnishing details, and this
must have stimulated Morris who already as an undergraduate had
revelled in Chaucer, Tennyson, and Rossetti.[10] Street at that time
was Diocesan Architect of Oxford. In 1852 he began the buildings
for the Cuddesdon Training College, in 1855 he worked on his
entry for the Lille Cathedral competition.

In the same year Morris started the *Oxford and Cambridge Magazine*.
He was the proprietor—he estimated that it would cost him £300![11]—
and in it wrote about Amiens Cathedral which he had visited on his
first foreign trip in 1854 with an enthusiasm which must have
pleased Street and would have pleased any partisan of the Second
Pointed. 'Intense exultation' was the effect of Amiens on him.[12]

As a counterweight to work at a desk and at a drawing board
Morris liked to make things with his hands. He carved occasionally
in stone (a capital) and in wood, and he illuminated.[13] His illumina-
tion Rossetti called 'quite unrivalled by anything modern',[14] and
it was due to Rossetti that Morris, disappointed with architecture
decided to be a painter and for some months, in a 'very desultory
way',[15] painted under Rossetti in London. This is how he joined
the team which in 1857 decorated the Oxford Union Library.
Morris did the decoration of the roof timbers—they are in their
present form his repainting in 1875—and Burne-Jones called it 'a
wonder' for its originality and fitness.[16] His only remaining painting
dates from 1858. *La Belle Iseult* (Tate Gallery; also known as *Queen*

[9] May Morris, op. cit., I, 68.
[10] He also incidentally read Kenelm Digby's *Mores Catholici*. See Henderson, *William Morris*,
14.
[11] Quoted from P. Thompson, *The Work of William Morris*, 6.
[12] *O. & C. Mag.*, I, 1856, 101.   [13] Mackail, *Life*, I, 106.
[14] Ibid., 118.   [15] Henderson, *Letters*, 185.
[16] Georgiana Burne-Jones, *Memorials of Edward Burne-Jones* (London, 1906), I, 161.

Guinevere) is obviously inspired by Rossetti and Burne-Jones, but it equally obviously shows a keen interest in the patterns on cloths and the pages of an illuminated book.[17] The painting illustrates a poem by Morris, the title-piece of his first volume of poetry *The Defence of Guinevere* which was published in 1858. Things came easily to Morris. Whatever he chose to do seemed to him no effort. 'If this is poetry', he said, 'it is very easy to write.'[18]

When Morris had left Oxford and settled down in London, he took rooms for himself and Burne-Jones in Red Lion Square, and he needed furniture. What was in the shops he evidently did not like—the 1851 Exhibition he had called 'wonderfully ugly'[19]—so they decided to have furniture made to their specifications. It looked, Rossetti said, 'like incubi and succubi', and a large table in particular Rossetti described as 'heavy as a rock'. Of the chairs he said they were 'such as Barbarossa might have sat in'.[20] One would give much to know what these pieces were like. Morris was not the only one at that moment to think in terms of simple specially designed furnishings instead of the kind of things one could buy in shops. Holman Hunt says that he, in 1847–8, 'declared that furniture . . . would remain as bad as for the last fifty years they had been, if we continued to leave the designing of them to tradesmen', that he 'drew Rossetti's attention' to his 'criticism upon the base and vulgar forms in contemporary furniture' and that they 'speculated on improvement in all household objects, furniture and fabrics'.[21] This is very interesting, or would be, if one could fully trust Holman Hunt on his dates. The only material evidence is an egyptianizing armchair now in the Birmingham Art Gallery. This dates from 1855.[22] There is a good deal more evidence about an early interest in honest furniture on the part of Ford Madox Brown. We know that he designed furniture for Seddon & Co. in the fifties, made an oak table for Holman Hunt in 1857 and resigned from the Hogarth Club when they would not let him exhibit furniture.[23] One chair

[17] On Morris's paintings see Janet Camp Troxell in *Journal of the William Morris Society*, II, no. 1, 4 ff.

[18] Mackail, *Life*, I, 54.

[19] Lewis F. Day, *Art Journal*, Easter Annual 1899, I, and of decorative art in general he said twenty years later that it was 'in a state of anarchy', *Coll. W.*, XXII, 9.

[20] Mackail, *Life*, I, 116.

[21] *Pre-Raphaelitism and the Pre-Raphaelite Brotherhood* (London, 1905), I, 76, 106.

[22] See R. Ormond in *Apollo*, July 1965, and Victoria and Albert Museum, *Catalogue of an Exhibition of Victorian and Edwardian Decorative Arts*, 1952 (I, 1). See also Holman Hunt's *Pre-Raphaelitism*, II, 137.

[23] F. M. Hueffer, *Ford Madox Brown* (London, 1896), 161.

of *c.* 1860 survives, and that is both elegant and honest.[24] Truth had been the motto of the Pre-Raphaelite Brotherhood in its short-lived journal *The Germ*, and truth was a motto of Ruskin. So when in 1858 Morris married, and when it became a question not of rooms but of a whole house, architecture and furnishings, Philip Webb designed Red House at Bexley Heath in Kent, some nine miles from London, in an equally truthful manner. It was called Red House first of all, because it was built of brick, and the brick was not to be hidden by 'the stucco abomination', as the *Journal of Design and Manufactures* had called it in 1850–1.[25] The plan, secondly, came before the elevations, as Pugin had already demanded, and one can see outside which windows will belong to major rooms, to a corridor, to the staircase. And, although the house, especially towards the garden, is unmistakably medieval in mood, there is little mere historicism. The monastic well-house—yes; the pointed arch of the doorway—yes. But otherwise Webb uses elements and motifs of the past, as they strike him as suitable. This is a very different thing from Kerr's mixed Renaissance, not only in that Webb is more discriminating and less obtrusive, but also because he had functional reasons for his choices: relieving arches are more effective if pointed, windows if of the William and Mary and Georgian types. And when it comes to the entrance side of Red House [Pl. 72] there is little left one can call period at all. Here is the beginning of the revolution against historicism altogether,[26] and even more inside, in the astounding chimneypiece with 'Ars Longa Vita Brevis' inscribed [Pl. 73], and in the stencilling of the staircase ceiling. In neither is there a single period motif. And Red House marks a new departure in yet one other way, at least for the historian of architecture. Until Red House and in most cases until much later the milestones in the development of secular architecture in England had been mansions and public buildings. Now they were to be houses of moderate size, whether one thinks of Webb's

---

24 See E. Aslin, *Nineteenth Century English Furniture* (London, 1962), 56, where the story is told and the chair illustrated. I have also illustrated the chair in J. Cassou, E. Langui, and N. Pevsner, *The Sources of Modern Art* (London, 1962), fig. 216 and *The Sources of Modern Architecture and Design* (paperback, London, 1968), fig. 9. At Kelmscott Manor there is bedroom furniture by Brown, stained green, but this dates from 1861–2, i.e. after the momentous year 1861, on which see below. See also Thompson, *The Work of William Morris*, 261, n. 10.

25 IV, 40, 'the stucco abomination, outfacing honest brick'.

26 But Dr. Paul Thompson has recently proved beyond any doubt that it is not quite the beginning; for Webb was inspired by certain parsonages and schools of Butterfield's of around 1850—see *Victorian Architecture*, ed. P. Ferriday (London, 1963). Street's parsonages and schools have the same character too.

Benfleet Hall, Smeaton Manor [Pl. 74] and Standen, or of Norman Shaw's Chelsea and Hampstead houses and his Glen Andred. Admittedly, this is a rough and ready generalization, but as such it stands.

The Morrises did not live long in Red House. The climate proved untoward, and they left in 1864. 'I cried,' he wrote to Burne-Jones.[27] That is Morris all over. He was a man of sudden and impetuous moods. A school-friend at Marlborough already knew of his 'fearful temper'.[28] Sir William Russell Flint had a friend who visited Morris in his later years, was received by a maid in tears, and told that Morris had pinched his finger in trying to close a travelling bag and in his fury kicked a panel out of a door.[29] Another time, in a rage against Val Prinsep he 'swallowed his anger, and only bit his fork . . . almost beyond recognition'.[30] Yet another time he hurled a fifteenth-century folio at a workman's head.[31] Once he bit nearly through a window frame, another time he banged his head against a wall so as to leave a deep dent in the plaster.[32] Allingham in 1864 and 1866 called him 'brusque [and] emphatic, often boisterously.'[33] Lady Burne-Jones tells that he painted a tree in their garden 'with such energy that it was long before the grass grew again on the spot.'[34] He was restless with his hands;[35] and even during meals could not sit still at table,[36] and he had an exceptional 'capacity for producing and annexing dirt', as, according to Mackail, Rossetti noted.[37]

But that is as much a matter of appearance as of character, and as for appearance one hears much and from many. He was not tall, thick-set, with plenty of nearly black hair. He had a high-pitched voice,[38] was 'very careless and unfinished in his dress[39] and wore butcher-blue shirts. A maid in a friend's house thought he was the butcher.[40] Vernon Lee (Violet Paget) found him 'like a railway porter or bargee'.[41] 'Anyway, he was out of place in a drawing room', said George Bernard Shaw.[42] In the *Washington Evening*

[27] Mackail, *Life*, I, 169.   [28] Ibid., 18.
[29] So Sir William told me in October 1959.   [30] 1857; Mackail, *Life*, I, 133.
[31] Ibid., 221.   [32] Ibid., 222.
[33] *William Allingham. A Diary*, ed. H. Allingham and D. Radford (London, 1907), 106, 139.
[34] *Memorials*, I, 157.
[35] J. J. Bruce Glasier, *William Morris and the early Days of the Socialist Movement* (London, 1921), 23.
[36] Mackail, *Life*, I, 221.   [37] Ibid., 223.
[38] So the late D. S. McCall told me.
[39] Percy Lubbock, *The Letters of Henry James* (London, 1920), I, 18.
[40] Mackail, *Life*, I, 224.
[41] Peter Gunn, *Vernon Lee* (London, 1964), 79.   [42] May Morris, op. cit., II, xviii.

Star on 4 November 1885 a reader writing from London described him thus: 'His clothes were . . . frayed at the cuffs and greasy at the seams. He wore a dirty blue linen shirt without collar or necktie, his iron-grey beard ragged and untrimmed . . . No watch-chain, sleeve-links or personal adornment of any kind relieved his shabbiness'.[43]

But that was written in 1885, and even the blue shirts appeared only after 1870.[44] We have left Morris so far installed in Red House. It was while he lived there that he made the most important decision of his life. In April 1861 he founded the firm of Morris, Marshall, Faulkner & Co., Fine Art Workmen in Painting, Carving, Furniture and the Metals. This then in the end was his way of founding a guild and of turning to good use what little he had learned of architecture and painting. True, Ruskin also, though later, had his St George's Guild, but Morris was a practical man, and Ruskin was not. So Morris & Co., as it was later re-named, could lead to European developments not only in theory but in practice as well. In the prospectus Morris referred to the recent 'growth of Decorative Art . . . owing to the efforts of English architects'—and he must have been thinking of Street, Bodley, Butterfield, and other serious Gothic Revivalists and perhaps even of Pugin. He also stated that the artists of the firm—Webb, Burne-Jones, Ford Madox Brown, Rossetti, Arthur Hughes—had 'for many years been deeply attached to the study of the Decorative Arts' and hence 'felt more than most people the want of some one place, where they could obtain or get produced work of a genuine and beautiful character'.

The firm was successful at once. Bodley saw to it that stained glass was commissioned, an exhibition was arranged in the Mediaeval Court of the 1862 Exhibition, in 1866 and 1867 work was executed in the South Kensington Museum (the Dining Room) and even in St James's Palace. Wallpapers were designed, and furniture designed and made [Pls. 75, 76]. The wallpapers have the same two-dimensional integrity as Pugin's, but at the same time a never-failing sense of the fulness of nature. The furniture is simple and inspired by the cottage and manor-house rather than the palace, and as for stained glass, Morris in 1883 stated for the Boston Fair some principles which are as true today as they were then:

As regards the method of painting and the design, our glass differs so much from other kinds that we may be allowed a word of apology. Glass

[43] Reprinted as a leaflet by the William Morris Society.   [44] Mackail, *Life*, I, 223.

painting differs from oil and fresco, mostly in the translucency of the material and the strength, amounting to absolute blackness, of the outlines. This blackness of outline is due to the use of lead frames or settings which are absolutely necessary for the support of the pieces of glass if various colours are used. It is therefore a condition and characteristic of glass painting. Absolute blackness of outline and translucency of colour are then the differentia between glass painting and panel or wall painting. They lead to treatment, quite peculiar in its principles of light and shade and composition. In the first place, the drawing and composition have to be much more simple, and yet more carefully studied, than in paintings which have all the assistance of shadows and reflected lights to disguise faults and assist the grouping. In the next place, the light and shade must be so managed that the strong outlines shall not appear crude, nor the work within it thin; this implies a certain conventionalism of treatment, and makes the details of a figure so much more an affair of drawing than of painting; because by drawing—that is, by filling the outlines with other lines of proportionate strength—the force of the predominant lines is less unnatural. These, then are the first conditions of good glass painting as we perceive them—well-balanced and shapely figures, pure and simple drawing, and a minimum of light and shade. There is another reason for this last. Shading is a dulling of the glass; it is therefore inconsistent with the use of a material which was chosen for its brightness. After these we ask for beautiful colour. There may be more of it, or less; but it is only rational and becoming that the light we stain should not be changed to dirt or ugliness. Colour, pure and sweet, is the least you should ask for in a painted window.[45]

By 1883 Morris & Co. had expanded into the making and selling of woven and printed textiles—the latter called chintzes—into *haute-lisse* tapestry and tufted rugs, and Morris himself, passionate craftsman by nature, learnt to dye and even learnt to make tapestry to be wholly *au fait* [Pls. 77, 78]. We know that in the course of four months he spent 516 hours at the tapestry loom.[46]

They were the summer months of 1879, and at that time Morris was engrossed in a new pursuit. On 4 December, 1877 he had delivered his first lecture on the theory and economics of art and design. The title of the first was 'The Lesser Arts', and later the political speeches absorbed much of his time.

[45] Quoted from Ray Watkinson, *William Morris as Designer* (London, 1967), 39. Morris in presenting this programme may well have thought of what Street had told the Oxford Architectural Society in February 1852 and had been printed in *The Ecclesiologist* in August of the same year (XIII, 247). Cf. pp. 135–6 above.

[46] Mackail, *Life*, I, 385.

So now, knowing what manner of man William Morris was and what manner of life he led, we can turn to his teachings. Like Ruskin's his initial start was 'hatred of modern civilization',[47] and what made him hate modern civilization was 'the study of history and the love and practice of art'.[48] His primary reactions were eye-reactions, against 'such monstrosities as your Manchester-Salford-Oldham',[49] against London seen as 'a whole county covered with hideous hovels',[50] and as 'masses of sordidness, filth and squalor, embroidered with patches of pompous and vulgar hideousness'.[51] Nor are the houses of the rich better at Bournemouth than in London. They are 'simply blackguardly' and built not for civilized people but for 'ignorant, purse-proud digesting machines'.[52] And go inside and what do you find: 'tons and tons of unutterable rubbish'.[53] 'I feel dazed', he said in another lecture, 'at the thought of the immensity of work which is undergone for the making of useless things',[54] and finally in a letter he called London 'this beastly congregation of smoke-dried swindlers and their slaves'.[55] These quotations show how short was the way from the visual to the social. Ruskin had gone it in 1857. Morris followed and never concealed how much he owed to Ruskin. In a lecture in 1884 he praised Ruskin's 'unrivalled eloquence and wonderful ethical instinct'[56] and in an article in 1894, he wrote: 'Ruskin was my master towards the ideal'[57] and when he had started the Kelmscott Press as his last venture in design he reprinted Ruskin's *The Nature of Gothic*.[58] That was only four years before he died.

Who else inspired him? Carlyle of course who, as we have seen, inspired Ruskin. To them we must add Robert Owen, as a few quotations from his *A New View of Society* and *Report on the County of Lanark*, published in 1813 and 1820 respectively, will prove.[59] You manufacturers, said Owen, while you take 'due care as to the state of your inanimate machines' don't pay 'equal attention to your vital machines'.[60] There is acute danger in the 'minute division

47 *Coll. W.*, XXIII, 279.
49 Henderson, *Letters*, 92.
51 *Coll. W.*, XXIII, 170.
53 *Coll. W.*, XXII, 23.
55 Henderson, *Letters*, 138.
57 *Coll. W.*, XXIII, 279.

48 Ibid., 280.
50 *Coll. W.*, XXII, 11.
52 Ibid., 149.
54 *Coll. W.*, XXIII, 194.
56 Lemire, *Unpublished Lectures*, 77.

58 Apart from *The Nature of Gothic* it must have been in particular 'A Joy for Ever', the first of the Manchester lectures of 1857, that inspired him.
59 References are to the recent Penguin edition, ed. V. A. C. Gatrell (Harmondsworth, 1970).
60 Ibid., 95.

of . . . manual labour' instead of the use of the 'extensive mental and manual powers in the individuals of the working-classes'[61] and also in the 'introduction of mechanism'[62]. Replace 'evil conditions by good [and] man might be . . . relieved from evil'.[63] But manufacturers, 'the money-making and money-seeking aristocracy of modern times'[64] will not do that. They have 'frittered down' all ties between employers and employed, and regard the workers as mere 'instruments of gain'.[65] The outcome of this is that 'the rich wallow in an excess of luxuries injurious to themselves, solely by the labour of men who are debarred from acquiring for their own use a sufficiency even of the indispensable articles of life.[66]

That is patent socialism, and Morris indeed read Owen in 1883, the year he joined the Democratic Federation. In the same year he read Marx (in French). What made him join the Federation in the first place, however, was again visual. In an article called 'How I became a Socialist', published in 1894, he wrote that he saw ugliness all round, and was 'driven to the conclusion that all these uglinesses are but the outward expression of the innate moral baseness into which we are forced by our present form of society'.[67] He found confirmation of these convictions more in Owen whom he 'praised immensely'[68] and 'placed first among early socialists'[69] than in Marx. Morris may have called himself a communist,[70] but he was not a Marxist. Reading *Das Kapital*, he suffered 'agonies of the brain' when it came to 'the pure economics of that great work',[71] and when, at a meeting, he was asked to comment on Marx's Theory of Value, he answered: 'To speak quite frankly, I do not know what Marx's theory of value is, and I'm damned if I want to know.'[72] How one would love to have been present. His socialism was not Fabian either. In his review of *Fabian Essays* in 1890 he blamed Sidney Webb for overestimating 'the importance of the mechanism of a system apart from the end toward which it may be used'.[73] State Socialism to him was 'but a dull goal',[74] and he disliked what

[61] Ibid., 238–9.
[62] Ibid., 53.
[63] Ibid., 41.
[64] Ibid., 44–5.
[65] Ibid., 49.
[66] Ibid., 57.
[67] *Coll. W.*, XXIII, 2.
[68] Mackail, *Life*, II, 104; from a private diary.
[69] *Commonweal*, 30 Oct. 1886; quoted from Thompson, *The Work of William Morris*, 228.
[70] So e.g. Shaw tells us in May Morris, op. cit., II, p. ix. See also E. P. Thompson, *The Communism of William Morris*, William Morris Society, 1965.
[71] *Coll. W.*, XXIII, 278.
[72] Glasier, op. cit., 32.
[73] *Commonweal*, 25 Jan. 1890.
[74] Henderson, *Letters*, 293.

he called 'that grievous flood of utilitarianism'[75] and 'gas and water Socialism'.[76]

Morris's Socialism was entirely *sui generis*. 'I want a real revolution, a real change in Society, a great organized mass of well regulated forces for bringing about a happy life for all.'[77] That sounds fine, but it is alas decidedly woolly. Did he mean a real revolution? Some times, as we shall see, he did. Did he mean organization and regulation? How did he visualize it? The answer is: like Ruskin in terms of the Middle Ages. 'I may say that I am fairly steeped in mediaevalism', he wrote in a letter to a student at Marburg,[78] and even in his late Utopia *News from Nowhere*, the bridge across the Thames still has 'gilded vanes and spirelets'.[79] The Renaissance he disliked, again like Ruskin. And as pigheadedly as Ruskin at his worst he said in 1873: 'Do you suppose that I could see anything in Rome that I cannot see in Whitechapel?'[80] In the end however he went to Italy, and he enjoyed himself though 'as a pig'.[81] He did admire and was moved by Verona,[82] St Mark's, Torcello, Fiesole, S. Miniato, and the Baptistery in Florence.[83] He saw even there, however, as Willis had done forty years before, that Italian Gothic 'is thoroughly neo-classical in feeling'.[84] As for all that followed he wrote: 'Let me confess and be hanged: with the later work of Southern Europe I am quite out of sympathy. In spite of its magnificent power and energy I feel it as an enemy'.[85] People, he said another time, have called the Renaissance 'a new birth, not a death sickness as they should have done'; for it was the Renaissance which 'first . . . imposed slavery on us'.[86] Ancient Roman art and architecture represents the 'hideous greed of the capitalist landowners',[87] the centuries after the Renaissance 'a caput mortuum of academical pedantry'.[88] St Peter's in particular, and also St Paul's in London, he loathed. They were to him 'the very type . . . of pride and tyranny, of all that crushes out the love of art in simple people'.[89]

[75] May Morris, op. cit., II, 315.
[76] Quoted from Henderson, *William Morris*, 319.
[77] Henderson, *Letters*, 228.   [78] Mackail, *Life*, I, 203.
[79] *News from Nowhere*, Coll. Works XVI, 1912, 8.
[80] Ibid., 302.   [81] Henderson, *Letters*, 56.
[82] S. Zeno in Verona he counted among 'the most beautiful buildings which the world has ever seen' (Lemire, *Unpublished Lectures*, 61) and hence regarded the Romanesque style as 'the first stage of actual Gothic art' (ibid., 62–3).
[83] Henderson, *William Morris*, 183.   [84] Henderson, *Letters*, 124.
[85] Ibid., 125.   [86] Lemire, *Unpublished Lectures*, 66, 54.
[87] Ibid., 99.   [88] Ibid., 55.
[89] *Coll. W.*, XXII, 208.

Now in all these passages there is again the step from the visual
to the social: simple people *versus* tyranny. And that is also what
determined his vision of the Middle Ages. In the Middle Ages 'all
handicraftsmen were artists' and 'everything that was made by man's
hand was more or less beautiful'.[90] Today art is 'divided among
great men lesser men and little men', and hence worthwhile art is
'made by conscious effort, the result of the individual striving
towards perfect expression of their thoughts by men very specially
gifted'.[91] whereas 'almost all ordinary wares that are made . . . are
shabbily and pretentiously ugly'.[92] Art today is 'an esoteric mystery',[93]
and the artists 'shut out . . . the everyday squalor that most of men
live in' and 'guard carefully every approach to their palace of art',[94]
and the architects are no better.[95] This is perhaps why Morris was
so aggressively against genius and even against divine inspiration.
'That talk of inspiration is sheer nonsense . . . there is no such thing;
it is a mere matter of craftsmanship . . . If a chap can't compose an
epic poem while he's weaving tapestry, he had better shut up.'[96]
His epics, no one could deny, suffer from this, and as for genius he
says in one place 'It is the happiness of the people that produces the
blossom of genius' and in another 'I would rather have a hundred
thousand happy persons than one genius made up of murder'[97]—
two questionable propositions.

Perhaps the finest statements of his ideal of the Gothic craftsman
are these: 'Consider, I pray you, what these wonderful works are,
and how they were made . . . They were common things . . . no
rarities . . . Did a great artist draw the designs for them, a man of
cultivation, highly paid, daintily fed, carefully housed, wrapped up
in cotton wool . . . By no means . . . They were made by common
fellows . . . in the course of their daily labour . . . And . . . many a
grin of pleasure . . . went to the carrying through' of their jobs.[98]

[90] *Coll. W.,* 9 and 145. Dyce had already said the same: 'In former times the artists were
workmen, and the workmen were artists . . . and it is very desirable to restore this happy connection.' W. Dyce and C. Wilson, *A Letter to Lord Meadowbank and the Committee of the Hon.
Board of Trade for the Encouragement of Arts and Manufactures* (Edinburgh, 1857), 28.

[91] *Coll. W.,* XXII, 55.

[92] Ibid., 9 and 146. The term 'cheap and nasty', which Morris used, was according to Professor Lemire created by Kingsley in 1850 (*Unpublished Lectures,* 84–5). His source is M. Ferrand
Thorp, *Charles Kingsley* (Princeton, 1937).

[93] *Coll. W.,* XXII, 133.   [94] Ibid., 39.   [95] Ibid., 41.

[96] Mackail, *Life,* I, 191–2.   [97] May Morris, op. cit., II, 203.

[98] *Coll. W.,* XXII, 40. It is interesting that Viollet-le-Duc said more or less the same in *Revue
Gén. de l'Arch.,* X, 1852, 377: 'Qui donc au moyen-âge a produit ces grands et admirables monuments? . . . Est-ce une caste privilegiée? . . . Point du tout. L'architecte, le peintre, et le sculpteur
sont les enfants du peuple.'

And: 'Not every day, you may be sure, was a day of slaughter and tumult, though the histories read almost as if it were so; but every day the hammer chinked on the anvil, and the chisel played about the oak-beam.[99]

All of this of course is straight Ruskin. In volume three of *Modern Painters* for example, he had written: 'The title "Dark Ages" given to the mediaeval centuries, is, respecting art, wholly inapplicable. They were, on the contrary, the bright ages; ours are the dark ones',[100] and the Middle Ages 'had their wars and agonies, but also their intense delights'. And if in one of his most famous statements Morris said 'Art is the expression by man of his pleasure in labour',[101] Ruskin had written in 'The Lamp of Life': 'The right question to ask . . . is simply this. Was it done with enjoyment, was the carver happy while he was about it?'[102] But the two other most famous statements of Morris go beyond Ruskin in their application to today: 'I don't want art for a few any more than education for a few or freedom for a few'[103] and 'Honesty and simplicity of life' are the prerequisites of any art which is to be 'by the people and for the people, as a happiness to the maker and the user'.[104]

It is this realism that distinguishes Morris from Ruskin, this sense of the urgency of effective action. In reading and rereading Morris's lectures, one finds nearly always answers to the question: What can be done? Totally negative radicalism is rare, and all the more moving where one finds it:

Years ago [he wrote in August 1874] men's minds were full of art and the dignified shows of life, and they had but little time for justice and peace; and the vengeance on them was not increase of the violence which they did not heed, but destruction of the art they heeded. So perhaps the gods are preparing troubles and terrors for the world (or our small corner of it) again, that it may once again become beautiful and dramatic withal: for I do not believe they will have it dull and ugly for ever.[105]

Even more Spenglerian is this in 1886: 'Maybe man may, after some terrible cataclysm, learn to strive towards a healthy animalism, may grow from a tolerable animal into a savage, from a savage into a barbarian, and so on, and some thousands of years hence he may be

99 *Coll. W.*, XXII, 42.   100 *Libr. Ed.*, V, 321. The date of volume three is 1856.
101 *Coll. W.*, XXII, 42.   102 *Libr. Ed.*, VIII, 218.
103 *Coll. W.*, XXII, 26.   104 Ibid., 46.
105 Henderson, *Letters,* 64.

beginning once more those arts which we have now lost.'[106] But Morris could never for long be so pessimistic. He was too busy, in Morris & Co. and in the socialist movement, ever consistently to contemplate a *tabula rasa*. Even saying 'It is the business of all of us to do our best to the end of preparing for the change, and so softening the shock'[107] is rare.

As a rule his advice is practical, and is directed to both, to the artist and to us as consumers. Architecture, he writes, is the 'master art'[108] and 'one of the most important things man can turn his hand to'.[109] 'Unless you are resolved to have good and rational architecture, it is . . . useless your thinking about art at all',[110] but 'noble as the art is . . . it neither ever has existed nor ever can exist alive and progressive by itself, but must cherish and be cherished by all the crafts whereby men make the things which they intend . . . shall last beyond the passing day.'[111] This, it will be noticed, is not Ruskin's equation of the beauty of architecture with the carving and painting applied to it, but an appeal to all to take the making of everyday things as seriously as architecture. And as seriously as the fine arts—for that is why in 1861 he got painters together to become 'Fine Art Workmen' and design things for us. As regards architecture today, he believed that 'there is only one style of architecture on which it is possible to found a true living art . . . and that style is Gothic'.[112] But he did not accept the common Gothic Revival of e.g. Waterhouse's Manchester Assize Courts ('a dreary pretentious heap'),[113] while on the other hand he did accept with reservations Norman Shaw's so-called Queen Anne—'quaint and pretty'[114] and even the Georgian because of its absence of pretence. After all he chose for himself a Georgian house to live in—Kelmscott House

[106] *Coll. W.*, XXIII, 95–6. Similarly: 'The arts have got to die . . . before they can be born again' (Henderson, *Letters*, 180) and 'Art must go under, where or however it may come up again' (Ibid., 157).

[107] *Coll. W.*, XXIII, 152. Similarly Lemire, *Unpublished Lectures*, 135: Let us 'help . . . that we may get out of the troubled waters speedily and with as little suffering to humanity as may be'.

[108] *Coll. W.*, XXII, 318. On Morris and architecture see my paper in *J.R.I.B.A.*, 3rd series, LXIV, 1957, reprinted in *Studies in Art, Architecture and Design* (London, 1968), II.

[109] *Coll. W.*, XXII, 119.   [110] Ibid., 73.

[111] Ibid., 119. Cf. 'All architectural work must be co-operative' (ibid. 301). Cf. Lemire, *Unpublished Lectures*, 40, on the 'collective genius' of the great Gothic buildings executed by 'a great body of men conscious of their union'.

[112] May Morris, op. cit., I, 266.   [113] Henderson, *Letters*, 303.

[114] *Coll. W.*, XXII, 73. Professor Lemire prints two lectures of 1884 called 'The Gothic Revival'. Here Morris allows the Elizabethan and Jacobean style 'homeliness and love of life' and confesses his love of it 'in spite of all defects'. Even in the Queen Anne style there is 'still some survival of Gothic'. 'The whimsical ghost of a style' he calls it, preceding 'the final degradation' (*Unpublished Lectures*, 67–8, 80).

in Hammersmith to which he moved in 1878. He called it 'without gross vulgarity'—that is all,[115] and there never developed that love in him which tied him to Kelmscott Manor. No more can here be said on his comments on actual architecture around him. An appendix on pp. 315–24 is a complete reprint of his 'The Revival of Architecture' published in the *Fortnightly Review* in 1888. It is reprinted *in toto* to follow after the reprint of Kerr's paper of 1883–4, because the two together give a comprehensive and fairly balanced account of the architectural styles of the years with which they deal, Morris being the idealist, Kerr the realist; Morris inspired, Kerr down-to-earth; Morris fervent, Kerr cynical.

Morris's comments on architecture are naturally less specific than his comments on design. Here the practician speaks, and what he says is still profitable today:

Be careful to eschew all vagueness. It is better to be caught out in going wrong when you have had a definite purpose, than to shuffle and slur so that people can't blame you because they don't know what you are at. Hold fast to distinct form in art. Don't think too much of style, but set yourself to get out of you what you think beautiful, and express it, as cautiously as you please, but, I repeat, quite distinctly and without vagueness. Always think your design out in your head before you begin to get it on paper. Don't begin by slobbering and messing about in the hope that something may come out of it. You must see it before you can draw it . . .[116]

And more generally; 'In these times of plenteous knowledge and meagre performance, if we do not study the ancient work directly and learn to understand it, we shall find ourselves influenced by the feeble work all round us . . . Let us therefore study it wisely . . . all the while determining not to imitate or repeat it.'[117] And his understanding was deep indeed. Of the Turks and the Persians designing rugs he said: 'In their own way they meant to tell us how the flowers grow in the gardens of Damascus, or how the hunt was up on the plains of Kirman.'[118]

So much for advice to the designer. It is confined to two-dimensional design. Webb who could have matched it for the design of buildings and furniture was not a man for formulating convictions. So we must now turn to Morris's advice to the consumer. 'Have nothing in your houses that you do not know to be useful, or believe

115 Henderson, *Letters*, 114.   116 Mackail, *Life*, II, 24.
117 *Coll. W.*, XXII, 15.   118 Ibid., 112.

to be beautiful.'[119] This is handsomely tolerant, and exceptional. In other places Morris is more determined. 'Let us make up our minds which we want, art, or the absence of art, and be prepared if we want art, to give up many things',[120] or, put more briefly: 'Learn to do without.'[121] In fact if you take a wealthy house today, it would be best if 'a bonfire [were] made outside of it of nine tenths of all that it held'.[122] If you find anything decent, it is more likely to be in the kitchen than in the drawing room.[123] For in the kitchen alone 'honesty and simplicity'[124] are likely to get a chance, and they should be your first principles. If he said in another context 'I for my part [would not mind] living in a tent in the Persian desert or a turf hut on the Icelandic hill-side',[125] he may have exaggerated. On the other hand he was no doubt entirely serious when he said that he 'would like a house like a big barn, where one ate in one corner, cooked in another corner, slept in the third corner, and in the fourth received one's friends'.[126] And indeed at the Morrises one ate at a table without a table-cloth, which was then a staggering innovation.[127] It is in line with this that Morris warned against too much furniture[128] and praised bare floors with small rugs as against close-cover carpeting.[129]

And apart from simplicity in all these aspects, what does Morris recommend? Keep our streets 'decent and orderly',[130] don't throw away sandwich papers,[131] don't tolerate smoke as it now poisons the towns,[132] don't start developing a site by cutting down all the trees,[133] and—first and foremost in Morris's mind—don't restore ancient buildings, preserve them.[134] With this we are back with Ruskin, but again where Ruskin preached and demonstrated, Morris acted and acted successfully. The Society for the Protection of

---

[119] *Coll. W.*, XXII, 76.   [120] Ibid., 117.

[121] Ibid., 150.   [122] Ibid., 48.

[123] Ibid., 24.   [124] Ibid., 47.

[125] Ibid., 76.   [126] W. B. Yeats; *Autobiographies* (London, 1926), 180.

[127] Introduction, 'William Morris as I knew him', by G. B. Shaw in May Morris, op. cit., II, p. xx. Shaw's Introduction was reprinted separately by the William Morris Society in 1966. One should also remember Morris's advice to leave 'oak just as it comes from the plane' (*Coll. W.*, XXII, 97).

[128] *Coll. W.*, XXII, 113.   [129] Ibid., 77, 93.

[130] Ibid., 138.   [131] Ibid., 72.

[132] Ibid., 138, also 70. Cf. 'Teaching Manchester how to consume its own smoke' (Ibid., 15).

[133] Ibid., 72–3, also 87, 129.

[134] And Morris added 'of all times and styles' (Mackail, *Life*, I, 354). He signed a letter of protest against the intended demolition of St Mary-le-Strand, together with Bentley, Bodley, Brooks, Street, Norman Shaw, Webb, and others. Reprinted in *The Century Guild Hobby Horse*, IV, July 1889. I owe this reference to Mrs. Lisa Tickner.

Ancient Buildings was founded by him in 1877, and it is still going strong, its principles having been accepted by everyone. On Oxford incidentally Morris was especially severe. Instead of 'that queer absurdity the Oxford Chair of Poetry' and 'those disasters the Slade Professorships of Art',[135] should not a chair of medieval archaeology be established before the town is totally ruined 'by the fury of the thriving shop and the progressive college'?[136] The function of the chair should be 'teaching the dons the value of the buildings of which they ought to be the guardians. In the thirty years in which I have known Oxford more damage has been done to art . . . by Oxford "culture" than centuries of professors could repair.' It all makes 'education stink', is his verdict,[137] and education was then as it is now the only safe remedy. The twentieth century, Morris prophesied in 1880, will be 'the century of education'.[138]

There is indeed much in Morris that is prophetic. But his is a Janus head. He looked back as intensely as forward. The archaic language for instance of his rhymes and his prose romances is entirely Victorian historicism and much harder to come to terms with than the architects' historicism. 'Unholpen', 'he spake', 'I hight', 'no city that I wot of'—it tires the reader.[139] Morris's designs may be evocative of the Middle Ages, but they are always fresh and never retrospective. His insistence on the other hand on the crafts only and his hatred of the machine are of the nineteenth, not the twentieth century.

But Morris was monumentally inconsistent. 'As a condition of life', he said, 'production by machinery is altogether an evil',[140] but 'it is not this or that tangible steel and brass machine which we want to get rid of, but the great intangible machine of commercial tyranny'.[141] Moreover he was ready to say not only that machines should be allowed 'for performing such labour as is revolting and destructive of self-respect',[142] but just once he even said that we had 'not near enough' machines and foretold that in the end 'pretty nearly everything that is necessary to men will be made by machines'.[143]

[135] Henderson, *Letters*, 261.   [136] *Coll. W.*, XXIII, 169.
[137] Henderson, *Letters*, 262.   [138] *Coll. W.*, XXII, 63.
[139] A. H. R. Ball's *Selections from the Prose Works of William Morris* (Cambridge, 1931) in fact has a glossary.
[140] *Coll. W.*, XXII, 335–6.   [141] Ibid., 352.
[142] *Coll. W.*, XXIII, 160. Cf., ibid., 193, also an unpublished lecture (B.M. Add. 45330) quoted by E. P. Thompson, *William Morris, Romantic to Revolutionary*, 758 n., and May Morris, op. cit. II, 134.
[143] *Coll. W.*, XXII, 166.

When that time has come everybody will have plenty of leisure. But 'what then shall we do with the leisure?'[144] We know the sad answer: a more and more vicarious life, and even that we find in Morris: 'Vicarious life is the watchword of our civilisation.'[145] So here is the Morris of the twentieth century speaking again.

Other inconsistencies are of a much more personal nature. Morris called himself—rightly—'an ornamentalist', yet he recommended to architects to be 'chary of ornament'.[146] He was a fervent socialist, but he was also a manufacturer and retailer. It worried him, and his answer was: Was it not more reasonable to keep his income and use it to foster social change? If he could reduce his income to £4 a week, that would only mean 5s. a week more for every workman.[147] At his workshops at Merton, south of London, he liked to pay by piece-work and offer an allotment to every piece-worker. There was also some profit-sharing, and George Campfield, the foreman of the glass painters called the conditions 'as near Paradise as anything well could be'.[148]

Very well—but however happy the workmen at Merton may have been, it is a fact that many of the designs of the firm were executed by manufacturers on machines and in the usual factory surroundings. This applies to wallpapers printed at Islington, silks woven at Macclesfield, chintzes printed at Leek, and carpets made at Heckmondwike and Wilton.[149]

Another and perhaps the most curious inconsistency is that

[144] *Coll. W.*, XXII, 33.

[145] Ibid., 338.

[146] He quoted this advice from William Richmond—see Lemire, *Unpublished Lectures*, 83.

[147] Which, it must be said, was quite something at the time. Henderson, *Letters*, 196-7. In a lecture of 1884 (Lemire, op. cit., 74) Morris spoke of the "desperate efforts' to revive the 'accessory arts' and of the fact that people—himself of course—were 'making money out of it'.

[148] Quoted from Henderson, *Letters*, xxiii.

[149] See Thompson, *The Work of William Morris*, 99 ff. The late Peter Floud was the first to draw attention to this inconsistency. Mr. Hugh McKenna on 13 Nov. 1947 told me that Anderson and Lawson of Glasgow made chenille body carpeting for Morris *c.* 1892, and Mr. John H. Lemon of Brinton's at Kidderminster on 5 Nov. 1947 that they made for Morris both Axminster and Wilton carpeting. Morris gave Brinton's in such cases the designs ready on squared paper. Frederick J. Mayers, a carpet designer, some time for Templeton's, some time free-lance, wrote to me on 11 Nov. 1947 as follows: 'I left Kidderminster in 1888 when I went to live in Paris . . . About 1884-7 I was working with Messrs. Brinton's Ltd. and during that time I made the working designs for 3 or 4 carpets, from Mr. Morris's sketches, which the firm was manufacturing for him.' Mr. Mayers suggested that Naylor's of Kidderminster and John Barton & Sons also worked for Morris. The Kidderminster carpets mentioned in the text were made at Heckmondwike, the Wilton carpets by the Wilton Royal Works, the silks by J. O. Nicholson of Macclesfield.

Morris who apart from being a manufacturer was without any doubt a designer had the lowest opinion of designers:

A highly gifted and educated man shall, like Mr. Pecksniff, squint at a sheet of paper, and . . . the results of that squint set a vast number of well-fed, contented operatives (they are ashamed to call them workmen) turning crank handles for ten hours a day . . . Well, from this system are to come threefold blessings—food and clothing, poorish lodgings and a little leisure to the operatives, enormous riches to the capitalists that rent them, together with moderate riches to the squinter on the paper; and lastly, decidedly lastly, abundance of cheap art for the operatives or crank-turners to buy.[150]

So much for 'by the people . . . as a happiness to the maker'.

Now concerning 'for the people'. What Morris designed was never cheap. He knew the reason: 'All art costs time, trouble and thought . . . and money is only a counter to represent these things'.[151] While he was working for Rounton Grange, Webb's mansion for Sir Lowthian Bell, he was asked what he was doing, and he answered looking 'like a mad animal': 'I spend my life in ministering to the swinish luxury of the rich'.[152] Moreover he knew that the many not only found his work inaccessible but also that they did not want it: 'I must admit that the people in general are not touched at all by any interest for decorative art'; only 'a few of the upper and middle classes' are.[153]

His last test was the Kelmscott Press, started in 1890. People go on pointing to the *Chaucer* of which the paper edition sold at twenty guineas, and of which all 425 copies printed were sold. But the majority of the other titles sold at two guineas on paper (some at thirty shillings and some at three and five guineas).[154] Even so, that

---

[150] *Coll. W.*, XXII, 114–15.

[151] Ibid., 75. Paul Bourget, when travelling in America, was nearer the mark, when he wrote of the new Chicago office buildings which so spectacularly foretell the twentieth century that they represent 'a new kind of art, an art of democracy, made by the crowd and for the crowd' (*Outre Mer* (Paris, 1895), 162; English translation by W. H. Jordy and R. Coe (Cambridge, Mass., 1961), 380). The French is 'par le foule et pour le foule'.

[152] W. R. Lethaby: *Philip Webb and his Work* (London, 1935), 94. Dr. Priscilla Metcalf drew my attention to Mrs. Russell Barrington *The Works and Life of Walter Bagehot* (London, 1915), X, 442–3. Bagehot got Morris to decorate his house in Queen's Gate Place, and he commented on 'Morris's autocratic attitude towards all questions of taste', on his views 'as to the morality or immorality of certain colours and designs', and on the slowness of finally completing an order for a blue damask silk which Morris was 'composing'. He was, Bagehot said, altogether 'composing the drawing room, as he would an ode'.

[153] Address given at Manchester in 1882, see *Mr. William Morris on Art Matters* reprinted from the *Manchester Guardian* by the William Morris Society, 1961, 5.

[154] The prices are noted in Mr. Briggs's *The Typographical Adventure*, 23.

clearly ruled out 'the people'. Was there no remedy? Obviously, price defeated Morris's object which was to make everyday things sound, sensible, and beautiful so that everyone could enjoy and use them.

The price of his products just as much as his faith in craft separates Morris from the twentieth century. But it seems as if in his last years he had found the way out—not, it may be said, without adding yet another inconsistency to his many. What he said to the Bibliographical Society on 19 June 1893[155] is this:

If you want to publish a handsome edition of a book as well as a cheap one do so; but let them be two books, and if you (or the public) cannot afford this, spend your ingenuity and your money in making the cheap book as sightly as you can ... Any book in which the page is properly set on the paper, is tolerable to look at, however poor the type may be—always as long as there is no 'ornament' to spoil the whole thing.

So here is a final plea for 'books whose sole ornament is the necessary and essential beauty which arises out of the fitness of a piece of craftsmanship for the use for which it is made'.[156]

Fitness for use—that was to be the slogan of the first half of the twentieth century. 'Form follows function' said Sullivan, 'the divine law of fitness', said Voysey,[157] and so we are on the way to the *Deutscher Werkbund* and to Gropius and the Bauhaus. The subtitle of a book which I wrote over thirty years ago on the pioneers of the twentieth-century style in architecture and design was 'From William Morris to Walter Gropius',[158] and so I may be excused if I do not continue this summary of nineteenth-century architectural writing to the year 1900. There is a good reason, I think, why Morris should remain the end, although, as I have shown in that other book, he is a beginning too.

In the last twenty years of the century two new movements appeared, both anti-historicist and in this closer to the twentieth than the nineteenth century: Art Nouveau and the School of

---

[155] May Morris, op. cit., I, 310–18.

[156] The readiness for less ornament appears in the field of interior decoration even earlier. It is a parallel to Webb's move from Red House to Smeaton Manor of 1877 which can only be called a personal variation on the theme of the plain William and Mary house. In *Making the Best of it* (*Coll. W.*, XXII, 30), i.e. in 1879 or a little before, Morris recommended whitewash for the external walls and white paint for the woodwork. Webb agreed.

[157] Quoted from J. Brandon-Jones, 'C. F. A. Voysey', *Architectural Association Journal*, 1957, 248.

[158] *Pioneers of the Modern Movement* (London, 1936), later editions *Pioneers of Modern Design* (New York, 1949 ff., also as a Penguin paperback).

Chicago. Art Nouveau started with Mackmurdo in 1883 and assumed sensational popularity with Horta and van de Velde in the nineties. It was totally novel in its forms, though certain passages in Morris's chintzes and wallpapers acted (against his will) as a stimulus,[159] but it was still highly personal and sophisticated, i.e. not 'for the people'. The Chicago office buildings were for the people, though Morris would probably have hated them.[160] And they were independent of the past in their forms too. The synthesis of the sensitivity of Art Nouveau with the functionalism of Chicago came in the first decade of the new century with van de Velde and Peter Behrens, who both had begun as painters and turned to design and architecture under the immediate impact of Morris's published lectures.

No wonder; for the impact of these lectures is irresistible even today and one intention I have had in compiling these twenty-five chapters is to induce their readers to become readers of Horace Walpole, of Whewell and Willis, of Pugin, of Ruskin, of Viollet-le-Duc, of Semper, and of Morris, and perhaps even of the others as well.

---

[159] Morris found Beardsley's *Morte d'Arthur* 'quite below contempt'. Quoted from Henderson *William Morris*, 378.

[160] He should not; for it was he who had written that the change he pleaded for would 'make life . . . rougher for the refined, and, it may be, duller for the gifted—for a while' (*Coll. W.*, XXII, 117). That he did hate the Forth Bridge which Gilbert Scott for instance would not have hated, is surprising. To mid-twentieth-century man it is so powerful an aesthetic thrill, yet Morris called it 'the supremest specimen of all ugliness'. (Quoted from Thomas McKay, *Life of Sir John Fowler* (London, 1900), 313–4), but then all modern engineering was to him 'horrible and restless' (Henderson, 210.)

APPENDIX I

English Architecture Thirty Years Hence[1]

By ROBERT KERR

THE question I am requested to submit is one that has a certain particular and practical importance just now:—What is the line upon which the profession of architects is moving in England? In other words, what is likely to be the position of English architects, say, thirty years hence? I am expected to confine your attention to the artistic aspect of the question, but to regard it in a practical light.

Now we pretty well understand in these scientific days that all continuous enterprises of human industry or skill, or of social or intellectual activity, when looked at in any degree under the surface of affairs, are found to be subject to the government of certain laws of progression; so that it is the critical study of the past that becomes the only means of forecasting the future. In the arts more particularly is the fact forced upon the notice of thoughtful observers that there has been a continuous current of development gliding through all the ages in one grand inevitable course: now in the sunshine, now in the shade; here swift and strong, there feeble and sluggish. But always the same: the same springs, the same issue; great men and great successes,—and great failures with them,—being but the greater bubbles on the surface of events, and even the humblest of workers adding every one his indispensable contribution to the tide.

Amongst the arts of which I venture to speak in this high tone, I may at once say that I regard architecture as one of the very greatest,—perhaps, indeed, beyond dispute, the most subtle and most glorious of all. It is nothing to me, standing before an assembly like this, if I should be told to moderate my language, and to ask you to veil your faces before the painter or the poet. I do nothing of the kind. I ask you, rather, to look back along an expanse of magnificent building, whose length is not to be measured by furlongs or feet, or its area by acres, but its unbroken continuity by the very ages of history, throughout at least 5,000 years, and in whose earliest and crudest works, such is the inherent majesty of the art, Queen of the Arts, the noblest of mankind aimed at never less than the noblest homage to the noblest conceptions of the Divine.

[1] Read on Friday, 9 May 1884, at the sixth and final Meeting of the General Conference of Architects held in London from 5 to 9 May. It was published in *Trans. R.I.B.A.*, XXXIV, 1883–4.

Along this splendid line of artistic manifestation we see exemplified, more clearly than in almost anything else that philosophy can quote, the operation of the process now known by the name of evolution. The simplicity of it is, indeed, perfect. Given the desire to build in beauty,—nothing more,—and the whole scheme of architectural history throughout the past is understood; and the persistent sequence of the self-same scheme throughout the future too. Out of the desire there comes at once a continual endeavour after novelty, the diversity which supplies the material for selection. That which is worthy is reproduced, that which is not is not, and hence arise schools and styles, in the most direct and palpable form, by the survival of the fittest. Thus it is that the study, the very studentship, of this art becomes so essentially bound up in the past; for no training worthy of the name can stop short of a review of the whole historical scheme of development. And thus it is again that the progress of change in this art appears to be so slow, the limits of even the most eager originality so narrow, and the disappointment of the too ambitious so complete.

Therefore, if we would try to understand our own position just now as representatives for the moment of this great art in England, and to foresee the attitude of our order in the next generation, the easiest mode of procedure,—perhaps the only one,—is to begin a generation back, and so work forward to the present day, in the hope that our research may acquire momentum enough to carry us still forward a little way into the future.

About fifty years ago, then, there happened certain occurrences which make the period a great landmark in English architectural history. In 1834 there was founded our professional guild, now so well known as the Institute of British Architects. In 1834 also the old Houses of Parliament at Westminster were burned down. The foundation of the Institute, and its incorporation by royal charter shortly after, indicated the arrival of the profession of architects in England at a significant stage of development and of organization. The destruction of the important edifice which had accommodated the business of the Legislature afforded an opportunity to that profession to enter upon a new career. The accession of the young Queen Victoria in 1837, involving the inauguration of a new national spirit, may be regarded as one more, and perhaps the chief, in this group of events; and if we further include the advent, within a short time afterwards, of Her Majesty's most admirable Consort, as an ally to the great cause of culture,—and more especially as regards our present purpose, with reference to the splendid new Palace of Parliament, by that time waiting for just such help as his,—we see, clustered within the compass of half a dozen years, a concurrence of circumstances by which there is constituted with remarkable precision just such a point of departure as we desire.

Let me remind you of the somewhat analogous combination of events under which English architecture started on a new line of development in the latter half of the seventeenth century: the overthrow of the gloomy Puritan ascendancy, the establishment of a new and brilliant royalty, then the disaster of a great fire—we will call it the burning of the Cathedral of London—and the rise of a great architect. So also at the time now before us we have, in the death of William IV, and the accession of the youthful Victoria, the old worn-out Georgian philistinism going down at last, rude and dogged as ever, and another social system arising, entirely new and bright, the hope of the world; and therewith another great fire, and the rise of another great architect. I am accustomed to speak of Wren and Barry as the two great architects of modern England, in whose especial eminence there is as yet no third great architect quite entitled to claim a share. With both of them alike, everything their hand touched seemed to turn to a certain personal graciousness of form not easily described or accounted for; neither of them, perhaps, attaining to the ideal which we are beginning to conceive of the perfect master of our wonderful art, with whom mechanical science and aesthetic grace advance hand in hand from the sketch to the consummation; each of them, indeed, in his degree very notably a designer of superficiation, if the truth must be told, but both accomplishing that superficiation with an infinite success of elegance altogether his own artistic quality. From the Great Fire of London, that is to say, and the career of Sir Christopher Wren to the burning of the old Parliament House, and the career of Sir Charles Barry, there extends a period of English architectural history which represents the whole development of popular Neo-Classicism, from its rise to its fall; from St. Paul's Cathedral and Greenwich Hospital to St. Pancras Church, the National Gallery, the British Museum, the Club-houses, and the plaster façades of the Regent's Park; when it was time at last that some change should come; and, if only as an enigma for your consideration, I think I see at the very beginning of this manifestation and at the very end the two most conspicuous masters of the situation, with no equal between. Perhaps I may go on to remark, as a coincidence, that from Barry's day to our own there extends the course of another remarkable architectural development, with its most powerful and characteristic exponents again at the beginning and at the end, Pugin and Street. I commend these circumstances to the curious: at the moment when Barry in his Club-houses offered us a new version of Wren's Classic, we threw it over and reverted to Gothic; and at the moment when Street in his Law Courts has brought Pugin's Gothic to supremacy, we now cast that aside and return to Classic. Such is the play of action and reaction: art is a long story, but its chapters are short.

At the commencement, then, of the Victorian age in which it is our privilege to live, this was the condition of architectural art in London.

Sir John Soane, in old age and retirement, was the efficient representative of the best commonplace Greek taste. Cockerell, his successor in the professorship of the Academy, was the much more brilliant and accomplished exponent of the higher theoretic level of the same school. Smirke and Hardwick, on the lower ground of mere successful business, were of still the same order of designers. Wilkins's National Gallery and University College had been produced as exemplars of what Anglo-Greek ought to be, and had failed to secure the popularity expected. Barry,—whose age was under forty when he stood on Westminster Bridge staring at the conflagration of the Parliament House, and dreaming inexpressible dreams,—had designed his two club-houses in Pall Mall in a novel mode, and had received the applause which had been denied to Wilkins. I need only add that at the newly-established Institute, Tite, as a representative of the rude energy of a prosperous commercial practitioner and an adherent of the convenient abstract eclecticism of the thorough man of business, divided the leadership with Donaldson, most indefatigable writer and speaker, to whose entranced intelligence the study of architecture was a worship, and its miraculous origin in far antiquity a faith that never could be shaken. The extreme refinement of the state of opinion which I have thus indicated was endowed with shape and purpose by the Society of Dilettanti, under whose authority the latest and most characteristic enterprize of a long series was undertaken a few years afterwards by Mr. Penrose, in his elaborate admeasurements of the optical corrections of the Parthenon, the supreme and final outcome of a system of criticism which the world can never now be at the trouble to revive.

The inevitable operation of the natural law of reaction and revolt had meanwhile been producing in many minds a feeling of antagonism to this attenuated and traditional Classic. Romanticism, in short, of the more robust order had begun to despise criticism so effeminate and so frigid. Now, English romanticism takes two forms: ancestor-worship and ecclesiasticism; and in both of these forms a change was coming over architecture. The Oxford movement, or High Church movement, or Mediaeval revival,—call it which you will,—was acquiring force in the Church; whilst, as regards the State, no sooner was it understood that a new palace of the Legislature was to be built on a grand scale, and that Sir Robert Smirke, as one of the standing architects of the Government, had been commissioned to prepare the design for it, than members of Parliament began promptly to agitate for a patriotic adoption of what was then designated the Baronial style,—'Gothic' or 'Elizabethan' was the phrase eventually accepted,—and for the transference of the architect's retainer from the hands of the prosaic Smirke to those of some unknown romanticist who should be selected by means of a public competition. Barry won the prize; and at the present moment, when an enthusiastic belief in the virtues of competition has been revived, in the hope that 'fair-play' will cure all evils (and fair-play seems as coy as ever in answering to the call), it is interesting to remember that the fairness of the selection of Barry's design was never challenged by any criticism more severe than this,—that the favour of influential friends at court had not been refused, and that the ablest specialist assistance had been wisely secured.

The adoption of this design for the new Houses of Parliament consummated the Gothic revival. The baronial idea instantly took the fancy of the public; it formulated an innovation, allayed a disquietude, and satisfied the demands of a genuine reaction. Churches, it was true, had been built for some time in various kinds of pointed arcuation; Castles also had been built for patriotic squires, even by Wilkins himself, with Gothic arches of no particular form, and some of them with Gothic cannon,—cannon of wood frowning ornamentally from embrasures of stucco; Cathedrals also had been restored by the help of cast-iron and compo; and London dining-rooms had been ingeniously adorned with tracery cut out of thin deal, and grained and varnished; but now all this was to be improved upon. Pugin fulminated his anathemas against everything that was spurious, everything that was pagan, everything that was modern; even the dainty engravings of Britton and Le Keux's cathedrals were supplanted by the masculine lithographs of a new school of travelling sketchers; Ruskin arose, as the prophet of a mysterious gospel unknown to the multitude; and England found itself at the commencement of an incomprehensible architectural civil war.

The contending parties gradually organized their forces. One called itself the Gothic party; the other the Classic party. There was a third, stronger than either in all but enthusiasm, which called itself the Eclectic party. At first, indeed, the Gothicists, like all originators of revolution, had to content themselves with the pleasures of hope, and to console themselves with the exercise of scorn. England is the home of compromise, and it was at length agreed that Gothic should be recognized as the proper mode for churches, Elizabethan for country houses, and Italian Classic for municipal buildings. It was agreed also that every individual practitioner should be permitted to do his best in all three styles, or, indeed, in any other he pleased, and to claim the respect of the world for so doing. Cockerell, in his Royal Academy lectures, pleaded earnestly for what he called catholicity, or universal forbearance. Donaldson, at the Institute, consented to accept the supernatural, to a reasonable extent, in Gothic as well as Greek; Tite had already actually taken a lead in Gothic design by his Scotch church in Regent Square; but, strange to say, Barry, the accepted prince of the practical revival, was at heart its enemy. I believe it is quite understood that, if the Government could have been persuaded by him, the Palace of Westminster would have been built after all in the stately style of the Italian

Renaissance. I ought not to omit to mention that at this time the architectural press, as we now understand the term, may be said to have been founded. I allude, of course, to the establishment of the first of our weekly newspapers. Previously, the *Civil Engineer and Architect's Journal*, a feeble monthly magazine, was the only organ of the profession, and necessarily one of very imperfect influence. The progress of architectural and engineering journalism separately, since that day, I need only say, has been most satisfactory; and I cannot help alluding especially to the remarkable development of the weekly illustrations of English architectural art, which cannot fail to be of immense artistic value throughout the world.

The year 1848 soon arrived. I need only remind you that it was a year of European revolution, out of which France, throwing off once more the embarrassments of tradition, entered upon a new and strange national career. For two hundred years Paris had been the focus of artistic culture, but of late the vivacity of the people had scarcely been seconded by the example of the Court. The Government now passed into the hands of a peculiar class of adventurous men of affairs, determined to purchase unlimited power for themselves at the price of unlimited luxury for the people. The arts do not inquire too closely into the character of their patrons; and whatever others may have to say of Napoleon III, architects must always hold his memory in honour for the artistic brilliancy (to say nothing of political wisdom) of the architectural operations which he so successfully conducted.

English architecture had not hitherto sought for inspiration in Paris. Neither, indeed, does it now, and I venture to think it never will; for, vastly as I admire all French art, I can never divest my mind of the feeling that I am admiring something whose charms are feminine. I say, therefore, that England, the very home of rough-and-ready muscularity, will probably never follow the precise formulas of French taste. But it was impossible that the new start which the French were making in social display in 1849 should fail to exert an influence upon English art in one way or another. The inauguration of the great system of international exhibitions brought this influence into play; and the years 1851 and 1855, taken together, produced a crisis in English architectural history which is now seen to have been almost more notable for its results than any other incident of the kind in modern times.

When the Exhibition of 1851 was opened, our professional world stood thus. The Prince Consort, now at the enterprising age of thirty-two, had become an important agent in the progress of general culture in his adopted country. It was soon understood that he had a considerable respect for architectural work, but that he had not the same regard for English architects. Perhaps this was partly due to the fact that the criticism of artistic building was in the confusion I have lately described, and that it occupied indeed what must be called low ground, a sort of unscientific squabbling ground to which a high-class German intellect might scarcely see its way to descend. Amongst the public duties which had come to be imposed upon him, one of the most prominent was the administration of the artistic completion of the new Houses of Parliament; and we may suppose him to have thus become deeply impressed with a sense of the tradesmanlike condition (if the phrase may be excused) in which he found popular English architecture and its auxiliary arts as a whole; a quality which is now candidly recognized as having been only too forcibly manifested in those days. I do not wish to attach to Prince Albert the character of a personal leader,—it would be false criticism to do so; but I think he was a particularly good representative of an impending change in the public intelligence of England; and it is no doubt the fact that the very peculiar unpopularity of the profession of architects, which, during the last fifteen or twenty years especially, has been so frequently exemplified to our cost, took its rise in the early days of the Prince's intervention in architectural affairs. The standard-bearers of the day, let us remember, were Barry and Pugin, Ruskin and Fergusson, Scott,—or rather Scott & Moffat,—and Donaldson and Tite at the Institute. Barry's work at the Houses of Parliament was advancing tediously and mysteriously, and a sort of philistine grumble against it was constantly being heard in the House of Commons, as if the architect and the legislature were not pulling together. Then Pugin, as the exponent proper of the Gothic Revival, although acting as Barry's very loyal ally in the great work itself privately, was, in his public capacity, simply a frantic enthusiast, whose fanaticism for the Mediaeval, in season and out of season, that and nothing else, made confusion worse confounded. Of Ruskin, again, one can only say,—and all the more confidently now that he has in age turned against himself in youth,—that the specious, reckless, often meaningless rhetoric of his charming writings stirred up a vague and spurious sentimentalism, which, without benefiting architecture, was doing infinite damage to the architect. Fergusson, next in order, although as dogmatic as Ruskin, was as prosaic and cool as Ruskin was poetic and impassioned, and as well disposed to the working architect as Ruskin was scornfully inimical. But he cannot be said to have helped the profession, by his very considerable services to the art, so much as he unconsciously disparaged in the eyes of the public an order of artists who required an amateur to teach them. I have next mentioned Scott & Moffat. For the moment I do not see the great ecclesiastical designer of a later date, but only the firm of reckless public competitioners, in whose hands the abuse of a practice, always signally open to abuse, had already attained dimensions which could not fail to bring down sooner or later a dignified aesthetic profession to the level of a grasping trade. Much as I revere the memory of Sir Gilbert Scott, I feel that I should be false to my duty at the present moment if I were to hesitate to blame him, and his too clever partner of forty years ago, for their introduction of a mode of struggling for work at any price, which I believe to have done an amount of injury to English architects only less than that which, I am sorry to say, I think it has yet to do. I have spoken lastly of Donaldson and Tite at the Institute. Of Professor Donaldson, I need only say that so far as a high-minded and fearless maintenance of the lofty character of our splendid art and its literature, and of the honourable historical position of our artists, antiquarians, and critics could defend us against assault, whether vulgar or refined, he never for an instant swerved from his duty as leader of the guild; and of Sir William Tite, although a man of very different qualities, I am glad to say, from personal knowledge, very much the same. By this time, I may add, Professor Cockerell, who never was wanting in courage to champion the cause of his order, could scarcely be called upon to be more than a looker-on.

I must now speak of that remarkable man, Henry Cole, whom I regard as having taken an exceedingly earnest and effective lead in the change that was coming over English art architectural. I use this term—*art architectural* —in order to suggest to you an important practical distinction between the academical *architecture* of the period preceding 1851, and the non-academical *architectural art* in general which then began to take its place,— a whole galaxy of constructive, formative, decorative, and industrial arts being now in question, amongst which the pure building-art of old traditions was but the central star.

Cole had for the work of his life the advancement of what we have been accustomed to call the minor arts; and there can be no doubt that he began upon the basis of a personal dislike to the professional practice of architecture, which he maintained to the end and bequeathed to his successors. Rightly or wrongly, he seems to have arrived at the conclusion that the architect was a fossil, whose functions in the streets of ancient Rome, or in the cloisters of Mediaeval abbeys, or in the market-places of modern but not too modern Italy, had no doubt been a useful function, judging by the remains of his performances, but who in modern London was a doer of nothing to speak of, or of nothing but what could be done quite as well without him. As a matter of business, we know this to be mere folly; there is perhaps nothing in the work of this world which the untrained intelligence can never hope to accomplish, if the proper design of a high-class building be not such a thing; and the continual endeavour of uninformed persons to do their own architecture, in spite of a thousand failures, is only evidence, indeed, of the fascination of the unattainable. Cole, however, seems never to have permitted himself, as so many do, to be an amateur architect, or even to have encouraged anyone else to be so; what he under-rated was, not art, nor even business, but men. His whole soul was wrapped up in detail, and he found the architects, as he thought, to be devoid of the knowledge of such detail, and content to trade upon a little experience merely in the drudgery of supervising building-contractors. When he fell in with an architect like Digby Wyatt, who knew all that he himself knew, or could wish to know, of the arts of detail, and who knew also that which he acknowledged to be beyond his own reach, the whole volume of the historical art of splendid building, he could honour him, and did honour him as far as was convenient; but if the mere art of building, without the arts of detail, were alone in question, his opinion was that the Royal Engineers could manage that quite as well as anyone need desire; and, indeed, all the better, because of one thing, that they were soldiers under discipline, and not like a good many architects he could name who were not under discipline, and whose successors, if we must tell the truth, are not under discipline yet.

The fact that the Prince Consort had built Osborne in 1848 without employing an architect (although the builder, of course, employed one) may have been encouraging to Mr. Cole when they came to compare notes; but the view of the matter which I prefer to take, as I have already suggested, is that both of these extremely intelligent and earnest men were in fact excercising shrewd foresight, and not merely cherishing a personal crotchet. At any rate, the immediate result of the Great Exhibition of 1851 was to open the eyes of Englishmen to the fact that the subtle spirit of artistic design ought to run through a great many branches of industrial production, which they had been accustomed to regard as scarcely worth the trouble. That many of these were more or less related to building, or to the decoration or occupation of buildings, was plainly manifest; and the triumph of Cole was that he had laid a foundation for the popularity of the whole world of decorative arts, and, amongst the rest, the minor arts architectural. The Exposition held in Paris in 1855 carried still further the same idea; and some English architects began to perceive that their studies must go more and more into the detail of general art. Architecture was therefore now on the move in a new direction.

Under the remarkably clever personal administration of Cole, the practical outcome of the exhibitions speedily acquired form and substance in the institution of National Schools of Design, and eventually of the South Kensington Museum. The establishment of the Crystal Palace also at Sydenham, for an artistic popular resort, ought to be coupled with these undertakings, as being a measure carried out with the same end in view As regards architects, it was no doubt a remarkable, and perhaps unfortunate, circumstance that a duke's gardener had to come in to design the Exhibition edifice, as if to show that it was not in artistic building alone that architects failed to keep pace with the times, but in scientific still more.

We are not bound, however, to accept this view of the incident, and certainly Paxton never made his mark in either art or science.

'South Kensington', as it has long been popularly designated, in the character of a somewhat self-assertive bureau of the Government, may, I think, be described as the head-quarters of art multifarious, no longer academical, but essentially non-academical. By academical art I mean to indicate, in the restricted sense, the old conventional circle of the arts' as accepted by the Renaissance academies, comprising painting, sculpture, architecture, and no more, and all on the high level only of dignified tradition. When, for example, no longer ago than 1854, we find Mr. Tite's contribution to the Royal Academy Exhibition to have been 'A Composition of the Works of Inigo Jones', and Professor Donaldson's 'An Architect's Dream, or Sketch of a Design for Opening the Crypt of St Paul's' (after the manner of the Invalides at Paris), we can acknowledge now that academicalism had reigned quite long enough. We can also acknowledge now, when we have in a great measure enfranchised the practice of the art from such inconvenient formalism, so that our Classic and our Gothic alike are often almost too free in treatment, and too demonstratively defiant of the categorical criticism of the schools, that the practical function of the architect has acquired, at the same time, extended limits. He can no longer rest content with having provided a building that is merely conveniently planned, properly constructed, and well proportioned, which other hands shall then clothe with decorative work, and furnish with ornamental accessories; there is finishing work everywhere, minor art work, which is part and parcel of his scheme, and which he must himself design and control; there is characteristic carving, for instance, and he must direct the carver; painting, still more; there may be even set pictures and statuary sometimes; there is metal-work, glass-work, plaster-work or some equivalent, even paper-hanging or some equivalent, and so on; there is floor-work, wall-work, cabinet-work, furniture-work; sometimes upholstery, carpets, tapestry; a multitude of miscellaneous fixtures and fittings, and even unfixed ornaments; all of these may more or less put in a claim to be 'endowed with artistic merit' by the one designer, lest anything unexpectedly awry should mar the effect of the whole design. And this great change in the scope of the architect's work has come about, I think, in response to a corresponding change in public feeling, which must be associated with the operation of South Kensington policy. Indeed, I am almost inclined to say that the *bric-à-brac* style, for such it is, of what we call Queen Anne architecture, is properly the South Kensington Museum style. Cole personally, the paramount genius of South Kensington, was originally, as Felix Summerley, content to devote himself for ever to *bric-à-brac*. There are cynical critics who will speak of the whole Museum as *bric-à-brac* still. And I, for one, have no objection to this, if I may take leave to identify with the name of *bric-à-brac* the idea of art multifarious and non-academical, that which underlies the entire range of the minor arts, unformulated often and unconventional, but constituting an inexhaustible source of everyday enjoyment which Academies, when inflated with the pride of empty traditions, are disposed to ignore rather than attempt to work.

But the Gothic revival, no doubt, is entitled to claim a considerable share in this expansion of the architect's work,—his work, let me say, as chief of all the workmen. Pugin, for instance, was especially an apostle of the minor arts. The Neo-Greek dilettantism that preceded his day, and the Georgian philistinism together, may be said to have shut the door upon them. It was under the successors of Pugin,—his direct successors in Gothic enthusiasm, —that they acquired the form and force they now possess in architectural business. South Kensington could never, perhaps, have converted the narrow connoisseurship of *bric-à-brac* into an expansive public interest in every possible kind of decorative and ornamental designership, but for the fanaticism, as it is called correctly enough, of Pugin and his school. And yet Coleism and Puginism were but unconscious allies, and are no better still. To this day South Kensington recognises little beyond Italian Renaissance, whereas even our Queen Anneists,—themselves stanch Mediaevalists quite recently,—would rather have turned to anything else they could find. At any rate, the point I desire to make is this,—that the epoch of the first great international exhibitions is to be identified in the history of English architecture with the rise of the minor arts, which have thus been progressing amongst us for about thirty years.

The Gothic revival must now be described for its own sake. In the language of our popular Protestantism, this great movement was simply a return to the artistic style of the Roman Catholic or Mediaevalist Church, of which it has been truly said that it is 'the Church of Poetry and Art.' At the date of the great exhibitions, Gothicism had got so far as to have acquired not only the undisputed possession of the whole ecclesiastical field in English architectural practice, but the disposition to claim whatever secular work was worth having. The theory that Italian art was only suited to Italian soil, that England required a style that was English, and that the only English style was the Gothic, was boldly advocated; and in 1857, when the Government instituted a public competition for the intended War and Foreign Offices at Whitehall, the competitors were found to be so equally divided in taste between Classicism and Gothicism that the adjudicators felt obliged to place the representatives of the two schools in alternate order for the prizes, to the number, I think, of fourteen in all, as an official acknowledgment of the absolutely equal value of secular Gothic and Classic in public esteem. We all know how in the end Scott's Gothic design was demonstratively selected for execution just before Lord Derby's Administration quitted office, and the style, almost still more demonstratively changed to Classic when Lord Palmerston came in. Such was the Battle of the Styles.

The chief merit, perhaps, to which the Gothic party laid claim was the resuscitation of the Mediaeval principle of truthful articulation, or the correct correspondence of the motive of superficial design with the motive of underlying construction. The stlyes of the Renaissance, they argued truly enough, were almost hopelessly entangled in shams, whilst the Mediaeval, they said, had nothing to conceal or to disguise. This was a great step in the right direction, for false architecture cannot be true art. It is not to be affirmed, however, that our Gothic architects quite acted up to the pretentions of their school; it was scarcely to be expected that they should; the habit of fibbing on the drawing-board, persisted in from the time of St Paul's Cathedral (which, with all its merits, is a mass of fibs), had become inveterate in England; and even now the Spartan principle that the facts of construction shall never be compromised in the design of superficiation is much too feebly recognised.

But the Gothic revival, as soon as it had acquired its full strength, brought about another result not so satisfactory to our professional repute. Architects were now divided into two 'camps' (to use the appropriate language of Sir Gilbert Scott), regarding each other with 'mutual scorn'. English people may fully appreciate in politics the advantages derived from the antagonism of parties, but in art they do not. Consequently, when Gothicists proclaimed Classicists to be, in plain language, foolish brothers, and Classicists said very much the same of Gothicists, the character of the whole profession was lowered inevitably, and the effect was only too distinctly apparent in Parliament and the press. Within the profession itself the authorities were divided in doctrine thus:—Gothicism rested its claims of superiority chiefly upon its qualities of honesty and masculine fortitude, which, in the work of Street and some others, were soon developed into something like a contempt for the graces; whereas Classicism relied upon the concurrence of all modern Europe in its adoption, and, while fully acknowledging the sin of sham, deprecated the substitution of ugliness for beauty, however masculine the one might appear to be, or however feminine the other.

There thus arose outside the profession a new philistinism. Before many years it acquired unexpected importance by reason of the appointment, quite accidentally, of Mr. Ayrton to the office of First Commissioner of Works. Ayrton was a very Goliath of the Philistines, and when Edward Barry had the temerity to encounter him he went down before him in the most melancholy manner; and unfortunately he dragged us all with him, so that the unpopularity of architects became established as almost a national principle. But it is due to South Kensington to give it most of the credit, or discredit, of this consummation. Cole may be said to have hated not only architects, but all classes whatever of professional artists of the academical order. He regarded their pretensions on all hands alike as a mere traditional, conventional, and spurious self-importance, impeding the progress of those minor arts which he considered to afford the true pabulum for national taste. Accordingly, as a rule, whatever had to be done artistically under Cole must be done, so to speak, non-professionally; and, inasmuch as architecture wa the most prominent of the professional arts, it was determined that, when building had to be done for South Kensington itself, the professional architect should be emphatically set aside. The military engineer was demonstratively substituted. Captain Fowke, a young officer of much general ability and of an amiable and well-disciplined nature, was made the representative of this policy. He became a favourite with the Prince Consort; he proved to be a man of large ideas; he entered thoroughly into the new system of artistic enterprise; he made a special study of new materials for design, such as iron and terra-cotta; and he was at once a judicious chief and a judicious subordinate. He died early; but if he had lived longer he could scarcely have accomplished more than he did. His successor, General Scott, carried on his work on the same lines; but Scott, being of a more genial temperament, allowed the arcihtectural world, if not the public, to discover at last the hollowness of the system, by acknowledging frankly that he himself was no architect at all, even although that very grand edifice, the Albert Hall, was nominally his personal work. But I need not remind you that, when the Albert Memorial had to be built, South Kensington discreetly made no attempt to commit it even nominally to the artistic mercies of the Royal Engineers.

We have now arrived at a period of less than twenty years ago; and the condition of English architecture was this, as illustrated in the great competitions for the Law Courts and the National Gallery. The Battle of the Styles was still in progress, and it cannot be denied that the Gothic party was victorious all along the line. Scott, Street and Burges were its most prominent champions. Scott had the unassailable leadership in ecclesiastical work everywhere. But the qualities which made him so popular socially with a body of men like the clergy rendered him incapable of maintaining that militant attitude which so much better suited the disposition of his eminent pupil Street. Again and again, in obedience to the call of partisanship, and to the dictates no less of his own sincere earnestness in the admiration of what we may call the milder Gothic, Scott came forward as a combatant Mediaevalist, and even made use at times of language that appeared to be strong. But no one was ever any the worse. In Street, however, the genius of the Revival possessed a soldier after its own heart. Even Ayrton had met his match; and, indeed, such has been the effect produced by the architect's undaunted attitude to the very end of his life, that the lawyers themselves in high places, exasperated at the universal anachronism and anomaly amidst which they are compelled, through sheer force of this one dead man's will, to perform their uneasy business, exclaim against him with bated breath. The third of our great Gothic trio, Burges, was not so much a man of power as of a certain playful fanaticism, which induced affectionate forbearance, and never provoked to wrath. With his intimates he was 'Billy'; I wonder if any one ever called Street 'Georgie'? But of the three, Burges was by far the most simple artistic spirit. Scott was a laborious and pushing man of business, with a congenial occupation; Street, a fighting ecclesiastic; Burges, an enamoured boy: one Low Church, one High Church, one No Church. But these three together represented the triumph of the great Gothic revival; and how strange it must appear to some of us that this triumph, which, like all our little mortal victories, seemed at the time so enduring, is now only an incident of history, and yet but a few years old!

By an ingenious contrivance of somebody's, the urgent demand for new Courts of Justice and the supposed desire for a new National Gallery were so combined together, and made the occasion of the brace of competitions alluded to, that Gothic should have its own way with one and Classic with the other. The Classic leaders of the day, however, were neither many nor strong; all the real artistic vigour was now Gothic—romantic. The result of the contest, after the customary vicissitudes, was the appointment of Street to build the Courts of Justice in an academic style, probably the most severely uncompromising that had ever been attempted in the world of archaeological art. The edifice has but recently been finished. It is a monument of artistic resolution, and, of course of artistic skill. But it is much more than this. Such is the fearless muscularity of its artistic attitude, such the vehemence of its characteristic Gothic force,—let me at once say ruthless violence,—that without it the whole process of the Revival had been quite incomplete. But, for that very reason, the consummation at length accomplished, it was fit that the great movement should confess itself exhausted. Street died at the very goal, and his cause died with him. Except in ecclesiastical work, our modern Gothic of any high pretension is now no more; it has done its service, and done it well.

A popular successor to the style of secular Gothic has necesssarily been growing up of late years by the mere action of natural law; indeed, such is the leisurely pace of architectural reform, that the new mode has been making its way slowly for more years than may be generally supposed. This is what is somewhat inexpressively and arbitrarily called by the name of the Queen Anne style, as if it were an act of mere revival. But I have suggested to you that it is really a *bric-à-brac* style peculiar to our own day, a minor art style which the influence of South Kensington may claim to have brought about, even if unconsciously. Within its own limits, and directly, no bureaucratic influence can do much in the way of producing a change of public architectural practice; it is a public demand which alone can have that effect. But it was South Kensington, as it seems to me, that created the public demand, now being satisfied by means of an infinitude of charming picturesque detail, chiefly appearing, however, in the design of small works. This is a much more philosophical way of accounting for the change than by attributing it to accident, or to any sort of personal authority. But Mr. Norman Shaw, whose modest and painstaking perseverance of character especially qualifies him, with the help of extraordinary dexterity of draughtsmanship, to be the unambitious agent of an artistic manifestation of this kind, fully deserves the credit of leadership; and he has been followed by a few equally brilliant men who have now unquestionably attained the status of a school, and one whose merits are becoming very considerable.

It is an exceedingly interesting exercise in criticism to inquire what is to be the outcome of this very peculiar movement. That it must gradually lose itself in a return to the universal European Renaissance, may probably be safely asserted. We must bear in mind,—neo-Mediaevalist criticism being here altogether unscientific,—that this great historical style, taken in its entirety, although often called Italian as an alternative title, was never such a thing as a merely local Italian, which by accident happened to spread over Europe. It was a Modern European style, which took its rise on the spot where modern Europe had its birth, and at the date when modern Europe was so born. To say that it spread westward until it had overrun the whole European world as a universally accepted mode of building, and that it has been maintained in use ever since, and still is maintained for all ordinary purposes without a question being raised,—except by people who are before the age, or behind it,—is to describe exactly the process by which every great style of design necessarily conquers its allotted territory; and when we in England claim credit with the world, as we do, and are fully entitled to do, for the exceptional merit of having originated and carried to great perfection the Gothic Revival, as a special act of characteristic motive which has now reached a turning-point after having fully satisfied our desires, what is this but a confirmation of the principle by a most unique exception?

If we now proceed to look a little more closely into the future, we have to account for three styles at present in use in England. First, there is the customary style of Modern Europe; secondly, the Revival Gothic; or the

21

style of Mediaeval Europe; and, thirdly, a certain popular and local mode which I say differs from both, but takes after both, essentially a minor-art style, and obviously transitional, prompting us already to ask ourselves what is, fourthly, to follow for a permanency?

In the first place, let us take the Gothic. Now the Gothic Revival,—which, as I have already said, was a return to the whole artistic system of the grand Mediaeval Church,—*par excellence* the church of the imagination,—so far as its ecclesiastical purpose extended, has not by any means exhausted itself. Architects of the type of Mr. Butterfield on the one hand, and of Mr. Pearson on the other, have, I think, a long career before them still; that is to say, Gothic churches show no sign of losing their popularity in England yet. But in municipal and domestic work the case is different, and the secular Gothic, having culminated in the London Law Courts, has surrendered its claims for ever. But let me put the case in another way. The movement of national sentiment which produced the Gothic Revival, and in its particular form, I observed once more, it was peculiar to England, other nations being mere imitators,—was partly ecclesiastical and partly social. It was the social phase of it which operated in 1834 in the demand that the new Houses of Parliament should be designed in what was called 'Gothic or Elizabethan.' This was for the sake of archaeology. Up to that date, and long after, when new churches were built in so-called Gothic, this also was not for any reason properly ecclesiastical, but on archaeological ground alone. The ecclesiastical motive, however, was all this time developing itself, chiefly in the universities; and in due course it came before the general public in the rise and progress of a powerful theological party. Now we are not theologians here, but artists; and the way in which we have to look at this very remarkable social phenomenon is, I think, to regard it as inevitable artistic reform, using the term in a very wide sense. It was the introduction of the infinite artistic element, or poetic element, into the English Church, as opposed to a dull and dismal philistinism which had been in possession of it for many generations. We were to have for the future artistic music, artistic decoration, artistic ceremonial, artistic architecture, and, as I venture to add, artistic doctrine and discipline. This, I may safely affirm, is the harmless way in which the people at large have always looked at the case; and it is especially proved to be so by the circumstance that even the Nonconformists and the Scotch Presbyterians have accepted the new system as far as they could. I need not remind you how earnestly it was embraced by English architects; in fact, we may say that architecture has been almost the helm of the enterprize, answering to every call with a readiness of resource for which English genius may justly claim the lasting admiration of the artistic world. It is the ecclesiastical Gothic, therefore, as the style of artistic religion, that I regard to be the only natural or historical form of the Revival. That it has taken a strong hold upon the affections of the people cannot be doubted, and I scarcely care to ask you to fix a period for the duration of its popularity. Like all other manifestations of sentiment, it must in time give way to something new; but let us hope at least that it may be something better rather than worse. Looking again at the influence of the minor arts, it must be borne in mind that, as they stand in practice, they owe almost all their present importance in England to their revivification by means of ecclesiastical architecture; so that, if it should be through the minor arts that the coming style of architecture is to be determined, there seems to be no reason why this should affect our revived ecclesiastical Gothic otherwise than by the continued amelioration of its sometimes too masculine manners, an effect which is not by any means to be discouraged.

As regards, in the next place, the exact position amongst us of the general Modern European mode, from which the French, the Italians, and even the Germans have never swerved, as we have done,—except in mere superficial imitation of ourselves,—I have only to repeat what I have already said, that we cannot help returning to it, and that, indeed, we are already so doing.

Turning now to our third manifestation,—the so-called 'Queen Anne,'— I think one motive which lies at the root of it may be thus described. Secular Gothic had for its principal basis the element of picturesqueness; it was, indeed, frequently designated the picturesque style, as thus distinguished in spirit from the Classic style or style of repose. When, therefore, it was found that municipal buildings and private dwelling-houses designed in this manner, unless all authenticity were expressly sacrificed, proved to be unacceptable to the ordinary feeling of the day, and that, in fact, English common sense, while admiring the picturesque greatly, pronounced against the practical inconvenience of obsolete forms and arrangements, it was necessary to find something to take the place for a time of the rejected style, without surrendering the picturesque character, Mr. Norman Shaw and his colleagues have accomplished this end, as I think, successfully; and it was done by means of the subsidiary art of what I will venture to call *sketchmanship*. The Gothicists had become enthusiastic sketchers; Street was the very prince of sketch-making out of doors; in fact, architectural sketching of the picturesque order was found to be the *forte* of Englishmen, bringing out in all its force the rough-and-ready national preference for experimental study instead of philosophical. So what was done was to make sketches of a new class of picturesque old buildings, not necessarily pure Gothic, or not even Gothic at all. I am afraid I must say that the specimens selected turned out generally to be Dutch. In a word, with the help of the good-natured name of Queen Anne, whose reign coincided sufficiently well with the use of a kind of Dutch art in England, there was at length brought about a certain popularity for red-brick buildings, with features neither Gothic nor Classic, but quaintly pleasing, and, so to speak of a sort of old English type. Nothing could be better suited for such an occasion. The recent development of the minor arts, moreover, was fully recognized; for Dutch art and *bric-à-brac* are never far apart. And so the Queen Anne architects are making very good innings, and just now are doing better and better work daily, although, no doubt, still leaving room for improvement. Some of the drawings of interiors more particularly, which are produced under names unknown to most of us, seem to me to evidence a degree of manual dexterity which ought to tell upon the artistic handling of a higher class of architectural style when the time comes.

What, then, is the higher style to be? I can only suppose, as I have said, that it must be the standard Renaissance in some form or other. We may now ask, therefore, whether England is to insist upon producing any modification of it to suit her own national character; and here a very interesting point comes into view. It is said that, in the history of modern intellectual development, the two races which occupy Europe, the Latin and the Teutonic, stand in this relation to each other, that the Latins initiate what the Teutons perfect. The more imaginative genius of the French and the Italians, that is to say, having its function in the origination of almost all great discoveries, it is the more practical scientific power of the Germans and English that assumes the task of their development. If this be true with reference to the arts, England in the coming generation may be destined to take the lead of even France; and I for one have no objection to look this possibility fairly in the face. Already the Ecclesiastical Gothic of England in our own day may certainly hold up its head beside anything that France has done; and, perhaps, in the coming Renaissance we may find ourselves no less able to compete with our gifted neighbours. Bright and joyous as the French Renaissance always is, there may be a certain vigour of manliness reserved for the English, which, in an age of increasing manliness and increasing English influence, shall accomplish unexpected results. It is of little use to speculate about the mere details of one academical style or another, and the introduction of this class of features and the rejection of that, as if personal authority were to govern the course of events; natural law will have its way in this as in all else, and if English intellectual enterprize is to be fairly challenged to accomplish an adaptation of the somewhat hard-worked forms of the Italian-European, I do not see why in the next century an English-European style should not take the lead throughout the world.

Let us further inquire what is the present drift of English architectural sentiment in the abstract. The Mediaeval romanticism which a few years ago was the dominant feeling has recently been disappearing with such a strange rapidity that it seems almost doubtful whether the secular Gothic party have not deserted to the enemy in a body. Now, I confess I should be sorry if this were really so; because I think the peculiar artistic enthusiasm which actuated Pugin, Scott, Street and Burges, cannot well be dispensed with for some time to come. No doubt a new enthusiasm will spring up; but the Queen Anne movement is not such a thing; it is an impulse of a much more feeble and evanescent character. The attitude which is assumed by the somewhat mysterious organization of 'The Society for the Protection of Ancient Buildings' seems for a moment now and then to be all that is left of the Gothic enthusiasm; but on closer acquaintance this impression is not confirmed. For it declines emphatically to be considered representative of Gothic alone, or, indeed, we may say, of Gothic at all. Its object is not even artistic, but historical; to preserve what is left of the past in the most indiscriminate way; whether good or bad, old or new, preserve it all, so that the reverie of the wayfarer may have not only something authentic, but everything veritable to dwell upon, even when the light of life, perhaps never a very bright light, has quite gone out. This, I need scarcely repeat, is not an enthusiasm of art,—indeed, scarcely one of archaeology; and it has become identified with architecture only because buildings are the most conspicuous relics for such a form of patriotic reverence. I may add, moreover, that the influence of archaeology itself upon architecture seems within the last few years to have given way; and I think this is to be regretted too, inasmuch as our archaeologists, like our old antiquarians the *dilettanti*, if only as matter of prestige, brought the element of learning into prominent connexion with our noble work. The minor-art architecture of to-day exhibits again in these respects its conformity with the South Kensington principle, which, in making art a thing of popular skill, and not of academical knowledge, widens the ground that is cultivated, but at the expense necessarily of the depth of cultivation. That our present age is one of superficiality in many other matters besides this, is a well-established fact; and I am not sure that it is to be regretted; for if we can see that the field of art, as actually enjoyable by the multitude of us, is thus being extended so largely, we may well be content to let the learning reappear in its own way and at its own time.

But there is another point to be noticed here, namely the way in which the architectural arts are being controlled and even directed by the artifices of draughtsmanship, or sketchmanship, regarded as a delightful, but delusive, sleight of hand. In the minor arts of decoration, such as glass-painting, carving, painted ornament, and so on, it is easy to see that clever drawing is in a great measure the essence of the artistic manifestation; but we cannot shut our eyes to the fact that in the now very pleasant work of furniture design, when in the hands of architects, the same clever drawing is fully accepted in the same way; and, as matters go, it is but a step in the style of the moment from furniture to building. Our architecture has thus come to be sketch-designed and sketchy, careless and vague in detail; a thing of scene-painting, picturesque at any price, restless and not necessarily anything else; exceedingly clever on paper, and, when carefully carried out, pretty and piquant in execution, but greatly wanting in the nobler qualities. I do not suppose, however, that this will last long; and, even before the so-called Queen Anne mode itself gives way, we may expect, I hope, to see a more careful manipulation of the modelling becoming universal: indeed, it is already making progress.

Another matter of sentiment to be noted is the abatement of that cynical poeticism which was introduced by Mr. Ruskin. I never could understand why this exquisite dream-painter should have ever taken up such a subject as architecture, except for the indomitable courage of the thing; but there can be no doubt that his visionary doctrines,—and the more visionary necessarily the more vague,—have had a great effect in helping what was weak English art to conquer strong English philistinism; and, if this involved a certain amount of inconvenient romancing when applied to the practical work of architects, such a result might be expected to appear, and the effect of the medicine must be allowed to wear off by degrees. At all events, now that the artistic spirit has taken possession of us, we need not grudge our thanks to the influence, perhaps upon the public mind more than the professional, of the writings of Ruskin.

But we have, nevertheless, still to face the fact that in high places in England a new philistinism has been for many years acquiring a certain force,—indeed for thirty years,—an influence antagonistic both to architecture and to architects. The building of the Houses of Parliament in a Gothic style was no sooner fairly under way than the common sense of the more utilitarian order of men connected with the Legislature revolted against it as an anachronism. The architect of the structure, even if he himself had been at first of the same opinion, had, of course, to take all the blame; and when the edifice came at length to be occupied, there was a cry raised of inconvenience and incongruousness, which has been kept up ever since. In course of time, when the son of the great architect, thinking he had acquired by his father's bequest the position of an hereditary successor, came into collision with Mr. Ayrton, and was ruthlessly defeated by that champion of the Philistines, backed by the unsympathetic logic of the Courts of Law, it would be idle to affect not to see that the pretensions of architects,—the Prime Minister himself had to say they were untenable,— had come to be seriously mistrusted. The immediate effect of it was that the Government determined to dispense with outside architects by making use of the officials of the Department of Public Works; and it is still understood that this rule is practically in force for a permanency. The charges made against the profession on this ground are shortly these,—that convenience and economy are sacrificed to monumental appearance, and that the severe character of the commercial contract with a builder is tampered with by the introduction of extras. Upon these questions I need only observe that the most successful architects in England from time immemorial,—I do not say the most artistic,—will be found to have been the most mercantile in their manners; and secondly, that the artistic element in architecture is not recognized by law, or recognizable in any way by the legal mind. I may also point out that the typical English gentleman,—and typical English legislator,—is a person whose ideas of building are still of primitive simplicity, and that his impression of an architect's business is equally devoid of sentimental considerations. But I do not consider that the so-called unpopularity of architects goes really deeper than this; and if any architect who happens to obtain Government employment,—scarcely ever a desirable thing by the way,—will condescend to bring his ambition down to the practical level of his private business, and to do everything in strictly commercial form, there is no reason why he should not give satisfaction.

One word more must be said here upon the influence of competitions. Looking at the eagerness with which these contests are entered upon, the disregard of commercial calculation that is manifested even by the leaders of the profession, and the unseemly bickering that invariably results, how is it to be expected that such men as are at the head of public affairs in a commonwealth of commercial common sense like ours should regard either architecture or architects with due respect? The logical conclusion obviously is that the designs which are so freely offered for nothing must be worth nothing, and that the men who are so ready to work for nothing must be taken at their own valuation. Nevertheless, although I believe it is almost invariably the case that it is not the proprietors that call for a competition for their own sake, but the architects who virtually solicit permission to compete against each other, I am afraid, in speculating upon the future of the profession, we must expect this practice of competing to increase rather than diminish. Sooner or later, however, some check must be put upon it, either by the good sense of the public, or by a feeling of shame on the part of the architects themselves; up to the present moment I do not see that any effective steps whatever have been taken towards that end. Still, on the other hand, I cannot but frankly acknowledge the opinion that, without the peculiar artistic exercise and enterprise which competitions induce, English architecture could not possibly have done all it has done during the last half-century. I chiefly object to the great waste the practice occasions, not only in money, but in time, temper and character.

I may now say a few words,—still keeping to the artistic view of my subject,—upon the position of architects in respect of business. I need not repeat in any way what I have said of the advancing popularity of minor-art architecture, and the increasing competency of our architects to deal with it. But what of the still more rapidly increasing numbers of the men who have to live by it? And what is the state of their organization?

In the first place, I may express my opinion that the Institute of Architects, established now fifty years ago under circumstances very different from those of the present day, does not display either the vigour or the intelligence which the service of the profession requires, whether we look to the interests of the art or to those of the artists. It is to be hoped that something may be done in that quarter before long; but it must take time: thirty years hence, at any rate, the Institute, we may safely say, ought to be much more earnestly devoted to the practical utilities of art than it is now.

The Royal Academy, also, if architectural art is to retain its connexion with it much longer, must, I venture to suppose, enlarge its views of the minor arts considerably; and here I think we may fortunately expect to see both painters and sculptors entering into the matter with understanding as well as with sincerity.

Turning next to the educational question, we find that examination tests are becoming the order of the day; but whether, in respect of architecture, the introduction of artistic design into the programme can be accomplished, seems still to be matter of doubt. That some kind of academical diploma for art-architectural in its expanding form must, however, sooner or later, be contrived, both to conciliate the artist and to meet a public demand, can scarcely be matter of doubt.

A circumstance that must not be overlooked is the still-increasing employment of professional architects all over the country, which, looking at the sum total, is so far encouraging, even if individual instances of dissatisfaction are numerous. Not many years ago there were but few architects of really good position, except in London and the larger provincial towns. Now the smaller towns, and some that are almost villages, are occupied by practitioners who are frequently quite equal to their metropolitan brethren in skill. The pupils also of provincial men have in some instances better work passing through their hands than those who are in average London offices; and, thanks to a study of the photo-lithographic illustrations of the professional journals, their draughtsmanship is often of quite as high an order as the best in London. All this points to a condition of things in the near future throughout England in which men architecturally educated are to do a vast amount of good art-work in one way or another, and, therefore, in many ways. Consequently, when I hear the question asked, as I often do, what is to become of the increasing host of young architectural pupils, my answer is that they will be drafted off more and more before long into the service of many charming arts. For there is a certain peculiar characteristic in architectural training, namely, the habitude of constructional design, which, even while as yet not so devoid of the old make-believe as we could wish, is still expressly calculated to prepare the mind for that association of the superficial with the substantial which becomes the most essential charm in all formative and ornamental art when once publicly understood, and which the mere counting-house designer acquires, if at all, under great disadvantages.

Another point of importance in our prospect of the next generation of architects is the work connected with so-called engineering construction. Perhaps the most regrettable weakness of English architects at the present time, in point of dignity, is their want of that higher scientific skill which they allow engineers to monopolise. To give a familiar instance, it is quite common for an architect of eminence, when he happens to have ironwork of any magnitude to deal with, to hand it over altogether to an engineer to design, like a solicitor employing counsel to draft a deed. Now this is to be regretted. The reason for the practice obviously is that there is no sufficient current of such work passing through the architect's own hands to keep him up to it, and that he, therefore, must call in a specialist who does nothing else. It would be useless and, indeed, unfair to reject such an argument; but what I want you to do is, to consider what a far superior position the architectural profession would occupy if it were publicly understood that they did all such work for themselves, even if the fact went no further than this,—that the aid came from a specialist architect and not from an engineer. Still, looking at art, what I should like to see is an architecturally-educated man designing such a thing as the most advanced ironwork, and introducing true architectural art into it as his design went on. Otherwise, if one of these two kindred professions has to call in the specialist aid of the other, why should it not be the engineering constructor who calls in the architectural designer? Why should all our building operations of the so-called, and improperly so-called, engineering order,—viaducts, bridges, great roofs, railway stations, piers, embankments and much more,—be left barren and unfruitful of grace because the designers of them, professing nothing of the artistic spirit themselves, assume that it has no connexion with their work? Here, I would fain hope we may see another sphere of business, and, indeed, one of vast importance and grandeur, opening out in the next generation to the English architect.

To conclude, in answering for yourselves the question what is to be the position of English architecture, let us say thirty years hence, I invite you simply to regard the profession as one that has been advancing during a corresponding period of the immediate past in a certain direction and at a certain pace, which a retrospect of recent history such as I have offered seems to indicate clearly enough, and then to follow forward the same line at an increasing rate of evolution. If the next thirty years should do as much as the last fifty have done, then it becomes easy to understand that the process of development would have to cover as much ground as has been covered since the time of the foundation of our Institute, and the inception of the design of the new Houses of Parliament, in the old-fashioned reign of King William IV. We do not require to imagine the occurrence of any catastrophe; but the change produced upon the face of our art and our profession must undoubtedly be great, and, perhaps may be greater than any argument such as mine suggests. For, during the last fifty years, Dilettantism has gone down before the Romanticism of the Gothic Revival; and this in its turn has at length given place, after adding a very glorious chapter to the history of the art. The old philistinism of the Georges has been vanquished by the South Kensington movement, as a movement of the people; and a new philistinism has arisen, which has to be vanquished, and will be, in due time. The empty conventional formulas of the academical arts have been vigorously assailed by the new non-academical substantial facts, and the minor arts are already so far triumphant before the common sense of England that architecture itself has taken service in their cause, and a great deal for the better if a little for the worse. In these campaigns the whole lives of such great men as Pugin and Barry, Scott and Street, have been expended, and the task of great writers like Ruskin and Fergusson exhausted. Cole has passed through his long and busy, masterly and masterful career. The genial influence of Prince Albert, infinitely beneficial to the artistic sentiment, has already survived his own august life for three-and-twenty years. This artistic sentiment has for the first time spread all over our country, one of the kindliest graces of the splendid Victorian age; and England is now ready to enter upon a new chapter of her magnificent history, not, let us hope, with arms in her hands, whether for conquest or defence, but with the fruits of science and the flowers of art. And possibly,—indeed, I venture to think not improbably,— it may be the destiny of England at a period by no means remote, in the development of the advancing scheme of Anglo-Saxon civilisation, to assume a leadership,—such as she already possesses in so much besides,— in the illustrious art which it is the pride and the joy of this assembly to represent.

APPENDIX II

The Revival of Architecture[1]

By WILLIAM MORRIS

AMONG cultivated people at present there is a good deal of interest felt or affected in the ornamental arts and their prospects. Since all these arts are dependent on the master-art of architecture almost for their existence, and cannot be in a healthy condition if it is sick, it may be worth while to consider what is the condition of architecture in this country; whether or no we have a living style which can lay claim to a dignity or beauty of its own, or whether our real style is merely a habit of giving certain forms not worth noticing to an all-pervading ugliness and meanness.

In the first place, then, it must be admitted on all sides that there has been in this century something like a revival of architecture; the question follows whether that revival indicates a genuine growth of real vitality which is developing into something else, or whether it merely points to a passing wave of fashion which, when passed, will leave nothing enduring behind it. I can think of no better way of attempting a solution of this question than the giving a brief sketch of the history of this revival as far as I have noted it. The revival of the art of architecture in Great Britain may be said to have been a natural consequence of the rise of the romantic school in literature, although it lagged some way behind it, and naturally so, since the art of building has to deal with the prosaic incidents of every day life, and is limited by the material exigencies of its existence. Up to a period long after the death of Shelley and Keats and Scott, architecture could do nothing but produce on the one hand pedantic imitations of classical architecture of the most revolting ugliness, and ridiculous travesties of Gothic buildings, not quite so ugly, but meaner and sillier; and, on the other hand, the utilitarian brick box with a slate lid which the Anglo-Saxon generally in modern times considers as a good sensible house with no nonsense about it.

The first symptoms of change in this respect were brought about by the Anglo-Catholic movement, which must itself be considered as part of the romantic movement in literature, and was supported by many who had

---

[1] Reprinted from the *Fortnightly Review*, May 1888.

no special theological tendencies, as a protest against the historical position and stupid isolation of Protestantism. Under this influence there arose a genuine study of mediaeval architecture, and it was slowly discovered that it was not, as was thought in the days of Scott, a mere accidental jumble of picturesqueness consecrated by ruin and the lapse of time, but a logical and organic style evolved as a matter of necessity from the ancient styles of the classical peoples, and advancing step by step with the changes in the social life of barbarism and feudalism and civilization. Of course it took long to complete this discovery, nor as a matter of fact is it admitted in practice by many of the artists and architects of to-day, though the best of them feel, instinctively perhaps, the influence of the new school of historians, of whom the late John Richard Green and Professor Freeman may be cited as examples, and who have long been familiar with it.

One unfortunate consequence the study of mediaeval art brought with it, owing indeed to the want of the admission of its historical evolution just mentioned. When the architects of this country had learned something about the building and ornament of the Middle Ages, and by dint of sympathetic study had more or less grasped the principles on which the design of that period was founded, they had a glimmer of an idea that those principles belonged to the aesthetics of all art in all countries, and were capable of endless development; they saw dimly that Gothic art had been a living organism, but though they knew that it had perished, and that its place had been taken by something else, they did not know why it had perished, and thought it could be artificially replanted in a society totally different from that which gave birth to it. The result of this half-knowledge led them to believe that they had nothing to do but to design on paper according to the principles the existence of which they had divined in Gothic architecture, and that the buildings so designed, when carried out under their superintendence, would be true examples of the ancient style, made alive by those undying principles of the art. On this assumption it was natural that they should attempt with confidence to remedy the injuries and degradations which the ignorance, brutality, and vulgarity of the post-Gothic periods had brought on those priceless treasures of art and history, the buildings yet left to us from the Middle Ages. Hence arose the fatal practice of 'restoration', which in a period of forty years has done more damage to our ancient buildings than the preceding three centuries of revolutionary violence, sordid greed (utilitarianism so called), and pedantic contempt. This side of the subject I have no space to dwell on further here. I can only say that if my subject could be looked on from no other point of view than the relation of modern architecture to the preservation of these relics of the past, it would be most important to face the facts of the present condition of the art amongst us, lest a mere delusion as to our position should lead us to throw away these treasures which once lost can never be recovered. No doubt, on the other hand, this same half-knowledge gave the new school of architects courage to carry on their work with much spirit, and as a result we have a considerable number of buildings throughout the country which do great credit to the learning and talent of their designers, and some of them even show signs of genius struggling through the difficulties which beset an architect attempting to produce beauty in the midst of the most degrading utilitarianism.

In the early period of this Gothic revival the buildings thus produced were mostly ecclesiastical. The public were easily persuaded that the buildings destined for the use of the Anglican Church, which was obviously in part a survival from the Church of the Middle Ages, should be of the style which obtained in the period to which the greater part of its buildings belonged; and indeed it used to be customary to use the word 'ecclesiastical' as a synonym for mediaeval architecture. Of course this absurdity was exploded among the architects at a very early stage of the revival, although it lingered long and perhaps still lingers amongst the general public. It was soon seen by those who studied the arts of the Middle Ages that there was no difference in style between the domestic and civil and the ecclesiastical architecture of that period, and the full appreciation of this fact marks the second stage in the 'Gothic Revival'.

Then came another advance: those who sympathized with that great period of the development of the human race, the Middle Ages, especially such of them as had the gift of the historical sense which may be said to be a special gift of the nineteenth century, and a kind of compensation for the ugliness which surrounds our lives at present: these men now began not only to understand that the mediaeval art was no mere piece of reactionary official ecclesiasticism or the expression of an extinct theology, but a popular, living, and progressive art—and that progressive art had died with it; they came to recognize that the art of the sixteenth and seventeenth centuries drew what vigour and beauty it had from the impulse of the period that preceded it, and that when that died out about the middle of the seventeenth century nothing was left but a *caput mortuum* of inanity and pedantry, which demanded perhaps a period of stern utilitarianism to form, as it were, the fallow of the arts before the new seed could be sown.

Both as regards art and history this was an important discovery. Undismayed by their position of isolation from the life of the present, the leaders of this fresh renaissance set themselves to the stupendous task of taking up the link of historical art where the pedants of the older so-called renaissance had dropped it, and tried to prove that the mediaeval style was capable of new life and fresh development, and that it could adapt itself to the needs of the nineteenth century. On the surface this hope of theirs seemed justified by the marvellous elasticity which the style showed in the period of its real life. Nothing was too great or too little, too common-place or too sublime for its inclusive embrace; no change dismayed it, no violence seriously checked it; in those older days it was a part of the life of man, the universal, indispensable expression of his joys and sorrows. Could it not be so again? we thought; had not the fallow of the arts lasted long enough? Were the rows of square brown brick boxes which Keats and Shelley had to look on, or the stuccoed villa which enshrined Tennyson's genius, to be the perpetual concomitants of such masters of verbal beauty; was no beauty but the beauty of words to be produced by man in our times; was the intelligence of the age to be for ever so preposterously lop-sided? We could see no reason for it, and accordingly our hope was strong; for though we had learned something of the art and history of the Middle Ages, we had not learned enough. It became the fashion amongst the hopeful artists of the time I am thinking of to say that in order to have beautiful surroundings there was no need to alter any of the conditions and manners of our epoch; that an easy chair, a piano, a steam-engine, a billiard-table, or a hall fit for the meeting of the House of Commons, had nothing essential in them which compelled us to make them ugly, and that if they had existed in the Middle Ages the people of the time would have made them beautiful. Which certainly had an element of truth in it, but was not all the truth. It was indeed true that the mediaeval instinct for beauty would have exercised itself on whatsoever fell to its lot to do, but it was also true that the life of the times did not put into the hands of the workman any object which was merely utilitarian, still less vulgar; whereas the life of modern times forces on him the production of many things which can be nothing but utilitarian, as for instance a steam-engine; and of many things in which vulgarity is innate and inevitable, as a gentleman's club-house or the ceremonial of our modern bureaucratic monarchy. Anyhow, this period of fresh hope and partial insight produced many interesting buildings and other works of art, and afforded a pleasant time indeed to the hopeful but very small minority engaged in it, in spite of all vexations and disappointments. At last one man, who had done more than any one else to make this hopeful time possible, drew a line sternly through these hopes founded on imperfect knowledge. This man was John Ruskin. By a marvellous inspiration of genius (I can call it nothing else) he attained at one leap to a true conception of mediaeval art which years of minute study had not gained for others. In his chapter in *The Stones of Venice*, entitled 'On the Nature of Gothic, and the Function of the Workman therein', he showed us the gulf which lay between us and the Middle Ages. From that time all was changed; ignorance of the spirit of the Middle Ages was henceforth impossible, except to those who wilfully shut their eyes. The aims of the new revival of art grew to be infinitely greater than they had been in those who did not give up all aim, as I fear many did. From that time forth those who could not learn the new knowledge were doomed to become pedants, differing only in the externals of the art they practised or were interested in from the unhistorical big-wigs of the eighteenth century. Yet the essence of what Ruskin then taught us was simple enough, like all great discoveries. It was really nothing more recondite than this, that the art of any epoch must of necessity be the expression of its social life, and that the social life of the Middle Ages allowed the workman freedom of individual expression, which on the other hand our social life forbids him.

I do not say that the change in the Gothic revivalists produced by this discovery was sudden, but it was effective. It has gradually sunk deep into the intelligence of the art and literature of to-day, and has had a great deal to do with the sundering of the highest culture (if one must use that ugly word) into a peculiarly base form of cynicism on the one hand, and into practical and helpful altruism on the other. The course taken by the Gothic revival in architecture, which, as aforesaid, is the outward manifestation of the Romantic school generally, shows decided tokens of the growing consciousness of the essential difference between our society and that of the Middle Ages. When our architects and archaeologists first mastered, as they supposed, the practice and principles of Gothic art, and began the attempt to reintroduce it as a universal style, they came to the conclusion that they were bound to take it up at the period when it hung balanced between completion and the very first beginnings of degradation. The end of the thirteenth and beginning of the fourteenth century was the time they chose as that best fitted for the foundation of the Neo-Gothic style, which they hoped was destined to conquer the world; and in choosing this period on the verge of transition they showed remarkable insight and appreciation of the qualities of the style. It had by that time assimilated to itself whatever it could use of classical art, mingled with the various elements gathered from the barbaric ancient monarchies and the northern tribes, while for itself it had no consciousness of them, nor was in any way trammelled by them; it was flexible to a degree yet undreamed of in any previous style of architecture, and had no difficulties in dealing with any useful purpose, any material or climate; and with all this it was undeniably and frankly beautiful, cumbered by no rudeness, and degraded by no whim. The hand and the mind of man, one would think, can carry loveliness (a loveliness, too, that never cloys) no further than in the architectural works of that period, as for instance in the choir and transepts of Westminster Abbey before it had suffered from degradations of later days, which truly make one stand aghast at the pitch of perversity which men can reach at times. It must be remembered too, in estimating the judgment of the Neo-Gothic architects, that the half-century from 1280 to 1320 was the blossoming-time of architecture all over that part of the world which had held fast to historical continuity; and the East as well as the West produced its loveliest works of ornament and art at that period. This development, moreover, was synchronous with the highest point of the purely mediaeval organization of industry. By that time the Gild-merchants and Lineages of the free towns, which had grown aristocratic, exclusive, and divorced from actual labour, had had to yield to the craft-gilds, democratic bodies of actual workmen, which had now taken the position that they had long striven for, and were the masters of all industry. It was not the monasteries, as we used to be told, which were the hives of the art of the fourteenth century, but the free towns with their crafts organized for battle as well as craftsmanship; not the reactionary but the progressive part of the society of the time.

This central period therefore of the Gothic style, which expressed the full development of the social system of the Middle Ages, was undoubtedly the fittest period to choose for the tree on which to graft the young plant of Neo-Gothic; and at the time of which I am now thinking every architect of promise would have repudiated with scorn the suggestion that he should use any later or impurer style for the works he had to carry out. Indeed there was a tendency, natural enough, to undervalue the qualities of the later forms of Gothic, a tendency which was often carried to grotesque extremes, and the semi-Gothic survivals of the late sixteenth and the seventeenth centuries were looked on with mere contempt, in theory at least. But as time passed and the revivalists began to recognize, whether they would or no, the impossibility of bridging the gulf between the fourteenth and the nineteenth centuries; as in spite of their brilliant individual successes they found themselves compelled to admit that the Neo-Gothic graft refused to grow in the commercial air of the Victorian era; as they toiled conscientiously and wearily to reconcile the Podsnappery of modern London with the expression of the life of Simon de Montfort and Philip van Artevelde, they discovered that they had pitched their note too high, and must try again, or give up the game altogether. By that time they had thoroughly learned the merits of the later Gothic styles, and even of the style which in England at least (as in literature so in art) had retained some of the beauty and fitness of the palmy days of Gothic amidst the conceits, artificialities, and euphuism of the time of Elizabeth and James the First; nay, they began to overvalue the remains of the inferior styles, not through pedantry, but rather perhaps from sympathy with the course of history, and repulsion from the pessimism which narrows the period of high aspirations and pleasure in life to the standard of our own passing moods. In the main, however, they were moved in this direction by the hope of finding another standpoint for the new and living style which they still hoped to set on foot; the elasticity and adaptability of the style of the fifteenth century, of which every village church in England gives us examples, and the great mass of the work achieved by it, in domestic as well as church architecture, ready to hand for study, as well as the half-conscious feeling of its being nearer to our own times and expressing a gradually-growing complexity of society, captivated the revivalists with a fresh hope. The dream of beauty and romance of the fourteenth century was gone; might not the more work-a-day 'Perpendicular' give us a chance for the housing of Mr. Podsnap's respectability and counting-house, and bosom-of-the-family, and Sunday worship, without too manifest an absurdity?

So the architects began on the fifteenth-century forms, and as by this time they had gained more and more knowledge of mediaeval aims and methods, they turned out better and better work; but still the new living style would not come. The Neo-Gothic in the fourteenth-century style was often a fair rendering of its original; the fifteenth-century rendering has been often really good, and not seldom has had an air of originality about it that makes one admire the capacity and delicate taste of its designers; but nothing comes of it; it is all hung in the air, so to say. London has not begun to look like a fifteenth-century city, and no flavour of beauty or even of generous building has begun to make itself felt in the numberless houses built in the suburbs.

Meantime from the fifteenth century we have sunk by a natural process to imitating something later yet, something so much nearer our own time and our own manners and ways of life, that a success might have been expected to come out of this at least. The brick style in vogue in the time of William the Third and Queen Anne is surely not too sublime for general use; even Podsnap might acknowledge a certain amount of kinship with the knee-breeched, cocked-hatted bourgeois of that period; might not the graft of the new style begin to grow now, when we have abandoned the Gothic altogether, and taken to a style that belongs to the period of the workshop and division of labour, a period when all that was left of the craft-gilds was the corruption of them, the mere abuses of the close corporations and companies under whose restrictions of labour the commercial class chafed so sorely, and which they were on the point of sweeping away entirely?

Well, it is true that at first sight the Queen Anne development has seemed to conquer modern taste more or less; but in truth it is only the barest shadow of it which has done so. The turn that some of our vigorous young architects (they were young then) took towards this latest of all domestic styles can be accounted for without quarrelling with their good taste or good sense. In truth, with the best of them it was not the differentia of the Queen Anne style that was the attraction; all that is a mere bundle of preposterous whims; it was the fact that in the style there was yet left some feeling of the Gothic, at least in places or under circumstances where the buildings were remote from the progressive side of the eighteenth century.

22

There I say some of the Gothic feeling was left, joined to forms, such as sash windows, yet possible to be used in our own times. The architects in search of a style might well say:

We have been driven from ditch to ditch; cannot we yet make a stand? The unapproachable grace and loveliness of the fourteenth century is hull down behind us, the fifteenth-century work is too delicate and too rich for the commonplace of to-day; let us be humble, and begin once more with the style of well-constructed, fairly proportioned brick houses which stand London smoke well, and look snug and comfortable at some village end, or amidst the green trees of a squire's park. Besides, our needs as architects are not great; we don't want to build churches any more; the nobility have their palaces in town and country already (I wish them joy of some of them!); the working man cannot afford to live in anything that an architect could design; moderate-sized rabbit-warrens for rich middle-class men, and small ditto for the hanger-on groups to which we belong, is all we have to think of. Perhaps something of a style might arise amongst us from these lowly beginnings, though indeed we have come down a weary long way from Pugin's *Contrasts*. We agree with him still, but we are driven to admire and imitate some of the very things he cursed, with our enthusiastic approbation.

Well, a goodish many houses of this sort have been built, to the great comfort of the dwellers in them, I am sure; but the new style is so far from getting under way, that while on the other hand the ordinary builder is covering England with abortions which make us regret the brick box and slate lid of fifty years ago, the cultivated classes are rather inclined to return to the severity (that is to say, the unmitigated expensive ugliness) of the last dregs of would-be Palladian, as exemplified in the stone lumps of the Georgian period. Indeed I have not heard that the 'educated middle classes' had any intention of holding a riotous meeting on the adjacent Trafalgar Square to protest against the carrying out of the designs for the new public offices which the Aedileship of Mr. Shaw-Lefevre threatened us with. As to public buildings, Mr. Street's Law Courts are the last attempt we are likely to see of producing anything reasonable or beautiful for that use; the public has resigned itself to any mass of dulness and vulgarity that it may be convenient for a department to impose upon it, probably from a half-conscious impression that at all events it will be good enough for the work (so-called) which will be done in it.

In short we must answer the question with which this paper began by saying that the architectural revival, though not a mere piece of artificial nonsense, is too limited in its scope, too much confined to an educated group, to be a vital growth capable of true development. The important fact in it is that it is founded on the sympathy for history and the art of historical generalization, which, as aforesaid, is a gift of our epoch, but unhappily a gift in which few as yet have a share. Among populations where this gift is absent, not even scattered attempts at beauty in architecture are now possible, and in such places generations may live and die, if society as at present constituted endures, without feeling any craving for beauty in their daily lives; and even under the most favourable circumstances there is no general impulse born out of necessity towards beauty, which impulse alone can produce a universal architectural style, that is to say, a habit of elevating and beautifying the houses, furniture, and other material surroundings of our life.

All we have that approaches architecture is the result of a quite self-conscious and very laborious eclecticism, and is avowedly imitative of the work of past times, of which we have gained a knowledge far surpassing that of any other period. Meanwhile whatever is done without conscious effort, that is to say the work of the true style of the epoch, is an offence to the sense of beauty and fitness, and is admitted to be so by all men who have any perception of beauty of form. It is no longer passively but actively ugly, since it has added to the dreary utilitarianism of the days of Dr. Johnson a vulgarity which is the special invention of the Victorian era. The genuine style of that era is exemplified in the jerry-built houses of our suburbs, the stuccoed marine-parades of our watering-places, the flaunting corner public-houses of every town in Great Britain, the raw-boned hideousness of the houses that mar the glorious scenery of the Queen's Park at Edinburgh. These form our true Victorian architecture. Such works as Mr. Bodley's excellent new buildings at Magdalen College, Mr. Norman Shaw's elegantly fantastic Queen Anne houses at Chelsea, or Mr. Robson's simple but striking London board-schools, are mere eccentricities with which the public in general has no part or lot.

This is stark pessimism, my readers may say. Far from it. The enthusiasm of the Gothic revivalists died out when they were confronted by the fact that they form part of a society which will not and cannot have a living style, because it is an economical necessity for its existence that the ordinary everyday work of its population shall be mechanical drudgery; and because it is the harmony of the ordinary everyday work of the population which produces Gothic, that is, living architectural art, and mechanical drudgery cannot be harmonized into art. The hope of our ignorance has passed away, but it has given place to the hope born of fresh knowledge. History taught us the evolution of architecture, it is now teaching us the evolution of society; and it is clear to us, and even to many who refuse to acknowledge it, that the society which is developing out of ours will not need or endure mechanical drudgery as the lot of the general population; that the new society will not be hag-ridden as we are by the necessity for producing ever more and more market-wares for a profit, whether any one needs them or not; that it will produce to live, and not live to produce, as we do. Under such conditions architecture, as a part of the life of people in general, will again become possible, and I believe that when it is possible, it will have a real new birth, and add so much to the pleasure of life that we shall wonder

22*

how people were ever able to live without it. Meantime we are waiting for that new development of society, some of us in cowardly inaction, some of us amidst hopeful work towards the change; but at least we are all waiting for what must be the work, not of the leisure and taste of a few scholars, authors, and artists, but of the necessities and aspirations of the workmen throughout the civilized world.

INDEX

1. Horace Walpole and others, Holbein Room, Strawberry Hill, Twickenham, 1759

3. James Essex, Detail of Screen, Lincoln Cathedral, 1761

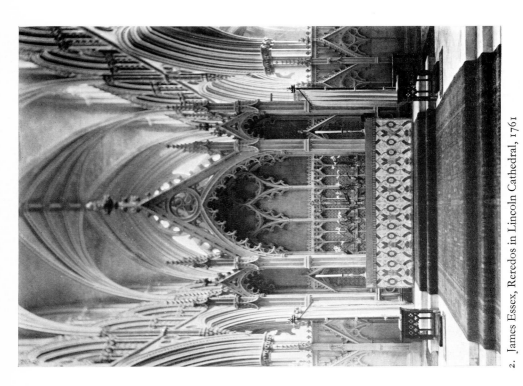

2. James Essex, Reredos in Lincoln Cathedral, 1761

5. James Wyatt, Fonthill Abbey, Wilts., begun in 1796. Drawn by J. P. Neale and engraved by W. Tombleson

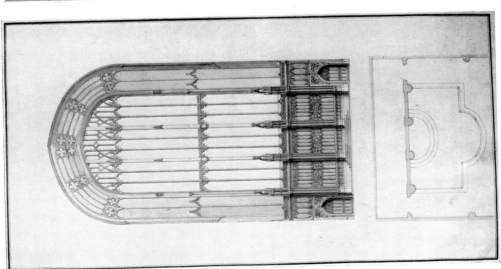

4. (*left*) James Essex, East Window of King's College Chapel, Cambridge, with Reredos executed 1770–5

6. Sir James Hall, Frontispiece to his *Essay on the Origin and Principles of Gothic Architecture,* 1813

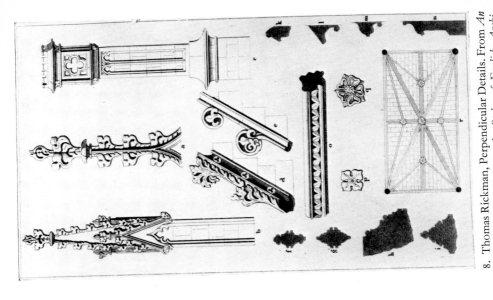

8. Thomas Rickman, Perpendicular Details. From *An Attempt to Discriminate the Styles of English Architecture from the Conquest to the Reformation*, 1817

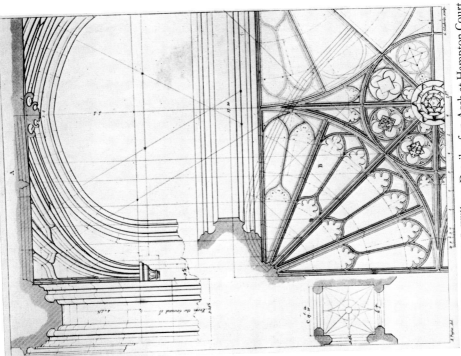

7. A. C. Pugin and E. J. Willson, Details of an Arch at Hampton Court Palace. From *Specimens of Gothic Architecture*, 1822

9. Thomas Rickman, Design for the Fitzwilliam Museum, Cambridge, 1829

10. Thomas Rickman, Design for the Fitzwilliam Museum, Cambridge, 1829

11. Thomas Rickman, Design for the Fitzwilliam Museum, Cambridge, 1829

12. Thomas Rickman, St. George, Everton, Liverpool, 1812–14

13. Thomas Rickman and Henry Hutchinson, South Aisle of Hampton Lucy Church, Warwicks., 1822–6

14. Thomas Rickman and Henry Hutchinson, Hampton Lucy Church, Warwicks., 1822–6

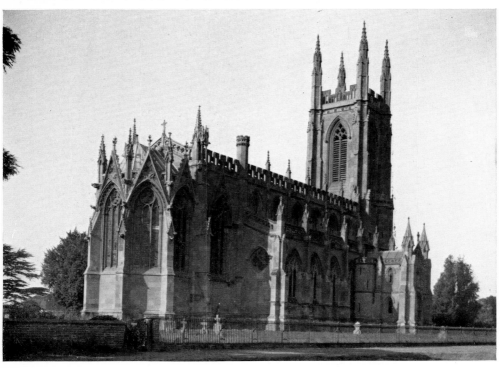

15, 16, J. Potter, St.
Mary, Sheffield, 1826–9

17. W. Thomas, St. Matthew, Duddeston, Birmingham, 1829–40

18. Arcisse de Caumont, Gothic Details. From *Sur l' Architecture du Moyen-Age, particulièrement en Normandie,* 1824

19. Arcisse de Caumont, Gothic Details. From *Cours d' Antiquités Monumentales,* 1831

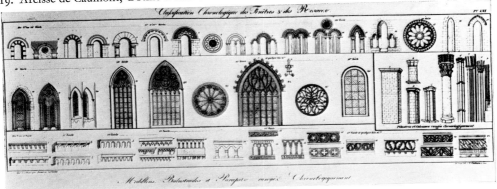

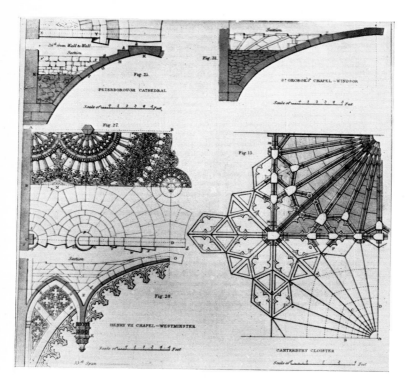

20. Robert Willis, Fan Vaults. From *On the Construction of the Vaults of the Middle Ages*, 1842

21. Robert Willis, Vault of Henry VII's Chapel, Westminster. From *On the Construction of the Vaults of the Middle Ages*, 1842

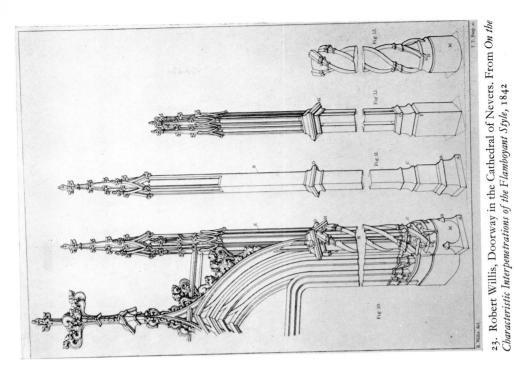

23. Robert Willis, Doorway in the Cathedral of Nevers. From *On the Characteristic Interpenetrations of the Flamboyant Style*, 1842

22. Robert Willis, King's Walk Cemetery Chapel, Wisbech, Cambs., 1841. From Neil Walker and Thomas Craddock, *History of Wisbech and the Fens*, 1849

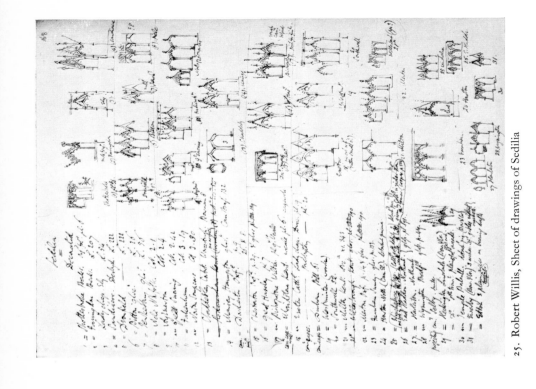

25. Robert Willis, Sheet of drawings of Sedilia

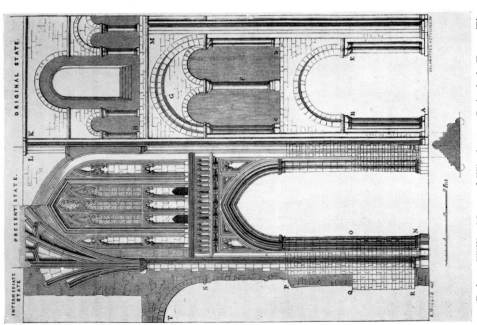

24. Robert Willis, Nave of Winchester Cathedral. From *The Architectural History of Winchester Cathedral*, 1846

26. Leo von Klenze, Allerheiligen Hofkirche, Munich, begun 1827. From an engraving by Poppel

27. T. H. Wyatt and D. Brandon, Wilton Parish Church, Wilts., begun 1840

28. Thomas Hope, S. Michele, Pavia. From *An Historical Essay on Architecture*, 1835

29. Ludwig Gruner, Casino, Buckingham Palace, 1844. From *The Decorations of the Garden-Pavilion in the Grounds of Buckingham Palace*, 1846

30. C. R. Cockerell, Design for the Royal Exchange, 1839

31. C. R. Cockerell, Tribute to Sir Christopher Wren, 1839

32. T. L. Donaldson, Dr. Williams's Library, formerly University Hall, Gordon Square, London, 1848

33. A. W. N. Pugin, 'The Present Revival of Christian Architecture', frontispiece to *An Apology for the Revival of Christian Architecture*, 1843

34. A. W. N. Pugin, St. Oswald, Old Swan, Liverpool, 1840–2, from a contemporary print

35. A. W. N. Pugin, St. Giles, Cheadle, Staffs., 1841–6

36, 37. A. W. N. Pugin, St. Augustine, Ramsgate, Kent, 1846–51

38. (*below right*) A. W. N. Pugin, St. Mary, Derby, 1837–9

39. Sir George Gilbert Scott, St. Giles, Camberwell, 1842–4

40. William Butterfield, Keble College Chapel, Oxford, 1868–76

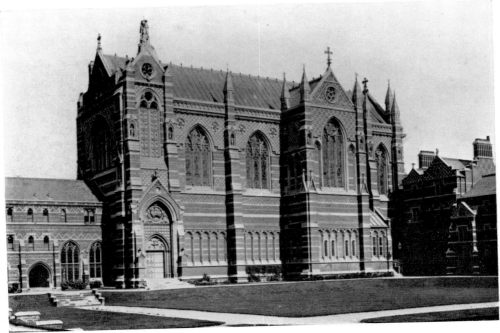

41. William Butterfield, All Saints, Margaret Street, London, 1849–59

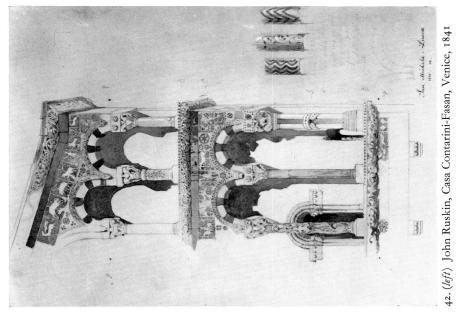

42. (*left*) John Ruskin, Casa Contarini-Fasan, Venice, 1841

43. John Ruskin, S. Michele, Lucca, 1845

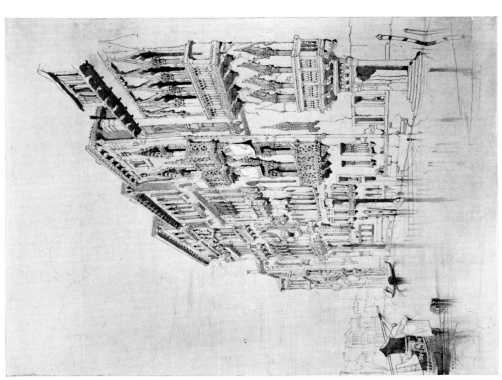

44. T. N. Deane, Garden front, Christ Church, Oxford

45. Owen Jones, Chestnut Leaves. From *The Grammar of Ornament*, 1856

46. Sir George Gilbert Scott, Aisle of St. Mary Magdalen, Oxford, 1840

47, 48. Sir George Gilbert Scott, St. George, Doncaster, 1854–8

50. Sir George Gilbert Scott, E. end of Oxford Cathedral, 1870–6

49. Oxford Cathedral before restoration, from a contemporary print

51. Sir George Gilbert Scott, Broad Sanctuary, Westminster, 1854

52. Sir George Gilbert Scott and Sir Matthew Digby Wyatt, Foreign Office from St. James' Park, 1868–73

53. Sir George Gilbert Scott, St. Pancras Station, 1868–74

54. W. H. Barlow, St. Pancras Station's iron roof, 1868–74

55. Sir George Gilbert Scott, Main Staircase, St. Pancras Station, 1868–74

56. Sir George Gilbert Scott, Glasgow University, begun 1866

57. Alexander Thomson, Caledonia Road Church, Glasgow, 1856 ff

58. Jacob Ignaz Hittorff, Gare du Nord, Paris, 1859–62

59, 60. A. J. Magne, Design for a Church. From *Revue Générale d'Architecture*, 1848

61. Henri Labrouste, Bibliothèque Sainte-Geneviève, Paris, begun 1842

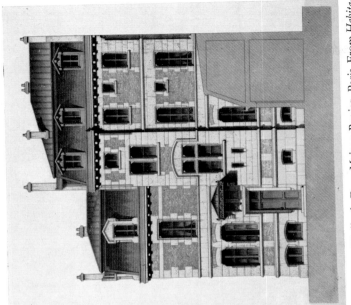

63. Eugène Viollet-le-Duc, Maison Rozier, Paris. From *Habitations Modernes*, 1875

62. (*left*) Eugène Viollet-le-Duc, Angel Choir, Lincoln Cathedral. From a drawing of 1850

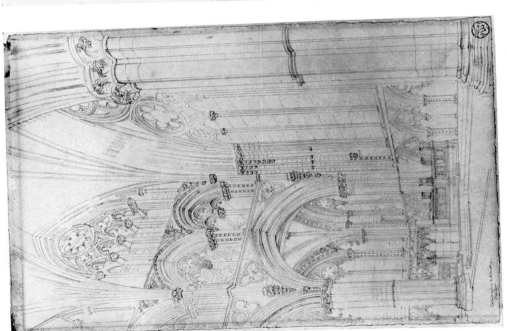

64. Louis-Auguste Boileau, St. Eugène, Paris, 1854-5

65. (*right*) Eugène Viollet-le-Duc, Façade for Clermont-Ferrand Cathedral. From a drawing of 1864

66. Thomas Harris, 155 New Bond Street, London. From *Examples of the Architecture of the Victorian Age,* 1862

67. Thomas Harris, Terrace at Harrow, Middlesex. From *The Builder,* 1862

68. Robert Kerr, Bearwood, Berks., 1861–8

69. Gottfried Semper, Opera House, Dresden, 1838–41, burned down 1869

70. Gottfried Semper, Opera House, Dresden, 1871–8
71. Gottfried Semper, Gallery, Dresden, 1847–54

72. Philip Webb, Red House, Bexley Heath, Kent, 1858

73. Philip Webb, Fireplace in Red House, Bexley Heath, Kent, 1858

74. Philip Webb, Smeaton Manor, Yorks., 1877–9

75. Sussex chair as revived by Morris & Co., before 1870

76. Table designed by Philip Webb for Morris & Co., *c.* 1870

77. William Morris: the Crompton Chintz, 1895

78. William Morris: the Lily Carpet, *c.* 1870